Pests and Diseases of Alpine Plants

Pests and Diseases of Alpine Plants

by
P. R. Ellis, A. R. Entwistle
and D. G. A. Walkey

ALPINE GARDEN SOCIETY

First published 1993

Published by the Alpine Garden Society
AGS Centre, Avon Bank
Pershore, Worcestershire WR10 3JP

Editor: Christopher Grey-Wilson
assisted by Christine Grey-Wilson

Designer: John Fitzmaurice

ISBN 0 900048 60 3

Typeset by Dorchester Typesetting Group Ltd,
Dorchester, Dorset.

Printed by the Friary Press,
Dorchester, Dorset

CONTENTS

Introduction

CURRENT ATTITUDES TO PEST AND DISEASE CONTROL PROBLEMS

Most books written about alpine plants say little about pest and disease problems. This is probably because the causes can be difficult to identify and information on specific control measures is not readily available.

This book attempts to remedy the situation. It gives a comprehensive account of the biology and control of pests and diseases of alpine plants and provides practical information on diagnosis of problems. Much of the information provided is also applicable to other garden plants.

Before describing the main pests and diseases we discuss certain general principles. Setting the scene in this way will help the alpine gardener or nurseryman adopt the right philosophy for coping with these problems. In the press and on radio and television we frequently receive news of the devastation by pests and diseases throughout the world. On a global scale these problems can inflict famine and total destruction of vegetation; for example, in 1988 plagues of locusts swept through many parts of Africa consuming every leaf and stem just at a time when rain had helped farmers produce promising crops. There was also the devastation caused by Dutch elm disease in the early 1970s which destroyed most of the mature elm trees in Britain and many parts of Europe and north America. More recently greenfly have hit the headlines and, in the late 1980s, farmers and gardeners were wondering how they were going to cope with these pests; indeed many suppliers ran out of stocks of insecticides and crops had to be ploughed in. All these events, and how we attempt to counteract them, emphasize the importance of crop protection and the principles we must adopt to control pests and diseases.

The first point is to realise that we share our gardens and farms with hundreds of different species of animals, plants and micro-organisms. They all live in a complex community involving food chains and the cycling of elements and it is easy to change the natural balance. The majority of organisms are harmless or beneficial and only a small fraction cause damage. A simple definition of a harmful organism is one (animal or plant) that interferes with man or his practices; with alpine plants, this means any pest or disease that prevents gardeners from growing plants to their satisfaction. However, no single definition describes all aspects of what we understand by the term “disease”. A “disease” implies a change from normal growth to one that harms the plant. Examples are premature death, rotting or collapse of the whole plant or rotting of roots, bulbs, leaves, flowers or fruits. Disorders of alpine plants can result from a wide range of factors acting either singly or in combination; the factors may be living organisms which use the plant as food (i.e. pests and diseases), chemicals which damage the plant (**phytotoxic**) or factors which affect plant growth such as abnormal light conditions, waterlogging, frost or nutrient imbalance. Knowing what constitutes normal plant growth is not always obvious especially when high altitude alpines are grown in lowland gardens. However, a reduction in plant growth is often a useful indicator of damage for example, microorganisms may reduce growth of the plant but cause no other obvious symptoms. This results in a smaller number of healthy roots which reduces the ability of the plant to take up water and nutrients. A plant in this condition is less able to cope with unfavourable environmental conditions or stress. It follows that a lack of vigour (‘unthrifty growth’) may be indicative of root damage especially when water and nutrients are in short supply. Other affects of root damage are premature flowering, premature autumn colouring and leaf fall, or poor survival during winter.

The technical terms used to describe the study of plant diseases include **Plant Pathology** or **Phytopathology** – individual aspects include **Mycology** (fungi), **Virology** and **Bacteriology**. The study of pests include, **Nematology** (nematodes or eelworms), **Acarology** (mites) and **Entomology** (insects). Definitions of other technical terms used in the book are provided in the glossary (p.287).

The reader should also realise that some organisms do good on one occasion but are harmful on another. For example, sparrows may peck at your primulas and aubrietia but they will also remove and eat hundreds of aphids from other valuable plants. Certain insects such as earwigs also fall into this category. What is needed is a harmonious balance in pest or disease prevention and control; to protect primulas and other alpines from sparrows cover them with netting to stop the damage while allowing them to assist in the removal of aphids from other plants. Thus the aim is to promote the activity of beneficial organisms and discourage harmful species.

Certain pests and diseases can present severe problems to the grower and nurseryman and there may be no easy answers to controlling them. We need to use nature and our ingenuity to a maximum so that we can cut down on the time wasted and minimise the use of pesticides. Sometimes it may be better to accept defeat and destroy a plant which is severely affected to prevent the problem spreading elsewhere.

It is often very difficult to eradicate a horticultural pest or disease from a garden or nursery. It may be possible to rid your rock garden of ants this year but there is a good chance that these insects will invade from some other part of the garden next year. Similarly, you may control an aphid infestation in your glasshouse early in the year but it is highly probable that aphids will migrate from elsewhere later on and again colonise your plants. So it is always necessary to be vigilant, inspect your plants frequently and accept the fact that pests and diseases will always be around – they are, after all, highly successful competitors. The aim should be to reduce pest and disease numbers to levels at which alpine plants can be satisfactorily grown.

A minority of pests and diseases live specifically on alpine plants with most infesting a wide range of plants. Only a few insect species such as root aphids and certain fungi are highly specific. Therefore any account of pests and diseases of alpine plants includes several which have a wide host range. As most alpine specialists grow other types of plants anyway, this book should help the keen gardener or nurseryman cope with practically all pest or disease situations.

Some alpine gardeners may be under the misconception that pests do not occur in alpine habitats. However, the account given in the AGS *Bulletin* (Vol. 58, No.2 p. 171, 1990) clearly illustrates problems which can be encountered in the wild, including, blackfly, froghoppers, slugs and snails. This explains why some plant collectors have been known to carry small quantities of pesticides to treat specimens in the field and thus ensure their survival.

The basis of all good gardening practice and, indeed, pest and disease control is the creation of a healthy soil or growing medium. Alpine plants grown in the right conditions will prosper and this should help them to resist attack by pest or disease. The soil and the scree-bed is a living community of countless numbers of microorganisms and other larger creatures. This community of organisms must be maintained in order that plants can be provided with the correct balance of nutrients and physical conditions to support healthy growth. Soils differ greatly from site to site depending on such factors as geology, pH and drainage, but every habitat can be maintained in a healthy state if its requirements are understood and each one will be suited to a particular range of plants. So it is necessary to learn as much as possible about the creation of appropriate soils and the requirements of individual plant species for vigorous growth.

The weather is probably the single most important influence on many of the pests and diseases in the garden, and it is the factor we have least control over. In fact, surprisingly little is known about the effects that changes in weather patterns can have on plant and animal populations. We know, however, that large changes in temperature or the occurrence of heavy rain can have far-reaching effects on certain plants and animals. For example, torrential rain can decimate populations of aphids and extremely cold winters can reduce the number of insects or fungi in soil and plant debris. Unfortunately, these adverse conditions also affect natural enemies as well. Nevertheless, well-directed heavy drenches or sprays of water can exert considerable control of aphids at times when predator and parasite numbers are low. We can also protect plants from rain or wind or excessive sun by using various types of cover.

The alpine glasshouse can provide the ideal environment for the development of high populations of pests and disease which can result in epidemics. This is partly due to the absence of many natural enemies and also due to the protection from the weather. Grey moulds, mildews, aphids, red spider mites, whiteflies and weevils are examples of organisms that can flourish in such a protected environment. The alpine gardener needs therefore to be especially vigilant to detect pest and disease outbreaks in the glasshouse.

CHAPTER ONE

Diagnosis

DIAGNOSIS OF PEST AND DISEASE PROBLEMS

This book provides descriptions of pests and diseases, the damage they cause and measures for their control. It also describes how the reader can diagnose a problem and select the correct solution to it. To positively identify the causal organism is not always straightforward and easy. For example, certain pests and diseases attack a wide range of plants growing under a wide range of conditions while others attack just one genus or species growing under specific conditions. Some pests and diseases occur under glass but rarely outdoors; some are confined to roots while others damage all parts of a plant. Furthermore, different disease organisms can cause similar symptoms particularly early on in the infection of the host. Consequently, there are few hard and fast rules governing pests or diseases and their attack on host plants. The reader should realise that there are other causes of disorders in plants besides pests and diseases which may induce similar symptoms. Examples include mineral deficiencies, weed killers, hail, frost, gales, drought, waterlogging or **inbreeding depression**.

Accurate diagnosis is dependent on good detective work. Anything which affects plant growth may be relevant and initially should be considered. Examine plants carefully and look at the type of symptoms on the different parts of the plant, the pattern of spread to other plants, and the time when the symptoms first occur. The environmental conditions and factors such as the type and origin of the soil or other growing medium, whether the plant is grown outside or inside a frame or alpine house are all relevant. The source of the plant and use of chemicals in the garden or surrounding areas may be important in diagnosis as is the identity of the plant.

The appearance of damaged tissue is often a good indicator of the cause. Symptoms may affect all the leaves or be limited to just a few. They may be related to the position of the leaf on the plant or to its age. Sometimes, only the leaves on one side of the plant are affected indicating damage to the connecting vascular system. The whole of the leaf or only a small area such as the tip or edge of the leaf may be affected and the damage may occur on one or both surfaces of the leaf. Pest damage to leaves may take the form of holes which are characteristics of a particular type of pest. Examples are illustrated in Fig. 9 on p.35).

Damage caused by leaf fungi often varies in a regular manner. It may start as pinhead-sized yellow spots, becoming bigger as the pathogen progresses eventually changing colour and texture as the spores develop. The edges of the damaged tissue are often coloured. Damage caused by pests is frequently less regular and usually more patchy in distribution. Root damage stunts plant growth sometimes without the presence of other obvious symptoms. Often leaves wilt during the day in times of water stress and recover at night. If root damage is pronounced, or the stress continues, the leaves will turn yellow (**chlorosis**) and die back from the tip. As seedlings have few roots they are likely to collapse and die when attacked by pests or diseases.

Symptoms which are confined to areas around the veins, including diffuse yellowing (**chlorosis**), reddening, and a browning (**necrosis**) may be caused by a virus or may indicate a mineral disorder. Mineral disorders are largely outside the scope of this book but are summarised briefly here. The minerals or nutrients most likely to be involved are Calcium (Ca), Nitrogen (N), Iron (Fe), Manganese (Mn), Magnesium (Mg) and Potassium (K). As with pests, viruses and fungi it is often possible to diagnose the nature of the mineral disorder from the type and pattern of symptoms on the leaves. Plants obtain inorganic nutrients from the soil solution via the roots and the vascular system. The availability of minerals may be insufficient for the needs of the plant if (a) there are insufficient amounts in the soil, (b) minerals are present but insufficiently available e.g. because their solubility is reduced at high or low soil pH or (c) if roots are damaged e.g. by insects or fungi hence reducing the capacity of the plant to extract water and minerals. When the uptake of minerals via roots is too low the parts of the plant with the greatest demand - those parts in active growth - try to obtain minerals from the older parts of the plant. Redistribution of nutrients within the plant is dependent on their mobility which in turn determines their availability and the patterns of symptoms on the plant. Old leaves are the first to show symptoms of mineral deficiency when the mineral is mobile enough to move from old to young leaves, e.g. Nitrogen, Molybdenum, Potassium, Boron. Conversely, young leaves show symptoms first when the mineral is less mobile, e.g. Calcium, Manganese, Iron, Zinc and Copper. Some common symptoms are given in Table 1.

Table 1: **Symptoms of mineral deficiency**

Nitrogen:	when deficient, plants are pale (**chlorotic**), starting with older leaves; in excess, plants become bright green.
Calcium:	when deficient leaves start to become pale at the leaf tip, gradually extending along the margin and affecting the rest of the leaf.
Manganese:	when deficient chlorosis extends along the areas next to the main veins in young leaves.
Magnesium:	when deficient interveinal chlorosis occurs in older leaves.
Iron:	when deficient veins in young leaves remain green, but interveinal chlorosis develops.
Potassium:	when deficient scorching of the leaf margins occurs starting with the older leaves.

There are two main ways of using the information in this book to diagnose a pest or disease problem. If you can positively identify the plant species that is affected you may find it easiest to look this species up in the index. Having done this you can refer to those pages which give information on the pests and diseases listed under that plant in the index. Alternatively, you can use the following diagnosis section and scan the information on the basis of the plant part damaged (for example, leaf, stem, tuber, etc.) and on the basis of the symptoms observed (for example, holes, spots, malformations, etc.).

When an unthrifty specimen is examined it is necessary to be careful not to jump to hasty conclusions. A systematic examination is required. The best evidence is the discovery of the causal organism. If the pest has departed tell-tail evidence may have been left behind. Always make a thorough search because several clues will help to narrow down the possible causes of the problem.

To help diagnose the problem its a good idea to obtain a hand lens and perhaps some scissors and needles for teasing apart folded leaves and dissecting stems, buds, roots, or other plant parts. A dissecting microscope can be very valuable. When examining a potted plant or one with dense foliage its worth placing a white tray or piece of white paper beneath the specimen to catch any pests or tell-tale clues which may be dislodged.

To begin with, search for the pest or disease organism itself. This often requires dissecting damaged tissues to find mycelial growth or a caterpillar or a maggot. Examine the soil around plants as many pests hide in the soil during the day and emerge at night to attack the plant. Also examine the damaged tissue of the plant carefully and, follow the systematic scheme described below.

Notes on scheme

Wherever possible specific pests, diseases or disorders are listed. When several species or causes produce symptoms a √ is given. Sprays include all types of pesticides (especially herbicides).

Tables 2-11 Scheme for the diagnosis of pests, diseases and disorders

Table 2

WHOLE PLANT

SYMPTOM	PEST, DISEASE OR DISORDER					
	INSECT	OTHER PESTS	BACTERIA, FUNGI	VIRUSES	PHYSIOLOGICAL DISORDERS, WEATHER	MINERAL DEFICIENCIES, SPRAY DAMAGE
Blisters	Aphids		Rusts, Smuts	√		Sprays
Chlorosis				√	√	√

WHOLE PLANT (continued)

SYMPTOM	PEST, DISEASE OR DISORDER					
	INSECT	OTHER PESTS	BACTERIA, FUNGI	VIRUSES	PHYSIOLOGICAL DISORDERS, WEATHER	MINERAL DEFICIENCIES, SPRAY DAMAGE
Collapsed or **severed**	Ants, Chafers, Cutworms, Leather-jackets, Sciarids Weevils, Wireworms	Millipedes, Mammals (Moles), Nematodes	Damping Die-back, Foot & Root rots, Wilts		Drought, Overwatered	√
Defoliated	Caterpillars, Sawflies	Mammals, Birds, Slugs, Snails				√
Discoloured	Aphids, Whiteflies	Nematodes, Mites		√	√	√
Flecks	Leafhoppers, Froghoppers, Thrips	Mites		√		
Galls, Tumours	Aphids	Nematodes	Bacteria, Fungi	√		
Honeydew	Plant bugs					
Lesions, necrosis			Damping -off Soft-rots	√	√	Sprays
Malformations, distorted	Mirids, Chafers, Plant bugs, Weevils	Mites		√		Sprays, Pollutants
Mosaics				√		
Slime		Slugs				
Spots	Plant bugs	Mites	Rusts, Smuts, Spots	√	Hail	Sprays, Pollutants
Stunted		Nematodes		√		
Waxy tufts	Aphids, Mealybugs		Mildews			
Webbing (silk threads)	Caterpillars	Mites				
Wilting	Root plant bugs, Cutworms, Sciarids, Ants		Foot & Root rots, Wilts	√	Drought, Overwatered	

Table 3

SEEDLING

SYMPTOM	PEST, DISEASE OR DISORDER					
	INSECT	OTHER PESTS	BACTERIA, FUNGI	VIRUSES	PHYSIOLOGICAL DISORDERS, WEATHER	MINERAL DEFICIENCIES, SPRAY DAMAGE
Blisters	Aphids		Rusts, Smuts	√		Sprays
Chlorosis				√	√	√
Collapsed	Collembola, Caterpillars, Cutworms, Leather-jackets, Wireworms	Millipedes, Woodlice, Birds, Mammals, Slugs, Snails	Damping -off, Foot and Root rot, Wilts	Drought		
Holes	Collembola, Fleas beetles	Millipedes, Woodlice				
Lesions, necrosis			Bacterial soft rots, Damping -off	√	√	√
Mosaics, flecks		Mites		√		
Spots			Mildews, Rusts, Smuts	√		√
Streaks			Smuts	√		
Stem constriction			Damping -off			
Stunted	Aphids	Mites, Nematodes		√	√	

Table 4

FRUIT or SEEDS

SYMPTOM	PEST, DISEASE OR DISORDER					
	INSECT	OTHER PESTS	BACTERIA, FUNGI	VIRUSES	PHYSIOLOGICAL DISORDERS, WEATHER	MINERAL DEFICIENCIES, SPRAY DAMAGE
Edges eaten	Caterpillars, Mirids	Birds, Mammals				
Galls, tumours	Aphids		Bacteria, Fungi			
Holes	Caterpillars, Mirids	Birds, Mammals				
Honeydew	Plant bugs					

FRUIT or SEEDS (continued)

SYMPTOM	PEST, DISEASE OR DISORDER					
	INSECT	OTHER PESTS	BACTERIA, FUNGI	VIRUSES	PHYSIOLOGICAL DISORDERS, WEATHER	MINERAL DEFICIENCIES, SPRAY DAMAGE
Lesions, necrosis			Bacteria, Fungi	√		√
Malformed	Aphids		Powdery mildew	√		
Mosaic				√		
Rots, decay		Millipedes	Bacterial soft rot, Grey mould		Frost, Overwatered	
Stains	Mirids		Bacteria, Fungi	√		
Waxy tufts	Aphids, Mealybugs		Mildews			

Table 5

FLOWER

SYMPTOM	PEST, DISEASE OR DISORDER					
	INSECT	OTHER PESTS	BACTERIA, FUNGI	VIRUSES	PHYSIOLOGICAL DISORDERS, WEATHER	MINERAL DEFICIENCIES, SPRAY DAMAGE
Colourbreaks				√		
Discoloured	Aphids	Mites		√	√	√
Eaten edges	Caterpillars, Earwigs, Weevils	Birds, Mammals				
Flecks	Mirids, Thrips	Mites		√		
Gall, tumours		Nematodes	√			
Holes	Caterpillars, Earwigs	Birds, Mammals, Slugs, Snails				
Honeydew	Plant bugs					
Lesions, necrosis			√	√		
Malformations	Aphids, Bulb flies, Earwigs, Mirids, Midges, Thrips	Mites Nematodes	Mildews, Rusts	√		

a. Springtail extracted from a soil sample

b. Adult common green capsid, *Lygocoris pabulinus*

c. Adult earwig, *Forficula auricularia*

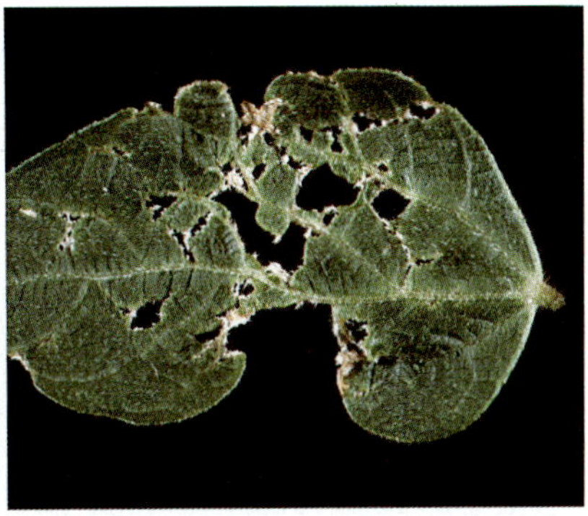

d. Damage caused by the common green capsid, *Lygocoris pabulinus*

e. Adelgid gall on Sitka spruce

f. Leaf distortion caused by the red currant blister aphid, *Crytomyzus ribis*

a. Peach-potato aphid,
Myzus persicae

b. The aphid, *Cinara* sp. infesting spruce

c. Elder aphid, *Aphis sambuci*
on saxifrage

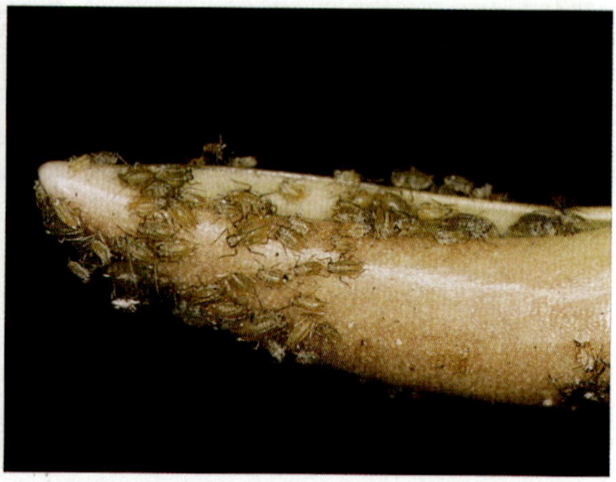

d. Tulip bulb aphid, *Dysaphis tulipae*
on tulip

e. Auricula root aphid,
Pemphigus auriculae on
Auricula

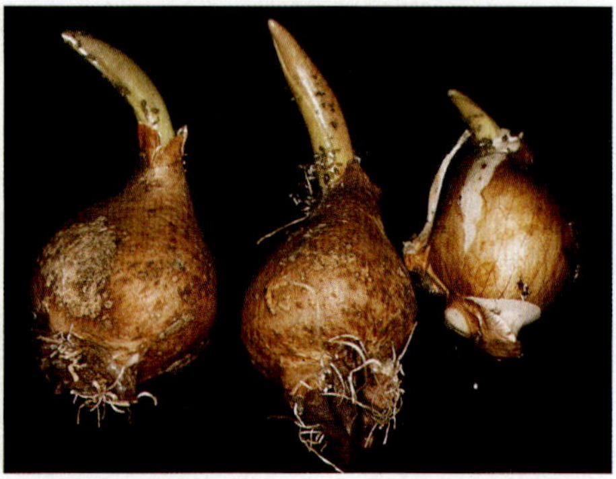

f. Tulip bulb aphid,
Dysaphis tulipae
on tulip

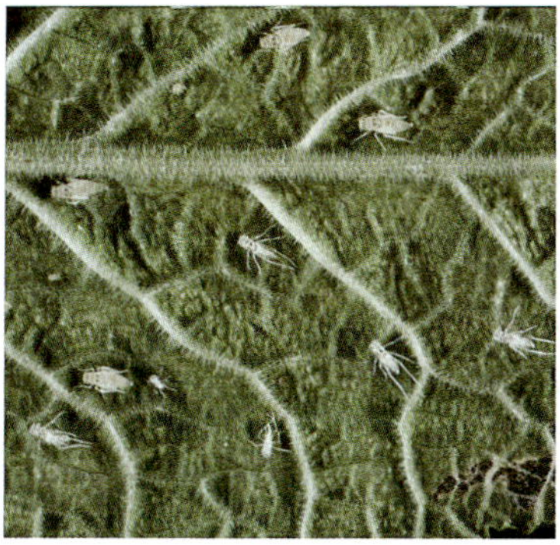

a. Nymphs and ghost flies of *Hauptidia maroccana*

b. Leafhopper damage to *Primula* sp.

c. Leafhopper damage to carrot leaf

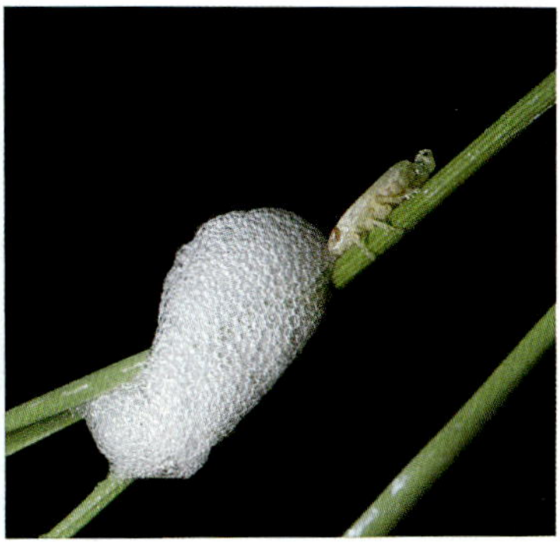

d. Cuckoo spit produced by froghopper nymph

e. Scale insects on bay leaf – note tiny crawlers

f. Mealybug on *Crassula*

a. Adult glasshouse whiteflies
Trialeurodes vaporariorum

b. Adult glasshouse whiteflies
Trialeurodes vaporariorum

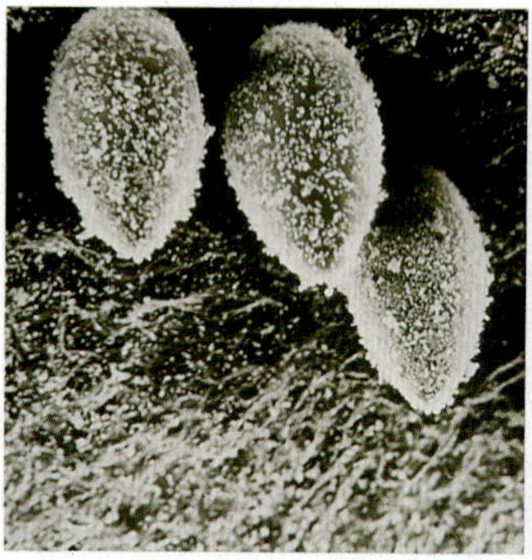

c. Eggs of glasshouse whitefly
Trialeurodes vaporariorum

d. Sooty moulds growing on honeydew produced by the glasshouse whitefly, *Trialeurodes vaporariorum*

e. Adult thrips, *Frankliniella occidentalis*

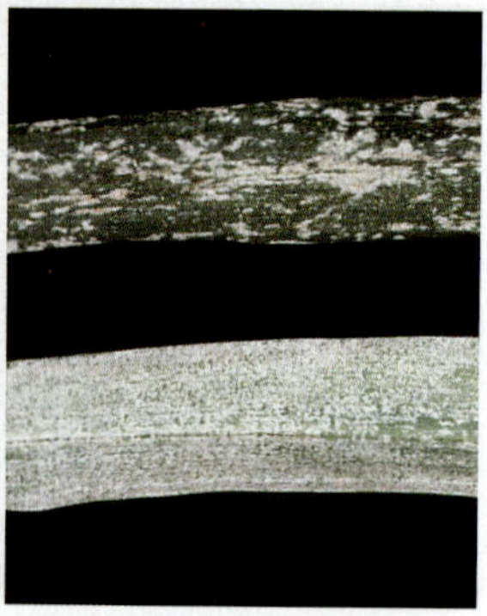

f. Damage caused by thrips, *Thrips tabaci* to *Allium* sp.

FLOWER (continued)

SYMPTOM	PEST, DISEASE OR DISORDER: INSECT	OTHER PESTS	BACTERIA, FUNGI	VIRUSES	PHYSIOLOGICAL DISORDERS, WEATHER	MINERAL DEFICIENCIES, SPRAY DAMAGE
Rots			Bacteria, Moulds		Frost	
Shrivelling	Aphids, Thrips	Mites, Nematodes	Cankers, Die-back			
Silvering	Thrips					
Slimes		Slugs, Snails				
Spots	Leafhoppers, Thrips	Mites	Rots, Rusts, Smuts	√	√ Rain	√
Streaks			Smuts	√		
Stunted				√		
Teared	Earwigs, Mirids	Birds			Weather	
Webbing	Caterpillars	Mites				
Waxy tufts	Aphids, Mealybugs	Mites	Mildews			

Table 6

BUD

SYMPTOM	PEST, DISEASE OR DISORDER: INSECT	OTHER PESTS	BACTERIA, FUNGI	VIRUSES	PHYSIOLOGICAL DISORDERS, WEATHER	MINERAL DEFICIENCIES, SPRAY DAMAGE
Eaten edges	Caterpillars	Birds, Mammals				
Flecks	Thrips	Mites				
Holes	Caterpillars, Earwigs	Birds, Mammals				
Honey dew	Plant bugs					
Lesions, necrosis			√	√		
Malformations	Aphids, Bulb flies, Midges, Mirids, Thrips	Mites	Powdery mildrew, Rusts	√		

BUD (continued)

SYMPTOM	PEST, DISEASE OR DISORDER					
	INSECT	OTHER PESTS	BACTERIA, FUNGI	VIRUSES	PHYSIOLOGICAL DISORDERS, WEATHER	MINERAL DEFICIENCIES, SPRAY DAMAGE
Rots			Bacteria, Grey mould	Frost		
Shrivelling	Aphids, Thrips	Mites, Nematodes	Canker, Die-back	√		
Spots			Rots, Rusts, Smuts	√	√	√
Waxy tufts	Aphids, Mealybugs		Mildews			

Table 7

LEAF

SYMPTOM	PEST, DISEASE OR DISORDER					
	INSECT	OTHER PESTS	BACTERIA, FUNGI	VIRUSES	PHYSIOLOGICAL DISORDERS, WEATHER	MINERAL DEFICIENCIES, SPRAY DAMAGE
Bleached dry	Leafhoppers	Mites				√
Blisters	Aphids, Leaf miners		Downy mildew, Rusts	√		√
Chlorosis				√	√	√
Discoloured			Mildews, Rots, Wilts	√	√	√
Edges eaten	Caterpillars, Weevils	Birds, Mammals				
Flecks	Leafhoppers, Thrips	Mites		√		
Galls, tumours	Aphids, Midges, Sawflies	Mites, Nematodes	Bacteria	√		
Holes	Caterpillars, Flea & lily beetles, Mirids, Weevils, Earwigs, Sawfly larvae	Birds, Mammals, Slugs, Snails, Snails, Woodlice	Bacterial canket			
Honeydew	Plant bugs					
Lesions				√	√	

LEAF (continued)

SYMPTOM	PEST, DISEASE OR DISORDER					
	INSECT	OTHER PESTS	BACTERIA, FUNGI	VIRUSES	PHYSIOLOGICAL DISORDERS, WEATHER	MINERAL DEFICIENCIES, SPRAY DAMAGE
Malformations	Bulb flies, Midges, Plant bugs	Nematodes	Powdery mildews	√		
Mines (tunnels)	Caterpillars, Leaf miners, Sawflies					
Mosaics				√		
Necrosis			Bacteria, Fungi	√		
Premature leaf fall	Plant bugs	Mites		√	√	√
Rolling	Aphids, Caterpillars, Sawflies		Powdery mildews	√		
Rots			Bacteria, Grey moulds			
Shrivelling	Plant bugs, Midges		Fungal wilts			
Silvering	Thrips	Mites				
Spots			Downy mildews, Rusts, Smuts	√	√	√
Streaks		Mites, Nematodes	Smuts	√		
Tears	Earwigs, Mirids	Birds, Mammals				
Waxy Tufts	Aphids, Mealybugs		Mildews			
Webbing	Caterpillars	Mites				

Table 8

SHOOT, STEM

SYMPTOM	PEST, DISEASE OR DISORDER					
	INSECT	OTHER PESTS	BACTERIA, FUNGI	VIRUSES	PHYSIOLOGICAL DISORDERS, WEATHER	MINERAL DEFICIENCIES, SPRAY DAMAGE
Blisters	Aphids		Rusts, Smuts			Spray
Flecks	Leafhoppers, Froghoppers, Thrips	Mites		√		
Galls, tumours	Aphids, Midges	Nematodes	√			
Holes	Caterpillars, Earwigs, Flea beetles	Birds, Mammals, Millipedes, Slugs, Snails				
Honeydew	Plant bugs					
Lesions			Cankers, Damping -off Die-back	√		
Malformations	Plant bugs, Midges	Nematodes		√		
Mosaics				√		
Necrosis			Bacteria, Fungi	√		
Silvering	Thrips	Mites				
Spots			Mildews, Rusts, Smuts	√	√	√
Streaks		Mites, Nematodes Smuts	Mildews, Rusts,	√		√
Waxy tufts	Aphids, Mealybugs		Mildews			
Webbing	Caterpillar	Mites				
Wilting			Fungal wilts	√		

Table 9

BULB

SYMPTOM	PEST, DISEASE OR DISORDER					
	INSECT	OTHER PESTS	BACTERIA, FUNGI	VIRUSES	PHYSIOLOGICAL DISORDERS, WEATHER	MINERAL DEFICIENCIES, SPRAY DAMAGE
Holes	Bulb flies, Caterpillars, Chafers, Leather-jackets, Weevils, Wireworms	Mammals, Millipedes, Slugs				
Malformations	Roots aphids	Nematodes	√	√		
Necrosis		Nematodes	Bacteria, Fungi	√		
Rings		Nematodes				
Rots	Bulb flies, Sciarids, Weevils	Millipedes, Mites, Nematodes	Bacterial soft rots, Mildews		Frost	
Scars		Bulb scale mites				
Sponginess	Bulb flies	Mites,	Mildew Nematodes			
Stunted		Nematodes	Fungi	√		
Waxy tufts	Roots aphids, Root mealybugs					

Table 10

CORM, RHIZOME, TUBER

SYMPTOM	PEST, DISEASE OR DISORDER					
	INSECT	OTHER PESTS	BACTERIA, FUNGI	VIRUSES	PHYSIOLOGICAL DISORDERS, WEATHER	MINERAL DEFICIENCIES, SPRAY DAMAGE
Holes	Caterpillars, Chafers, Leather-jackets, Weevils, Wireworms	Mammals, Millipede, Slugs				
Malformations	Nematodes		√	√		√
Rots	Sciarids	Millipedes, Nematodes	Bacterial soft rots, Mildews		Frost	

CORM, RHIZOME, TUBER (continued)

SYMPTOM	PEST, DISEASE OR DISORDER					
	INSECT	OTHER PESTS	BACTERIA, FUNGI	VIRUSES	PHYSIOLOGICAL DISORDERS, WEATHER	MINERAL DEFICIENCIES, SPRAY DAMAGE
Sponginess	Nematodes	Mildew				
Waxy tufts	Roots aphids, Root mealybugs					

Table 11

ROOTS

SYMPTOM	PEST, DISEASE OR DISORDER					
	INSECT	OTHER PESTS	BACTERIA, FUNGI	VIRUSES	PHYSIOLOGICAL DISORDERS, WEATHER	MINERAL DEFICIENCIES, SPRAY DAMAGE
Eaten away	Caterpillars, Chafers, Cutworms, Weevils, Wireworms	Mammals, Millipedes				
Galls, Tumours	Root aphids	Mites, Nematodes	√	√		
Holes	Caterpillars, Chafers, Wireworms	Millipedes, Slugs				
Malformations		Nematodes		√		
Necrosis		Nematodes	Bacteria, Fungi	√		
Rots		Bacterial soft rots, Foot rots				
Stunted		Nematodes	Fungi	√		
Tunnels	Caterpillars, Weevils	Slugs				
Waxy tufts	Root aphids, Root mealybugs					

CHAPTER TWO

Pests

GENERAL INFORMATION

How do we define a pest and why are they so successful? A pest is any animal which competes with man for his food, clothing, fuel or shelter or which interferes with his health, livestock or way of life. The majority of pests are found in a small number of animal classes. These classes are formed on the basis of common characters which indicate their position in the evolution of animals. Most pests belong to the nematode, mite, mollusc, insect, bird and mammal groups. The numbers of species of serious pests is small – for example, about 5,000 out of more than 1,000,000 species of insects. It should be emphasized that the majority of animals do not compete with man and most are beneficial or harmless.

Attempts have been made to determine which characteristics of an animal contribute to its success as a pest. The one factor which is common to virtually all pests is their ability to exploit new situations that man has created, for instance, the vast monocultures of crops which, in the case of cereals or forest trees, may represent millions of hectares. These monocultures present to any animal that feeds on the crop a boundless supply of food. Pests are opportunists and adapt to changes in agricultural practices. One form of adaptation is the development of new races or biotypes when the environment exerts an adverse selection pressure on the pest. The existence of races of pests resistant to pesticides is a good example of such adaptation.

Another trait which most pest species possess is the ability to reproduce rapidly from small populations. If all the progeny of a single aphid survived, then after one year the population would encircle the earth hundreds of times!

The ability to disperse efficiently also contributes to the success of insects. Most species fly and this enables them to escape predation, find members of the opposite sex, and to migrate and locate new supplies of food.

Nomenclature

All pests have unique latin names which are based on Linnaeus's binomial system of genus and species. This is discussed in greater detail in Chapter 3.

Animals are classified according to the International Code of

Zoological Nomenclature (1985). The example of the vine weevil illustrates categories in the hierarchy:

Phylum	Arthropoda (jointed-limbed animals)
Class	Insecta (insects)
Order	Coleoptera (beetles)
Sub Order	Polyphaga
Superfamily	Curculionoidea
Family	Curculionidae (weevils)
Subfamily	Otiorhynchinae
Genus	*Otiorhynchus*
Species	*sulcatus* (vine weevil)

The animal phyla described in this book include:

Arthropoda	–	insects, mites, crustaceans (woodlice), spiders, centipedes and millipedes
Mollusca	–	slugs and snails
Nematoda	–	nematodes
Vertebrata	–	amphibians, reptiles, birds and mammals

As well as having a latin name which is internationally recognised, pests also have common names. A single pest can have several common names depending on the country, region or locality in which it is found. A pest can also have separate names for adult and immature stages, e.g. **click beetle** (adult) and **leatherjacket** (larva). Common names may describe the host plant (e.g. vine weevil, lily beetle), the part of the plant attacked (e.g. root fly, leaf miner), the symptom of damage (leaf roller, webworm, borer), or the appearance of the pest (woolly aphid, whitefly).

Pest Life Histories

Pests display a wide range of life histories or life cycles some of which are extremely complex. All species have an egg stage, although eggs may be rarely found for species which breed largely by asexual means. In many animals, for example, birds and mammals, development from the egg stage through to adult is a continuous process with no distinct intermediate stages. Thus a young bird or mammal resembles the adult in most basic characteristics. The change from an egg to an adult varies considerably in invertebrate animals such as nematodes, mites and insects, often with several different life stages evident; this change is known as **metamorphosis** and several different types occur. There are three basic types in the case of insects:

Ametabolous. In these insects there is no true metamorphosis and the adult develops progressively first from an egg then a **larva** which it closely resembles in nearly every way except for size and maturity. Growth is achieved by a series of moults. The adults and larvae also live and feed in the same habitat. Examples of ametabolous insects include silverfish (Order **Thysanura**) (Fig. 1) and **Collembolans** (springtails).

Hemimetabolous. In these insects the larvae, sometimes called **nymphs**, hatch in a form which resembles the adult but differ in several important characteristics such as the absence of wings and functional sexual organs. The larvae are smaller than the adult and usually possess characteristics which are not found in the adult and are lost on the final larval moult. Many plant bugs (Order **Hemiptera**) such as aphids examplify this type of metamorphosis (Fig. 2) as do grasshoppers and locusts (order **Orthoptera**) (Fig. 3).

Holometabolous. These insects have a life cycle in which the larva is totally unlike the adult and there is an additional stage in the cycle known as the **pupa** or **chrysalis**. The pupa is a stage in which there is extensive re-organisation of the body tissues and although it is often considered to be a resting phase it is actually a period of intense activity within the body of the insect. Several important pest Orders have this type of life history, for example beetles (Order **Coleoptera**), moths and butterflies (Order **Lepidoptera**) (Fig. 4), flies (Order **Diptera**) (Fig. 5) and ants, bees and wasps (Order **Hymenoptera**).

A complete life cycle is often known as a **generation** and insect species developing through a single generation in a year are termed **univoltine** (literally 'single flight') and those with several generations **polyvoltine**. Mites may also display egg, larva and pupal life stages while nematodes have egg, larva and adult stages.

Insects, slugs, snails, millipedes, mites and nematodes are cold-blooded animals (**poikilothermic**) and their activity is controlled mainly by temperature but also clearly by the availability of food and a suitable habitat. To help them overcome unfavourable periods these pests may enter resting phases when normal activities slow down. This condition

Figure 1 Life cycle of silverfish *Lapisma saccharina*

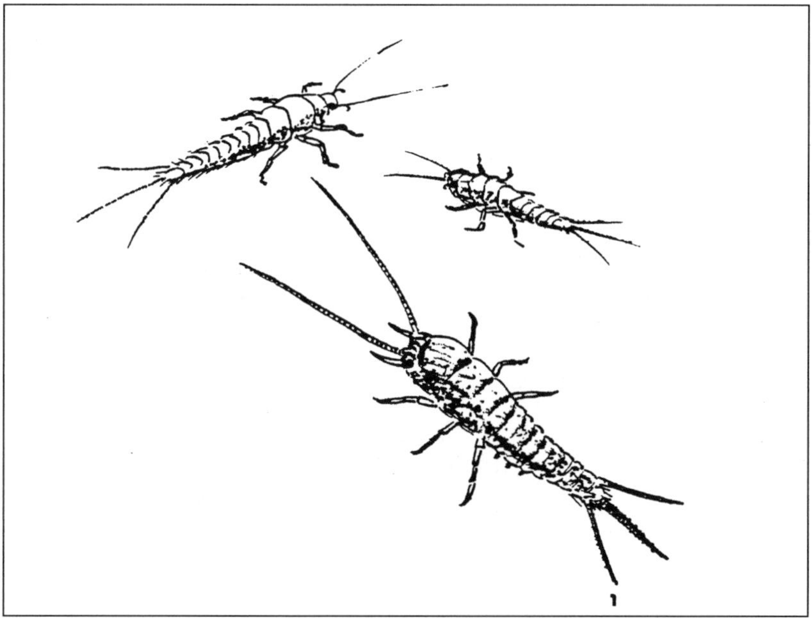

may be stimulated by cold weather, conditions which are too hot, changes in daylength or lack of food. Many insects enter a state known as **diapause** which is an extended resting period.

Feeding

Pests feed in a number of different ways and an appreciation of the methods is important in studies of pest control. The mouthparts of a pest are related to the diet. There are two basic types in insects – those adapted to biting and chewing and those used in piercing and sucking up the contents of a plant or some other substrate. The more primitive or generalised condition is illustrated by the mouthparts of a locust in Fig. 6.

These consist of:

1. The upper lip (**labrum**), which bears sense organs and holds the mouthparts in position. The labrum forms a cover over the jaw area where food is cut up and chewed.
2. The jaws (**mandibles**), which move with a scissor action to cut up food and usually have a sharp cutting surface.
3. The sensory organs for testing the quality of food (**maxillae** with **palps**) and for manoeuvring food material; these can also be used for

Figure 2 Life cycle of lettuce root aphid *Pemphigus bursarius*

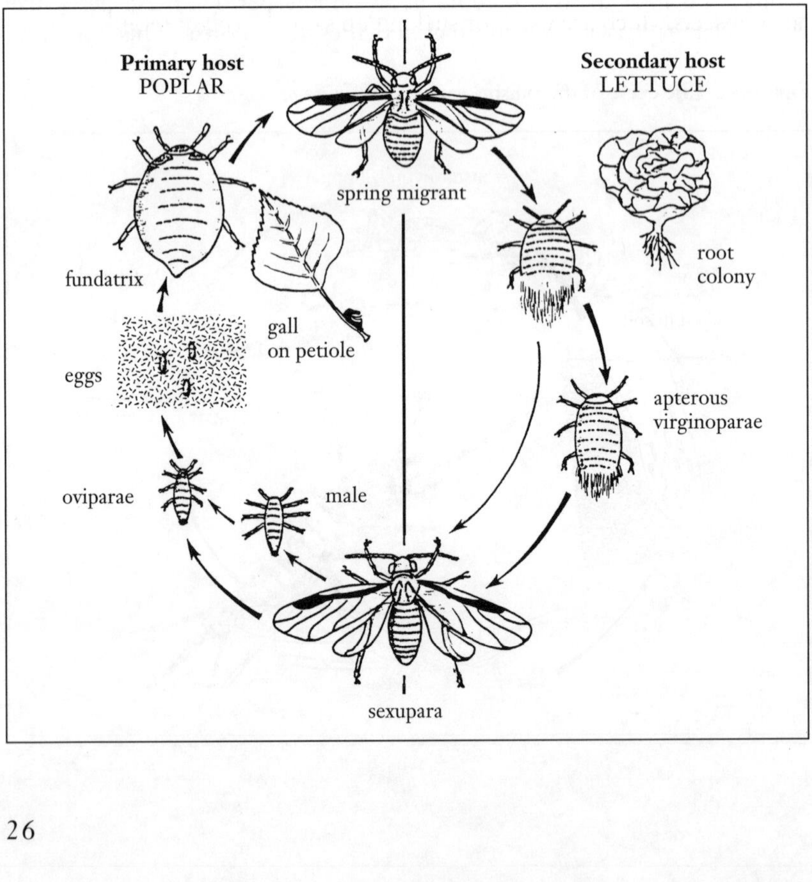

cleaning **antennae** (see Fig. 6), legs or other parts of the body. They are situated behind the mandibles.
4. The lower lip (**labium**) which also may bear palps. Both the maxillae and the labium help the insect to catch and hold food and then to direct the food into the mouth.
5. The mouth.
6. The **hypopharynx** a lobe behind the mouth which often contains sclerotinised plates.

Insects possessing these biting or chewing mouthparts include beetles, crickets, grasshoppers and locusts. The terms described above are related to mammalian mouthparts and equivalent organs can be recognised in birds and slugs.

The mouthparts of certain insects, mites and nematodes which feed on fluids are modified to form a sucking tube up which liquids may be drawn. The mouthparts of aphids are a good example of those adapted to this method of feeding (Fig. 7). In this condition the mandibles and maxillae are bristle-like and form the **stylet** bundle which is a flexible, double-channelled, needle-like organ which can be used to pierce tissues and suck up the sap from the plant. Saliva also passes down the stylet and forms a sheath inside the pierced tissues. A pump is often associated with these mouthparts for sucking liquids up into the mouth. Some of the most important insect pests have piercing mouthparts including mirids, aphids, plant hoppers, whiteflies, scale insects and mealy bugs.

Many nematodes (Fig. 8) and mites have piercing mouthparts similar to insects which are used for sucking up sap from plant tissues.

Figure 3 Life cycle of the migratory locust *Locusta migratoria*

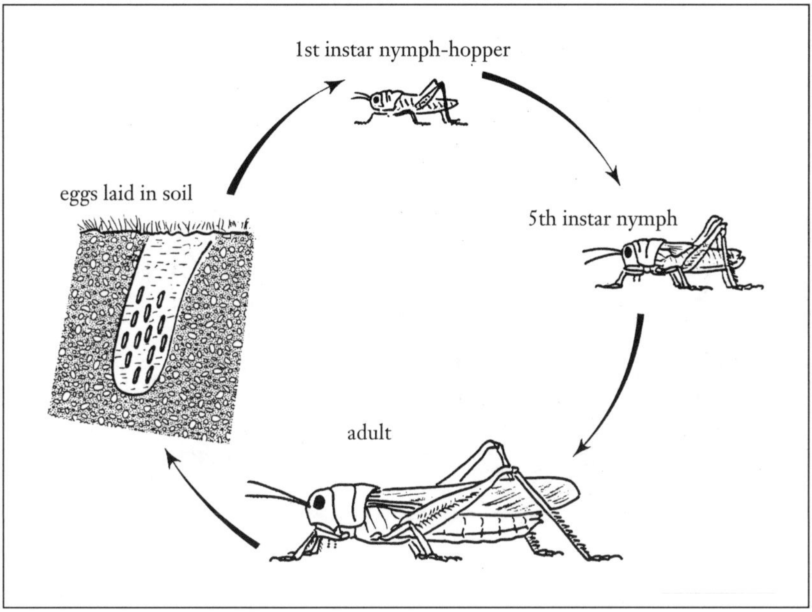

The specificity of pests for plants varies considerably. Certain pests feed on a single species of plant and are called **monophagous**. Examples include the holly leaf miner, *Phytomyza ilicis* Curtis and the auricula root aphid *Pemphigus auriculae* (Murray).

Many pests feed on a restricted range of plants, for example a single family of plants; these are called **oligophagous**. The lily beetle, *Lilioceris lilii* (Scopoli) feeds only on members of the Liliaceae and is attracted to volatile compounds characteristic of this family.

Other pests which feed on a very wide range of plants from many different families are called **polyphagous**. The peach-potato aphid, *Myzus persicae* (Sulzer), is polyphagous and is known to colonise and feed on more than 300 different crops from many different plant families. Rabbits, slugs and vine weevils are also polyphagous.

Behaviour

Pests differ from plants and the pathogens described in this book in that they exhibit behaviour which is a characteristic of all animals. The subject of animal behaviour is fascinating and a knowledge of certain aspects of it can be of great help in devising prevention and control methods for pests. Animal behaviour results from the perception and integration of external and internal stimuli followed by a course of action taken in response to those stimuli. The animal perceives environmental stimuli through its sense organs. The senses include **olfaction** (smell), vision (sight), **thigmoreception** (feeling and touch), **gustation** (taste) and hearing (vibration

Figure 4   Life cycle of large white butterfly *Paris brassicae*

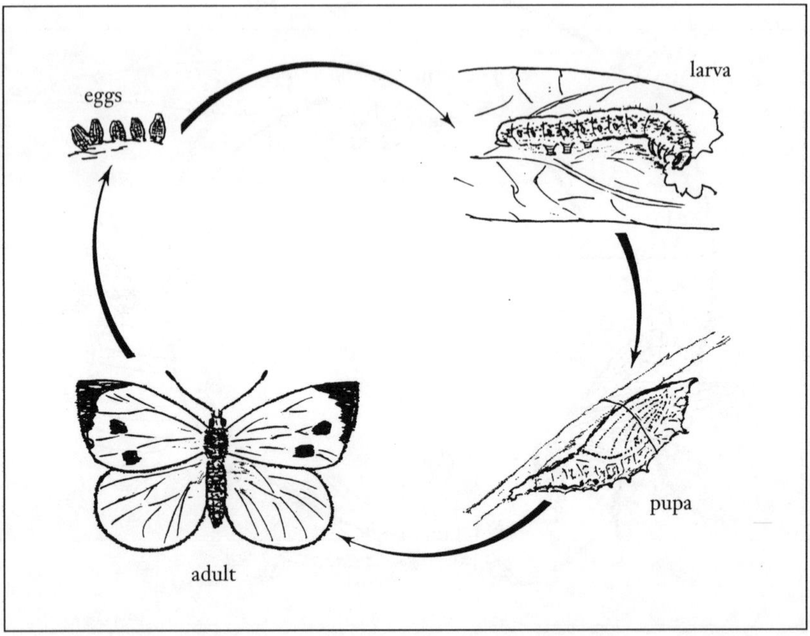

or sound). Internal factors may be innate e.g. the urge to migrate or result from the animal's condition e.g. feeling hungry. The different senses are developed to different degrees in each animal species. For instance many mammals have keenly developed senses of touch and sight whereas a moth may have a well developed sense of smell – e.g. a male moth can detect a few molecules of an attractive odour released by a female of the same species situated a kilometre upwind. These odours, known as **pheromones**, have been identified for certain pest species and are used in traps to catch the insects. Having received all this information the animal responds and takes a course of action. Thus an animal can show a preference for certain plants or certain conditions and can avoid unfavourable situations. A disease organism does not possess this array of senses and cannot take this course of action; its distribution in the environment is passive and determined by factors outside its control. Observations of pest behaviour can indicate pest activity and preference. We have learnt that a large number of pests are active at night or at dawn and dusk (**crepuscular**). Indeed a high proportion of all damage to the aerial parts of plants occurs when the gardener or nurseryman is asleep. Good examples include damage done by cutworms, earwigs, vine weevils, millipedes, woodlice, slugs, snails and rodents. So if you want to observe damage by these pests and to catch the pest, it is best to operate after dark (See article in AGS *Bulletin* 60, 1992). Other valuable observations concerning behaviour have contributed greatly to the development of traps for the monitor-

Figure 5 Life cycle of house fly *Musca domestica*

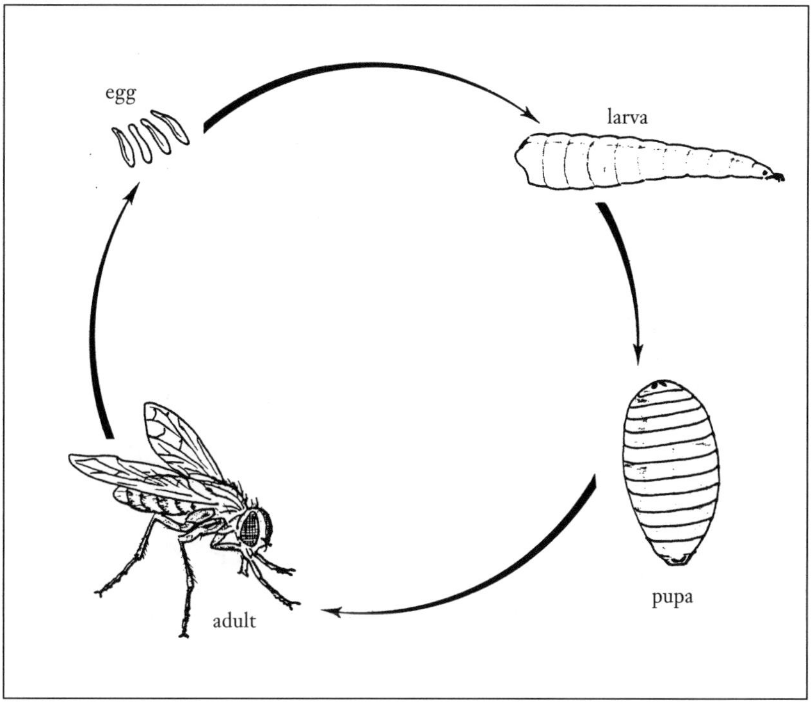

ing and control of pests and in the area of breeding crops resistant to pests. Aspects of animal behaviour are referred to under individual pests.

Identification

Correct pest identification is very important. In the past, crop protection programmes have gone astray as a result of the mis-identification of the pest organism. For example, there are many uncertainties and errors concerning the identity of host ranges of aphid pests. Failure to recognise that several different species feed on closely related plants can lead to the use of the wrong control measures.

Pests can be classified according to the severity of their attack on crops and a consideration of this status can be relevant to crop protection.

Key pests. These cause a significant reduction in yield every season and require regular attention. There are usually few of these pests for any crop. Integrated control programmes are devised primarily for them. Examples include the Colorado potato beetle, *Leptinotarsa decemlineata* (Say), and *Globodera* spp. of cyst nematodes, some of the most severe pests of the potato crop; the carrot fly, *Psila rosae* (F.), which is the major pest of carrots in temperate regions; and red spider mites, *Tetranychus urticae* Koch, on tomatoes and ornamentals. The vine weevil *Otiorhynchus sulcatus* (F.) is an important pest of cyclamen.

Occasional or sporadic pests. Populations of these pests flare up from time to time and cause severe crop losses when they do attack. They are

Figure 6 Insect head and appendages

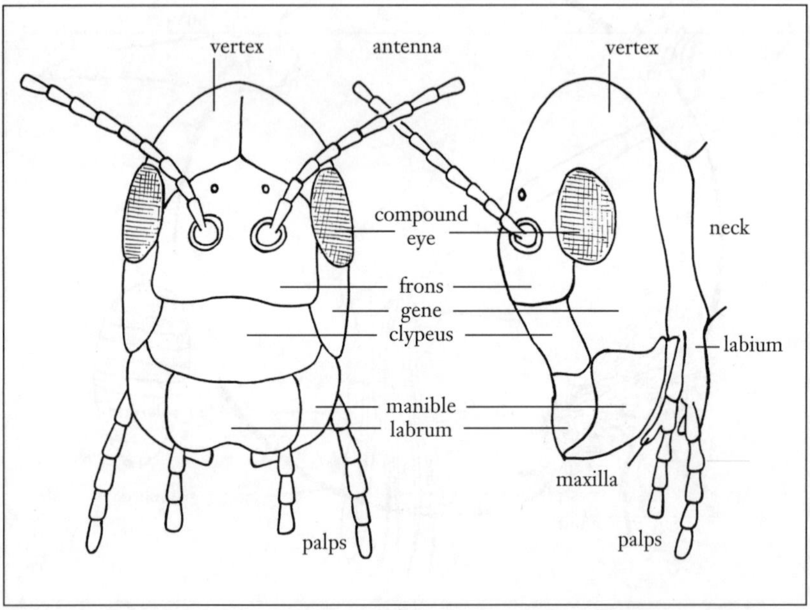

unpredictable and hence difficult to control. Monitoring of pest populations is the key factor in coping with these species as the information gathered can be used to predict outbreaks. An example of this type of pest is cutworm attack on horticultural crops. Their populations are greatly affected by weather conditions and when these conditions are favourable their numbers increase rapidly and damage is severe. Entomologists try to predict outbreaks of cutworm attack by monitoring insect populations and studying weather patterns.

Minor pests. Minor pests occur frequently or sporadically but the damage done to the crop is minor and only in exceptional circumstances will control measures be needed. In other cases the pest occurs at very low numbers and is not a threat. A minor pest of carrots in Britain is the carrot root aphid, *Pemphigus phenax* Borner & Blunch. Only in exceptional circumstances will the grower have to take steps to control this species. Many nematode pests also fall into this category. The carrot cyst nematode, *Heterodera carotae* Jones, is a minor pest of the carrot crop and only occurs in a few localities.

Potential pests. These comprise the vast majority of species which feed on plants. Normally they cause little damage and rarely need to be controlled. If conditions change however, they may have the potential to become more important pests.

These are all general terms and a key pest in one country may be only a minor or potential pest in another, and vice versa.

The identification of pests down to the species, genus and even family level presents greater difficulty. The real experts are either dedicated amateurs who belong to natural history societies or nature conser-

Figure 7 Mouthparts of an aphid

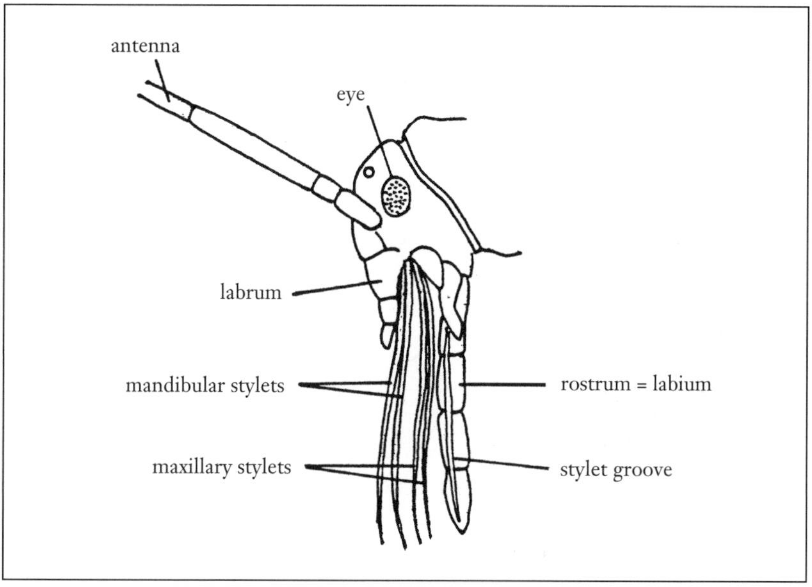

vation trusts or they are employed as professionals at research institutes, universities or centres such as the British Museum. Many gardening societies or nurseries know of useful contacts and will offer advice. To become an expert there is no alternative but to devote many hours of study of pest specimens, identification keys, illustrations and descriptions in text books. To identify specimens you may have to purchase identification keys and a microscope to see the fine morphological characters of a specimen. Clearly you can learn from the experts by accompanying them on forays and discussing problems with them. A list of useful text books to aid in identification is provided in the chapter on further reading.

INSECT PESTS

About half of the million or so insect species described feed on plants, and these are mainly in the **Orthoptera** (crickets, grasshoppers and locusts), **Lepidoptera** (butterflies and moths), **Hemiptera** (mirids, aphids, whiteflies, hoppers, scale insects and mealy bugs), **Thysanoptera** (thrips), **Phasmida** (stick insects), **Isoptera** (termites), **Coleoptera** (beetles including chafers, weevils), **Hymenoptera** (ants, wasps, bees and

Figure 8 Head and anterior end of nematode

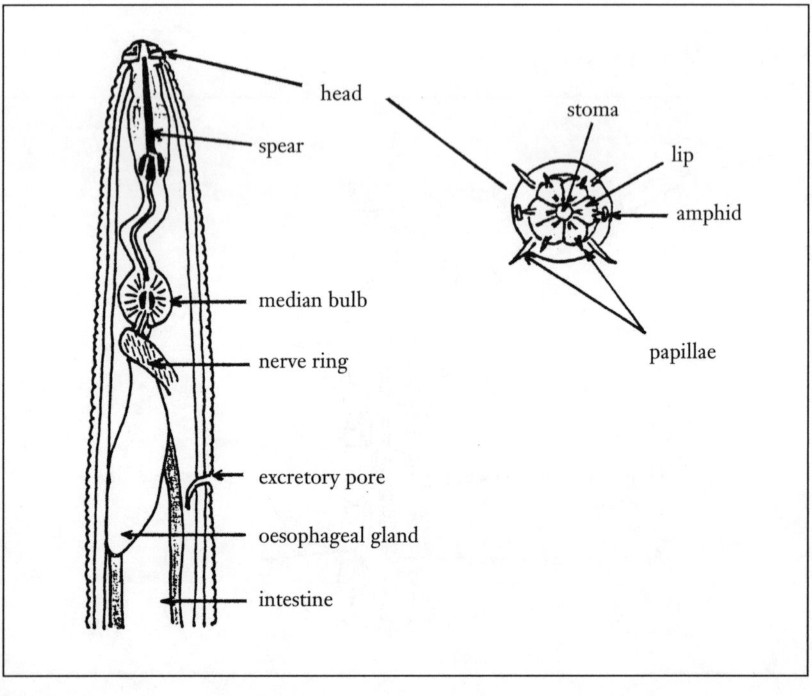

sawflies) and **Diptera** (true flies). In this book we have included certain minor Orders as well as the most important of those listed above.

Springtails (Order Collembola)

The most common pest species are *Bourletiella hortensis* (Fitch), occurring in the garden, and species of *Hypogastrura*, *Onychiurus* and *Orchesella* which occur mainly in the greenhouse and indoors.

Springtails are minute (1.25 – 2.5 mm long), wingless animals which have fewer segments than other insects (Plate 1a). Their name is derived from the highly characteristic springing organ (**furcula**) situated at the rear of the body. This appendage is shaped like a tuning fork and is released forcibly against the ground when the insect is disturbed. The action shoots the insect forward through the air. The springtail body is usually clothed in scales or hairs which give certain species a velvety appearance. Springtails are brown, green, grey or white. They do not possess compound eyes. These insects are distributed throughout the world and are mainly confined to soil and leaf litter but they also colonise the surfaces of ponds and rock pools. They are particularly abundant in wet, acid soils and in frames and glasshouses. Eggs are laid in the soil singly or in groups. The young hatch into miniature adults and there is no metamorphosis. They grow, moult and become adult in a few months.

The majority of springtails are beneficial members of the soil and leaf litter fauna, feeding on dead plant tissues and fungal mycelia thus assisting in the re-cycling of organic matter. However, a few species attack emerging seedlings causing minute lesions and holes in cotyledons, stems and young leaves. Severe attacks result in the collapse of seedlings. *Bourletiella hortensis* can be a severe pest of conifer seedlings particularly *Pinus contorta*. Damage to seedlings results in stunted plants bearing many distorted and swollen needles. Subsequent growth produces a multi-leadered plant. In the glasshouse and frame a wide range of plants may be affected by springtails including *Chrysanthemum*, *Cineraria*, conifers, *Cyclamen*, orchids and *Viola*. Damaged seedlings are prone to fungal and bacterial disease. Springtails also invade plant tissues injured by other organisms.

Infestations can be reduced by improving soil drainage, reducing acidity and by treating soils with insecticides (see Table 44, p.247).

Earwigs (Order Dermaptera)

Earwigs are familiar to most gardeners and are very common pests. They are capable of damaging all parts of a plant. The species most frequently seen in the garden or glasshouse is *Forficula auricularia* L. (Plate 1c).

The adults grow to 25 mm in length and have an elongated brown body which ends in a pair of pincers. They also have a single pair of delicate wings which are folded into wing cases along the back. Earwigs rarely use these wings and prefer to drop to the ground and scurry away when disturbed. The females overwinter in crevices in the soil, piles of stones and garden debris where they lay a cluster of 50-100 eggs. The females guard their eggs as well as the white nymphs which hatch in the spring. The young moult several times and become mature in about 10 weeks. They leave the care of the females and disperse to other feeding sites. The females lay a second batch of eggs in May or June. Earwigs, like many other pests, feed mainly at night. Up to 20 earwigs have been observed feeding on the young flowers of *Buddleia globosa* tearing and distorting the flowers. During the daytime they may be found in flower heads, folded leaves or other crevices. The most serious damage is done to flower petals which they tear and destroy but they will also eat holes in buds, leaves and stems.

Earwigs can be trapped by taking advantage of their habit of hiding during the day. Plant pots loosely filled with straw inverted over the end of bamboo canes, or rolls of newspaper are examples of traps used by gardeners and these can be examined regularly to remove the insects. Insecticidal dusts are effective in reducing their numbers (See Table 44, p.247). Although they can be a troublesome pest they are also predatory and feed on small insects including aphids. So they are beneficial in some circumstances and should only be controlled when they cause damage.

Plant bugs (Order Hemiptera)

This Order of insects includes many important plant pests such as shield bugs, mirids, cicadas, frog hoppers, leafhoppers, aphids, psyllids, whiteflies, scale insects and mealybugs. All these insects are characterised by the possession of a piercing beak (the **rostrum** or **stylet**) formed by the modification of mouth parts to form a structure like a hypodermic needle (see Fig. 7). This is used to penetrate plant tissues and withdraw the sap. The most important plant pests are described below:

Mirid or Capsids (Family Miridae)

These constitute the largest family of the plant bugs and they are very active. Most species are **herbivorous** and the majority overwinter as eggs. They feed on a wide range of garden plants and the damage leads to distortion of buds, leaves and flowers. The two most common species are the common green capsid, *Lygocoris pabulinus* (L.), (Plate 1b) and the tarnished plant bug, *Lygus rugulipennis* Popp.

Mirids have slender relatively-soft bodies, about 6 mm long, conspicuous 4-jointed antennae and membraneous wings. The common green capsid lays eggs in the autumn in the young shoots of a woody host plant. The nymphs hatch out in the spring and feed for a few weeks on these woody plants before moving to herbaceous plants. Adults are produced in June which give rise to a second generation.

Mirids pierce plant tissues with their rostrum, release a toxic saliva, and then suck up the sap from the damaged cells. Initially their feeding activities in leaves and buds pass un-noticed but as the tissues grow and expand a highly characteristic type of damage develops (Fig. 9). Leaves become torn and distorted or puckered because of unequal growth of tissues (Plate 1d). Feeding punctures appear as brown, calloused spots while buds and flowers are distorted. A very wide range of garden plants are damaged, particularly members of the Compositae, the daisy family.

Mirids are not easy to control as the insects may well have left by the time the damage is noticed. Plants may be treated in the spring with certain chemicals (See Table 44, p.247) and may require several treatments if mirids are numerous. Again, chemicals should only be used as a last resort because several species of mirids are important predators of mites, aphids and other small insects.

Aphids (Family Aphididae)

Aphids also known as blackfly, greenbug, greenfly, plant lice and blight, are some of the most important pests in the rock garden and in the alpine house. There are something like 500 species in Britain and many more in Europe and north America, some of them being highly selective in the plants they infest while others feed on practically all garden plants. The most widespread and damaging species in the garden and on the nursery are the peach-potato aphid, *Myzus persicae* (Sulzer) (Plate 2a), the potato aphid, *Macrosiphum euphorbiae* (Thomas) and the glasshouse potato aphid, *Aulacorthum solani* (Kaltenbach).

Aphids vary in length from 1-5 mm, they are typically soft-bodied,

Figure 9 Damage to leaves caused by various pests.

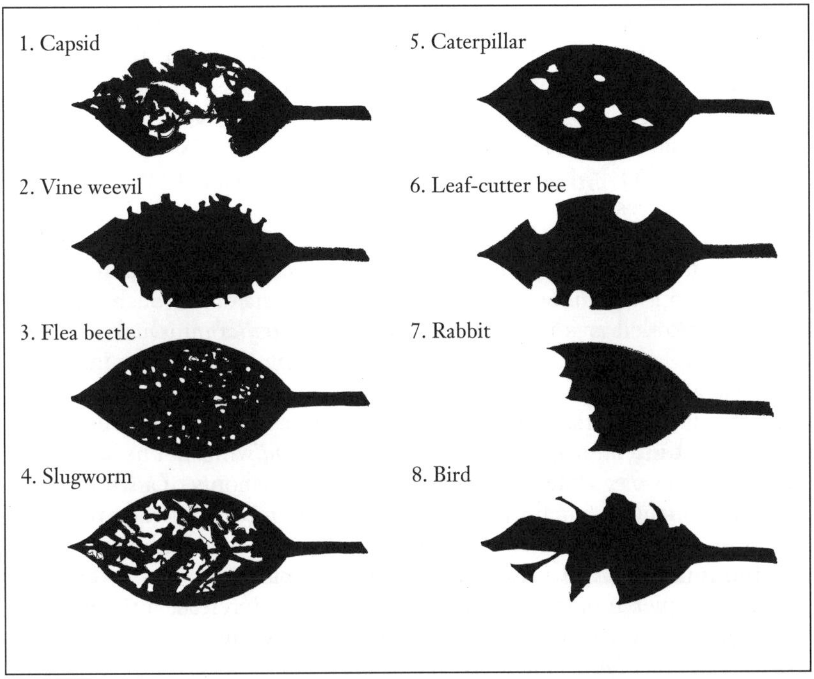

have two antennae, well developed compound eyes, six long legs and at the end of their bodies there are a pair of tube-like extensions, the **siphunculi**. The siphunculi release chemicals used in communication and defence. Aphid life cycles may be very complicated involving numerous different stages which quite often alternate between a woody, winter host and herbaceous plants in the spring, summer and autumn; an example is illustrated in Fig. 2. Certain species overwinter in the egg stage while in mild winters or in the sheltered alpine glasshouse aphids may breed continuously. An infested plant may have winged forms, wingless adults, nymphs, young and eggs but the larger stages are the most conspicuous. Aphids vary greatly in colour – they may be red, yellow, orange, green, brown, blue or black – some colonies may consist of individuals of several different colours. From a distance, however, colonies appear as an amorphous mass. Aphids usually reproduce most rapidly by asexual means and the majority of those seen on plants are **parthenogenetic** females which produce live young. Their powers of reproduction are amazing and in summer outdoors, or in the greenhouse, young aphids mature in a week and then themselves reproduce so that large populations build up very rapidly. Juvenile and adult aphids feed on plants by inserting their stylets into the tissues and sucking the sap (Fig. 7). Large quantities of sap are taken into the body and excess water and sugars are excreted in the form of **honeydew** which is flicked away or falls onto the leaves and stems. This honeydew is greatly sought after by ants which tend the aphids like we tend dairy cattle and this herding instinct leads the ants to protect the aphids from parasites and predators. The sugary honeydew which collects on the plant is soon colonised by sooty moulds which produce black patches (Plate 4d). This fouling of the leaves and stem is not only unsightly but also reduces the leaf's efficiency for manufacturing nutrients and the appearance of alpines grown for exhibition. Primary damage is done to plants by the aphids' feeding activities which lead to distortion, discolouration and malformation of leaves and buds (Plate 1f). Secondary damage results from the honeydew associated with sooty moulds and from viruses which the aphids transmit from plant to plant during feeding (See virus diseases Chapter 4).

Apart from the species mentioned above which are common and widespread, the fern aphid, *Idiopterus nephrelepidis* Davis, infests species of *Cyclamen* and *Viola* under glass and outdoors in warm parts of the country while the mottled arum aphid, *Aulacorthum circumflexum* (Buckton), also occurs in the greenhouse on *Cyclamen* and many other plants including liliaceous and bulbous plants; it is responsible for transmitting a mosaic virus of primula. Sexual forms of this aphid have not been recorded. One species, the tulip bulb aphid (Plate 2f), *Dysaphis tulipae* (Fonsc.) infests the bulbs or corms of a wide range of species including *Crocus*, *Galanthus*, *Iris*, *Scilla* and *Tulipa*. It is mainly a pest of stored bulbs or corms in winter but can cause severe distortion of young shoots when they begin growth in the spring (Plate 2d). Certain aphids only colonise conifers, for example *Juniperus communis compressa* which is severely infested by the aphid *Cinara juniperi* (De Geer) while spruce can be severely damaged by a very large species of *Cinara* (Plate 2b).

There are several species of aphids which infest the roots of alpine plants in the garden, nursery and glasshouse. The colonies of these pale-coloured aphids are surrounded by a powdery, white wax. They can build up to very large numbers on the roots causing severe stunting and wilting. Ants carry these aphids from plant to plant. The most troublesome species are the auricula root aphid, *Pemphigus auriculae* (Murray), which infests *Auricula* and *Primula* species (Plate 2e) and the elder aphid, *Aphis sambuci* L., on *Dianthus* and *Saxifraga* species (Plate 2c).

Because they are so widespread and reproduce so rapidly aphids fall prey to numerous natural enemies (see Chapter 5 for details). Spiders, ladybirds, hoverfly larvae, lacewing larvae and birds all eat large numbers of them and these natural enemies should be encouraged. A predatory midge is now available commercially for the biological control of aphids under glass (see Chapter 5). Also, several species of insects parasitise aphids. However, very few other non-chemical methods appear to work efficiently. Aphids can be killed by squashing them on stems and foliage. Some gardeners spray plants regularly with large quantities of soapy water and this may help. Proprietary compounds containing soaps or detergents (fatty acids) are now widely available at garden centres. Several insecticides can be used to kill aphids, including non-persistent and persistent contact insecticides as well as systemic compounds (See Table 44). Certain products like pirimicarb are especially effective against aphids and have little effect on most aphid parasites and predators – this compound does, however, kill hover flies. **Systemic** compounds are valuable when the insects have invaded inaccessible parts of the plant. In all cases prompt action is essential and regular inspections should be made to detect infestations of aphids as early as possible in their development.

Root aphids are very difficult to control. Frequent checking of the collar region of the plants and of roots around the edges of pots is essential. Infested pot plants should be tapped out and all aphids and soil removed from the roots, this infested material should not be scattered about but very carefully disposed of by burning or placing in the dustbin. The roots may then be dipped in a solution of a contact insecticide. Alternatively plants may be drenched with an appropriate insecticide. Systemic compounds can be particularly effective when the plants are growing actively.

Further reading: 'Aphids on the World's Crops. An Identification and Information Guide' (Blackman & Eastop, 1984).

Adelgids (Family Adelgidae)

Adelgids are closely related to aphids and similar to them in most aspects of their biology and life history. However they are much smaller insects (little more than 1 mm long) and appear as tiny specks on the plant. Colonies of adelgids, produce a woolly wax. Many of the pest species have a two-year life cycle which alternates between spruce (*Picea* species) as a primary host and other conifers as secondary hosts.

The spruce gall adelgids or conifer woolly aphids *Adelges abietis* (L.),

Adelges viridis (Ratzeburg), are severe pests of spruce. Nymphs overwinter on trees and mature in the spring. Females lay batches of eggs which are covered by white woolly wax. The young emerge after a few weeks and feed at the base of needles at shoot tips. The plant's respond by forming a gall which takes on the appearance of a miniature pineapple (Plate 2e). This occurs at the tip of the shoot in the case of *A. viridis* while the gall caused by *A. abietis* is found at the shoot base. In late summer and early autumn winged adelgids leave the galls. Those of *A. abietis* fly to other *Picea* trees while those of *A. viridis* seek out larch trees. These insects produce nymphs which spend autumn and winter on the foliage.

Adelgid feeding leads to yellowing and distortion of the needles and eventually to defoliation. Most stages secrete a woolly wax and produce honey dew which is soon colonised by sooty moulds. The galls disfigure trees and reduce their value. All infested trees are reduced in vigour and, in some cases, severe infestations kill trees. Other species of adelgids attack silver fir (*Abies* sp.) and pine (*Pinus* sp.) plantations.

Trees can be protected from adelgids by spraying the foliage in mild conditions during the period between early November and the end of February (see Table 44).

Leafhoppers (Family Cicadellidae)

Leafhoppers cause considerable damage to many garden plants outdoors and in the greenhouse. The most troublesome species to the alpine gardener is the glasshouse leafhopper, *Hauptidia maroccana* (Melichar) (Plate 3a). Other very widespread species in gardens include *Empoasca* spp.

Adult leafhoppers are like elongated aphids, about 3 mm long but they differ in their ability to jump off a plant and fly away when disturbed. The resting insect is well camouflaged and inconspicuous. The glasshouse leafhopper adults are long, pale yellow with dark bands on their back. The front end of the body is rather frog-like in appearance with prominent eyes and a tapered body. Adults and young have a **proboscis** which they use to pierce plant cells and suck up the sap. Females lay up to 50 eggs which are inserted singly in the veins on the underside of a leaf. The eggs hatch after a few days and the wingless nymphs feed on the underside of leaves. Nymphs are small, wingless insects which are sluggish to begin with but later very active (Plate 3b). They moult 5 times and become winged adults in 4-8 weeks. The cast skins of the nymphs are left attached to the leaves by the proboscis and are sometimes mistaken for insects being known as '**ghost flies**' (Plate 3a). Breeding continues all the year round under glasshouse conditions while outdoors the insects are active in the warmer months.

The feeding damage causes a mottling made up of coarse, pale yellow or white spots (Plate 3c). Seedlings may be killed outright but the tissues of larger plants are distorted and leaves may be completely 'bleached'. Numerous ornamental plants are attacked including *Calceolaria*, *Chrysanthemum*, *Fuchsia* while some species of *Primula* are particularly susceptible (Plate 3b).

Certain species of leafhopper transmit diseases to plants including viruses (See Chapter 4). The aster leafhopper, *Macrosteles fascifrons* (Stal.), transmits a mycoplasma which causes aster yellows in many important crops in the USA.

To reduce leafhopper numbers, badly infested leaves should be removed and burnt. Insecticidal sprays will kill adults and nymphs but need to be used at 2-week intervals. Sprays should be directed at the underside of leaves.

Froghoppers (Family Cercopidae)

Froghoppers are closely related to leafhoppers and very similar to them in details of biology and life history. However, they are stouter, more robust bugs, mostly brown and have horny, pitted forewings. Like leafhoppers they have well-developed hind legs which enable them to jump considerable distances. They all feed on plants.

The most widespread pest species, the common froghopper, *Philaenus spumarius* (L.), is familiar to most gardens as cuckoo spit, a frothy mass produced by the nymphs during the period they are feeding on plants (Plate 3d). This froth prevents dessication and obviously protects the insects from most predators. By late July the nymphs have completed development and emerge from the cuckoo spit as dark brown, tough, jumping froghoppers (Plate 3d). These adults continue to feed, lay eggs in the stems of woody and herbaceous perennials and then die. The life cycle is completed in the following May when the eggs hatch and the nymphs emerge.

Damage results from piercing of plant tissues and removal of sap but is rarely severe – the moulting disfigures leaves. The cuckoo spit is highly conspicuous and may be a nuisance particularly in greenhouses on alpines grown for shows. However, these insects are easily found within the froth and can be squashed.

Mealybugs (Family Pseudococcidae)

Both foliage- and root-feeding species occur in glasshouses or indoors, causing damage to a wide range of plants. The most troublesome foliage feeders include the glasshouse mealybugs, *Pseudococcus obscurus* Essig, and the citrus mealybugs, *Plannococcus citri* (Risso) (Plate 3f), while most root mealybugs are species of *Rhizoecus*, for example, *R. falcifer* (Kunckel d'Herculais).

These pests are tropical and sub-tropical in origin and only occasionally cause problems outdoors in Britain, usually in the south. They are soft-bodied, oval, flattish insects and the females in particular are rather like a woodlice in appearance particularly as females and young have no wings (Plate 3f). They grow to a length of 4 mm and are pale yellow or pale pink in colour. Their bodies are covered with white, woolly, meal or wax which is water-repellent and the wax forms filaments that stick out from the body in a fringe. They feed by sucking sap from stems and foliage and, unlike scale insects, they are mobile although they do spend most of their time in one feeding site. They secrete honeydew on which sooty moulds develop. Males are winged and very rare so most reproduction occur parthenogenetically. Eggs are laid in clumps and covered with wax. Both adult females and young occur together on plants and eight generations can be produced in a year.

Mealybugs are particularly common on plants in the Family Crassulaceae such as *Sedum* and *Sempervivum* and they seem to prefer the most inaccessible parts of a plant – leaf axils, crevices or buds and this makes them very difficult to control. Infested plants grow poorly, are often distorted and lose their leaves. It is extremely difficult to spray and kill these insects particularly because of their position on the plant but also because of their repellent wax covering. Certain systemic chemicals are used to reduce their numbers (Table 44). Malathion sprays damage plants of the Crassulaceae. If you have the time and patience you can pick off the mealybugs or dab them with a paint brush dipped in methylated spirits, surgical spirit, or a contact insecticide. If an infestation is too severe it may be necessary to trim off the worst affected parts of the plants and burn them.

Root mealybugs have a similar life history to foliage-feeding species. They are also extremely difficult to control as populations build up unnoticed and the first symptom is when plants wilt. As with root aphids, pot plants need to be tapped out and all mealybugs and infested soil carefully removed. The root system should then be washed in an insecticide solution. Alternatively plants may be drenched with systemic insecticides.

Once again prevention is better than cure. Newly-acquired plants should be examined for mealybugs before placing them in the greenhouse.

Scale insects (Family Coccoidea)

Scale insects are widespread and common pests of many fruit trees and ornamental plants particularly in greenhouses. The more common species include the brown scale, *Parthenolecanium corni* (Bouché), the soft scale, *Coccus hesperidum* L., the mussel scale, *Lepidosaphes ulmi* (L.), the hemispherical scale, *Saissetia coffeae* (Walker), the oleander scale, *Aspidotus nerii* Bouché which attacks pot *Cyclamen* and two species which infest *Juniperus* and *Thuja*, the Juniper scales, *Carulaspis juniperi* (Bouché) and *Carulaspis minima* (Targ.).

The mature females and nymphs form the characteristic brown, white or yellow waxy scales, up to 5 mm long, which protect their bodies (Plate 3e). These scales are usually sedentary, have no sharply-defined body segments and feed by penetrating the plant stem or leaf with their stylets and sucking the sap. The males which are minute, short-lived and winged are extremely rare or absent in certain species. Females lay hundreds of eggs under the scale or in some species in a white, waxy egg sac. The young nymphs or '**crawlers**' which emerge from these eggs are the dispersive stage and move about on the plants or get carried by the wind, birds or insects to other plants before settling and feeding (Plate 3e). Scale insects are not easy to identify but the shape, size and colour of the adult females are useful diagnostic characters.

Most damage results from the direct feeding action by the scales which reduces plant vigour. In addition, the scales produce copious quantities of honeydew and so the leaves become sticky and have a glistening appearance; ants like to feed on this honeydew and later on sooty moulds colonise the honeydew and the sticky patches turn black. All these effects can ruin alpine plants grown in the greenhouse; few species in the rock garden are likely to be infested.

All newly-acquired plants should be examined for scales and action taken immediately if these pests are discovered. In the greenhouse, plants can be treated individually and the scales wiped off using a soft cloth or fine brush dipped in soapy water; this action is particularly effective on plants with large flat robust leaves such as cyclamen. Crawlers are more easily killed by insecticides than scales, and a contact insecticide (Table 5.5) can be effective, particularly if the timing is right. Spraying may have to be repeated two weeks later to kill all the crawlers. A systemic insecticide will kill the adult scales but the label should be examined to check that the chemical does not harm the plant.

Whiteflies (Family Aleyrodidae)

These small, moth-like insects are covered with a pure white, powdery wax and are familiar to most gardeners. The glasshouse whitefly, *Trialeurodes vaporariorum* (Westw.) is a severe pest of many plants in the glasshouse and in warm sheltered parts of the garden; it is commonly found on *Fuchsia* and *Primula* (Plate 4a). It should not be confused with the cabbage whitefly, *Aleyrodes proletella* (L.), which is confined to various brassicas and related crucifers species, or with certain other species which occasionally infest shrubby plants in the garden.

The tobacco whitefly (cotton whitefly), *Bemisia tabaci* (Gennadius), is a subtropical species which has been introduced recently into Britain and is widespread in the southern United States and other subtropical regions. This species can severely damage greenhouse crops or crops grown outdoors in warmer regions and transmit several important virus diseases (See Chapter 4).

The glasshouse whitefly is not a native British insect although it has been established in the country for many years. It maintains its populations under glass, in polytunnels or in sheltered areas outdoors. The adults are about 1 mm long and covered in the pure white, mealy wax (Plate 4b). They settle on the underside of leaves and rise in a cloud when disturbed. Their eggs are laid in circles on the underside of leaves (Plate 4c), each female producing 200-250 eggs. The eggs hatch after about 10 days and a pale green, flat larva or nymph emerges which, to begin with, is quite active in searching for a suitable feeding site but then settles down and becomes firmly anchored until maturity. The nymphs feed in a similar way to aphids and possess a stylet which is used to pierce cells and suck up the sap. They also excrete the sticky, sugary honeydew which fouls the leaves and is quickly colonised by black sooty moulds (Plate 4d). The larvae are often called **scales** because of their flat, waxy bodies. The nymph passes through four stages, the last being the pupa when the scale becomes thicker, heavily coated with wax and bearing long waxy filaments. Adult flies emerge from these pupae about 10 days later, the complete life cycle taking about 28 days at 21°C.

Damage to plants results from the direct feeding action of whitefly nymphs and the honeydew infested by sooty mould; these problems prevent leaves from functioning properly and in severe outbreaks leaves shrivel and die. Recently the glasshouse whitefly has been shown to be the vector of Beet Pseudo Yellows Virus (BPYV), a notifiable disease of lettuce and cucumber. Several weed species e.g. chickweed, groundsel, shepherd's purse and sowthistle also carry the virus and serve as sources of infection.

It pays to examine plants and deal with infestations before they are introduced to the glasshouse. Several different insecticides in the form of drenches or fumigants are used against whiteflies (See Table 44) but treatments usually have to be repeated several times because the scales are difficult to kill. Glasshouse whiteflies can be controlled using the parasitic chalcid wasp *Encarsia formosa* Gahan, which is introduced into the glasshouse and provides an excellent example of biological control. The wasps lay their eggs in the whitefly scales which are subsequently killed by the parasitic larvae. Affected scales turn black and an adult wasp emerges from each through a hole cut in the top of the scale. At about 22°C the reproductive rate of the parasite is greater than the pest whereas at lower temperatures the whitefly is favoured. Whitefly parasites can be bought from several suppliers (See Table 41).

Further reading: 'Whitefly of the World. A Systematic Catalogue of the Aleyrodidae (Homoptera) with Host Plant and Natural Enemy Data' (Mound & Halsey, 1978).

Thrips (Order Thysanoptera)

Thrips are minute insects which, from time to time, build up in large numbers on plants in the garden and in the glasshouse causing damage to flowers and foliage. The commonest species include the carnation thrips, *Thrips atratus* Hal., the gladiolus thrips, *Thrips simplex* (Mor.), the glasshouse thrips, *Heliothrips haemorrhoidalis* (Bouché), the onion thrips, *Thrips tabaci* Lind. and the rose thrips, *Thrips fuscipennis* Hal. The western flower thrips, *Frankliniella occidentalis* (Pergande), has recently gained a foothold in glasshouses in Britain where it attacks a wide range of crops. This species is more common in parts of Europe and north America and was introduced into Britain in 1986. It is particularly serious on *Cyclamen* and *Primula* collections. It can also transmit tomato spotted wilt virus (See Chapter 4).

Thrips adults are tiny, slender insects, 1-2.5 mm long, with narrow strap-like wings fringed with long hairs (Plate 4e). Although they are tiny they are irritating when they crawl across your skin. They are often called '**thunderbugs**' or '**thunder flies**' as they disperse in very large numbers from cereal fields in stormy weather. Many species are parthenogenetic and the eggs are laid in slits made in plant tissues. The young resemble the adults but do not possess wings; they develop through two nymphal stages, a pre-pupa and a pupal stage before becoming adult. Up to one third of their life cycle may be spent in late larval and pupal stages in the soil.

Thrips feed by puncturing the surface layer of leaves, shoots, flowers or buds and sucking up the sap. This damage drains the cells of their contents and the empty cells fill with air giving them a silvery or pale yellow colour, characteristic of thrips attack (Plate 4f). White flecks on petals later turn brown. Where infestations are severe extensive patches of tissue become discoloured and distorted. Leaves may be shed and buds and flowers are malformed. Seedlings are distorted by attack and take a long time to recover.

Reproduction is fastest in warm, dry conditions and several species build up in large numbers in the glasshouse where conditions are particularly favourable. Severe damage occurs on species of *Chrysanthemum*, *Cyclamen*, *Dianthus* and *Lilium*. Thrips may live in deep crevices on the plant and this makes them hard to detect and difficult to control. Various sprays or dusts are available to control thrips and are listed in Table 5.5. Anthocorid bugs and the mite *Amblyseius cucumeris* are being developed for the biological control of thrips in glasshouses (See Chapter 5 on Natural Enemies of Pests, p.).

Further reading: 'Thrips, their Biology, Ecology and Economic Importance' (Lewis, 1973).

Moths (Order Lepidoptera)

The caterpillars of several species of moths are important pests in the garden and glasshouse. Butterflies and moths are characterised by having two pairs of membraneous wings which, together with the body, are covered in tiny scales. The mouthparts are modified to form a sucking tube, the **proboscis**, through which nectar is drawn. When not in use this tube is coiled beneath the head. The life cycle consists of egg, larva (**caterpillar**), pupa (**chrysalis**) and adult stages (Fig. 4).

In practically all species, the caterpillars are plant feeders equipped with a well-developed head bearing a strong pair of cutting **mandibles** or jaws. The thorax has three pairs of true legs and the abdomen usually five pairs of fleshy **prolegs**. All caterpillars have glands which produce silk threads used in life-lines, tents, webbing or in cocoon production. Most caterpillars moult four or five times. The final stage of the life cycle is the pupa or chrysalis which is usually formed within a **cocoon**. Most species overwinter as a chrysalis but some remain in the caterpillar stage and then pupate in the spring.

Only the caterpillar stage damages plants and the different species feed in a variety of ways:

a) Defoliation – biting out holes (See Fig. 9) or cutting up and eating pieces of leaf, bud, flower and stem.
b) Webbers – spinning webs which pull leaves together to form tents. Caterpillars are then protected when they feed (Plate 5a).

c) Leaf miners and stem borers.
d) Root feeders.

The most common pest species include:

1) Garden swift moth, *Hepialus lupulinus* (L.) and ghost swift moth, *Hepialus humuli* L., which feeds on roots or underground parts of *Campanula, Chrysanthemum, Iris, Narcissus* and *Phlox*. Large cavities may be excavated inside tap roots in which the larvae feed. The caterpillars of swift moths are white with a reddish-brown head (Plate 5b).
2) Garden tiger moth, *Arctia caja* (L.) (Plate 5c), whose caterpillars are known as woolly bears.
3) Several **tortrix** moths which bind leaves together, for example, the flat tortrix moth, *Cnephasia interjectana* (Haworth), which damages species of *Chrysanthemum, Phlox* and *Primula* and the carnation tortrix moth, *Cacoecimorpha pronubana* (Hubner) which attack glasshouse plants; the carnation tortrix moth is described below.
4) A range of **noctuid** moths including the angle shades moth, *Phlogophora meticulosa* (L.), which occurs both in the garden and under glass feeding on species of *Anemone, Chrysanthemum, Iris, Primula* and a wide range of other host plants; silver Y moth, *Autographa gamma* (L.) (Plate 5e), the bright line brown eye or tomato moth, *Lacanobia oleracea* (L.) (Plate 5d) and the cabbage moth, *Mamestra brassicae* (L.) which feed on a large number of plants. The cabbage moth is described in more detail below.
5) **Cutworms** for example the turnip moth, *Agrotis segetum* (Dennis & Schiffermuller) and the large yellow underwing *Noctua pronuba* (L.). The caterpillars of these moths (Plate 5f) cause considerable damage to seedlings, bulbs, corms, tubers and established plants. The turnip moth and large yellow underwing are both noctuid moths and are described in more detail below.

Carnation tortrix moth (*Cacoecimorpha pronubana* (Hubner)). The carnation tortrix moth is one of the leaf-tying species of moths which attacks a wide range of plants in the garden and glasshouse. The moth is distributed in the south of Britain, in central and southern Europe around the Mediterranean and has been recorded in North America, South Africa and Japan. As it also occurs frequently in the glasshouse its range is extended to cooler areas of many countries. Adult moths have a wingspan of about 20 mm, the forewings are brown with darker markings and hind wings orange. The eggs are laid on foliage or other suitable surfaces in overlapping batches of 100 – 200 and covered in a jelly. After 2 to 3 weeks they hatch and the larvae commence feeding. They are bright green or greyish brown and grow to a length of almost 20 mm. Fully fed caterpillars pupate in a dense web of silk amongst foliage or flowers.

The adults are on the wing in May to July or August to November. The broods of caterpillars overlap each other due to variations in emergence of moths. Under glass up to 5 generations of caterpillars can be produced in one year. Damage results from the feeding activities of the caterpillar and from the webbing which constricts growth and detracts from the appearance of the plant. On *Daphne* plants they bind the foliage together with silk and feed inside the bundles. On larger leaved plants they may feed in leaf axils or in rolled leaf tips. they burrow into young tissues destroying flowers and shoots. The caterpillars can escape rapidly from infested plants and drop on a silk thread. The best way to control these pests is to break the webbing, pick off the caterpillars and the bundles of leaves or shoots and destroy them.

Turnip moth, common cutworm (*Agrotis segetum* (Denis & Schiffermuller)). The turnip moth is distributed widely in temperate regions of Asia, Africa and Europe. It is not a pest in the Americas or in Australasia. In western Europe the turnip moth is a most serious and widespread pest.

Adult moths have a wing span of about 40 mm. The forewings are pale greyish-brown with dark brown markings which include rings (**stigmata**) and lines (**fascia**). The hind wings are white in the male; the female's are similar in colour but suffused with brown towards the edge. The robust body and head are brown and the collar region has a black band. Up to 1000 ribbed eggs with a **reticulate** patterning are laid in small irregular masses. They are globular, about 0.5 mm in diameter, milky-white and later turn cream-coloured with reddish-yellow markings and an orange band. Fully-grown larvae are about 40 mm long. The body is plump and rather greasy in appearance, greyish-brown and sometimes tinged with green (Plate 5f). There is a dark dorsal line and a lighter spiracular line. The thoracic legs are yellowish-brown and the abdominal prolegs pale greyish-brown. The pupa, about 15 mm long, is reddish-brown with dark brown spiracles and the **cremaster** has two short, divergent prongs.

Adults emerge in May and June and fly at night. Females lay their eggs on plants, soil or plant debris. They hatch in 10-28 days and young larvae in the first two instars feed on plant foliage. In the later stages, the larvae descend to the ground and feed nocturnally as cutworms, remaining by day in soil crevices or under stones or plant debris. Feeding occurs at or below soil level. These caterpillars either produce a second generation or feed slowly throughout the autumn and winter and become fully-fed in the following spring. About 80% of the food consumed by larvae is eaten in the final **instar**, that is after the last moult. In Britain there is a partial second generation in September or October while further south in Europe there are two generations. Up to 5 generations occur in warmer climates. The larvae pupate in the soil in cells formed from particles of earth. The time spent in this stage varies considerably depending on the time of year but it may be as little as 10 days and in warm conditions, the life cycle being completed in 6 weeks.

This polyphagous species is the most important cutworm in Britain and Europe. Most damage occurs in late summer and early autumn. Seedlings and young plants are severed from the roots and die (Plate 6e). Severe infestations result in patches of devastated plants. Cutworms create cavities in the stems, rhizomes, tubers and roots of larger plants, the damage being similar to that caused by slugs but is not accompanied by the slime characteristic of molluscs. Cutworm damage is most severe in light, sandy soils where the larvae can burrow easily. In Britain, outbreaks of cutworm attack occur sporadically.

Turnip moth attacks are forecast in several countries in order that growers can more accurately time insecticide sprays or, in some years, avoid the use of chemicals. Early monitoring of moth activity was based on light trap catches but the development of baited pheromone traps has improved the efficiency of forecasting.

Weedy ground harbours most cutworms, as the moths prefer sites providing dense plant cover for egg-laying. Thus alpines planted immediately following a dense weed cover are much more likely to be seriously damaged by cutworms than those planted in weed-free soil. It may be possible to hand-pick the caterpillars from the soil near infested plants. Digging over the border injures some larvae and brings many others to the surface of the soil where they are vulnerable to desiccation and predators. As rain reduces larval survival, copious watering of vulnerable plants in mid-summer provides a useful method of checking infestations.

In the past, cutworms were controlled with poison baits containing Paris green (a compound prepared from copper and arsenic salts) mixed with bran or beet pulp moistened with water and spread over infested areas or placed under covers to retain moisture. Gamma HCH was then substituted for Paris green but baits are now rarely used. High volume sprays with DDT have also been effective but treatments aimed specifically at young larvae before they move underground are now based on high volume sprays containing carbamate, organophosphorus and synthetic pyrethroid insecticides (Table 5.5). The bacterium *Bacillus thuringiensis* is effective against caterpillars and several proprietary compounds contain this organism and are approved by organic gardeners (Table 5.1).

Large yellow underwing (*Noctua pronuba* (L.)). This species is widespread in the Palaearctic region as far north as Iceland and Finland. It also occurs in North Africa and was reported recently from Nova Scotia. It is found throughout the British Isles. Like the turnip moth it is a pest of many garden plants.

The adult moth has a wing span of 50-60 mm. This species is sexually **dimorphic** and, although the sexes may be similar in size and shape, they differ in other respects. Thus dark specimens are males while pale ones are females. The forewing ranges from yellowish-brown to dark brown and may have spots and ring markings. The hind wing of both sexes is orange-yellow with a black border. The head and thorax are a similar colour to the forewing while the abdomen is brown. The eggs are about 0.75 mm in diameter, hemispherical, ribbed and reticulated above the middle and smooth below. Initially, they are yellowish-white but they later become reddish-grey. The larva is robust and may grow to a length of 50 mm. It varies in colour from yellow-brown to green and is finely marked with black above the spiracles; it is pale beneath. The lines along the dorsal surface and both sides of the upper part of the body are narrow and pale. The head is light brown and has reddish-brown markings (Plate 6f). The pupa is smooth, glossy and reddish-brown with dark brown spiracles and the cremaster has two spines and two pairs of minute bristles.

Moths have a prolonged emergence in Britain, beginning in mid-June and reaching a peak in August. They are active at night, feeding on the nectar of flowers, and they hide during the day in leaf litter. When disturbed, they fly off wildly and display the bright orange patches on their hindwings. Females lay up to 1000 eggs in flat masses of 100-150 on the underside of leaves, most eggs being laid in July-August. After 10-28 days, the larvae hatch and start feeding on plants during the day (Plate 6f) but later instars feed as typical cutworms. Fully grown larvae remain active during the winter months in Britain and pupation occurs in an oval cell in the soil during late spring.

This species is polyphagous, feeding on most crops and many wild and garden herbaceous plants; the larvae attack the roots and foliage of plants. The caterpillars are frequently found on top of cushion alpines such as saxifrages on mild winter nights browsing the foliage (Plate 6f). The host plants include *Chrysanthemum*, *Dianthus*, *Viola*, *Primula* and numerous species of cushion plant.

Cabbage moth (*Mamestra brassica* (L.)). Caterpillars of the cabbage moth, (also known as the cabbage army worm in Japan) attack many species of alpines and damage all parts of the plant. This moth's range extends from Europe to Japan and into subtropical Asia including India; it is very common in the British Isles and continental Europe. The adults fly at night, appear in late May and early June and have greyish brown forewings mottled with dark brown; the wingspan is 42 mm. The hind wings are greyish brown and pale towards the base with a terminal white line. The globular, finely reticulated, and ribbed pale eggs are laid singly or in groups of 20 to 100 on the undersides of leaves (Plate 6a). The young caterpillars are light green but vary in colour as they grow older (Plate 6b); they may remain light green or change to a darker green, brown or even black (Plate 6c) on the dorsal surface while the under surface and legs vary from green to yellow. The caterpillars feed from 4 to 5 weeks and may grow to a length of 50 mm. They burrow into the soil and form a glossy reddish-brown pupa (Plate 6d) enclosed in a delicate **cocoon**. Sometimes these conspicuous pupae are found when digging in the garden.

There is usually one generation a year but occasionally there may be a partial second generation, the caterpillars feeding until October before pupation. These caterpillars defoliate plants outdoors and under glass. A range of insecticides, as well as *Bacillus thuringiensis* Berliner, can be used to control the caterpillars (Tables 5.1 & 5.5).

The most satisfactory way of dealing with practically all caterpillars is to hand-pick those infesting the foliage, to crush leaf miners and to search for root feeding caterpillars such as cutworms and remove them from the soil. Regular examination of plants for caterpillars or for signs of wilting is advisable.

Further reading: 'Pest Lepidoptera of Europe with Special Reference to the British Isles' (Carter, 1984).

True flies (Order Diptera)

Several species of two-winged flies (Order Diptera of the insects) are pests of alpine plants grown outdoors or under glass. The adults are characterised by the possession of only one pair of wings (the forewings), the hind wings being modified to form a pair of balancing organs, the **halteres**, which are used in flight. Adult flies mostly feed on nectar, honeydew or decaying organic matter, none of them damage plants. Eggs are laid near, in or on plant tissues and it is the larva or **maggot** which emerges that causes the damage. The maggot grows rapidly, moults three times and, when fully grown, forms a pupa. The life cycle (Fig. 5) is completed when the adult insect emerges from the pupa. The larvae or maggots feed on different parts of the plant and this provides a convenient way of grouping them.

Bulb flies (Family Syrphidae)

Certain species of flies are important pests of bulbs. The maggots of these flies burrow into the tissues causing severe damage which kills the plant. The most common species are the large narcissus fly or bulb fly, *Merodon equestris* (F.) (Plate 7a), and the two species of small narcissus flies or lesser bulb flies, *Eumerus strigatus* (Fall.) and *Eumerus tuberculatus* (Rond.) (Plate 7). These three species are all members of the hoverfly Family, the Syrphidae.

The life cycles of these flies are similar. The adults are quite like bees in appearance and they emerge from pupae in late April and May. Their food is nectar and they may be seen hovering near flowers in the garden or hedgerow. Females lay eggs on the plants or in the soil nearby. The young larvae emerge from the eggs after a few days and they burrow into the bulb. The tissues are excavated and eaten, the larvae growing rapidly and moulting several times before becoming fully grown; they overwinter as a larva. Pupation takes place in the soil near the bulb in spring.

The large narcissus fly differs from the smaller species in having only one brood a year, it is also a primary pest and attacks healthy bulbs, and the larvae, which attain a length of 19 mm (Plate 7b), occur singly in a bulb. In contrast, the small narcissus flies have two or three broods a year and the larvae which grow to a length of 8 mm are invariably found in groups (Plate 7d). The adult females of the small narcissus fly always lay their eggs on or near already diseased or damaged bulbs.

The large narcissus fly attacks several species of bulbous and some tuberous plants including *Amaryllis*, *Cyrtanthus*, *Eurycles*, *Galtonia*, *Galanthus*, *Habranthus*, *Iris*, *Leucojum*, *Scilla* and *Vallota*. However, *Narcissus* species are the principal hosts. Maggot damage affects growth and survival of the plants. Small bulbs may be killed but larger bulbs grow poorly and commonly fail to produce a flower. The foliage is distorted and often slender giving rising to the symptoms known as 'grass' by nurserymen.

The small narcissus flies attack a wider range of plants including

a. Webworm caterpillar on pine

b. Ghost swift moth, *Hepialus humuli*

c. Adult garden tiger moth, *Arctia caja*

d. Bright line brown eye moth caterpillars

e. Adult silver 'Y' moth, *Autographa gamma*

f. Caterpillar of turnip moth, *Agrotis segetum*

a. Eggs of cabbage moth, *Mamestra brassicae*

b. Caterpillars of cabbage moth, *Mamestra brassicae*

c. Caterpillar of cabbage moth, *Mamestra brassicae*

d. Chrysalis of cabbage moth, *Mamestra brassicae*

e. Damage to rows of young plants by turnip moth, *Agrotis segetum* caterpillars

f. Caterpillar of large yellow underwing moth, *Noctua pronuba*

a. Adult of large narcissus fly, *Merodon equestris*

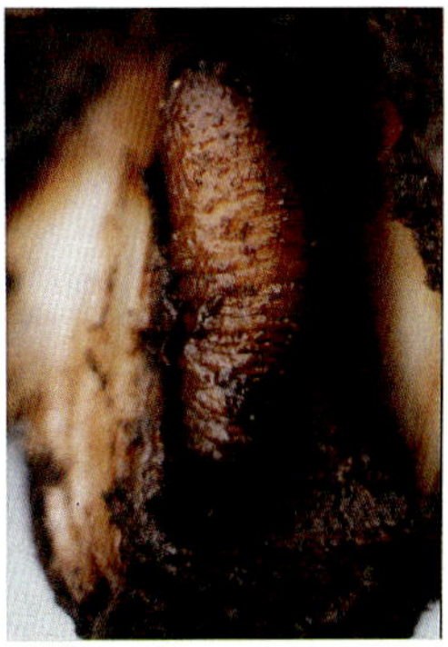

b. Larva of large narcissus fly, *Merodon equestris*

c. Adult of lesser bulb fly, *Eumerus strigatus*

d. Larva of lesser bulb fly, *Eumerus strigatus*

e. Adult crane fly, *Tipula paludosa*

f. Larvae (leatherjackets) and pupae of crane fly, *Tipula paludosa*

a. Adult sciarid fly (fungus gnat), *Bradysia paupers*

b. Larva of sciarid fly (fungus gnat), *Bradysia paupers*

c. Damage to cyclamen by sciarid fly (fungus gnat), *Bradysia paupers*

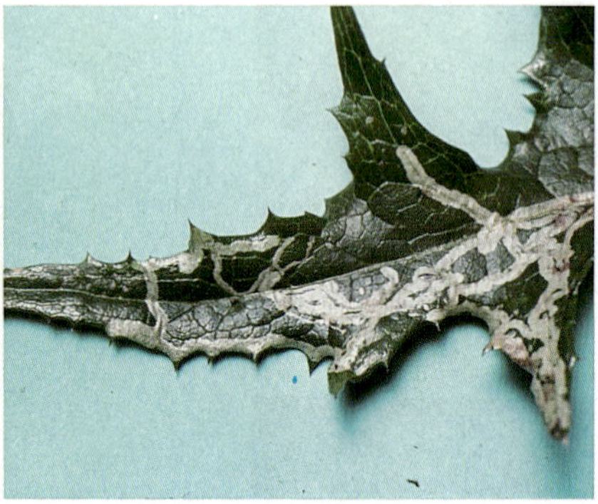

d. Damage to dandelion by leaf miner

e. Damage to pear leaf by pear slugworm, *Caliroa cerasi*

f. Caterpillar of Solomon's seal sawfly, *Phymatocera aterrima* and damage to plant

Hyacinthus, *Iris*, *Lilium*, carrot, *Narcissus*, onion, parsnip and potato. Bulbs are commonly destroyed by the maggots and the associated disease organisms.

Bulb flies are difficult to control and little can be done to save plants infested with maggots. It is important to examine all bulbs that are lifted from the garden or acquired from friends or garden centres. Any suspect, soft bulbs should be destroyed. Reputable suppliers of bulbs are likely to have treated their stock using hot water dips or chemicals and this kills any maggots within the tissues. Bulbs which produce distorted, weak or abnormal foliage should be lifted and examined. Any larvae discovered should be destroyed.

Leatherjackets (Family Tipulidae)

Leatherjackets are the larvae of crane flies or daddy longlegs. They are primarily pests of grassland but occasionally damage other crops or garden plants including alpines. Adults of several species are very commonly seen in gardens and in houses during the evening particularly the marsh or common crane fly, *Tipula paludosa* Meig. (Plate 7e), which is on the wing in September and the two closely related species *Nephrotoma appendiculata* (Pierre) and *N. flavescens* (L.) which emerge in May or June. The life cycle of the common cranefly is typical.

Adult flies are large with long, slim bodies (12-25 mm), very long spindly legs and one pair of narrow wings (Plate 7e). Females lay up to 300 eggs in soil crevices or drop them in flight. After 10 to 14 days the tiny brown or grey legless larvae emerge and crawl to reach plant roots on which they feed during autumn, winter and spring. By the spring they may have reached 4 cm in length and typically are brown to greyish-black, fat, soft but with a tough skin – hence the description **leatherjackets** (Plate 7f). The larvae pupate in the soil but protrude slightly above the soil surface. Adults emerge from these pupae; the latter are illustrated in Plate 7f. It is only the larval stage which damages plants and feeding occurs on roots just below the soil surface or on foliage and stems at the surface; bulbs, corms and tubers are also attacked. Most damage is done in the spring and seedlings or young plants are particularly vulnerable; it only requires a few larvae to cause serious damage. Affected plants turn yellow, wilt and die. This damage is similar to that caused by cutworms and in fact the larvae of both pests may be of a similar size and resemble each other. It is important to search for the larvae in soil near damaged plants. Leatherjackets differ from cutworms in not having legs or a distinct head and they do not curl up when handled.

Leatherjackets are usually only troublesome in areas of the garden brought recently into cultivation which had previously been a lawn or pasture, although an example was recently brought to the author's attention of an infestation in the gravel bench of an alpine house. Leatherjackets were removed from underneath pots standing on the gravel. Either the adult craneflies laid eggs in the house or soil was introduced which contained eggs or larvae. The larvae have been reported as severe pests of mossy saxifrages.

If a new rock garden or raised bed is being constructed much of the damage caused by leatherjackets can be prevented by thorough and repeated cultivation in the spring or in July/early August followed by a fallow period. Many leatherjackets are killed by natural enemies such as viruses and birds, particularly starlings, which probe lawns for the larvae or pupae. Repeated cultivation of the soil exposes larvae to birds. Insecticidal dusts or drenches around plants reduce their numbers as do pellets put down to control slugs.

Sciarid flies (Family Sciaridae)

Sciarid flies, also known as mushroom flies, fungus gnats and Mycetophilids, have increased in importance with the advent and widespread use of soil-less compost as a growing medium for pot plants. Although they are believed to feed primarily on decomposing vegetable matter there is no doubt that they can do serious harm to a wide range of seedlings and pot plants. The species most commonly associated with damage is *Bradysia paupers* Tuom.

Adult flies are black, delicate, gnat-like and only 2.5-3.5 mm long (Plate 8a). Their behaviour is highly characteristic as they are more frequently observed running over the surface of plants or the soil than they are flying; in fact they are weak fliers. When at rest their wings are held flat along the body. Mating occurs within hours of emergence and soon afterwards females lay eggs. Between 100 and 300 of the tiny eggs are laid in clusters in soil crevices and these hatch in a few days. The emerging larvae have white segmented bodies, a black shining head and they pass through four larval stages, the final stage being about 5 mm long (Plate 8b). With the aid of a lens the gut of the larva is visible in the milky white body. It is only the larval stage which damages plants, both roots and stems being invaded. Fully-grown larvae form pupae in the soil and adult flies emerge about one week later. The entire life cycle may be completed in as little as 4 weeks when conditions are favourable and breeding continues throughout the year in greenhouses or in the home.

These pests are particularly troublesome in the alpine glasshouse attacking seedlings, rooted cuttings and established plants of *Cyclamen*, *Dianthus*, *Saxifraga*, *Sempervivum*, *Primula* and numerous other alpines incuding cushion plants. Seedlings collapse and die as a result of damage by the larvae (Plate 8c) while larger plants grow poorly, wilt and eventually die when infestations are severe.

Additives to compost such as perlite, plastic foam and vermiculite appear to have increased the sciarid problem and it is known that females are attracted to, and may lay their eggs in freshly sterilised soil and composts incorporating dried blood. Potting composts should therefore be kept in closed containers. It is advisable to monitor the presence of the flies using yellow water-traps. Plants which are pot-bound appear to be more susceptible to damage than those with a free root run. Certain chemicals available to the amateur as sprays or fumigants are used against the adults while drenches or sprays may kill some of the larvae (Table 44).

Gall midges (Family Cecidomyiidae)

The larvae of certain species invade leaves and stems causing galls or other types of malformation. The chrysanthemum gall midge, *Rhopalomyia chrysanthemi* (Ahlb.), is a common pest of chrysanthemums grown in greenhouses and polytunnels. Other species include the violet leaf midge, *Dasineura affinis* (Kieff.) and the arabis midge, *Dasineura alpestris* (Kieff.).

The adults are tiny flies which lay their eggs on buds and leaves. After hatching the larvae feed on tissues which become distorted and galled. The larvae continue to feed within the galls for 2-3 weeks before pupating. In the case of the chrysanthemum gall midge infestations in leaves, buds and stems produce characteristic thorn-like projections. Flowers may be malformed while cuttings are weakened and do not root well. The pest is particularly troublesome in glasshouses and numerous generations may be completed each year.

Newly-acquired plants should be examined for symptoms of attack and infested leaves and shoots removed. Similarly, affected parts of plants should be removed and destroyed by burning as soon as they are noticed.

Leaf miners (Family Agromyzidae)

The larvae of flies from several families mine the foliage and stems of garden plants. The damage is rarely sufficient to kill plants but the blisters in the foliage ruin the appearance of the plant and reduces their vigour (Plates 8d). The most common species include the carnation fly, *Delia cardui* (Meigen), the chrysanthemum leaf miner, *Phytomyza syngenesiae* (Hardy) and the iris leaf miner, *Cerodontha ireos* (Goureau). Two leafminer pests *Liriomyza bryoniae* (Kaltenbach) and *Liriomyza trifolii* (Burgess in Comstock) are important outdoors in the USA and occur in glasshouses in Britain; they severely damage crops such as tomatoes. Recently the leaf miner *Liriomyza huidobrensis* (Blanchard) has been introduced into Britain and is causing crop losses in glasshouses. Adult females lay their eggs on leaf surfaces, in leaf axils or they are inserted in the tissues. When the larva emerges it starts tunnelling in the leaf or stem. When fully grown the larva pupates either in the tissues or in debris on the ground. If a leaf is held up to the light the translucent larva may be seen inside the blistered area. If infestations are severe leaves may shrivel and die. The most satisfactory means of control is to remove infested leaves and burn them. Under glass, tomato leafminers are controlled by the parasitic wasps *Dacnusa sibirica* Telenga and *Diglyphus isaea* (See also Chapter 5 on Biological Control of pests, p.215).

Ants, Bees and Sawflies (Order Hymenoptera)

Ants (Family Formicidae)

Ants are very common insects and can be pests in the garden, house, or alpine house although certain species are beneficial or harmless. About 35 species live in Britain, the most troublesome in the garden being the common black ant, *Lasius niger* (L.), the mound ant, *Lasius flavus* (Fabricius), while in the glasshouse and indoors the most common are the Pharaoh's ant, *Monomorium pharaonis* (L.), and the Argentine ant, *Iridomyrmex humilis* (Mayr).

Ants live in nests which often contain several thousand individuals, most of them are workers (sterile females). It is the workers that care for the nest, tend the larvae, collect food and ward off enemies. Winged males and females are produced when conditions are favourable in the summer months and swarms of these insects crawl about on paving slabs or on the rock garden. They fly off to mate on the wing. Males die soon after mating but fertilised females (young queens) return to the ground, shed their wings, and crawl away in search of an existing nest or find a site suitable for founding a new colony. Queen ants may live for several years and in that time lay several thousands of eggs. The legless, soft-bodied larvae are reared in the nest and when fully grown develop into a pupa enclosed in a silk cocoon. The adult insect emerges from this pupa to complete the life cycle.

Ants occasionally damage plants by feeding on buds, leaves and flowers; they also collect seeds which are taken back to the nest. They swarm over plants infested with aphids, mealybugs and scale insects, collect the honeydew and protect these pests from attack by natural enemies; they may even carry aphids from plant to plant. Ants probably cause most damage when constructing their nests in the rock garden because they tunnel among the roots and remove soil. In dry borders and rock gardens on light soils root systems may be seriously effected and the plant dies.

Direct action on the nest is the best control method. If it is accessible you may be able to dig out the nest. If not then water a solution of a suitable insecticide into the nest entrance using sufficient liquid to permeate the nest and then close the entrance. If nests are inaccessible, for example, under paving slabs or in the alpine house, you will have to use baits although some gardeners recommend drenching the ground with liquid insecticide. Most bait's contain a sugary substance or other attractant mixed with a persistent insecticide which is placed on a piece of card or wood. The worker ants carry the poisoned bait back to the nest. The bait should be replenished regularly and protected from water splashed about in the glasshouse. Several insecticides are available (Table 44).

Sawflies (Family Tenthredinidae)

Sawflies belong to the same insect order as ants, bees, ichneumon flies and wasps (Hymenoptera). The caterpillars are all plant feeders and can be important pests in the garden. They occasionaly attack alpine plants. Common garden pests include the geum sawfly, *Metallus gei* (Brischke), the iris sawfly, *Rhadinoceraea micans* (Klug), the Solomon seal sawfly, *Phymatocera aterrima* (Klug), the pear slugworm, *Caliroa cerasi* (L.) and the common gooseberry sawfly *Nematus ribesii* (Scopoli).

Adults look like flying ants, about 10 mm long with two pairs of membraneous wings, dark body and legs and they possess a saw-like organ which is used to cut plant tissues during egg-laying. Unlike other members of the Order they do not have a waist-like constriction between thorax and abdomen. Males are found in most species but others reproduce parthenogenetically. The geum sawfly only has one generation each year and adults are found in May – early June. Eggs are inserted in the leaves of host plants. They hatch after a few days and the larvae mine the leaf tissues. Many sawfly larvae are very similar in appearance to the caterpillar of certain species of butterflies and moths (Plate 8f) but on close inspection they are seen to have at least 6 sucker feet (prolegs) without rings of hooks and have only a single pair of simple eyes. Butterfly and moth caterpillars only have five pairs of prolegs and have four or five pairs of simple eyes. Other sawfly larvae may look like small slugs (Plate 2.70). When fully-grown most sawfly larvae pupate in a cocoon in the ground.

The type of damage depends on the plant/insect species and includes defoliation (Plate 8f), leaf mining, leaf-rolling, removal of the leaf epidermis or galling of tissues.

Caterpillars can be picked off plants by hand, mining larvae can be crushed while certain chemicals deter egg-laying females and kill many larvae (See Table 44).

Leaf-cutter bees (Family Megachilidae)

Occasionally leaf-cutter bees cause damage to alpine plants. The commonest garden species is *Megachile centuncularis* (L.).

Leaf-cutters are solitary bees and do not form a hive or swarm. The adults are about 10 mm long and similar to honey bees except that their bodies are stouter and more hairy. Females have a distinctive bright orange pollen brush under the abdomen. The adults emerge in the spring and soon after mating the females commence nest building in either hollow plant stems, decaying timber or the soil. The hollow, cylindrical cells are formed from rolled sections of leaf cut with the mandibles from certain species of plant. The cells are filled with honey and pollen, an egg laid on the top and the cell capped with another leaf section. Several cells are constructed in this way. The female then dies. The larvae feed on the rich mixture of honey and pollen and eventually pupate inside the cell.

The young bees eat their way out of the cells in the following spring males being the first to emerge. They wait on neighbouring flowers for the females to emerge which are then mated.

The symptoms of leaf-cutter bee attack are highly characteristic. The females cut almost perfectly symmetrical semi-circular sections from leaves (Fig. 9) of a range of plant species. Host plants include *Fushsica*, *Geranium*, *Laburnum*, lilac, privet, rhododendron, rose and *Viola*. Damage is seldom severe enough to warrant control measures.

Beetles (Order Coleoptera)

Beetles form the largest order of insects in terms of number of species and are familiar to most gardeners. Practically all adults have two pairs of wings, the forewings being modified to form tough wing cases under which the membraneous flight wings (hind wings) are folded. The first segment of the thorax is normally large and mobile. Beetles have biting mouthparts. Like many other insects the life cycle consists of egg, larva, pupa and adult stages. The larvae or grubs have well developed heads with strong biting mouthparts and usually three pairs of legs. The pupae have free legs, antennae and mouthparts. Most species have only one generation a year and they overwinter as young larvae, pupae or adults. Beetles vary considerably in size and both larvae and adults feed on plants. However, a large number of species are predatory and of considerable value to the gardener as they consume many pests. Ground beetles are examples of beneficial species which should be encouraged.

The main pests belong to four groups of beetles which are described below.

Chafer grubs (Family Scarabaeidae)

These grubs are the larvae of certain beetles and the following species attack plant roots and are occasionally a nuisance in gardens: the summer chafer, *Amphimallon solstitialis* (L.), the cockchafer *Melolontha melolontha* (L.), and the garden chafer, *Phyllopertha horticola* (L.).

Many people will be familiar with the adults of these insects particularly the **cockchafer** or **Maybug** which is attracted to lighted windows on spring evenings and crashes repeatedly against the glass. The life cycle of this species is fairly typical of the group. The adult insects are large and heavy, about 25 mm long with a dark head and thorax, light reddish-brown wing bases, strong bristly legs and prominent antennae and eyes. The males have elaborate fan-like antennae. The adults emerge in the spring and feed on foliage at night but rarely do any significant damage. Eggs are laid in the soil near plants. The grubs (larvae) are large and powerful having white bodies with three pairs of legs and strong biting mouthparts. They moult through several stages and live underground for about 3 years. These grubs are easily found in the soil and lie in a characteristic curved position. The fully-grown grub forms a cell in the soil and changes into a soft-bodied white pupa. The following spring the adults emerge from their pupae, crawl up to the surface of the soil and fly away. The life cycles of the other two species differ in that it takes one year for the garden chafer and two years for the summer chafer to complete their development.

It requires only a small number of these grubs to destroy a plant and the infestation results in the appearance of patches of wilting or stunted plants. Roots, corms, tubers and stems of plants such as *Alyssum*, *Anemone*, *Draba* and *Iris* are attacked.

The beetles are usually controlled using dusts of derris or gamma HCH which is applied to the foliage and surrounding soil.

Leaf beetles (Family Chrysomelidae)

Leaf beetles are brightly coloured, sometimes metallic, usually small insects. Many species have grubs (larvae) which are soft-bodied and are almost slug-like in appearance. World-wide there are about 25,000 species in this family and in Britain we have more than 250 species. As a group they are practically all plant feeders in the adult and larval stages. There are several important pests in the Chrysomelidae including cereal leaf beetles, flea beetles, the Colorado potato beetle, the asparagus beetle as well as lily beetles.

Flea beetles. Both the larvae and adults attack plants and are occasionally pests of alpine plants. The most common species all belong to the genus *Phyllotreta*.

Adult flea beetles are small, up to 3 mm long, with shining wing cases which may be black, black with a yellow stripe down each case or black with green, blue or bronze sheen depending on the species (Plate 10b). When disturbed they jump off the plant in a similar way to a flea jumping off its host – hence the common name flea beetle. Adults spend the winter in crevices in plant debris, trees, and undergrowth. At the onset of spring they emerge and fly off to colonise host plants feeding on the foliage. During May and June eggs are laid in or on the soil near plants. The larvae crawl and invade the roots or foliage of the plant. Fully-grown larvae are 4-6 mm long and they pupate in the soil. After 2-3 weeks adults emerge and begin feeding. The time taken from egg to adult is 6-8 weeks and there is one generation a year.

Most of the damage is done by the adults which eat holes in leaves, stems and young seedlings and plants may be 'peppered' with feeding holes (Fig. 9). Amongst the alpine plants damaged are species of *Alyssum*, *Anemone*, *Draba*, *Iris* and *Matthiola*. To reduce damage seedlings should be given ideal conditions for rapid establishment, such as well-prepared ground containing adequate moisture and nutrients. Insecticidal dusts applied to leaves and surroundings of plants will deter beetles (Table 44).

Lily beetles. Several members of the Alpine Garden Society have reported devastating attacks of **lily beetles**.

There are two species of lily beetle which attack lilies and related plants: *Lilioceris merdigera* (F.) and *Lilioceris lilii* (Scopoli). They were both formerly included in the genus *Crioceris* and they are sometimes known as lily criocerans. Some of the most important host plants of lily beetles are listed below:

Fritillaria meleagris	Snake's head Fritillary
Lilium auratum var. *virginale*	Golden-rayed Lily
L. candidum	Madonna Lily
L. giganteum (*Cardiocrinum giganteum*)	

L. hansonii	
L. martagon	Turk's cap Lily
L. philippinense var. *formosanum*	
L. regale	Regal Lily
L. tigrinum	Tiger Lily
Nomocharis saluenensis	
Polygonatum multiflorum	Solomon's Seal

Lilioceris merdigera also attacks *Convallaria majalis* lily of the valley, and various *Amarallydaceae* including onion and shallot.

Lily beetles are distributed widely throughout Europe extending as far east as Asia and south to North Africa; they also occur in Canada and the north eastern USA. They are particularly important in western Europe and cause severe damage to crops in France. Britain is really on the northern fringe of their range. They were first reported as far back as 1890 in Kent and, subsequently, they were recorded in other parts of England. Adult beetles are thought to have been introduced into Britain on lily bulbs and in packing material. At present they are largely confined to southern England but sporadic attacks have been reported from Cheshire, Cumberland, Middlesex, Surrey and Kent.

Adult beetles are 8 mm long and the upper parts of their bodies are almost entirely bright vermilion (Plate 10a). This brilliant colour fades after the beetles die. The head, antennae and lower parts of the body are black. *L. merdigera* has reddish legs; those of *L. lilii* are black, the different permitting the two species to be easily distinguished. The front part of the face is extremely flat and streaked, the eyes are small but prominent. The front part of the thorax is more than half the size of the wing cages and strongly indented near the middle of each side. The adults **stridulate** (produce sounds by rubbing two parts of the body together) on lily plants in the spring so you are as likely to hear them as catch sight of them at this time of the year.

The eggs are about 1 mm long, shining and dirty yellow. The grubs are a similar colour with a slightly curved, thick, short body and six black-brown legs; the head is also black-brown. When fully grown the grubs are 8-10 mm long. The segments of the body possess small, regularly-arranged black plates which bear two hairs. The excrement of the grub accumulates in a mass above these plates probably as a form of camouflage but also possibly to protect themselves from the heat of the sun and to retain body moisture. The grubs pupate in the soil in a polished, oval cell lined with a varnish-like coating.

Adults emerge in the spring and they aggregate on plants where they nibble the leaves and flowers. Shortly after emergence the adults mate and females soon begin to lay their eggs. Females lay up to 300 eggs during the seasons and if they survive to the following year, they lay more eggs in the spring. The eggs are glued to the border of host plant leaves either singly or in small irregular groups. Incubation usually lasts 7-10 days, sometimes longer, and after emergence the young grubs immediately feed on the leaves or flower buds of host plants. The growth of the grubs is rapid and they can be fully developed in 16 days. Having completed their development the grubs descend to the ground and bury themselves in the surface layers of the soil where they hollow out a cavity which is lined with saliva. This lining which has a varnish-like appearance, forms the pupal cell. The grubs pupate and remain in this state for 20-22 days after which the adults emerge.

In warmer areas, the first generation in the spring gives rise to adults in mid-May and, eggs laid later, produce a second generation in June-July. A third generation may follow in the autumn. The generations tend to overlap and it is possible to find eggs, larvae and adults on plants during most of the growing season. Many insects overwinter as adults in leaf litter and organic debris near damaged plants.

At first grubs feed gregariously upon the leaf tissues moving along in regular rows but separating as they grow larger. Considerable damage can be done by these grubs and leaves are shredded. Sometimes plants are stripped bare by heavy infestations. Adult beetles nibble at leaves, stems and flowers and this damage is less extensive than that caused by the grubs but nevertheless still unacceptable. Sometimes the seed capsules are damaged.

The fact that the grubs and adults are conspicuous on lily foliage means they can be seen, collected and disposed of as soon as infestations occur. This is by far the safest and surest method of dealing with them. The commercial grower and some amateur gardeners may not have enough time to collect beetles and so they resort to chemical control. There are several compounds which are used as dusts, including derris and gamma-HCH. Sprays of synthetic pyrethroid insecticides have also been found to kill these insects.

Weevils (Family Curculionidae)

Weevils are amongst the most serious pests of alpine plants in both rock gardens and glasshouses, the most troublesome species being the vine weevil, *Otiorhynchus sulcatus* (F.) and the clay-coloured weevil *Otiorhynchus singularis* (L.). Most alpine gardeners and nurserymen are only too well aware of the havoc they cause.

Outdoors, weevils overwinter either as adults in leaf litter and other debris in the hedgerows and the garden or as grubs in the soil. In the glasshouse during winter the weevils may be found at all stages of development. Adult weevils (Plate 10b) are about 9 mm long, dark brown-black with longitudinal ridges down their backs covered with small yellow specks. They are wingless. The head is typical of most weevils in being elongated and it bears two long antennae. Males are rare and reproduction occurs without fertilisation. The female lays several hundred eggs near plants in soil or potting compost. After 1-3 weeks the grubs (larvae) hatch and begin feeding on plant roots, corms, stems and tubers. These grubs are legless, have a brown head and a wide body (Plate 9d); they feed for about 3 months, moulting several times and eventually grow to a length of nearly 10 mm. The larva makes an earthen cell in the soil beneath the plant and changes into a white pupae which has many features of the adult including legs and head appendages (Plate 9e). The life cycle is completed when the adults emerge from the pupa, crawl to the surface of the soil and disperse. The vine weevil is the species usually found in glasshouses and in dwellings. In these situations the majority of eggs are laid in the spring but females lay more eggs during the summer so that grubs can be found over a period of several months.

The leaves, flowers and stems of plants are eaten by adult weevils and the leaf notching can occur on many alpine plants (Fig. 9; Plate 9a). However, the most severe damage is done by the grubs and it may be too late to save a plant when the first symptoms are discovered. The foliage turns yellow, flags during the day and persistent wilting occurs. Plants often die as a result of the attack and whole plant collections can be lost. Grubs sever roots, remove the cortex from underground stems and burrow into corms or tubers. Amongst the alpine plants damaged are *Begonia*, *Crassula*, *Cyclamen*, *Lewisia*, *Polyanthus*, *Primula*, *Saxifraga* and *Sedum*. The *Cyclamen* plant illustrated in Plate 9c was infested with half a dozen grubs which consumed practically the whole corm.

There is no doubt that vine weevils have increased greatly in numbers with the rapid growth of the container-grown plant industry. Associated with this development there has been a great increase in the number of greenhouses and polytunnels at garden centres which favours weevil reproduction during many months of the year.

In the glasshouse adult weevils hide during the day under pots and in other crevices. It is a good idea therefore to search for them from time to time and kill any that are caught. Infestations of precious plants may be prevented by mixing insecticidal dusts in the potting compost. Later, applications of the dust or a drench will extend the period of prevention and may control the grubs. When potting-on plants you should keep an eye open for the distinctive white grubs. If a plant is infested by grubs all the compost from the container should be sifted and the weevils removed. Susceptible plants such as *Saxifraga* and *Sedum* should be treated with an insecticidal dust that is incorporated into the surrounding soil (See Table 44). Biological control by parasitic eelworms and parasitic fungi is being developed for the control of vine weevil and certain of these organisms are now on the market (See Tables 40 & 41).

Wireworms (Family Elateridae)

Wireworms are the larvae of **click** beetles or **skipjacks**. They are mainly pests of grassland but are occasionally troublesome in gardens. The most common species are the common click beetle, *Agriotes lineatus* (L.), and the garden click beetle, *Athous haemorrhoidalis* (F.).

Click beetles have earned their name as a result of their unusual behaviour. When the adult beetles are laid on their backs, they struggle and then flick themselves into the air with an audible click. They are commonly seen scurrying around in grass and among plant debris, although they are most active by night. These beetles are dark brown or black and about 10-15 mm long. They feed on leaf bases of grasses and do little harm. Females lay eggs singly or in small clusters in the soil around plants. The larvae emerge a few weeks later and, to begin with, are white and about 1.3 mm long. As they grow they develop into the typical golden brown wireworm which has a distinct dark brown head, three pairs of legs close behind the head, and a shining cylindrical body with a tough skin (Plate 9f). The larval stage lasts four to five years and they spend this time in the soil feeding on the underground parts of plants. When fully grown, that is after four or five years, the larvae burrow deeply into the soil where pupation takes place. The adult beetles emerge in the same autumn and hibernate over winter.

There are two periods of the year when wireworms feed most actively, firstly in the spring when many plants are seedlings and vulnerable, secondly in the autumn when most plants are mature. They injure plants by biting holes into tissues below ground and burrow into bulbs, tubers, corms, rhizomes and tap roots. Wireworms feed on practically all plants, especially species of *Anemone*. Small black pits or holes are typical symptoms. Seedlings are often destroyed. As with leatherjackets, the highest populations occur in areas of the garden brought recently into cultivation from a lawn or pasture and much of the problem can be prevented by thorough and repeated cultivation in the spring or in the July or August followed by a fallow period. An insecticidal dust worked into the surface of the soil or a drench of the insecticide also reduces localised infestations (See Table 44).

MILLIPEDES, SYMPHYLIDS AND WOODLICE

Millipedes (Order Diplopoda)

Millipedes are often grouped in the class **Myriapoda** of invertebrate animals which also includes centipedes and symphylids but some authors now place them in a Class of their own – the Diplopoda. They are arthropods and therefore similar to insects in having segmented bodies, a tough **exo-skeleton** (external skeleton) and jointed-limbs but they differ in not possessing wings and in having an elongated body consisting of a large number of segments each bearing two pairs of legs. The group name, millipede would suggest these animals have a 1000 legs but there are usually fewer than 100. The body segments are circular in cross section but flat-backed millipedes appear flat because the segments have lateral extensions on the upper surface. **Repugnatory** glands are situated on certain body segments and these produce a repellent fluid which is emitted when the animal is threatened by predators. The body is protected by a hard and horny **integument** (skin) which is impregnated by phenolic tannins and deposits of calcium but it is not as water proof as the integument of insects. Millipedes are therefore confined to moist, humid habitats so that water can be conserved – in this respect they are similar to centipedes, symphylids and woodlice. In dry conditions they move deep into the soil or plant litter to avoid dessication. They also resemble centipedes and woodlice and avoid light. Millipedes have a distinct head which bears short antennae, two pairs of mandibles (jaws) and certain species have eyes. Some millipedes lay eggs in soil crevices while others construct a nest made from saliva, soil particles and excrement. Millipedes grow through a series of moults, the number of legs increasing with age until the full adult complement is attained; they may live for several years. They move along with a rippling motion of the legs.

Millipedes are primarily feeders on decaying vegetation and rotting substances and therefore help to decompose organic matter; they are an important part of the soil leaf litter fauna. The flat-back millipede, *Brachydesmus superus* Latz. (Plate 11a) is very common in gardens and can be seen at night even in winter browsing on decaying leaves or feeding on bird droppings. Although millipedes' main food is decaying animal and vegetable matter they also damage plants. Their mouth parts are not strong enough to penetrate a tough plant epidermis and they are therefore not usually considered as primary pests of plants. However, if a root, seedling, bulb, corm, rhizome or tuber is damaged in some other way they invade the tissues and can destroy the plant. When soil is enriched with manure, millipede populations build up rapidly, colonise the abundant food supply and help to break down the organic matter making it available to plants – in this role of recycling materials they are beneficial. However, as the manure is exhausted the millipedes use living tissues for food and become a pest.

There are about 50 species of millipede in Britain the most common being the flat millipede, *Brachydesmus superus* Latz. (Plate 11c), the spotted millipede, *Blaniulus guttulatus* (F.) (Plate 10c), and the glasshouse millipede, *Oxidus gracilis* (Koch). The black snake millipede, *Tachypodoiulus niger* (Leach) (Plate 10d) is common in gardens but feeds mainly on algae and mosses on the bark of trees. When disturbed this millipede coils up tightly like a watch spring into a flattened ball and if it is threatened by predators it emits a foul-smelling fluid from its repugnatory glands. The spotted millipede is the commonest species in gardens and glasshouses. It grows up to 10 mm long and is easily recognised by the bright orange spots on its body and by the fact that it coils up when at rest. Eggs are laid in clusters and the larvae have only a small number of segments. There may be 2 or 3 broods each year. Millipedes have many enemies including centipedes, spiders, amphibians, reptiles, birds and mammals. Frogs, toads and birds, especially starlings, are important predators.

Seeds, seedlings and large plants can be protected with soil insecticides (See Table 44). It is important to distinguish millipedes from their close relatives, centipedes which are nearly all predators and therefore beneficial. Centipedes are nearly always fast moving and they possess only one pair of legs per segment. A brief description of centipedes is given later (See p.231).

Symphylids (Order Myriapoda)

Symphylids are small, pallid arthropods resembling tiny centipedes in appearance and activity. They live in damp places under stones, leaf litter and in soil crevices. They are about 1 cm long, have long antennae and 12 pairs of legs. Symphylids appear at any time of the day but retreat quickly into shelter if disturbed. They are similar to centipedes, millipedes and woodlice in that moisture is the most important environmental factor determining their behaviour. When conditions are dry these animals descend to a depth of up to 1.5 m in the soil. The young grow through five stages, moulting their skin and becoming adult in about 40-60 days. Between 4 and 25 eggs are laid in crevices in the soil.

Symphylids eat decaying, succulent organic matter but also feed on a variety of materials including fungi, mosses and higher plants.

The most troublesome species is the glasshouse symphylid, *Scutigerella immaculata* (Newport) which can be a serious pest, sometimes reaching plague proportions (200 million per hectare). They browse root hairs, fine roots and may excavate root tissues. Seedlings collapse and larger plants wilt and become stunted. Foliage discolouration is another symptom of attack and the wounds created by the invasion may facilitate the entry of root pathogens. *Anemones*, lilies and primulas can be seriously affected. These animals are easily detected by digging in the surface layers of the soil or, by plunging a potted plant in water when the symphylids float to the surface. Preventive measures include strict hygiene, isolation of plants on raised benches, soil sterilisation and the use of soil insecticides (See Table 44).

Woodlice (Order Isopoda)

Woodlice belong to the class **Crustacea** of the invertebrate animals and are the only terrestrial members of this diverse group which includes many aquatic animals such as crabs, lobsters, shrimps and water fleas. Like all arthropods they are segmented animals with an exo-skeleton and jointed limbs (Plate 11c). They differ from insects in the absence of wings and in having more legs. These animals have dozens of local names, for example in America they are known as sow bugs.

The head bears two pairs of antennae, a smaller pair of antennules anterior to them and large dark eyes composed of many small units – these are similar to insect compound eyes and they build up a mosaic image of the surroundings. The mouthparts include mandibles, armed with heavily sclerotinised teeth, and various jointed appendages used in the manipulation of food. The thorax has seven segments each one carrying a pair of walking legs. In the female, segments 2-5 bear plates which form a broad pouch in which, first the eggs, and later the young, are carried. The abdomen has six segments. The body is covered by a series of protective plates arranged along the back.

As many as 200 eggs are laid by some species but 20 is more usual.

The young which resemble miniature adults remain in the pouch for a week or two. After release from the brood pouch they disperse and feed, moulting at intervals before reaching full size. Certain species of woodlice can produce several broods a year in favourable conditions such as in a warm glasshouse. However, many species have only one brood each year.

The cuticle differs from that of insects in not being entirely waterproof. They are very sensitive to changes in humidity and for survival it is essential they remain in moist conditions. Their activity is largely governed by this over-riding influence of water retention. Woodlice also avoid bright light whenever possible. Thus, their commonest habitats are damp, dark crevices where large numbers congregate to conserve moisture. On certain occasions they may need to lose excess moisture because they lack a normal excretory system. Thus they will emerge at night and climb walls, tree trunks and buildings.

The natural habitats of our commonest species are soil crevices, leaf litter, behind bark and in piles of stones. They are particularly common in rock gardens and in glasshouses, for example amongst seed trays and stacks of pots.

Woodlice are omnivorous their diet including live or dead plants, animal remains, fungi and dung. The damage includes holes in leaves, fruit and mushrooms and destruction of seedlings (Plate 11b). Although they are pests they also serve a valuable function in helping to decompose organic material.

Woodlice have many enemies. Predators include centipedes, spiders, amphibians, reptiles, birds and mammals. Parasites include worms, flies and microorganisms. They defend themselves by running away, clamping to a surface, rolling up in a ball (for example, the pill woodlouse) feigning death or by discharging a repellent fluid. The most common species include *Oniscus asellus* L. (Plate 11c), *Philoscia muscorum* (Scopoli) and *Porcellio scaber* Latreille. The common pill bug *Armadillidium nasatum* Budde-Lund is widespread in the countryside.

Infested rock gardens and other crevices can be treated with insecticidal dusts (See Table 44). To reduce their numbers in glasshouses, good hygiene is essential. All plant and soil debris, old seed trays and rotting wood should be cleared away. Pots should be lifted regularly and any woodlice removed.

MITES AND SPIDERS

Mites (Order Acari)

Mites belong to the Class Arachnida which includes harvestmen, scorpions, spiders and ticks. They are widespread and common animals and they reproduce extremely rapidly; certain species are important pests of plants. They have a tough external skeleton and jointed limbs as do insects but can be distinguished by their lack of wings and antennae and by the fact that their head is not distinctly separated from the abdomen. The body is usually sac-like or globular with few segments and in most species the adults have eight legs. Mites are tiny, few of them being visible with the naked eye. The gardener needs a hand lens to see them properly and identification of species is very difficult. Species which are plant pests feed in a similar way to aphids and their allies by piercing plant tissues and sucking the sap. Some species produce webbing which is a characteristic feature of their activity.

There are four main groups of mites: 1) Red spider mites, 2) Tarsonemid mites, 3) Acarid mites and 4) Gall mites. The first three groups include several important pests of alpine plants grown in the rock garden or in the glasshouse.

Red spider mites (Family Tetranychidae)

Bryobia mites (*Bryobia*). Adults are 0.7 mm long, flattened and range in colour from yellow-green to bright red or dark red-brown and their front pair of legs are particularly long (Plate 12a). On close inspection adults are frequently seen on the upper surface of leaves. These mites sometimes swarm in glasshouses particularly in late summer and early autumn. Most species breed parthenogenetically, males being unknown. The globular red eggs are laid in crevices of plants, rocks or the glasshouse structure. The larvae, nymphs and adults feed on plants particularly when conditions are warm. There may be as many as five to eight generations a year and the mites overwinter either as eggs or more often in the active stages.

Bryobia mites damage many alpine plants including *Androsace*, *Campanula*, *Crocus*, *Cyclamen*, *Dianthus*, *Gentiana*, *Iris*, *Narcissus*, *Polyanthus*, *Primula* and *Saxifraga*. Damage takes on the appearance of fine, yellow speckling which spreads until leaves become yellow, silver or bronze. Leaves dessicate and drop off prematurely. These species of mites do not produce any webbing on the plants. Certain acaricides are available to control these mites.

Glasshouse red spider mites (*Tetranychus urticae* Koch and *Tetranychus cinnabarinus* (Boisd.)). These two species have been introduced from warmer countries. They are severe pests in glasshouses in Britain and outdoors in the summer months. Adult females of *T. urticae* reach 0.6 mm in length and are green to straw-yellow coloured (Plate 11f, Fig. 10) but turn bright red if starved or when ready to hibernate, hence their common name red spider mites. Males and juvenile stages are straw-yellow or pale green; eggs are translucent white. Females of *T. cinnabarinus* are red-brown while males and juveniles are straw-yellow; their eggs are pale white tinged with pink or red.

Some mites, particularly those of *T. cinnabarinus* may remain active throughout the winter in glasshouses if conditions are favourable while most *T. urticae* hibernate in crevices. As temperatures rise in the spring the mites breed rapidly and, in favourable conditions, the development from egg to adult is completed in less than 10 days. Many generations are completed each season. All stages of the life cycle can be seen on infested plants together with accumulations of egg shells and moulted skins. The mites feed mainly on the underside and along the veins of the leaf piercing cells with their **stylets**, sucking the sap from tissues and producing webbing. Leaves become mottled with fine white speckles (Plate 11e) dry up 'wither' and in severe infestations the tops of plants are completely shrouded with **webbing**. Mites may be seen in festoons clinging to the web and they move from plant to plant on the silk threads (Plate 11d). Plants become severely stunted and are killed. Because the mites are so tiny an infestation can become established or introduced without being noticed. Plants should be examined regularly with a hand lens.

Many plants are attacked by red spider mites including alpine species of *Androsace*, *Chrysanthemum*, *Cyclamen*, *Dianthus*, *Primula* and *Viola*. Whole collections of precious plants are known to have been lost because of red spider mites. Families Campanulaceae and Primulaceae (especially the Asiatic primulas and androsaces) are particularly susceptible. Red spider mites thrive in hot, dry conditions and so their increase can be prevented or reduced by regularly spraying plants with water. They thrive on unthrifty, overcrowded plants. Weeds growing near a glasshouse should be removed as they commonly harbour mites. Several acaricides are available to the gardener and professional grower (See Table 44) but unfortunately mite populations are resistant to certain products. It may be necessary to try several different compounds before finding one which is effective. There is increasing uses of red spider mite predators to control these pests. The predatory mite, *Phytoseiulus persimilis* Athias-Henriot, is now mass-reared by several companies and can be purchased. If introduced early on in the growing season the predators rapidly overcome an infestation of the mites. The predators work best at temperatures of about 25°C and they can be killed by certain pesticides used to control other types of mite. The predators will not overwinter in the glasshouse unless temperatures are high and supplementary lighting is provided. Therefore, new supplies have to be bought next season.

Tarsonemid mites (Family Tarsonemidae)

Several species of these mites damage alpine plants but particularly the broad mite, *Polyphagotarsonemus latus* (Banks), the bulb scale mites *Steneotarsonemus laticeps* (Halbert), and the cyclamen mite or strawberry mite, *Phytonemus* ssp. *fragariae* (Zimmerman) (= *Tarsonemus pallidus*) (Fig. 10).

Tarsonemid mites are extremely small, only about 0.25 mm long, and easily escape notice until the symptoms of damage appear and infested plants are closely inspected. The mites are slow-moving, round, shiny cream to light brown in colour. Males are considerably smaller than females and less common, reproduction being parthenogenetic for most of the time. Eggs are laid singly or in clusters on buds, leaves and flowers and they hatch after a few days. Six-legged larvae emerge and, after a period of feeding, they enter a resting stage. Males sometimes carry these quiescent pre-adults around and thus spread infestations. The pre-adults eventually moult to produce adults. When temperatures reach 21-25°C the life cycle takes about five days but at other times much longer. Tarsonemid mites breed continuously in the glasshouse but outdoors individuals remain dormant within plant tissues during colder periods. Several generations each season can be completed in favourable conditions.

The broad mite is an important pest of ornamental plants grown in glasshouses and damages several species of *Chrysanthemum* and *Cyclamen*. Mites infest buds and leaves and stunt growth. Leaves may be puckered taking on a shiny, brittle appearance and the edges curl downwards. Leaves and flowers developing from damaged young buds are distorted and may drop off. The bulb scale mite is more specific in its host range and only damages *Narcissus* and *Hippeastrum* species. It is particularly

Figure 10 Mite pests of crops

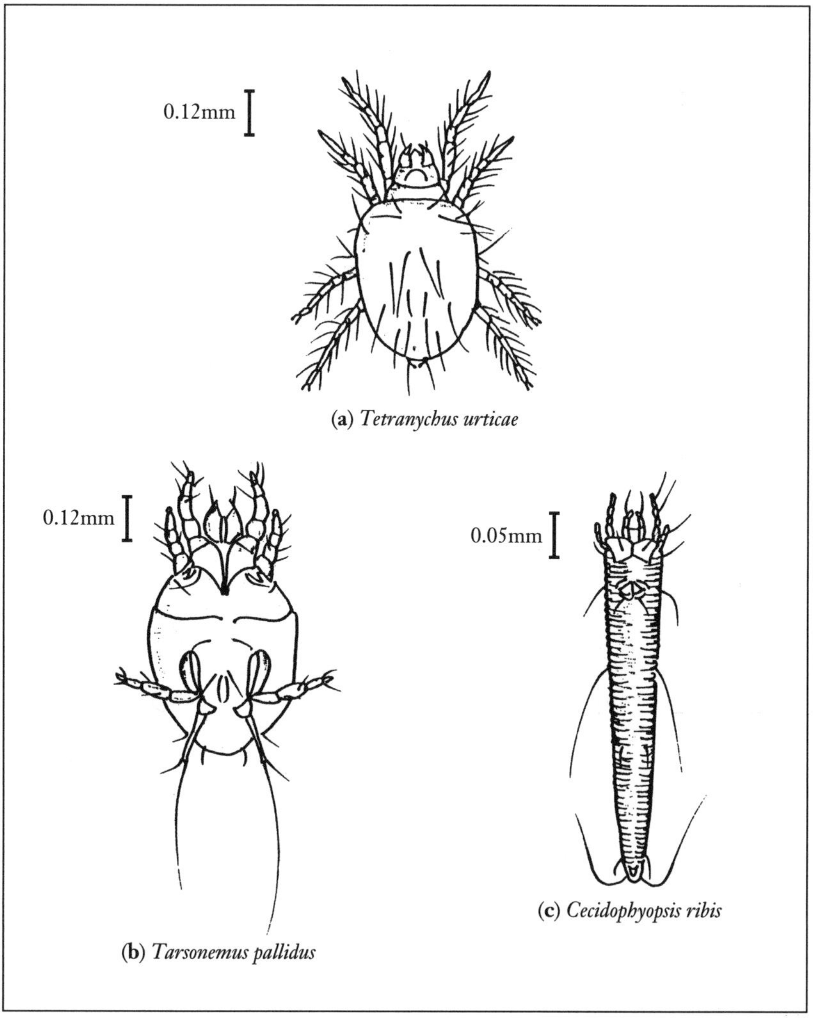

severe under glasshouse conditions. Leaves growing from infested bulbs are streaked and flecked with yellow as a result of mite feeding and become distorted. Flower stems bear similar marks and often have the characteristic 'saw-edged' symptoms. The flower bud is commonly deformed and in severe cases the stem and buds are killed soon after emergence from the bulb. If infested bulbs are cut horizontally near the neck, brown scars resulting from mite feeding can be seen on the scales. Colonies of mites may also be seen in the neck region. *Narcissus* grown outdoors and infested by these mites lack vigour, have poor growth and small deformed flowers. Only in warm weather will symptoms become as marked as those in the glasshouse.

The cyclamen mite exists in the form of different races. The race which occurs under glass is likely to be the most troublesome for the alpine specialist as it attacks many ornamental plants especially *Cyclamen* species. Mites feed in young leaf and bud tissues and as these expand the damage shows up as distorted, hardened areas covered with small brown scales. Flowers which have been infested at the bud stage are disfigured by blotches and streaks and often fail to open.

Control of tarsonemid mites is not easy. Good hygiene is essential and infested bulbs, tubers and young plants should be disposed of if possible and as mites are carried on plant debris great care must be taken not to scatter infested material. Removal of infested buds also reduces mite multiplication. Unfortunately chemical control is not practical in the garden because none of the products approved for commercial growers are available to the amateur gardener. Commercial growers use dicofol/tetradifon sprays or aldicarb granules.

Acarid mites (Family Acaridae)

The most important species are the **bulb mites**, *Rhizoglyphus callae* Oudemans, and *Rhizoglyphus robini* Claparàde, which attack corms, bulbs and tubers. It is likely that these mites have been introduced in infested plant material from warmer countries.

Adult mites have yellow-white, glistening, globular bodies about 1 mm long; they are larger and slower moving than the bulb scale mites described above. Males are usually a little smaller than females. Both sexes have four pairs of stout legs. The female lays up to 100 eggs, 0.2 mm long, each one being laid singly on plants. The young resemble the adults but have only three pairs of legs. They feed on the plant tissues and moult three times before becoming adult. The whole life cycle may be completed in less than 30 days in favourable conditions. A specialised immature stage in the life cycle, the **hypopus** may develop in adverse environmental conditions. Hypopi are minute, shiny brown and can attach themselves to insects or other animals by which they are dispersed.

The bulb mite causes damage to *Narcissus*, *Tulipa* and other plants which form bulbs, corms or tubers. It is mainly associated with tissues damaged by some other pest, disease or mechanical injury or with senescing parts of the plant such as leaves or scales. Only on loosely formed bulbs such as *Lilium* is the pest thought to be a primary cause of damage.

Once established, colonies of mites build up rapidly and bulbs may be reduced to a rotten, brown pulp.

Good hygiene and careful handling of plants offer the best prospects for the amateur gardener and nurseryman to prevent these mites from ruining plants. Infested and damaged bulbs should be destroyed and no debris scattered about.

Gall mites (Family Eriophyidae)

Several different species of **gall mite** (or **eriophyid mite**) are common in gardens and nurseries, the most familiar being the black currant gall mite, *Cecidophyopsis ribis* (Westwood), which causes 'big bud' and reversion disease of black currant (Fig. 10). Certain species attack woody plants grown by alpine specialists. Nail galls on lime and sycamore leaves are commonly seen symptoms of their damage (Plate 12b). Two species attack *Chrysanthemum* species in glasshouses. The chrysanthemum leaf rust mite, *Epitremus alinae* Liro, causes russetting of stems and premature leaf fall while *Paraphytoptus* retards the growth of cuttings.

The adult gall mites are minute, elongate, semi-transparent or pale yellow, only 0.1-0.25 mm long, and therefore invisible to the naked eye. They have two pairs of legs situated close to the head which bears palps and a rostrum through which the needle-like mandibles project. The body is divided into a short thorax and a long tapering abdomen which has many annular rings (Plate 12d). The females lay large, white, semi-transparent eggs. Young mites pass through two nymph stages before becoming adult. Mites disperse by crawling across the surface of the plant or over longer distances by rain, air currents or attached to insects.

Damage results from the feeding activity of the mites which stimulates production of a gall containing several thousand individuals. Most galls contain a mass of deformed hairs, thickened and twisted and may occur on either side of a leaf or in a bud. The galls turn red or black as they age. The mites live amongst the leaf hairs draining sap from the tissues. The shape of the gall is often quite characteristic – nail galls, pouch galls, felt galls and dimple galls. Other species cause leaf rolling or live on plant surfaces. Certain species invade flower heads and their feeding activity causes dehydration and withering (Plate 12c).

These mites are difficult to control. Infested leaves can be collected and destroyed. No chemical control measures are available for ornamentals or hardy nursery stock.

Spiders
(Class *Arachnida*, Order Araneida)

Like earthworms, spiders are almost entirely beneficial; they are important predators of many pests. However, they are sometimes a nuisance in the glasshouse or frame when they produce webs on and around plants grown for exhibition. If they become a nuisance they can be collected and transferred to the open garden where their beneficial activities will be appreciated.

SLUGS AND SNAILS

Slugs and Snails (Order Gastropoda)

These animals belong to the group known as molluscs. They are familiar to all of us, occur in most gardens and nurseries and can be the most troublesome of pests in the rock garden or alpine glasshouse. There is little doubt that international trade has been responsible for the worldwide distribution of certain pest species. A very small number of species are responsible for a high proportion of the slug and snail damage to plants. These include the field slug *Deroceras reticulatum* (Mull.) (Plate 12e), the garden slug, *Arion hortensis* Fer. (Plate 12f), the keeled or subterranean slug, *Tandonia budapestensis* (Hazay) (*Milax budapestensis*), the garden snail, *Helix aspersa* Mull., (Plate 13d) and the strawberry snail, *Trichia striolata* (Pfeiff.).

Slugs and snails have soft unsegmented bodies and move about on a slimy muscular foot. Their head bears two pairs of long retractile tentacles, the longest pair carrying the eyes at their tip. Snails possess a shell into which they can retreat to avoid danger or to survive unfavourable periods of weather. Slugs have no shell. These animals secrete mucus or **slime** which prevents them from dehydrating and assists in locomotion.

These animals are hermaphrodyte having both female and male reproductive organs and, although self-fertilisation occurs in some species, most species pair and cross fertilise. Some species breed all the year round when conditions are favourable. Batches of pale, translucent eggs are laid in the soil (Plate 13c). Those laid in winter may not hatch until the spring but at other times of the year and in the glasshouse the young slugs or snails emerge after a few days. Young slugs and snails resemble adults in most respects except size and may be lighter in colour. They take several months to reach maturity. Snails breed mainly in the spring and hibernate during winter whereas slugs are active all year round.

Both slugs and snails flourish in damp conditions and are most troublesome in wet seasons. Slugs in particular live in close contact with the soil and prefer heavy soils and the damper parts of gardens or in glasshouses. They feed mainly at night and during the day hide in crevices in the rock garden, under plants, especially cushion plants, and under pots in the glasshouse or frame. Slugs are known to occupy favoured niches and return 'home' after each night's foraging. Snails are particularly abundant in calcareous soils.

Apart from causing enormous damage to plants, slugs and snails also play an important role in disposing of waste plant and animal matter. Some species have been observed eating cabbage root fly eggs, aphids and other slugs. The slugs belonging to the Family Testacellidae are largely carnivorous.

The **field or netted slug**, *Deroceras reticulatum* (Müller) (Family Limacidae) is distributed throughout the world and is probably the most common species in fields, gardens and nurseries (Plate 12d). It is variable in colour, light grey-brown, cream, fawn or yellowish white and measures 3-5 cm in length. Its body is slender and has a short ridged keel at its pointed end. The body is marked with a network of brown grooves, spots and streaks and is covered in a milky white, sticky slime (mucus) which glistens.

The field slug has a complex life history which is largely dependent on temperature. This severe pest remains active at temperatures as low as 1°C and breed at 3°C. It requires less than 12 months to complete a generation, mating and egg-laying taking place in spring, summer and autumn. Peaks of breeding take place in April-May and September-October each individual being capable of laying 200-500 eggs.

The **garden or yellow soled slug**, *Arion hortensis* Ferussac (Family Arionidae) is as common as the field slug in many areas and is an important pest which feeds above and below ground. It is dark brown, grey or black and yellow to orange underneath. It is 2-3 cm long (Plate 12f). The hind end is rounded. The garden slug is less active than the field slug at low temperatures. This species matures in early autumn and breeds throughout the winter and spring. Peak egg hatch occurs in late spring, and young slugs grow rapidly. Each slug lays up to 300 eggs.

The **keeled or subterranean slug**, *Tandoniax budapestensis* (Hazay) (Family Milacidae) and several other closely-related species are mainly subterranean but also feed above ground. They are most important as pests of field crops but attack plants with fleshy roots, rhizomes or tubers. The body is black or brown with a dirty yellow or orange keel running down the centre of the back. The under surface or sole has a dark central area flanked by light edges. The keeled slug grows to a length of 6-7 cm. This species mates in autumn, winter or spring and lays up to 30 eggs between December and April. Most eggs hatch in May and June. The young develop through the summer, autumn and following spring and summer laying eggs in the autumn.

The **large black slug**, *Arion ater* (L.) is much larger than any of the species mentioned above and grows to 10-13 cm in length. Its body is dark brown or black, it is marked with longitudinal ridges or tubercles and has a grey sole; the immature stages are yellowish brown. This species causes a moderate amount of damage in gardens and nurseries.

The **garden or brown garden snail**, *Helix aspersa* Müller (Family Helicidae) is very common in gardens and easily distinguished by its greyish brown shell with pale markings and flecks or streaks. The shell reaches

3.8 cm in diameter. The animal's body is greyish-black (Plate 13d).

The **strawberry or ruddy snail**, *Trichia striolata* (Pfeiff.) (Family Helicidae) is much smaller than the garden snail its flattened shell only reaching 1.3 cm in diameter. The shell is grey to dark red-brown in colour, and the snail's body is grey-brown.

The **smaller banded or white-tipped snail**, *Cepaea hortensis* (Müller) (Family Helicidae) has a shell which is glossy yellow, light brown or reddish with one to five darker bands. The shell grows to a diameter of 2.0 cm. The closely related banded wood snail or brown-tipped snail, *Cepaea nemoralis* (L.) (Plate 13e), is a little larger than *C. hortensis* and, as the name implies, the lip of the shell differs in colour for the two species.

Slugs and snails feed on decaying vegetable matter but also browse buds, flowers, stems, leaves and roots of a very wide range of garden plants including many alpines. Their food is detected by its smell. Slug and snail damage usually occurs close to the ground although snails may climb plants to browse the foliage. The damage takes on the appearance of irregular, often ragged holes either in the centre or around the edges of leaves (Fig. 9, Plate 13a) and/or flowers (Plate 13b) and is usually associated with the tell-tale silvery slime left behind after feeding (Plate 13a). An example of damage to *Primula* is illustrated in Plate 13b. Some alpine plants such as *Armeria*, *Campanula zoysii*, *Omphalodes*, *Lilium*, *Phyteuma comosum*, *Silene schafta* and *Viola* seem to be highly preferred as food and are so severely damaged they may be killed. They also show preferences for certain cruciferous plants, hostas and *Lamium maculatum* 'Beacon Silver'. Trays of seedlings in frames and glasshouses can be destroyed overnight by a few individuals. They tend to avoid plants containing cyanogenic (release cyanides when crushed) compounds. There can be as many as 200 slugs per square metre.

There are many factors which regulate slug and snail populations. Extremes of drought and cold kill many individuals. In warm, dry conditions they move to greater depth to avoid desiccation. Snails congregate and **aestivate** (summer quiescent period) under these conditions. Certain cultural practices reduce damage. For example, repeated cultivations and firming of seed beds will restrict their activities and may kill some slugs and snails. Conversely, these pests thrive in rough lumpy soils. Spot watering of plants rather than broadcast irrigation could reduce their foraging range across flower borders or rock gardens. Slug barriers can be placed around precious plants. Some gardeners cut the bottom off plastic lemonade bottles and then slip the cylinder around the plant. Slugs are unable to reach the plant. These are unsightly and rather cumbersome and you have to make sure there are no slugs trapped inside the barrier. Other growers put wood ash, lime, sand or other material around plants to act as a barrier. A search of the literature reveals many different types of trap which have been used in the control of slugs and snails in the past. An efficient trap provides an attractant and a refuge or container for them. These devices range from grapefruit halves to saucers filled with beer to plastic containers sunk in the ground, the last two are periodically removed and disposed of. Collecting by hand can be a highly effective means of removing large numbers of slugs and snails. The best time for collection is after dark. Individuals can be picked up with tweezers, dropped into water containing a drop of detergent and then disposed of. In one April in the author's garden slugs were collected on three successive mild, damp evenings from one rock garden. In less than a quarter of an hour 55, 35, and 40 slugs were removed on the three occasions. One specimen of *Silene schafta* had 9 fully-grown slugs browsing its leaves and stems and there were 10 small slugs under a large *Aubrieta* plant. Removal by hand is a most satisfactory organic method of controlling these pests.

Slugs and snails have many natural enemies including badgers, foxes, hedgehogs and other small mammals, birds (particularly thrushes), frogs, toads, newts, carabid beetles, sciomyzid flies, centipedes, parasitic

Figure 11 *Ditylenchus dipsaci*

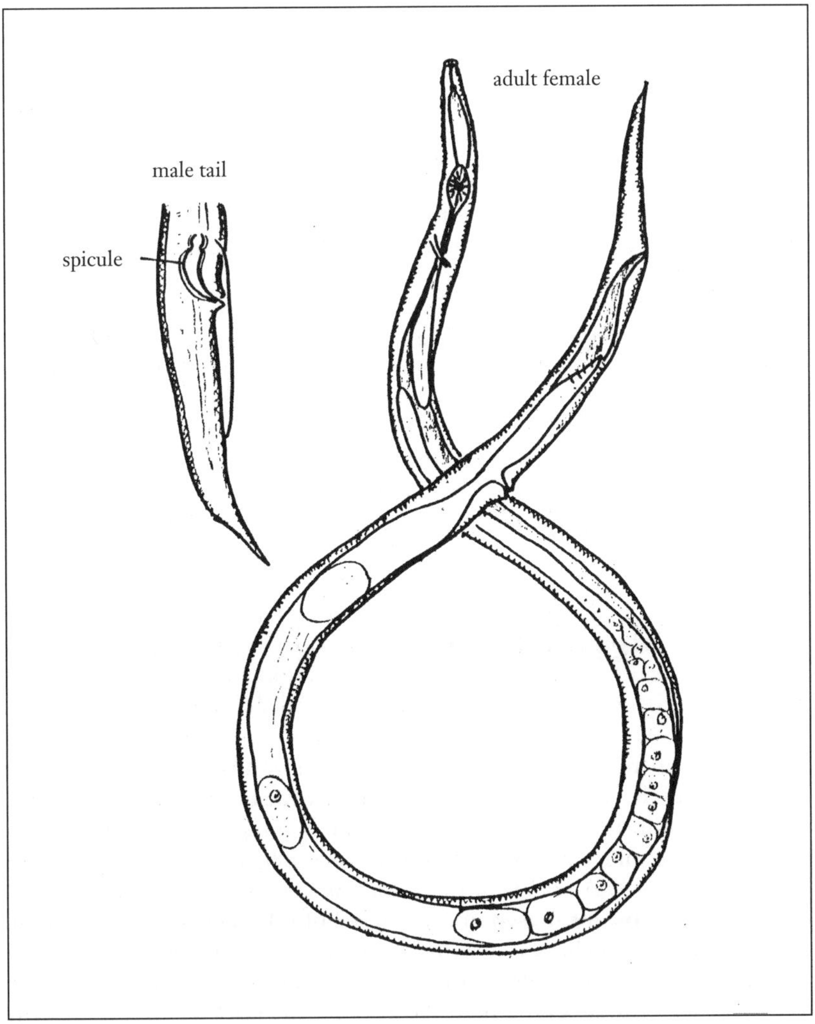

worms, protozoans, and various fungi, bacteria and viruses. One particular ground beetle *Abax parallelepipedus* (P. & M.) is the subject of investigation for biological control.

At present slugs and snails are mainly controlled using chemicals (See Table 44). Most materials incorporate a bait such as bran for attraction, a binding compound and an antibiotic. Baits containing a molluscicide such as methiocarb or metaldehyde are widely used in the form of pellets or impregnated tapes. Methiocarb is the most widely used compound and acts as a stomach poison with a partial contact effect. This compound also kills leatherjackets, earthworms and beetles. Metaldehyde, discovered in the 1930s, is primarily a contact molluscicide. The impregnated tapes are sold in reels and a barrier around frames or vulnerable plants can be formed from the tape. These are thought to be safer than pellets and remain active for several weeks. However molluscicides, particularly metaldehyde, are a hazard to pets. Certain plant extracts such as saponin compounds are potential molluscicides while other types of extract may be developed to prevent feeding. Contact molluscicides such as aluminium sulphate which cause shrinkage of the slime-forming organs in these animals are now available. They are claimed to last for up to six months, kill above and below ground, kill eggs, young and adult molluscs and are harmless to humans, livestock, pets and most wildlife. Crystals of these compounds are scattered around infested areas. Considerable research effort is being invested to improve baits and molluscicides. One idea is to incorporate iron or aluminium, two metals highly toxic to slugs, within a pellet.

Further reading: 'Pest Slugs and Snails. Biology and Control' (Godan, 1983).

NEMATODES AND EARTHWORMS

Nematodes or eelworms (Phylum *Nematoda*)

Several eelworm species are pests of garden plants. The tiny worms invade the plant and build up to enormous populations. The damage caused by feeding leads to distortion of buds, stems, leaves and roots and plants die as a direct result of attack and from associated disease organisms. The most troublesome species for the alpine specialist is the stem and bulb eelworm, *Ditylenchus dipsaci* (Kühn) Filipjev (Fig. 11). This species and several others which damage alpines are listed in Table 12.

Most eelworms which damage ornamentals are minute, elongated worm-like or eel-like animals less than 2 mm long (Plate 13f). Even with a hand lens they are hard to see, especially inside plant tissues. The eelworms have a spear-like stylet in the head end which pierces plant cells and through which the sap is sucked (Fig. 8). They reproduce by means of eggs which hatch into miniature worms which grow rapidly and moult several times.

Table 12: **Eelworm species known to damage alpine plants**

Common name	Latin name	Host plants
Chrysanthemum eelworm	*Aphelenchoides ritzemabosi* (Schwartz) Steiner & Buhrer	*Chrysanthemum*, *Phlox*, *Calceolaria*, *Penstemon*
Leaf eelworm	*Aphelenchoides fragariae* (Ritzema Bos) Christie	*Lilium*, *Primula*, *Viola*
Scabious bud eelworm	*Aphelenchoides blastophthorus* Franklin	*Anemone*, *Iris*, *Narcissus*, *Trollius*, *Viola*
Root-knot eelworm	*Meloidogyne* species	*Dianthus*, *Chrysanthemum*, *Cyclamen*
Stem and bulb eelworm	*Ditylenchus dipsaci* (Kühn) Filipjev	Numerous species
Potato tuber eelworm	*Ditylenchus destructor* Thorne	*Iris*, *Tulipa*
Root lesion eelworm	*Pratylenchus penetrans*	Roots of *Anemone*, *Lilium*, *Narcissus*, *Ranunculus*
Needle eelworm	*Longidorus* species	Browse on exterior of roots of many hosts. Can transmit viruses to plants
Dagger eelworm	*Xiphinema* species	
Stubby-root eelworm	*Trichodorus* species	

The stem and bulb eelworm (Fig. 11) has been recorded as a pest of at least 400 species of wild and garden plant which includes bulbs such as *Galanthus*, *Hyacinthus*, *Iris*, *Narcissus*, *Scilla* and *Tulipa* as well as *Aubrieta*, *Campanula*, *Dianthus*, *Gypsophila*, *Phlox*, *Primula* and *Saxifraga* species. Eelworms survive unfavourable periods by forming **'eelworm wool'**. this is formed from a mass of the pre-adult larvae which aggregate on the base plates or between the scales of bulbs. In this state they can survive dry conditions for several years, reviving when moistened. The damage done to bulbs by this pest is highly characteristic. During the growing season the leaves develop gall-like swellings, **'spickels'** and streaks on leaves and stems. Foliage may be much smaller and distorted and in severe cases flowers are not produced. Affected bulbs are pulpy and when cut across they show a characteristic brown ring of dead tissue;

these areas of dead tissue may spread to make the whole bulb rotten. Symptoms are similar in hyacinth species while in tulip and phlox the leaves often split and flower stems are stunted and twisted. Eelworms commonly migrate from plant to plant and in this way patches of bulbs become infested. Aizoon and Porophyllum saxifrages are severely attacked by leaf and bud eelworms (*Aphelenchoides* sp.) and stem and bulb eelworm (*Ditylenchus dipsaci*). Whole collections of alpines can be destroyed by these pests. The symptoms of damage are described by Horny, Webr & Byam-Grounds (1986). Infested plants cease to make fresh growth and rosettes, stems and inflorescences become distorted. Daughter rosettes either become greatly diminished in size, more numerous and deformed in the centre or, in extreme cases, they are no longer produced. Infested daughter rosettes make no growth, often become chlorotic, gradually die and rot. Sometimes swollen or pouchy leaves are produced, especially at rosette centres and rooting is slow or non-existent. In Aizoon saxifrages symptoms of eelworm infestation include reddish tints on the leaves. On some saxifrage varieties which are naturally tinted red, stem or leaf distortion accompanied by discolouration indicates eelworm attack. These authors have reported that certain porophylla saxifrages are more susceptible to eelworm attack than others. These include all varieties, forms and cultivars of *S. marginata*, *S. luteo-viridis*, 'Rosea', 'Oberon', 'Camyra', 'Faust', 'Alfons Mucha' and 'Roxanne'. Resistant species include *S. juniperfolia* and related species and *S. burserana*.

There are no satisfactory chemical treatments for gardeners to use against eelworms. Nurserymen use aldicarb and metham sodium which are not available to the amateur. Commercial growers also use hot water treatments for bulbs but this is a highly specialised technique. Important measures to adopt include strict hygiene coupled with frequent inspection of plants. Affected plants should be removed (rogued) during the growing season and destroyed. If bulbs are lifted they should be examined and any soft ones discarded. As the eelworms are commonly found in the debris associated with the plants strict hygiene should be practised and any plant remains burnt. Stock plants should always be purchased from a reputable supplier and it is wise to quarantine new plants before they are arranged in the alpine house.

Earthworms (Phylum *Annelida*, Class *Oligochaeta*, Order Terricolae)

Earthworms are beneficial in the production of a healthy soil, particularly with regard to fertility, structure and drainage. However, they are a thorough nuisance when incorporated in the soil of pot plants. The worms literally plough up the compost and disturb plant growth. The inclusion of a perforated zinc disc in the bottom of pots may prevent mature worms entering a pot from below but it will also prevent young worms which have developed in the pot from escaping. Therefore, all worms should be removed from loam, leaf mould and sand before mixing up composts.

BIRDS AND MAMMALS

Birds (Class *Aves*)

Several common birds damage alpine plants. These include the blackbird *Turdus merula* L., bullfinch, *Pyrrhula pyrrhula* (L.), collared dove, *Streptopelia decaocto* (Frivaldsky), house sparrow, *Passer domesticus* (L.), starling, *Sturnus vulgaris* L., wood pigeon, *Columba palumbus* L., and several different domesticated and game birds; peacocks can even be a major problem in some gardens. The damage includes pecking and eating of buds, leaves (See Fig. 2.9), flowers and seed, tearing away of straggling parts of plants for nest material, and scratching of areas underneath or around plants to disturb invertebrates or to dust bathe. For example, blackbirds will strip the berries off *Cotoneaster* and *Pernettya* species and they will scratch up rosettes of *Saxifraga* and *Sempervivum* species to find food. The soft rosettes of *Androsace primuloides* 'Chumbyi' may be carried away and used in nests. Sparrows can be particularly destructive to *Crocus*, *Draba*, *Polyanthus*, *Primula*, *Viola* and certain cushion plants; they can almost completely disbud *Aubrieta* and *Lavandula* on a raised border in the spring. Birds will also attack plants in the alpine house or frame plants and growers have reported the destruction of cushion plants and mossy saxifrages under glass by birds.

It seems that the worst damage occurs in the spring at the time of nesting and for a short period in the autumn.

There are no satisfactory methods of prevention and control other than netting or the continuous presence of cats or humans. Bird repellents such as aloe and anthraquinone are usually ineffective and so are bird scaring devices which rapidly lose their deterrent effect as the birds became used to them. Most gardeners welcome birds particularly as many species do more good than harm. A range of netting materials which are not too conspicuous are available to the gardener; netting will also exclude birds from the alpine glasshouse. Black cotton criss-crossed above and around precious plants is certainly effective in deterring attack by birds and has been used by generations of gardeners to protect *Crocus* and *Primula* species which appear to be preferred hosts.

Mammals (Class *Mammalia*)

Certain mammals are pests of alpine plants and damage can occur outdoors or under glass. The most important pest species are described below.

Mice, rats and voles

The house-mouse, *Mus musculus* L. (Family Muridae), is probably the most common and widespread of our smaller mammals. It is particularly abundant in the neighbourhood of human habitation and can be highly destructive. The mouse is believed to have originated in Asia and spread to all parts of the world inhabited by humans.

The mouse's head and body are 7-9 cm long and its flexible, tapering tail the same length. Its bright beady eyes are black, nose pointed and large ears almost half the length of the head. The fur is brownish-grey and only a little lighter on the under parts of the body. The gestation period is 19-20 days, the litter size averages five or six young and breeding may be continuous; under favourable conditions a female may have ten litters a year.

This mouse is extremely adaptable and highly successful and is commonly a pest in the alpine house or propagating frame. It is largely nocturnal in its activity. Mice severely damage bulbs, corms and tubers especially *Crocus* and *Cyclamen* species and also nibble the shoots or buds of plants.

The wood-mouse, or long-tailed field-mouse, *Apodemus sylvaticus* (L.) (Family Muridae) is a real nuisance in the garden where it steals seeds and digs up bulbs. It is particularly fond of lilies, narcissi and tulips. This mouse stores foods of all kinds and therefore will frequently carry away plant material to its burrow. This species also consumes weeds, seeds and invertebrate pests and therefore is sometimes beneficial. The wood-mouse is larger than the house-mouse, growing to a total length of 19 cm and the upper parts are dark, yellow-brown while the underparts are white. The gestation period is 25-26 days. It occupies burrows underground, often amongst tree roots and stores large quantities of food in the burrow. It is less active during the cold months than the house-mouse and breeding is only continuous when winters are mild. Sometimes it will enter buildings in the autumn and become a nuisance by chewing wires and consuming food.

The yellow-necked mouse, *Apodemus flavicollis* (Melchior) (Family Muridae) is a close relative of the long-tailed field mouse but is larger (body up to 12 cm long) and is distinguished by the pattern of yellow markings on the chest, which, in this species, are in the form of a cross. The yellow-necked mouse is most common in southern England and it frequently enters buildings or stores in the autumn. This species occasionally damages bulbs, corns and tubers.

The common rat, *Rattus norvegicus* (Erxleben) (Family Muridae) needs no introduction and is associated with human habitation throughout the world. It is believed to have originated in the Middle or Far East and reached Britain from the Continent in the early 18th century and north America soon afterwards. Although rats are normally associated with farms and particularly barns which store corn, they do occur in small numbers in hedgerows and shelter belts. They are also frequently found beneath sheds in gardens, outhouses, garages and sometimes in glasshouses. Rats cannot be considered severe pests of alpine plants but their diet includes many plant storage organs such as bulbs, corms and tubers which they dig from borders or steal from the alpine house or propagation frame. They are also known to strip the buds from shoots. The rat may grow to a length of 26 cm and the tail is of a similar size. The ears and eyes are small, the head short and the fur is grey-brown above and greyish-white on the underparts. The gestation period is about 21 days and the litter size varies from 4 to 10 young. There are 3-5 litters per year and individuals are capable of reproducing when 3-4 months old. It is not surprising therefore that populations can build up rapidly under favourable conditions. Mice and rats can be deterred from entering the glasshouse or frame by closing holes and erecting wire-netting barriers. Some gardeners protect bulbs with netting either by covering the soil surface or by enclosing the bulbs in netting buried in the ground.

Poisons are commonly used against these rodents and warfarin which stops the blood from coagulating has been used extensively. However, resistance to warfarin is now widespread in both rats and mice. There are more effective toxicants for mice such as calciferol and difenacoum and for rats bromadiolene, brodifacoum and difenacoum. However, there are pockets of infestation where mice and rats have developed resistance to these second generation toxicants. These chemicals also present great hazards to other animals because of their increased toxicity and persistence. A more satisfactory method of controlling these animals is to use traps of which many different types are available.

Traps can be baited with a range of foods but when they are set outdoors, they should be covered to protect birds, pets and other animals. The ideal location for trapping is in the shed, frame or glasshouse which should then be locked to prevent pets and children from being poisoned.

The short-tailed vole *Microtus agrestis* (L.) (Family Cricetidae). This small rodent, known in the past as the field vole, field-mouse or grass-mouse is extremely widespread and periodically very common, sometimes even reaching plague proportions. It is highly destructive and can be a severe pest in the garden.

The fully-grown adult attains a length of 13 cm (including tail) and its blunt, oval head, short, round ears and short, stiff tail easily distinguish it from the related mice species described above. The female makes a dome or cup-shaped nest of shredded grass which is usually sited next to a tuft of grass. The gestation period is 21 days, the litter size averages six and there may be several litters in the breeding season which extends from February to September. The young mice start breeding when six weeks old so it is not surprising that vole populations can build up rapidly when food supplies are abundant, weather conditions favourable and predators scarce. Voles excavate underground burrows and create a network of runs above ground through grass and herbage. They can move rapidly throughout this network sheltered from predators.

The short-tailed vole's habitat is typically damp pastures or meadows but it is also common in gardens, orchards, plantations and open woodland. This vole eats practically any plant material including bark, bulbs and seeds and probably also some insects. When populations reach plague proportions, extensive damage can be done to many garden plants. In some countries they cause severe damage to young plantations and orchards. Voles have been known to cause extensive damage to orchids and numerous other precious plants in lawns rich in wild flowers. Plants in the borders surrounding wild flower `meadows' have also been destroyed.

Voles can be trapped but this has little impact on the population in a garden or on a nursery. Baits containing anticoagulant poisons are not suitable for voles and are hazardous to use where pets and wild animals are present. Most alpines shrubs are too small to protect with tree guards. Probably the most appropriate method of reducing vole infestations is to deny them the cover they require for normal activities and so long grass or herbage in the vicinity of alpines should be cut down periodically and removed.

Occasionally the bank vole *Clethrionomys glareolus* Schreber invades gardens and damages plants.

Rabbits and hares

The rabbit, *Orycotolagus cuniculus* (L.), also known as the cony, (Family Leporidae) is an extremely important pest of agricultural and horticultural crops and was estimated in 1984 to be causing between £95m and £120m damage annually to crops in Britain. Since then populations have increased. In situations where rabbits are abundant on land next to gardens or nurseries, they are serious pests.

The earliest accounts of rabbits are from Portugal, Spain and islands in the Mediterranean. Rabbits are believed to have spread, or to have been introduced, into Britain at the time of the Norman invasion. The rabbit was not present in many parts of Scotland until about 1850 but rapidly spread to all regions of the British Isles soon afterwards. Rabbits are burrowing animals and the network of tunnels is called a warren. They are largely nocturnal in activity.

The rabbit is familiar to all gardeners and growers. The fully grown adult is about 40 cm long and has large ears which may be 9 cm long. The doe usually chooses a site well away from the warren to build her nursery and excavates a short burrow about 0.5 m long just under the surface of the ground. A nest of fur plucked from the doe's underside is made at the blind end of the burrow. The gestation period is 28 days and litters of 2-8 young are produced at about monthly intervals from January to June. Breeding occasionally occurs in other months as well. The young are capable of an independent existence within one month and become sexually mature in about four months. The rabbit is almost exclusively vegetarian, apart from taking the occasional earthworm or snail. They eat practically any garden plant and can very quickly gnaw through the stems of dwarf rhododendrons or conifers. What is more they always seem to gnaw off more stems than they could possibly consume in one day.

Hares (*Lepus europaeus* Pallus) are considerably larger than rabbits often reaching 61 cm in length. Hare populations are also most unlikely to reach the plague proportions so typical of rabbits. The two animals have similar diets and hares can be very destructive in gardens, nurseries and plantations. Hares are believed to show a preference for certain plants including *Chrysanthemum* and *Dianthus* species as well as most conifers.

The most effective way of preventing damage by rabbits and hares is to fence the garden or nursery. Wire-netting should be at least 1.5 m high with a 2.5-3.0 cm mesh and be buried 30 cm deep to prevent burrowing. The netting should be well supported. If the erection of a perimeter fence is too expensive then individual trees, shrubs, frames or borders can be protected with tree guards or wire-netting.

Squirrels, moles and deer

The grey squirrel, *Sciurus carolinensis* Gmelin (Family Sciuridae) is another widespread and familiar mammal in forests, parks and gardens. It is a pest of forestry and can cause extensive damage in gardens and nurseries.

Grey squirrels grow to a length of almost 30 cm, the tail being an additional 20 cm long. They have grey fur and the underparts are white. The hind legs are much longer than the fore-limbs and the feet well adapted to climbing. The tail is bushy and commonly held high over the back. The breeding season lasts from December to June and there are usually two litters a year. The gestation period lasts 44 days and litter size averages four young. Squirrels cause considerable damage by up-rooting corms, tubers and bulbs, consuming buds, shoots and flowers, by stealing berries and other plant parts and by stripping bark from shrubs and trees. Ring barking low down on the stem will kill trees and shrubs and less extensive damage facilitates the entry of pests and diseases. The severity of damage to young trees has been found to be correlated with phloem thickness which, in turn, is determined by growing conditions. The greater the thickness and therefore the volume of phloem the worse the damage. Young plantations established in clear-felled areas which are well-spaced and which receive maximum sunlight and nutrients produce saplings with the greatest volume of phloem. These trees are most vulnerable to damage. In north America squirrels appear to be less of a problem because most deciduous woodlands regenerate from self-seeded understorey saplings. Under these conditions the young trees have a thin phloem layer and grey squirrels are not an important pest.

Warfarin is used by foresters to poison these pests and many squirrels are shot. Various traps are also available. If grey squirrels are a problem it may be necessary to protect bulbs, corms and tubers with wire-netting.

The **common or European mole**, *Talpa europaea* L. (Family Talpidae). Adult moles grow to a length of about 15 cm (120-170 mm) and are covered with thick, silvery black fur. They have tiny beady eyes, strong sensitive whiskers but no external ears. They have a flexible, pink, sensitive nose and stout, powerful spade-like front legs equipped with claws which are used in burrowing. The snout also possesses sensory organs, the **Eimer's organs**, which are sensitive to humidity and temperature as well as touch. The female rears about four young in a litter during the breeding season (February to June). The gestation period lasts four weeks. When juveniles are about nine weeks old, they leave the maternal burrow and disperse. This is a critical phase in their life and many starve or are taken by predators.

The main function of a mole's burrow is to act as a food trap. Their principal food is earthworms and other small invertebrates which fall into the network of tunnels. Tunnels are often greatly extended during periods of cold weather as the moles need to dig deeper in order to catch earthworms and soil insects which retreat to greater depths in the ground.

Moles do not consume plants but cause damage to them in several different ways. Their burrowing activity disturbs plants and covers others with piles of soil. These mounds of soil rapidly become invaded with weeds. Underground, the raising of the tunnel roof uproots plants, killing them outright or depriving the roots of water and nutrients. Roots and bulbs which are in the way of tunnel construction will be destroyed or exposed to frost and other animal species will invade the network of tunnels and eat any exposed roots or bulbs. Occasionally extensive tunnelling activity will lead to soil erosion or the collapse of part of a rock garden. The mounds of loose earth interfere with lawn mowing.

The mole has many natural enemies such as owls, other birds of prey and foxes but the opportunities for predation are few and far between except when they are searching for water or during the time of dispersal of the young which are expelled from the territory by their mother.

Trapping is widely used to reduce mole infestations, the two most popular types being scissor (caliper or pincer) traps or half-barrel traps. These traps are carefully laid in the tunnel. Poisons have also been used extensively, for example, strychnine-baited earthworms, alphachoralose thallium sulphate, various gases, soil fumigants and pesticides. In gardens a wide range of techniques are used to control moles, several of them relying on the production of vibrations or noises which are believed repel moles. Even milk bottles or tins sunk in the runs are claimed to be effective as the wind blows across the mouth of the container producing a resonance which deters moles. Most of these devices are likely to provide only a brief respite in the problem, however, as moles will block off tunnels that have been interfered with and excavate new sections of run to by-pass the obstruction.

Various species of deer may be troublesome in gardens and it is necessary to erect high fences or plant dense hedges to keep them out. Some gardeners have trouble with dogs, cats and foxes the usual problem being scratching of the soil, disturbance of alpine plants fouling of borders and removal of plant labels. Chemical repellents are available for dogs and cats but usually have only short term effects.

a. Damage by vine weevil, *Otiorhynchus sulcatus*

b. Adult vine weevil, *Otiorhynchus sulcatus*

c. Damage to cyclamen by vine weevil, *Otiorhynchus sulcatus*

d. Larva of vine weevil, *Otiorhynchus sulcatus*

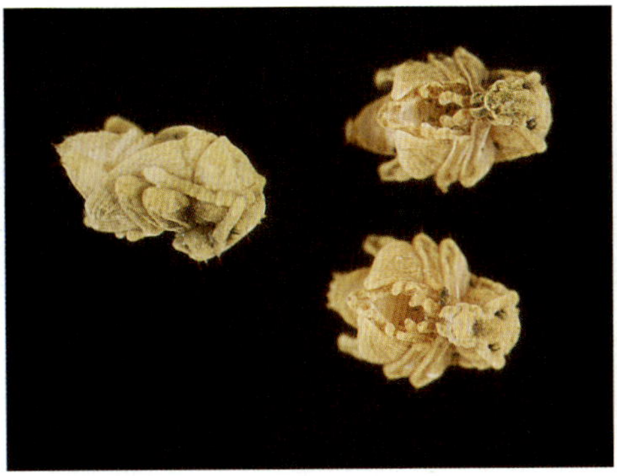

e. Pupae of vine weevil, *Otiorhynchus sulcatus*

f. Larva (wireworm) of click beetle, *Agriotes lineatus*

a. Adult lily beetle, *Lilioceris lilii*

b. Adult flea beetles, *Phyllotreta* sp.

c. Spotted millipedes, *Blaniulus guttulatus*

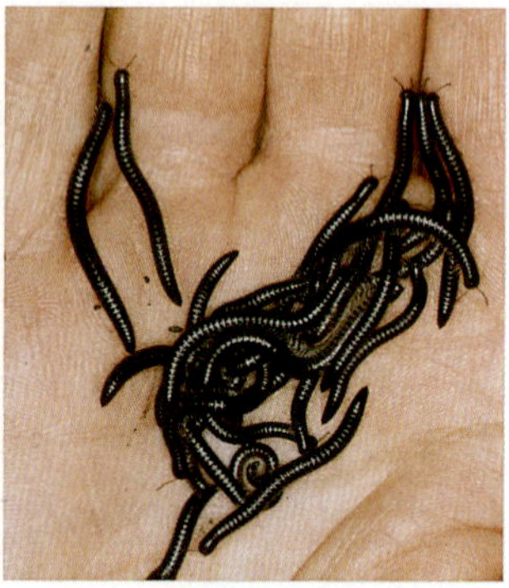

d. Black snake millipedes, *Tachypodoiulus niger*

e. Adult centipede, *Lithobius forficatus*

f. Adult centipede, *Geophilus* spp.

a. Flat back millipede, *Brachydesmus superus*

b. Damage to seedling by woodlice, *Oniscus osellus*

c. Woodlice, *Oniscus osellus*

d. Webbing produced by red spider mite, *Tetranychus urticae*

e. Damage to leaf by red spider mites, *Tetranychus urticae*

f. Red spider mites, *Tetranychus urticae*

a. *Bryobia* mite

b. Lime leaf damaged by gall mites, *Eriophyes tiliae*

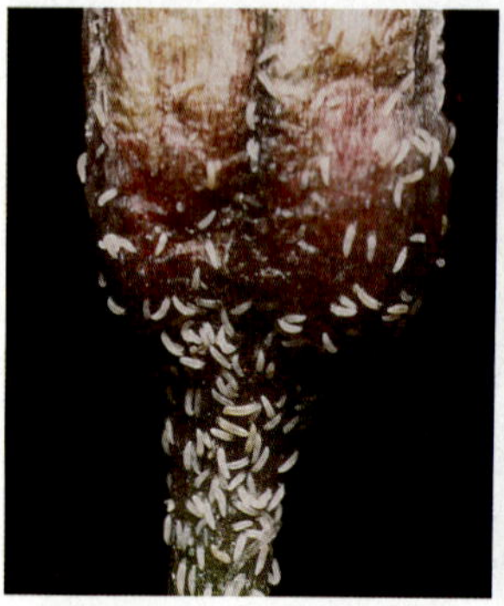

c. Gall mites on *Allium* flower head

d. Scanning electron micrograph of gall mite, *Eriophyes* sp.

e. Field slug, *Deroceras reticulatum*

f. Garden slug, *Arion hortensis*

CHAPTER THREE

Fungi and Bacteria

GENERAL INFORMATION

This chapter describes the characteristics of fungi and bacteria -

- the appearance and structure, nutrition, survival and effects of fungi on plants;
- the classification and nomenclature of fungi (See p.92)
- the specific diseases caused by fungi (See p.95)
- the characteristics of bacteria, and the diseases they cause (p.152)

Whilst the information contained in this chapter necessarily refers to garden plants in general, much of it is also applicable to alpines particularly those in similar families for example Cruciferae and Compositae, or genera for example *Narcissus* and *Tulipa*.

Characteristics of fungi

Appearance and Structure. Fungi are organisms which are neither animals nor plants and are classified in the Kingdom Fungi (Table 14; See p.91). They differ from plants by not possessing chlorophyll, and their dependence on the infection or colonisation of live and dead organisms for a supply of carbon-containing nutrients. By breaking down plant and animal tissue they provide nutrients for other organisms and, consequently, are an essential part of the ecosystem contributing to soil fertility. Fungi differ from most animals by absorbing nutrients, rarely ingesting them; also they are usually non-motile although some have motile stages. Most have cell walls which contain cellulose and chitin. Fungi are multinucleate (**eukaryotic**) and have different genetic states; they reproduce sexually and asexually.

Only a small proportion of fungi affect living plants directly. They can be beneficial and promote growth or, in contrast, they may be harmful and reduce growth, damage or kill the plant. Many fungi affect man and animals: *Eurotium repens* is the fungus which is often responsible for mouldy jam; *Claviceps purpurea* infects rye which, when eaten, causes hallucinations or 'St Anthony's Fire'; *Amanita phalloides*, the death cap fungus and *Aspergillus flavus* produce dangerous toxins which may cause death or cancer; *Tinea* species (syn. *Trichophyton*) infect the skin causing ringworms such as athletes foot; and *Candida albicans* produces the throat infection called 'thrush'. Fortunately, the fungi which infect plants do not infect man or animals. However, the spores sometimes cause allergies, or even more serious lung diseases and should not be inhaled. Some fungi form **lichens** in partnership with algae, obtaining complex carbon compounds via photosynthesis of the algal partner. Many fungi produce materials which are valuable in medicine and the food industry e.g. alcohol (yeasts), cheese manufacture (*Penicillium camembertii*, *P. roquefortii*), antibiotics (penicillin from *P. chrysogenum*, griseofulvin from *P. griseofulvum*) and enzymes such as pectinase.

The 'body' of a fungus is called a **thallus**, and is composed of filaments called **hyphae** (Fig 12) which are aggregated into a **mycelium**; the latter two terms are often used synonymously. In contrast, yeast fungi are unicellular, not filamentous. The hyphae of most fungi are divided into cells by cross-walls or **septae** but those of the Oomycetes and Zygomycetes have few if any septa, that is the hyphae are **coenocytic**. Hyphae are organised into a variety of structures adapted to different functions in the life cycle such as vegetative growth, reproduction and survival. Fungi do not produce stems, roots or a vascular system although some larger fungi have structures which are superficially similar for example the stalks of mushrooms or the **rhizomorphs** of the honey fungus (*Armillaria mellea*).

Most fungi grow best between 10-30°C although some are able to grow outside this range. They also prefer acid conditions whereas bacteria grow best in alkaline conditions. The only time that light is required is for spore production. The various fungi are adapted to life in different environments. Activity may be favoured by wet (*Pythium*) or warm (*Corticium rolfsii*) conditions; or the fungus may be adapted to an aerial (pow-

Figure 12 Fungal hyphae, the threads from which fungi are formed

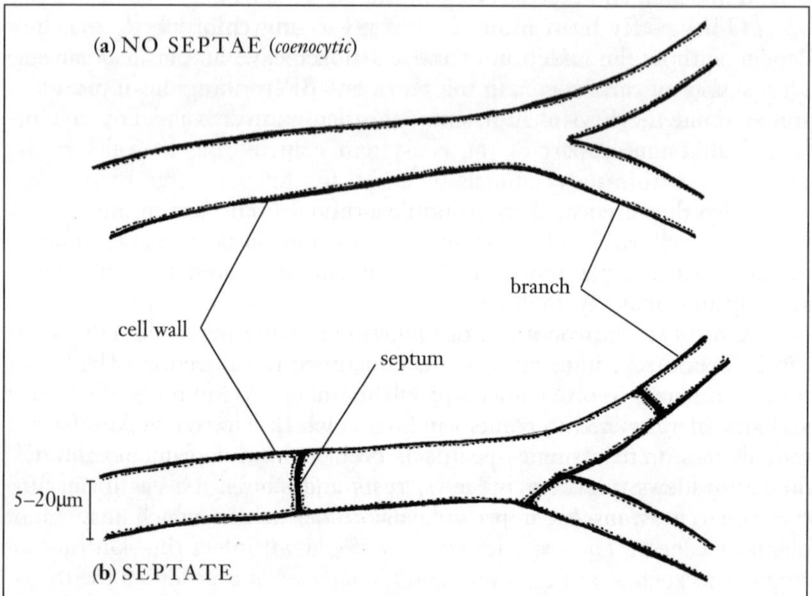

dery mildews) or soil environment (clubroot).

It is important to know how environmental conditions affect the activity of plant pathogenic fungi because this provides a logical basis for control measures.

Nutrition. Fungi require major elements (carbon, hydrogen, nitrogen, potassium, phosphorus, magnesium and sulphur) and minor elements (iron, zinc, copper). They obtain their carbon in the form of complex molecules such as sugars and cellulose that is to say they are **heterotrophic**. Fungi obtain nitrogen from proteins and amino acids or from inorganic nitrogen-containing compounds. Fungi are said to be **saprophytes** or **saprobes** if they obtain carbon from dead plant or animal tissue, **necrotrophs** if from both living and dead tissue and **parasites** or **biotrophs** if from living organisms. Most necrotrophic fungi and many biotrophic fungi cause considerable damage to plants. If the fungus has only one mode of nutrition it is said to be **obligate**. When the mode of nutrition changes according to the prevailing ecological circumstances, the fungus is **facultative**. Summarising, fungal nutrition is classified as:

- **obligately saprotrophic** – only dead tissue colonised;
- **facultatively necrotrophic** – saprophytic but, in appropriate environmental conditions, also parasitic. Examples are *Pythium*, and *Thanatephorus* (*Rhizoctonia*) causing seedling damping-off, and *Botryotinia fuckeliana* (*Botrytis cinerea*) causing grey mould;
- **obligately necrotrophic** – specialised parasites attacking living plants but with a limited capacity for growth in dying tissue e.g. formae speciales of *Fusarium oxysporum*;
- **facultatively biotrophic** – restricted to living host but with an independent mycelial stage in the field;
- **obligately biotrophic** – restricted to growth in a living host and without an independent mycelial stage. Examples include the downy mildews and blister rusts (Peronosporales), powdery mildews (Erysiphales), smuts (Ustilaginomycetes) and rusts (Urediniomycetes).

These differences in nutrition give rise to differences in the types of plant which are affected. A single species of fungus may be able to infect several species of plants which are botanically unrelated and is then said to be **plurivorus**: examples are *Pythium ultimum*, *Botryotinia fuckeliana* (syn. *Botrytis cinerea*), *Sclerotinia sclerotiorum* and *Corticium rolfsii*. As mentioned previously, fungi may be dependent on the infection of different unrelated plants in order to complete the life cycle (See p.140); or a fungus may be restricted to plants which are closely related e.g. *Mentha* and *Calamintha*, or to a single species or even variety of plant, notably the downy mildews, powdery mildews, rusts and smuts. This is in marked contrast to most insects, mites and eelworms which affect a wide range of plants.

Reproduction in Fungi. Reproduction in fungi is the formation of new individuals and has similarities with the reproduction of most other forms of life. There are two distinct processes:

(1) **Sexual reproduction** in which genes are exchanged between individual parents. The resulting new individuals have different combinations of genes and therefore differ from the parents in characteristics such as growth rate, competitiveness, survival and infectivity. Thus, sexual reproduction provides the variability that allows a species to adapt to different environments.

(2) **Asexual**, or **vegetative reproduction**, is the production of new individuals with identical characteristics to the parent. Genes are not exchanged. Asexual reproduction often occurs when conditions are favourable, large numbers of individuals are produced and hence is often associated with the spreading phase of plant pathogens.

The information needed to control fungal growth, is, as in most forms of life, carried by DNA in genes (See Chapter 4 for description of RNA genomes in viruses); the genes are located on chromosomes within the cell nucleus. The collection of genes can be likened to a language which translates or organises the many biochemical processes of a living

Figure 13 General life cycle of a disease causing fungus

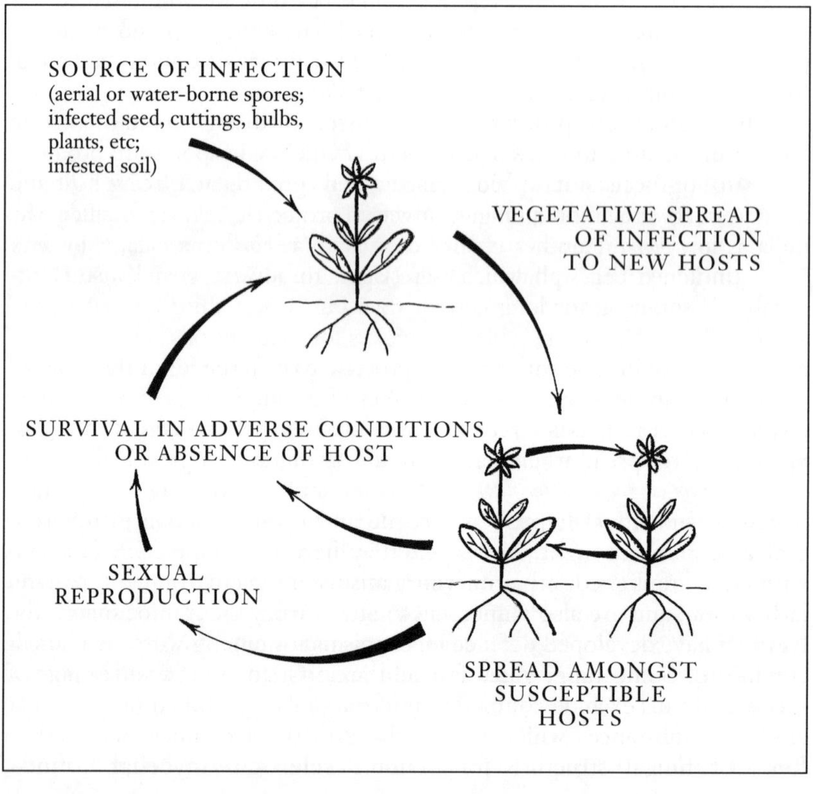

organism. To succeed in a different range of growth conditions, different combinations of genes are needed. These different combinations of genes are obtained, as mentioned above, by exchange between individuals during sexual reproduction whereas asexual reproduction allows fungi with a suitable genetic complement to produce large numbers of similar individuals which can take advantage of prevailing favourable conditions.

In sexual reproduction, nuclei, each with a single set of chromosomes (called **haploid**), are brought together from different cells and fuse to give a double set (called **diploid**). Later, the nuclei undergo a special process called **meiosis** or **reduction division** dividing twice to produce nuclei with the original single set of chromosomes but with a different combination of genes. The spores formed during this type of reproduction are named after the taxonomic group which produces them. Thus ascospores are produced by Ascomycetes, basidiospores by Basidiomycetes, and oospores by the Oomycetes.

Some fungi do not have a true sexual cycle but exchange genes by a process called **parasexuality**. Parasexuality is common in *Fusarium*, *Verticillium* and *Penicillium*. Such fungi adapt readily to new resistant varieties of plants and, as a result, plant resistance is overcome by the new fungus variant (See also Chapter 5).

Asexual or vegetative reproduction. The main function of asexual reproduction is the dispersal of genetically identical individuals, often in very large numbers. This form of reproduction is based on hyphae modified into specialised spores or sclerotia. Some spores have thin walls and hence are vulnerable and short-lived because of adverse climatic conditions and attack from other microorganisms. Examples are the urediniospores of rust fungi (See p.138), oidia of powdery mildews (See p.110) and conidiospores or conidia of the grey mould fungus (See p.126). Conidiospores are produced at the tips of specially modified hyphae called conidiophores, either directly in air as in the grey mould fungus, or within protective structures called pycnidia as in *Phoma*. Another type of asexual spore, called a chlamydospore, has a thickened cell wall which is resistant to adverse environments and capable of surviving for long periods (See Fig. 17). A third type of asexual spore, called a sclerotium, typically survives for long periods, and consists of aggregations of hyphae with an outer protective rind (See Fig. 16).

In summary, sexual reproduction enables fungi to adapt to new conditions, whereas asexual reproduction enables populations to increase rapidly and to spread when conditions are favourable.

Survival. Individual hyphae are fragile and do not survive extremes of temperature or drought. Moreover, they have to compete for nutrients with large numbers of other microorganisms in the environment, particularly in soil, and are also vulnerable to attack from them. Not surprisingly, fungi have developed defence mechanisms for coping with such hostile conditions. Some fungi grow fast and are first to occupy an ecological niche, and thus exclude competing microorganisms, while others produce antibiotic substances which inhibit the growth of competitors. Certain types of fungal structure for example **sclerotia**, **mycelial strands**,

rhizomorphs, **chlamydospores** and various types of **resting spore** also help them to survive unfavourable environmental conditions.

Sclerotia range from simple aggregations of a few hyphal cells in species such as *Verticillium dahliae*, to more complex structures differentiated into an outer dark, resistant rind and a centre made of compact hyphae in genera such as *Sclerotinia*, and *Helicobasidium*. All three fungi attack a wide range of mostly herbaceous plant species. The sclerotia of some fungi such as *Sclerotium cepivorum*, which can only attack *Allium* species, can survive for more than 15 years and consequently are difficult to eradicate. Fortunately, not all sclerotia are so resistant. Sclerotia contain reserves of nutrients and these attract other microorganisms such as the fungi *Trichoderma harzianum*, *Coniothyrium minitans* and *Sporidesmium sclerotivorum*; these fungi weaken and destroy the sclerotia by using up their stored nutrients. Sclerotia are also weakened by sub-lethal environmental conditions – conditions which are harmful but not harmful enough to kill e.g. sub-lethal temperatures of about 40°C. Weakened sclerotia are vulnerable to attack by other organisms, germinate more slowly in soil and are less able to infect the host. Consequently, the fungus is then at a competitive disadvantage to other antagonistic organisms.

Mycelial strands and rhizomorphs are hyphae which are aggregated into strands. Mycelial strands are pale-coloured and able to grow for considerable distances across nutrient-poor or unfavourable substrate regions. **Rhizomorphs** have a dark rind, similar to sclerotia, and look rather like thin boot laces or the roots of certain plants such as birch (*Betula*). Both types of structure are common in the wood-rotting Basidiomycetes, such as the honey fungus (*Armillaria mellea*), and allow the fungus to grow between woody roots and tree stumps in soil. Such structures commonly invade the garden from neighbouring infected hedges.

Chlamydospores and **resting spores** have thick protective walls, and also survive for long periods in the absence of the host. Chlamydospores are produced within the old mycelium and are released when the intervening cells die; they are usually produced in soil or in infected plant tissue and are common in *Trichoderma*, *Fusarium* and *Thielaviopsis basicola* whereas resting spores are found in *Phytophthora*, *Pythium*, *Plasmodiophora* and *Synchytrium*. The tissue of the infected plant gives additional protection to the fungus from high temperatures, desiccation or attack by other microorganisms.

Effects of fungi on plants. It was only in the late 1880s that some plant diseases were definitely attributable to the harmful effects of microorganisms, for example, the downy mildews which commonly infect many alpine plants.

Fungi grow on the surface of plants or within the tissues, and penetrate or grow between host cells. They harm plants by reducing the amount of photosynthetic tissue, by reducing the numbers and size of flowers and damaging the petals, by reducing the production of seeds or by damaging the roots and vascular system. Often, they cause spots on leaves, stems, roots, flowers or fruits which, to begin with, resemble the damage caused by viruses or bacteria. Later, a whitish mycelium may grow over the leaves, plant base or roots, and dust-like spores, reproductive and survival structures may develop. The cut-like damage produced by grazing insects, slugs etc. or the inter-veinal yellowing caused by viruses are not typical of fungi. Sometimes the damage is easily recognised and attributable to a particular organism e.g. clubroot of Cruciferae (*Plasmodiophora brassicae*), white rot of *Allium* (*Sclerotium cepivorum*) or various rusts and smuts. At other times, the damage may be indirect and more difficult to detect and identify the cause. For example, some fungi invade roots but cause only a slight reduction in plant growth. However, infection reduces the size of the functioning root system hence lessens the capacity of the plant to take up water and nutrients. As a result, wilting is often the first sign of attack. (See also Chapter 1: Diagnosis of Pest and Disease Problems.)

Beneficial microorganisms. Fortunately the numbers of species of fungi and bacteria which damage plants are greatly outnumbered by those, often unnoticed, which have beneficial effects. Examples are the nitrifying bacteria which convert nitrogen gas from the atmosphere into N-containing compounds such as nitrates, or amino acids which are essential for plant growth; root colonising bacteria or **rhizobacteria** which protect roots from attack by fungi or stimulate plant growth; **mycorrhizae** which colonise roots and improve nutrient uptake in poor soils, or improve seed germination in orchids. Also many fungi or bacteria are able to attack and destroy other harmful organisms such as fungi, insects and eelworms and are therefore used in biological control.

Recommended reading: 'The Advance of the Fungi' (Large, 1958); 'Introduction to Fungi' (Webster, 1986).

Life cycles

In common with other organisms, fungi have life cycles with clearly recognisable stages of birth, growth, reproduction and death. In fungi, these correspond to infection of the host plant followed by establishment and growth of the fungus, vegetative and sexual reproduction and finally a resting stage for survival in unfavourable conditions. Reproduction is accompanied by dispersal to other parts of the same plant or to different plants, followed by the initiation of new cycles of infection, growth and reproduction. Ultimately, the fungus dies if it is unable to find a source of nutrients or if the unfavourable conditions persist. Thus, the life cycle of a fungus is comparable to that of a flowering plant: plants start growth in spring when the weather improves, they grow, spread vegetatively by runners etc. or form shoots for the production of flowers, and finally they produce seed; the seed enables the plant to survive unfavourable conditions.

The form of a fungus which is potentially able to infect a plant is called **inoculum** examples being mycelium, vegetative or sexual spores, resting spores, or sclerotia.

The first function of inoculum is to initiate infection, and establish growth; logically enough, this is called **primary inoculum**. The second function is for inoculum to disperse to fresh host tissue and repeat the cycles of infection, growth and reproduction; this is called **secondary inoculum** (Fig. 14,). Understanding the difference between these two functions of inoculum provides clues to the correct control measures for a disease.

Primary inoculum. Plant infection starts when (a) inoculum is present, (b) a food supply in the form of susceptible host tissue becomes available and (c) temperatures and moisture favour fungal activity. Primary inoculum is often present when the plant is dormant and attacks the new host growth in the spring or after periods of unfavourable environmental conditions. Therefore the primary inoculum is often in the form of survival structures such as chlamydospores, sclerotia, resting spores etc. (See Table 13). However, primary inoculum can also be in a form with little capacity to survive e.g. as with infected plant cuttings. It is important to remember that susceptible, healthy, plants may be attacked when they are brought into the alpine house, garden or nursery and dormant primary inoculum is already present. Conversely, primary inoculum may be introduced into the alpine house, garden or nursery on infected new plants or bulbs, allowing the disease to become established. In temperate climates, rising temperatures in spring have the dual effect of stimulating the production of susceptible host tissue and providing conditions which favour fungal activity. As a result, primary inoculum has the opportunity to initiate infection. For example, in the UK, the production of roots by ornamental *Allium* plants in spring coincides with the time when the white rot fungus, *Sclerotium cepivorum*, becomes active. As a result, the worst effects of white rot generally occur in spring and early summer. In arid countries, primary inoculum may initiate infection as plants start to grow when rain falls after a long period of drought.

Secondary inoculum repeats the cycles of infection, growth and reproduction, hence its function is essentially that of propagation or spread of the disease (Fig. 14). Secondary spread occurs when there is an abundant source of susceptible host tissue and when environmental conditions favour fungal activity. Therefore, secondary inoculum is usually in the form of vast numbers of thin-walled spores or hyphae growing in pieces of plant tissue such as petals e.g. grey mould (*Botryotinia fuckeliana* (syn. *Botrytis cinerea*)). When repeated rapidly, cycles of secondary infection give rise to an 'explosion of infection' called a disease **epidemic**. For example, one primary colony may produce secondary inoculum which starts, say, 10 secondary colonies; each of the ten secondary colonies produces 10 more colonies and so on. At the end of 3 cycles there would be more than 10,000 colonies! Bearing in mind that each colony of the grey mould fungus produces large numbers of spore-bearing hyphae, that each spore-bearing hypha produces several hundred vegetative spores and that each spore is capable of starting a new colony, it becomes obvious how rapidly the fungus can spread when provided with favourable conditions.

Transition between secondary and primary inoculum. Ultimately, secondary spread slows down as supplies of susceptible host tissue diminish, either because of the attack or because plants become dormant in winter. Fungi have evolved methods for survival in the absence of a host or in unfavourable conditions. White mould (*Sclerotinia sclerotiorum*), which attacks a wide range of herbaceous plant species, produces sclerotia on infected plants at the end of summer. The sclerotia are released into soil as the plant decays and remain inactive during the winter. Sclerotia germinate the following spring producing apothecia (Table 17, Fig. 16) which, in turn, produce primary inoculum in the form of ascospores.

Figure 14 Initiation and spread of a disease causing fungus

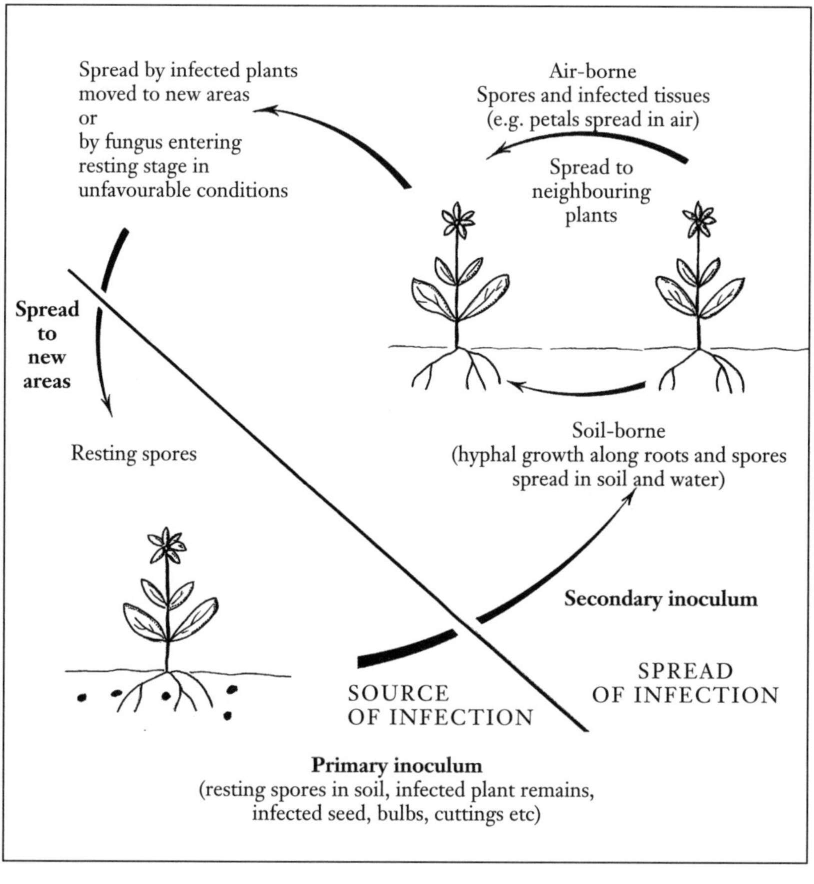

Table 13 **Function of inoculum and type of fungal structure**

Function of inoculum	Type of fungal structure
Primary inoculum	**Vegetative**
Starts a cycle of infection at the beginning of an epidemic	Sclerotia which produce hyphae or vegetative spores
	Chlamydospores
	Hyphae in plant tissue, hence planting material such as seeds, bulbs and plant cuttings
	Sexual
	Ascospores produced on apothecia from sclerotia
	Basidiospores
	Oomycete resting spores
Secondary inoculum	**Vegetative**
Repeats the cycles of infection during the growing season causing the disease to spread	Spores
	Plant tissue such as petals colonised by hyphae

Figure 15 Spread of soil-borne fungi

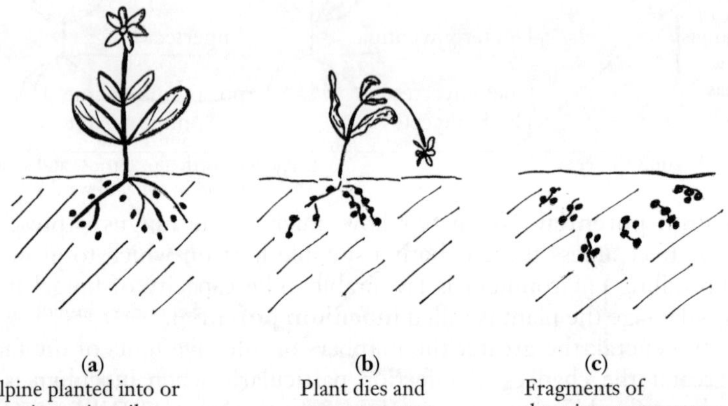

(a) Alpine planted into or germinates in soil contaminated with fungal spores which germinate allowing fungal hyphae to infect plant

(b) Plant dies and new spores are formed on roots

(c) Fragments of decaying roots carry fungal spores which are dispersed to new areas as the soil is cultivated

Table 14 **Classification of fungi**

Taxonomic group	Classification	Common name
Kingdom	Fungi	Fungi
Division	Myxomycota	Slime moulds
Class	Plasmodiophoromycetes	
Division	Eumycota	True fungi
Sub-division	Mastigomycotina	no common name
Class	Chytridiomycetes	Water moulds
Class	Oomycetes	
Sub-division	Zygomycotina	no common name
Class	Zygomycetes	no common name
Sub-division	Ascomycotina	Ascomycetes
Class	none recognised	
Sub-division	Basidiomycotina	Basidiomycetes
Class	Hymenomycetes	Toadstools and bracket fungi
Class	Gasteromycetes	Puffballs, earthstars and stinkhorns
Class	Urediniomycetes	Rusts
Class	Ustilaginomycetes	Smuts
Sub-division	Deuteromycotina	Imperfect fungi
Class	Coelomycetes	no common name
Class	Hyphomycetes	no common name

Inoculum potential. No matter how much of the fungus is present, it has no effect unless there is both a suitable host on which to grow, and the prevailing environment is favourable. The capacity of fungal inoculum to damage the plant is called **inoculum potential**.

In general, the greater the numbers of infective units of the fungus the greater the chances of infection particularly when inoculum is dispersed over a wide area. However, the infective units of soil-borne fungi – sclerotia, chlamydospores, etc. – are produced on roots or stems and, as a result, are in clusters. The infective units are released when the host decays, become incorporated into soil and are subsequently dispersed during cultivation; successive cultivations result in a progressively wider dispersal. Initially, clustered inoculum is in contact with only a small number of susceptible plants and it hardly makes any difference whether the inoculum comprises 1, 10 or 1000 infective units, because only the small number of plants are available for infection. During dispersal, the infective units come in contact with larger numbers of plants and hence the inoculum potential increases. In effect, the same number of infective units is now in a position to attack more plants (Fig. 15).

Inoculum potential is also affected by the inherent activity of individual infective units which in turn is dependent on the size of their food reserves, and their 'vigour'. Vigour results from the capacity of the fungus to resist attack by antagonistic microorganisms, to withstand adverse environmental conditions, to germinate promptly in response to favourable conditions and to grow rapidly on the host. This is comparable to the situation which occurs with seed or bulbs which, for example, at one extreme are large and vigorous hence likely to grow and flower well, at the other small and weak, therefore less likely to succeed.

Given that a suitable host is present and that the fungus is vigorous, the effectiveness of inoculum (inoculum potential) is dependent on a favourable environment, such as temperatures and moisture suitable for germination, infection, growth and reproduction of the particular fungus. Less obviously, the activity of other microorganisms also forms part of the environment affecting the interaction between pathogen and plant. Thus root-colonizing bacteria or rhizobacteria can reduce infection from disease fungi.

Control measures are based on manipulating these three types of effect. Hence it may be sufficient to tip the ecological balance slightly against the pathogen and in favour of the host for the disease to be reduced. For example, host resistance reduces the availability of susceptible host tissue, physical treatments such as hot water treatment of the infected host, or treatment of infected soil, reduces the capacity of the fungus to grow, and treatment of the host with fungicides or biological control organisms changes the environment and reduces the chance of infection.

Recommended reading: 'Biology of Root Infecting Fungi' (Garrett, 1956).

Classification and nomenclature of disease fungi

Classification

Classification indicates the evolutionary relationships between different organisms. However, it becomes necessary to revise both the classification and nomenclature as knowledge increases and this is one reason why the names of some higher plants change so frequently. The system of classification and nomenclature of different organisms in use today is based on the system published by Linnaeus in 1753. Organisms are allocated to a series of descending taxonomic groups or **taxa** (singular, taxon; See also Chapter 2): Phylum, Kingdom, Division, Sub-division, Class, Order, Family, Genus and Species. Originally fungi were considered as part of the Plant Kingdom. Nowadays they are thought to be sufficiently different to be placed in a separate Kingdom, the Fungi. It is important to realise that the Linnaean system of classification is not applicable to viruses (See Chapter 4).

The Kingdom **Fungi** is divided into two main Divisions the **Myxomycota** and the **Eumycota** or true fungi (See Table 14), the latter forming the main topic of this book. Of the Myxomycota, only *Plasmodiophora* is described in this book.

The true fungi are arranged in four main Sub-divisions: **Mastigomycotina**, **Zygomycotina**, **Ascomycotina** and the **Basidiomycotina**, plus the **Deuteromycotina**. You may come across older classifications with different arrangements. For example, the Phycomycetes corresponds to a combination of the current Mastigomycotina and Zygomycotina. Within the Sub-divisions there are a series of **Classes**, **Orders** and **Families**. On the basis of their structure, evolutionary development and behaviour, the Myxomycota, Chytridiomycetes, Oomycetes, and Zygomycetes are described as **lower** fungi and the Ascomycotina and Basidiomycotina as **higher** fungi.

Many fungi exist in different forms and produce different types of spore and hence are said to be **pleomorphic**. The form which produces sexual spores is described as the **perfect** state and the form which produces asexual, vegetative spores or no spores as the **imperfect** state. Nowadays the sexual and vegetative states are called the **teleomorph** and **anamorph** respectively, and collectively the **holomorph**. As a general rule, a particular species of fungus may have several different anamorphs and often it is the anamorph which causes the most damage in plants and hence is most often seen. Sometimes, however, the teleomorph may not be known – possibly because it has been lost in evolution or simply because it has yet to be discovered. This situation becomes confusing because it is not very obvious that the different forms are from one and the same organism. When only the vegetative (anamorph) state was known the fungus was originally placed in a **form** taxon the Deuteromycotina or **Fungi Imperfecti**. Then, when the sexual state (teleomorph) was discovered, the fungus was transferred to its appropriate place in the classification, usually to the Ascomycotina or Basidiomycotina. However, even in the absence of a known sexual stage, it may be possible to classify a particular fungus, at least provisionally, by comparing it with similar fungi whose sexual state (teleomorph) is definitely known. Similar rules of classification apply to animals such as insects (See Chapter 2).

As mentioned earlier, classifications such as the Linnaean system which reflects evolutionary changes in organisms are called 'natural' classifications. However, there are other classifications designed for practical purposes. Fungi, particularly those which harm plants, are classified on the basis of their methods of dispersal and survival, for example soil-borne or air-borne fungi, or on the part of the plant which is affected, for example leaf or root fungi. Classifications intended solely for practical convenience are called 'artificial' for example those based on symptoms – leaf spots, wilts, seedling diseases, etc.

Nomenclature

The nomenclature or **taxonomy** of fungi and pests is based on the characteristics of the organisms and is governed by the **International Code of Botanical Nomenclature** (latest versions 1978, 1981, 1988) or the **International Code of Zoological Nomenclature**. The main aim of these Codes is to provide a stable and unambiguous method of naming organisms, and to avoid or reject names which are likely to cause error or confusion. Each distinct organism – plant, fungus or insect, but excluding viruses – has a pair of names or **binomial** which is unique. The first part of the binomial is called the **genus** followed by the second part, called the **species**. Some fungi have an additional taxon below the rank of species that is they have three names called a **trinomial**. This additional taxon may be based on morphological features such as **variety**, or on differences in growth or host response (physiological differences) e.g. **formae speciales** as in *Fusarium oxysporum*, **physiological races** or **strains** as in the downy mildews, **anastomosis** or **incompatibility groups** as in *Thanatephorus* (*Rhizoctonia*) and *Verticillium*.

For precision, each name is followed by the **authority**. The authority is a citation of the author who first described and published the name and is abbreviated in a standard manner e.g. L. (= Linnaeus), Fr. (= Fries E.M), Sacc. (= Saccardo P.A.), Pers. (=Persoon); an example is *Puccinia graminis* Pers. The inclusion of the authority minimises the chances of confusion if the same name were to be used inadvertently for a different organism – as has happened in the past when the communication of published names was slow. When fungal names are subsequently revised, the authority comprises two or more names. The name of the earlier author is given in round brackets before that of the author making the revision e.g. *Fusarium avenaceum* (Fr.) Sacc. The method of describing the authority for insect names differs slightly in that it is sometimes included in parentheses even though there has been no change of name. The inclusion of the authority is essential for a description to be definitive but, nevertheless, is often omitted in more general texts.

The choice of fungal names is based on the priority of publication in Linnaeus's *Species Plantarum* (1753), Persoon's *Synopsis methodica fungorum* (1801), and Fries's *Systema mycologicum* (1821) and *Elenchus Fungorum* (1828). Names are valid only when published in the appropriate Code and formally adopted by an International Botanical or Zoological Congress; revisions of nomenclature are adopted in a similar manner. About 64,000 species of fungi are known, and more than one million insect species.

The appearance of the sexual (teleomorph) and vegetative (anamorph) states differs considerably and in addition a single species of fungus may have several anamorphs each producing a different type of spore. To add to the confusion, the different fungal states may depend on different species of plant in order for completion of the life-cycle. An example is the group of **heteroecious** rust fungi where the sexual and asexual states often grow on totally different plants such as pines and grasses (See p.140). As mentioned before, there was initially no means of knowing that a fungus occurred in different states. As a result, fungi often have two or more names, one for each state or spore type. Under the Botanical Code, names based on the sexual (teleomorph) state have priority over the names based on the vegetative (anamorph) state. Since the vegetative state is often the most common form of the fungus, the 'correct' teleomorph name is often qualified by the 'vegetative' name e.g. the **oidium** state of *Erysiphe*, the **botrytis** state of *Botryotinia*, the **fusarium** state of *Nectria*, etc. Whilst the teleomorph name has priority, anamorph names often persist because of their familiarity by established use e.g. *Botrytis* (=*Botryotinia*), *Fusarium* (=*Nectria*), *Rhizoctonia* (=*Thanatephorus*), *Oidium* (=*Erysiphe*).

The simple rules listed below ensure that names are used in a consistent manner:

The initial letter only of the genus is written in upper case (capital) whereas the species name is in lower case; this is true even if the binomial is derived from a proper name or noun; both parts of the name are underlined when written or *italicised* when printed e.g. *Fusarium oxysporum*. The name is written in full when first used. Subsequently, the genus may be abbreviated to the initial (upper case) letter (e.g. *F. oxysporum*); if more than one species of the same genus are described together, the initial letter may be repeated e.g. *FF. culmorum*, *oxysporum*, *solani*; however, if this is ambiguous, for example if different genera have the same initial letter, the name is repeated in full;

When the genus name is not used as a proper noun, the initial letter is usually in lower case and the name is not italicised e.g. the fusaria.

Large organisms – aphid, white fly, oak etc. – are often known by common names. Common names are also given to the major groups of fungi for example the rusts, powdery mildews, downy mildews and smuts. However, individual species of fungi, excepting those with obvious structures such as toadstools, do not have common names. With harmful organisms, the name of the disease is used as a common name and may be linked to the organism e.g. the white rot fungus, the grey mould fungus, the mildew fungus etc.

An example of the classification of an insect is given in Chapter 2 and the classification and nomenclature of viruses is described in Chapter 4.

THE MAIN GROUPS OF FUNGI

There are four main Sub-divisions of fungi, plus the Deuteromycotina (Fungi Imperfecti), and their classification and the type of symptoms they cause are described in Table 15.

Table 15 **Main groups of fungi and the diseases they cause in plants**

Main group	Order	Example	Symptom
Myxomycota Plasmodio-phoromycetes	Plasmo diophorales	*Plasmodiophora*	clubroot in cruciferae
Eumycota: Mastigomycotina Chytridiomycetes	Chytridiales	*Synchytrium*	wart disease
Oomycetes	Peronosporales	*Albugo*	white blister or white rust: distortion and powdery white mould on aerial parts
		Peronospora	downy mildew : leaf rot
		Phytophthora	downy mildew : root, seedling, leaf rot
		Plasmopara	downy mildew : leaf mildew
		Pythium	water mould : seedling damping-off
Eumycota: Zygomycotina Zygomycetes			
Eumycota: Ascomycotina	Eurotiales	*Eupenicillium* *Penicillium*	blue-green moulds: bulbs, corms or rhizomes rot or mummify
	Erysiphales	*Erysiphe*	powdery mildew: yellow to brown spots, white powdery mould mainly on leaves
		Sphaerotheca	mildews of stem and leaf
	Hypocreales	*Fusarium*	: some species associated with seedling damping-off and decay of roots and stem base; : formae speciales block and stain the vascular system causing wilting
		Verticillium	: similar wilts to Fusarium
		Trichoderma	: often associated with biological control of fungal pathogens
	Helotiales	*Botryotinia* *Botrytis* *Ovulinia* *Sclerotinia* *Stromatinia*	: form large (0.25-20 mm) resistant sclerotia; sclerotia produce hyphae which infect roots and stem and leaves at soil level (Sclerotium, Sclerotinia spp.), or aerial spores either directly from the sclerotium ('Botrytis grey mould') or from an intermediate apothecium; spores infect soft aerial tissue such as seedlings, leaves and flowers; : cause root, stem and leaf rot and spots on leaves and petals
	Dothideales	*Ramularia* *Didymella* *Septoria* *Alternaria* *Macrophoma* *Venturia* *Mycosphaerella*	spots on leaves, often with concentric rings (zonate) or dark coloured edges
	Ophiostomatales	*Thielaviopsis*	black root rot in a wide range of species; weakens the plant which is more vulnerable to drought
	Polystimatales	*Colletotrichum* *Gleosporium*	small black ascervuli on plant surfaces
Eumycota: Basidiomycotina	Exobasidiales	*Exobasidium*	obligate parasites causing galls on leaves especially in the Ericaceae

Main groups of fungi and the diseases they cause in plants (continued)

Main group	Order	Example	Symptom
	Uredinales	*Coleosporium* *Ochropsora* *Puccinia* *Uromyces*	obligate plant parasites: rusts
	Ustilaginales	*Entyloma* *Ustilago*	facultative plant parasites: blister smuts : smuts of anthers, seed capsules
	Tulasnellales	*Rhizoctonia* *(Thanatephorus)*	facultative plant parasites with a wide host range often causing seedling damping-off, or sclerotia on corms, rhizomes etc.

Lower fungi

Background. This group contains fungi in the Sub-division **Mastigomycotina** which includes the Classes **Oomycetes** (e.g. *Phytophthora*, *Pythium*, downy mildews and white rusts), the **Chytridiomycetes** (e.g. *Olpidium*) and **Zygomycetes**; the latter Class contains fungi such as *Mucor* and *Rhizopus* which attack *Narcissus* bulbs in store or during 'chipping' (Plate 15).

For convenience, the Class **Plasmodiophoromycetes** is included here although it correctly belongs to the **Division** Myxomycota – amoeba-like organisms which include *Plasmodiophora brassicae* the clubroot organism.

Most of the lower fungi in this group produce zoospores or related structures. Zoospores are spores which swim in films of water. Swimming is achieved by the movement of minute whip-like threads called **flagellae** (singular: flagellum) and their numbers, position and structure are used for further classification within the group. Actually, zoospores only swim for very small distances and movement over greater distances is by irrigation or drainage water, floods, and rivers. There is an evolutionary trend away from the total dependence on water for growth and spread, to tolerance of drier conditions. At its simplest, the **zoosporangium** – a minute bag containing zoospores – remains attached to the parent mycelium. More advanced species have zoosporangia which become detached and are dispersed in air before germinating and releasing zoospores; examples are *Albugo*, *Phytophthora* and *Plasmopara*, *Bremia* and *Peronospora*, two of the downy mildew genera, are even more advanced and do not produce zoospores. Instead, the 'zoosporangium' behaves as a spore or conidium; after dispersal, the conidium germinates by a germ tube, produces hyphae and infects the aerial parts of the host. Clearly, the combination of aerial dispersal and infection of the host without the need for water films improves the capacity of the fungus to spread to and become established on distant hosts. However, high atmospheric humidity is still necessary for growth, consequently these fungi are mostly active in moist habitats. This is in contrast to the powdery mildews (See p.110) and rusts (See p.138) which thrive in dry conditions – although, again, moisture is essential for certain stages of their life cycles.

All the fungi in this group are coenocytic, that is the mycelium does not have cross walls. The amount of mycelium which is produced varies with the particular group, the Chytridiomycetes producing very much less than Oomycetes such as *Pythium* and *Phytophthora*. In common with other groups of fungi, there are distinct phases of vegetative, non-reproductive growth, asexual (vegetative) and sexual reproduction. At its simplest, the whole vegetative body or thallus converts to a reproductive body and is said to be **holocarpic**; evolutionary-wise, this is a primitive character. In contrast, the more advanced **eucarpic** fungi have distinctive vegetative and reproductive mycelia, only part of the vegetative thallus being converted for reproduction.

The Class Oomycetes is important because it contains *Phytophthora* and *Pythium*, the downy mildews, and the white rusts which together infect a wide range of garden plants. The Chytridiomycetes contain *Olpidium*, *Polymyxa* and *Synchytrium*, fungi which mainly damage agricultural crops and are discussed only briefly. A third Class, the Hyphochytriomycetes feed on algae and fungi, or on dead plant or insect tissue and are not discussed further.

At one time, the Oomycetes formed part of the Phycomycetes, a group which also included the **Zygomycetes**. Nowadays, the term Phycomycetes is only used in a general sense to describe the lower fungi, that is fungi which have not evolved far from their aquatic ancestors.

Symptoms. Infected host tissue generally dies and this gives rise to a wide range of types of lesion. Pre-emergence damping-off occurs when seedlings are attacked below soil level, consequently emergence is patchy or fails. Post-emergence damping-off describes seedlings which emerge normally and look healthy, then suddenly collapse. Soft wood cuttings rot at the base, and new shoots wither. (Note, however, that other types of fungi can also cause problems during propagation e.g. *Botryotinia fuckeliana* (*Botrytis cinerea*), *Cylindrocarpon destructans*, *Glomerella cingulata*, *Monochaetia karstenii*, *Pestalotiopsis*, *Thanatephorus (Rhizoctonia) solani*.) A rot which affects the base of the plant is called a foot rot or, if the plant is woody, a collar rot. Infected leaves develop pale spots or blotches on the upper surface followed later by patches of white, grey or purplish mycelium in similar positions on the under leaf surface. (Similar symptoms are also caused by powdery mildews (See p.110) and rusts (See p.138)). When infection is severe or prolonged, leaves wither and drop off, and young plants die, as do young shoots on established plants. Distorted, swollen shoots or leaves, covered with chalky white spores are characteristic of white rust caused by *Albugo* species (Plate 14b). Swellings or galls are produced on roots, stems or leaves by the repeated division of infected host tissue and are indicative of the fungus *Synchytrium*. (Galls may be caused by other pathogens such as clubroot (See p.108) or bacteria – (See p.152). Infected roots turn from creamy white to dull brown, and rot. Alternatively, the root vascular tissue – called the stele or core – stains brown, giving rise to a 'brown core' symptom. Often, the vascular tissue protrudes from the decaying outer fleshy root tissue, giving rise to the so-called 'rats-tail' symptom. There is also a syndrome of indirect effects arising from the reduced capacity of infected roots or stems to supply water and nutrients to the aerial parts. Shoot growth nearly always slows down and leaf colour fades. At other times plant growth appears normal until whole branches begin to die from the tips backwards, even though others on the same plant look healthy. This type of selective branch death occurs when infected roots cut off the water and nutrient supply to branches connected by the same vascular trace. In contrast, a rot which girdles the stem at soil level is likely to affect all branches. Plants become 'bushy' when infection kills the main shoot, and side and basal shoots become dominant.

A particular pathogen may infect plant tissue which is either soft or hard, but generally not both. Seedlings are likely to be infected by *Pythium* species, less commonly by downy mildew or white rust, whereas hard tissue in soil may be infected by soil-inhabiting *Phytophthora* species. Young leaves and shoots on established plants are often infected by downy mildew or white rust, but may also be infected by soil-borne *Phytophthora* species if splashed with contaminated soil; *Pythium* is unlikely to infect aerial tissue. Of course, fungi from other taxonomic groups also attack roots, shoots and leaves etc.

Life cycle. Infection of a host starts from primary inoculum (See Fig. 14; p.89) comprising resting spores in soil or host tissue, mycelium surviving in infected plant debris, or infected propagating material. Secondary inoculum is provided by zoospores or conidia which repeat the cycles of infection causing the disease to increase rapidly. Asexual reproduction is by sporangia which either produce zoospores, or germinate directly and infect the plant. Asexual thick-walled chlamydospores (See p.86) help some species, particularly *Phytophthora*, to survive during unfavourable conditions. Sexual reproduction is either by fusion of zoospores, which function as gametes, to produce a zygote, or by fusion of a male (♂) gamete with a female egg (♀) cell to produce an **oospore** contained in a protective structure called an oogonium.

Individual fungi which cause important diseases of alpine and other garden plants are described below and in Table 27, Table 28; at the end of this chapter.

Phytophthora, *Pythium*, downy mildews and white rusts

These fungi belong to the Class Oomycetes and affect a wide range of alpines and other garden plants. Most are widespread and common. They range from those such as *Pythium* which lives only on dead tissue (saprotrophs: See p.83), to those like *Phytophthora* living on either dead and live tissue (facultative necrotrophs) and finally the downy mildews and white rusts which spend the whole life cycle on living plants (obligate biotrophs or parasites). Species in the first two categories often live in soil and infect roots and seedlings whereas the downy mildews and white rusts attack the aerial parts of the plant, at least in the spreading phase. However, there are exceptions to this generalisation, and some soil-borne *Phytophthora* species also infect aerial plant parts when, for example, they are splashed with soil. When conditions are moist, oomycete fungi increase and spread rapidly. However, they often have only a limited capacity to compete with other microorganisms. As a result, fungi such as *Pythium* may be first to colonise new substrates – where there are few antagonistic microorganisms – but are subsequently easily displaced by other microorganisms. This secondary colonisation often makes it difficult to isolate and identify the primary cause of damage, and consequently special selective laboratory growth media are needed.

Most species are dispersed by infected plant propagating material, stock plants, dead plant tissue, or by contaminated soil found in used seed trays or other containers. Seed-borne infection is unlikely, except possibly by downy mildews, when seed may become contaminated with infected plant debris. Soil-borne *Phytophthora* and *Pythium* species usually infect a range of host plant species and this provides ample opportunity for cross infection. Individual species of downy mildew or white rust are limited to a single host plant species, or at most to their close relatives, and cross infection from other host species is unlikely.

Phytophthora and *Pythium*

These two genera have many similarities. However, *Phytophthora* species are mostly parasitic, rarely saprophytic, and attack both young and old host tissue. The genus *Pythium*, with about twice as many species as *Phytophthora*, attacks mostly soft tissue, and can be either saprophytic or parasitic. Most species of *Phytophthora*, and all species of *Pythium*, are adapted to life in soil and roots; *Phytophthora infestans*, the cause of potato and tomato blight, is a notable exception because it mainly attacks leaves and spreads in air. In favourable conditions, repeated cycles of infection, the production of sporangia and release of huge numbers of zoospores, and infection cause a rapid increase in populations. Dispersal is by movement of zoospores in irrigation and drainage water, and by oospores and mycelium in infected tissue and soil. *Pythium* species survive unfavourable environmental conditions, or the absence of suitable host plants, by growing in dead plant tissue, or as oospores in plant tissue and soil. *Phytophthora* also survives as oospores, and as chlamydospores, but the mycelium has less capacity for saprophytic growth than *Pythium*, surviving only as long as the host tissue takes to decay; consequently, survival is greatest in large pieces of dead tissue. Most species of either genus survive freezing.

Pythium species are generally homothallic, that is sexual reproduction occurs on a single mycelium. However, a few *Pythium* species such as *P. sylvaticum*, together with the majority of *Phytophthora* species require two different mycelia for sexual reproduction, that is they are heterothallic.

Symptoms. *Phytophthora* species mostly affect the roots of plants which are woody, consequently symptoms are initially not very obvious and often take several years to appear; by this time root infection is well-established and difficult to control. Early signs of infection are poor growth, faded leaf colour, whereas later signs are withered leaves and branches; all the symptoms result from the impaired capacity of infected roots to supply water and nutrients. However, careful diagnosis is needed, because leaves can also turn brown for a variety of other reasons, for example because of excessive nutrient release from slow-release fertilizers during hot weather. Leaves and berries also develop blotches and rot when splashed with contaminated soil during heavy rain or watering, for example leaf infection by *P. ilicis*. Infection of herbaceous plants shows more quickly than in woody species generally as a wilting or collapse as in *Campanula persicifolia* infected by *P. porri* Foister, or *Primula vulgaris* infected by *P. primulae*. The crown of *Campanula* plants also turns brown and becomes loose in the soil as the roots are killed. The root vascular system of *Primula* turns brown, and the outer part of the root decays leaving a protruding stele or core, or rat-tail symptom.

Pythium species attack soft plant tissue and are often responsible for pre- and post-emergence damping-off. Some *Pythium* species infect and kill the tips of roots but this does not show, or shows only as a slight reduction in plant growth.

As mentioned above, *Phytophthora* and *Pythium* are both adapted to life in soil, or on roots or stem base tissue and depend on wet soil for growth and spread. *Phytophthora* species can be grouped according to their temperature requirements (See Table 16, p.104). Those species which grow best at 'low' temperatures – *P. cactorum* (4-29°C; optimum 20°C), *P. ilicis* (3-25°C; 20°C), *P. primulae* (1-20°C; 15°C), *P. syringae* (1-25°C; 20°C) – are active in cool weather. Others need warmer temperatures for example *P. cinnamomi* (5-36°C; 20-25°C), *P. citricola* (3-32°C; 25°C), *P. cryptogea* (3-25°C; 25°C) and hence are active in warm weather; growth does occur at lower temperatures, but is slower. A third group requires temperatures of 25-38°C, for example *P. parasitica* and *P. nicotianae* which, in the UK are more likely in glasshouses, or occur in warmer climates abroad. Differences in soil pH have little effect on the growth of *Phytophthora* or *Pythium*. *Phytophthora* and *Pythium* both cause a considerable amount of damage to a wide range of garden plant species (See Table 16, Table 27, Table 28). The soil-borne *Phytophthora* species commonly attack *Chamaecyparis* and *Cupressus*, and Ericaceae such as *Rhododendron* (including *Azalea*), *Erica* or *Calluna*. Species such as *Phytophthora cinnamomi* Rands affect huge numbers of plant species. Others are limited to a single species or to a small number of close relatives, notably *Phytophthora ilicis* Buddenhagen & Young on *Ilex*, *Phytophthora primulae* Tomlinson on *Primula vulgaris*, and *Phytophthora richardiae* Buisman on *Zantedeschia aethiopica* (*Z. africana*; arum lily). Not surprisingly plants are often susceptible to several different *Phytophthora* species and are sometimes infected by several at once. *Pythium ultimum* Trow (= *P. debaryanum* Hesse emend. Middleton), the commonest of the *Pythium* species, infects most plant species providing the tissue is soft and the soil is wet.

Sources of infection. The soil is a reservoir of inoculum for most of the *Phytophthora* species, both for root infection and, for species such as *P. porri* which infects leaves which come in contact with soil; *Pythium* originates from similar sources. Ultimately the fungi return to the soil in decayed tissue. Thus primary inoculum may exist as pieces of infected root or other plant debris, or contaminated soil. Any of these sources may be present in seed trays, plant pots, benches, or water butts. Drainage water from infected plants is often a recurrent source of infection. Containers for propagation and growth are easily contaminated, and, unless disinfested, are a source of infection. The lack of early symptoms in woody plants means that they may be infected when distributed and themselves become new sources of infection.

Because these fungi are able to grow fast in the absence of competition from other microorganisms, they may cause problems when they enter growing media with low populations of microorganisms, for example peat based compost, loam compost which has been steamed too long, or fumigated soil (See Chapter 5). This is one reason why seed and potting composts are pasteurised rather than sterilised. Obviously it is essential that growing media and containers are kept away from potential sources of fungal contamination.

Control. A variety of factors make the control of *Phytophthora* difficult: (1) early infections in woody plants are difficult to detect, (2) most *Phytophthora* species attack roots and are inaccessible to treatment, (3) established infections are difficult to eradicate, (4) a wide range of unrelated plant species can be infected by a single species of *Phytophthora*, (5) contaminated soil, plant debris or irrigation water can re-new infection, (6) effective chemicals are few and the methods of application limited. As described in Chapter 5, control measures aim to prevent infection, to stop infection from getting worse, and to eradicate established infection. Treatment is more likely to succeed when applied early and carefully, and takes into account all aspects of the problem such as sources of inoculum, growth conditions and fungicide. Overlooking one factor, for example re-infection by contaminated water, can easily nullify control measures. Because of these difficulties it is best to concentrate on preventing infection rather than trying to cure infections which have become established. Hygiene and sanitation are the key factors, the aim being to delay the development and spread of *Phytophthora* as long as possible. Essentially this means (1) excluding infected plants, soil, water and containers from the garden or nursery, (2) alleviating bad drainage, and minimising soil wetness to stop small amounts of infection from increasing, (3) timely application of fungicides and (4) sanitation by destroying infected plants, and sterilising plant pots, seed trays, benches, plunge beds and water butts. First, the sources of infection must be identified and this depends on whether plants are obtained from outside the garden or nursery, or whether they are propagated on site. Bought-in plants may already be infected, even if this is not apparent, and the aim then is to reduce the severity of symptoms and to stop the disease from spreading to healthy plants. This latter point is particularly important for amateur gardeners because the most effective anti-*Phytophthora* chemicals are available only to professional horticulturalists. Those who propagate and distribute plants, particularly nurserymen, will wish to minimise infection, and hence the possibility of distributing infected plants to customers. Used plant containers should be washed thoroughly and soaked in bleach or sodium hypochlorite. This technique is usually successful with plastic pots which are smooth, but less so when containers are made from other materials such as polystyrene, or if pots are damaged, because infected roots and spores can survive in small cracks. The disinfectant must be replaced when it becomes dirty otherwise it is inactivated.

Recurrent infections can be traced by monitoring possible sources of contamination – e.g. water, re-useable containers, nursery stock, by growing seedlings as test plants. The root systems are then compared with those grown in conditions kept free of *Phytophthora*. Healthy plants can be isolated from sources of infection by standing them on inverted plant pots. Contaminated irrigation water, as in re-cycled water on modern nurseries, can be treated by injecting chlorine compounds (1 mg chlorine per litre water). Theoretically irrigation supplies can be sterilised by UV light, but the equipment is expensive to buy and run. Finally, infection is also kept in check by ensuring that plants are not stressed due to inadequate or unbalanced feeding, poor light, drought, or excessive temperatures.

Pythium species are easier to control because they only infect soft tissue, and seedlings are only vulnerable for a short time and become increasingly resistant with age. As with *Phytophthora*, the key factors for control are hygiene and sanitation. Control by fungicides is described later (See p.106).

Most of the *Phytophthora* damage to garden plants in the UK is by four out of the 50 or so species, and these, together with *Pythium*, are described below. Other species of *Phytophthora* are listed in Table 16.

Phytophthora cryptogea Pethybr. & Lafferty is common in conifers, and ericaceous plants such as *Rhododendron* and *Erica*. Root infection reduces plant growth, shoots and leaves wilt and isolated branches die. The fungus also causes damping-off and foot or collar rots causing a wide variety of young plants to wilt or collapse, and is common on propagating material. Growth is best at 25°C but occurs as low as 3°C. Infection is said to pre-dispose the host plant to infection by *Phytophthora cinnamomi*; pre-infection by *Phytophthora cactorum* (See Table 16) is said to have a similar effect.

Phytophthora citricola Sawada causes die-back in a wide range of plants including *Antirrhinum majus*, *Hibiscus*, *Malus pumila*, *Pieris japonica*, *Primula japonica*, *Rhododendron*, *Rubus*, *Syringa*, *Chamaecyparis*, *Cupressus*, and *Pinus*. The fungus is active at similar temperatures to the preceding species.

Phytophthora cinnamomi Rands attacks about 1000 plant species, more than any other species of *Phytophthora*, and occurs throughout the world.

Table 16 **Phytophthora species found in gardens**

Species of *Phytophthora*	Hosts	Optimum growth temperature
cactorum	about 100 species including *Cornus*, *Cotoneaster*, *Gladiolus*, *Rhododendron*, *Lilium*, *Phlox*, *Tulipa*	25°C
cinnamomi	>1000 species, especially conifers; rarely monocots	25°C
citricola	common in conifers	25°C
cryptogea	many especially conifers; *Tulipa*	25°C
erythrospetica	*Tulipa*	28°C
fragariae	*Dryas*, *Geum*, *Potentilla*	15-22°C
ilicis	*Ilex*	20°C
lateralis	conifers	15-22°C
porri	*Allium*, *Campanula*, *Dianthus*, *Gladiolus*	20-28°C
primulae	*Primula*; also *Asparagus* and parsley	15°C
richardiae	*Zantedeschia*	20-28°C
syringae	woody Rosaceae; *Syringa*	20°C
verrucosa	*Primula*, *Dahlia*	20-28°C

Hosts which are often affected include *Chamaecyparis lawsoniana* var. *ellwoodii*, *Cupressus*, and Ericacaeae such as *Rhododendron*, *Erica* and *Calluna*. The fungus causes root and foot rots, leaf discoloration, wilt and death, but symptoms rarely occur until infection is well-established. With conifers, the leaves first turn pale, then brown, or wilt, desiccate and die. The fungus persists in soil for many years even when hosts are absent. Growth is best at 20-25°C but also occurs down to 5°C and up to 35°C, and in slightly drier soils than other *Phytophthora* species. Infection by *P. cinnamomi* can be detected by mixing samples of suspect roots in water and then baiting the water with seedlings of the blue lupin (*Lupinus angustifolius*), or with young shoots of *Hebe pinguifolia* 'Pagei', which rot when infected. Root infection by other *Phytophthora* species seems to increase the ease of attack by *P. cinnamomi*.

Phytophthora primulae Tomlinson causes brown core disease in *Primula*. It is unusual in that it has a much more restricted host-range than the previous three species being found only on certain *Primula* species or on parsley. *Primula* plants become stunted and the leaves wilt and collapse in succession from the outside to the centre. The root system is poorly developed and there are few lateral roots. When the main root is cut, the root vascular tissue is seen to be stained brown – the so-called brown core symptom – and the brown colour extends into the crown. Later on, the vascular tissue protrudes from the end of the broken root. Oospores are produced in the roots and enter the soil as the tissues decay. Root infection takes place in autumn, but wilt and collapse symptoms do not usually appear until the following spring. *Primula vulgaris* is susceptible but *P. denticulata*, *P. veris* and *P. wanda* appear to be resistant. Seedlings become infected from contaminated soil in seed trays, or when planted into contaminated soil in the garden. The same fungus also attacks parsley causing the crowns to turn brown and rot. *Primula* plants are also attacked by *Phytophthora citricola* and *P. verrucosa* Alcock & Foister.

Of the hundred or so *Pythium* species, *P. ultimum* probably does the most damage affecting virtually any soft young tissũe when the soil is wet, particularly if plant growth is slow. Aerial parts of the plant are not affected unless in contact with soil, and then only if the soil is wet. Three other species also cause trouble: *Pythium mammilatum* Meurs on a wide range of plants including *Aquilegia*, *Papaver*, and *Viola*; *Pythium oligandrum* on *Antirrhinum*, *Papaver* and *Viola*; and *Pythium violae* on *Viola*. All grow in a wide range of temperatures, and all require wet conditions.

Phytophthora and *Pythium* also cause bulb rots, although mostly in warm glasshouses, or outside in warm climates. Thus, *Phytophthora cryptogea*, together with the closely-related *P. erythroseptica* Pethyb. var. *erythroseptica*, infect flower stalks causing a rot called **shanking**; it occurs mainly in forced tulips but is occasionally found in the open. *Pythium ultimum* Trow var. *ultimum* attacks tulip roots and *Phytophthora nicotianae* van Breda infects lily bulbs but, as with *P. erythroseptica*, both fungi only cause damage in warm conditions. *Phytophthora richardiae* causes a root rot in *Zantedeschia aethiopica* (=*Z. africana*).

Downy mildews

These only affect living plants, usually the leaves and thus are markedly different from *Phytophthora* and *Pythium*. Plants which are already infected with downy mildew provide the sources of inoculum for starting repeated cycles of infection and spore production on leaves. Spores from leaves are dispersed in air thereby spreading the fungus. Resistant oospores are produced in infected plant tissue and ultimately return to the soil as the tissue decays. Oospores are also capable of initiating infection. Although the downy mildews are adapted to aerial dispersal, the air must be humid, both for infection and for spore production, and hence for continuation of the repetitive stages of the disease. Consequently, downy mildews usually do little damage, the chief risk being with seedlings where crowding causes both a local high humidity and films of water to form on cotyledons and leaves. It follows that providing plenty of space and minimising air humidity do much to control downy mildews. Control with fungicides is described below.

Symptoms. The first signs of downy mildew infection are pale yellow spots on the upper leaf surface which later turn downy, then brown (See Plate 14). A whitish felty growth of mycelium and spores develops on the under side of the leaf in areas corresponding to the spots; the fungal growth is often faintly purple. When infection is severe, the leaves wither and drop off and, if young, the plant dies; older plants survive but are disfigured. Downy mildew infection sometimes becomes systemic in rhizomes or buds, causing a general yellowing or withering of the leaves and shoots, and stunting of plant growth; examples are *Peronospora lamii* in *Lamium* (See Plate 14f) and *Peronospora pulveracea* in *Helleborus niger*. The systemic mycelium overwinters and provides inoculum the following year. Multiple shoots grow from the base of the plant if the apical bud is killed by systemic infection for example in *Antirrhinum* (*Peronospora antirrhini*) or *Buddleja* (*Peronospora hariotii*). Most of the downy mildew fungi which are likely to affect alpine plants belong to one of three genera *Bremia*, *Peronospora* or *Plasmopara*. With few exceptions, individual downy mildew species are restricted to a single plant species, or to closely related species. Cross infection from unrelated plant species is therefore unlikely. This is in marked contrast to the situation described for *Phytophthora* and *Pythium*.

There are large numbers of species of downy mildew and selected examples are listed in Table 27, Table 28.

White blister or white rust

The name is misleading because this group of fungi have no relationship whatever to the true rusts (See p.138). Only two species are likely to cause trouble. *Albugo candida* (Pers.) Kuntze causes white powdery galls or blisters on stems and leaves of Cruciferae; often the stems and leaves are stunted and distorted (See Plate 14b). As with some of the downy mildews, hyphae invade the dividing tissue and become systemic; *Albugo tragopogonis* (DC.) Gray causes similar symptoms on Compositae and is commonly seen on groundsel.

Fungicidal control of *Phytophthora*, *Pythium*, downy mildews and white rusts

Whilst fungicides are an essential aspect of controlling Oomycetes, success depends on the amount of infection that is present – well-established infections being the most difficult to control. Therefore it is best to treat plants as soon as possible to prevent infection, preferably as seedlings, cuttings or at transplanting.

Oomycete fungi are controlled by fungicides containing copper, thiram or – for professional use only – etridiazole (Aaterra, ICI), fosetyl-aluminium (Aliette, Embetec), furalaxyl (Fongarid, Ciba-Geigy) or propamacarb hydrochloride (Filex, Fisons). Furalaxyl is a phenylamide compound – also called acylanaline – one of the two classes highly effective against these fungi, particularly the soil-borne *Phytophthora* species; fosetyl-aluminium belongs to the second class, the phosphonates, used for control of *Phytophthora* on hardy ornamental plants. Etridiazole, furalaxyl and propamacarb hydrochloride (from now on abbreviated to propamacarb) are used to protect plants from infection and hence are applied with the compost before planting; even mixing is essential. Furalaxyl and propamacarb are also applied as drenches, the former compound to treat established infection, the latter to extend the duration of protection. Furalaxyl should not be applied to plants grown in open ground; propamacarb should not be watered onto seedlings, and etridiazole should be applied only after seedlings have established. Propamacarb may be used to treat bulbs against root rot, either as a dip treatment, or as a drench before planting. Some plant species are known to be sensitive to fungicides – for example *Viola* to etridiazole, but the reaction of most alpine species is unknown and selected plants which are not too valuable should be tested first for evidence of distortion or scorch. Dichlofluanid is also active against this group of fungi. In summary, the fungicides for use in professional horticulture are as follows:

Herbaceous plants – fosetyl-aluminium (in combination with captan + thiabendazole) against damping-off or downy mildew; etridiazole, fosetyl-aluminium, furalaxyl or propamacarb against *Phytophthora*; furalaxyl against *Pythium*.
Plants in containers, or **bulbs** – Etridiazole or propamacarb against *Phytophthora* or *Pythium*.

Only thiram and copper fungicides are available to amateurs. Thiram is supplied either mixed with rooting hormone for the treatment of cuttings, or with gamma-HCH and rotenone insecticides for general use. Copper fungicides such as Cheshunt compound, or copper oxychloride are watered on seedlings to control damping-off. The lack of more effective chemicals, particularly against deep-seated root infection by *Phytophthora*, is a distinct drawback for amateurs.

Soil fumigants such as formaldehyde and metham sodium, are active against a wide range of fungi and are used to kill pathogenic fungi in soil; formaldehyde is also used to disinfest glasshouses. In addition, soil fumigants kill weed seeds, insects and eelworms. Unfortunately, beneficial soil microorganisms such as mycorrhizae are also killed, consequently plants may be stunted. Moreover, if fumigated soils become re-contaminated with *Phytophthora* or *Pythium* there is a risk that the lack of competition will lead to their rapid multiplication and infection. Neither fumigant chemical is authorised for use by amateur growers.

Chytridiomycetes

Four genera, *Olpidium*, *Physoderma*, *Polymyxa* and *Synchytrium*, are pathogenic, and are classified in the Order Chytridiales. None of the Chytridiales form extensive mycelium. The whole fungus changes into a zoosporangium which germinates releasing zoospores into soil to start another infection cycle. Zoospores also fuse to form a motile zygote which infects the host, later forming a resting sporangium within the cell. Dispersal and survival is by resting spores, infected plant tissue and contaminated soil. These fungi mostly affect agricultural crops and are only described briefly.

Olpidium and ***Polymyxa*** damage the host plant by transmitting viruses during infection by zoospores (See Chapter 4). Typical symptoms are enlarged yellowish veins (e.g. big vein virus of lettuce: *Olpidium brassicae* (Woron.)), leaf yellowing and stunted growth (barley yellow mosaic virus carried by *Polymyxa graminis* Ledingham), and root proliferation and reduced sugar production in beet, called rhizomania (beet necrotic yellow vein virus carried by *Polymyxa betae* Keskin.).

Synchytrium and ***Physoderma*** cause warts or galls on aerial or below-grown parts of a wide range of plants. The fungal thallus converts to a sporangium producing summer spores (sori), sporangia, zoospores and resting spores. Thus, the spores are known by their function rather than by differences in appearance. Summer spores repeat the cycles of infection and increase disease incidence. In autumn, zoospores fuse to form motile zygotes which infect the host forming resting spores, and become embedded and hence protected, by repeated cell division in the host. These spores are extremely resistant and almost impossible to eradicate. *Synchytrium endobioticum* (Schilberszky) Percival causes potato wart disease – a disease which must be notified to the plant health authorities – but may also infect other Solanaceae such as *Petunia* and *Physalis*, at least experimentally. There are large numbers of species affecting wild plants for example *Synchytrium macrosporium* Karling forms blue-red galls on leaves and stems of *Lavendula* in America, and *Synchytrium mercurialis* affects dogs mercury (*Mercurialis perrenis*) in the UK. *Physoderma* species also cause galls but only on agricultural crops such as alfalfa (*P. alfalfae*) or sugar beet (*P. leproides*) and are not discussed further.

Clubroot

Most gardeners and nurserymen are familiar with this disease caused by *Plasmodiophora brassicae* Woronin. Clubroot symptoms are of two types – galls or swollen roots ('finger and toe' symptom) caused by the proliferation of infected cells, and wilt or stunted growth resulting from the inability of infected roots to supply sufficient water and nutrients. Clubroot symptoms develop in the Cruciferae, many of which are alpine plants grown in the garden for example *Cheiranthus*. The first cycle of infection also occurs on *Holcus*, *Papaver* and *Rumex* weeds but it is not known how important this is for survival and increase of the clubroot organism.

Clubbed and swollen roots contain large numbers of resting spores which remain in the soil as the root decays, and which can survive for many years. Resting spores germinate to produce zoospores which penetrate root hairs and produce a multinucleate mass of cell material called a **plasmodium**. The plasmodium grows, divides and starts a second cycle of zoospores and plasmodium, but this time deeper in the root, ultimately leading to the production of resting spores.

The key factors for control are the exclusion of the pathogen from the nursery or garden, in combination with hygiene and sanitation. There are three main sources of clubroot – contaminated soil, contaminated manure and compost, or infected plants. Soil from clubroot sites, for example on footwear and tools from infected gardens or allotments, should be kept out of clubroot-free areas. Similar precautions should be taken with manure and compost because clubroot resting spores survive ingestion and composting. It is very likely that clubroot symptoms will not show on infected young plants or transplants and so the disease can be introduced without knowing; clubroot develops later as the plants become established. It is best not to accept plants from areas with clubroot, even if the plant appears healthy, as the soil may be infested with resting spores. Infected plants, together with the soil around them, should be carefully removed, placed in a polythene bag and then either transferred to a tip for burial, or burnt; as before, precautions are needed to stop the spread of contaminated soil on footwear and tools. Once the clubroot organism has become established in the garden, the soil is likely to remain infective for ever. Adding lime to the soil is the traditional and effective method of reducing the severity of attack; however, liming does not kill the pathogen and the soil becomes infective again as the soil acidity returns. Plants grown in pots of clubroot-free soil, or other growing medium, remain free of symptoms for longer when transplanted to contaminated soil, in comparison with those planted directly into contaminated soil. Dipping seedlings or young plants in thiophanate-methyl (See Table 45) also reduces the severity of symptoms but does not cure the disease.

Ascomycetes

The Ascomycetes (Sub-division Ascomycotina: Page 92: Classification and nomenclature) contains just under half the total numbers of fungal species, and is by far the largest of the four main Sub-divisions of the fungi. As might be expected in such a large group, the fungi differ considerably, including the powdery mildews, vascular wilts, yeasts, leaf curls, and the fungal partners of lichens.

Only the fungi which affect garden plants are described here and no attempt is made to describe the whole Sub-division.

The diagnostic feature of the Ascomycetes is the **ascus** (plural asci), a minute sac containing sexually derived ascospores (Fig. 16).

Classification within the Ascomycetes is based on the methods of development and the microscopical structure of the ascus together with the type of structure they are protected by called **ascocarps**, **ascomata** or 'fruiting bodies' (Table 17).

Powdery mildews

The **powdery mildews** belong to the Family Erysiphaceae in the Order Erysiphales. They are very common and cause considerable damage to both garden and wild plants (Table 27, Table 28). Powdery mildews only infect living tissue (obligately biotrophic) and cannot be cultured on artificial media. They are restricted to the aerial parts of flowering plants (Angiospermae) and are never found on roots. Powdery mildews are easily recognised because of the characteristic whitish-grey growth of hyphae and profuse production of white spores on leaves, stems and buds (Plate 14d, f). This is the vegetative or anamorph stage and it is the most

Figure 16 Fungal structures which produce and protect with ascospores

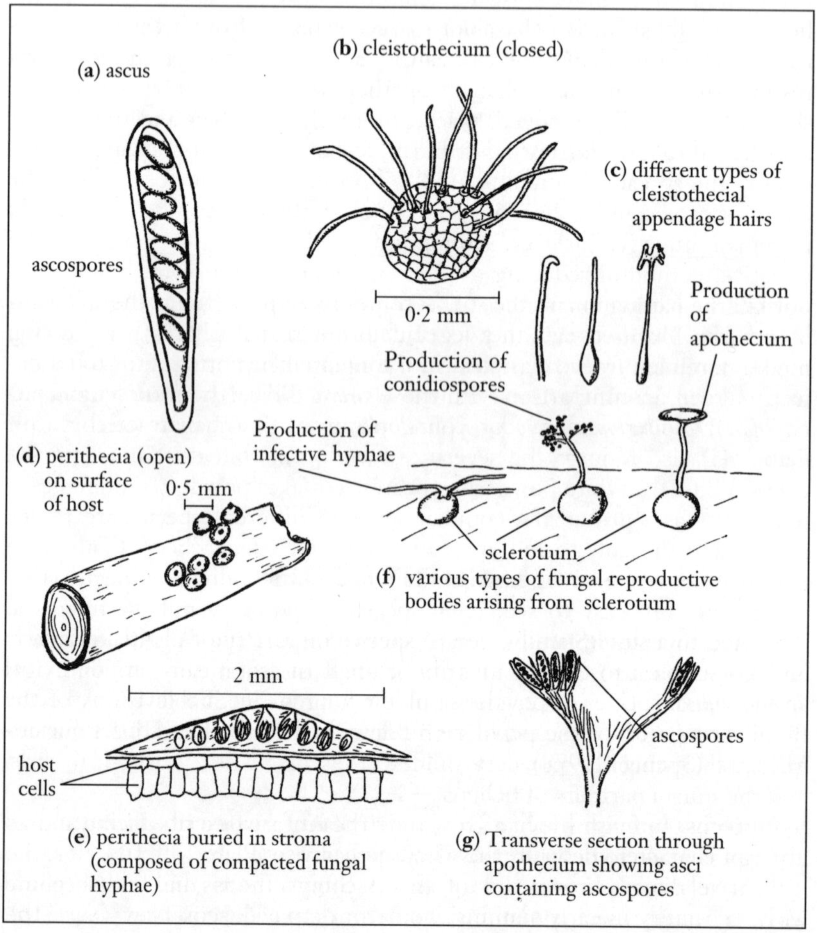

Table 17 **Types of structure which produce or protect asci**

Type of structure	Characteristics	Main groups
Cleistothecium	spherical with no special opening	Erysiphales Eurotiales
Perithecium	flask-shaped with a definite opening	Hypocreales Sphaeriales
Pseudothecium	stroma containing asci in cavities (locules)	Pleosporales
Apothecium	saucer-shaped disc with asci in layer on upper surface, asci exposed when mature, spores dispersed in air	Helotiales
Stroma	mass of vegetative hyphae containing asci	several e.g. Hypocreales
Pseudostroma	stroma containing remants of host tissue	several e.g. Hypocreales
Sclerotium	mass of hyphae with protective dark rind; they produce vegetative spores (conidia) or germinate to produce hyphae or an apothecium which produces sexual ascospores	Helotiales

obvious and common state of the powdery mildew fungi. As a result, before the link between the vegetative and sexual phases was known, powdery mildews were classified in the Deuteromycotina (Fungi Imperfecti: Order Moniliales) and named *Oidium* (sexual stage (teleomorph) *Erysiphe*), *Ovulariopsis* (teleomorph *Phyllactinia*) or *Oidiopsis* (teleomorph *Leveillula*).

Whilst the white powdery appearance makes powdery mildews easy to identify as a group, the conidial states of different species are rather similar and difficult to tell apart and identify. Cleistothecia (Table 17) have distinctive appendages which help to identify individual species (Fig. 16) but are not easy to see. Each species of powdery mildew fungus is restricted to a single family, genus, species or variety of plant. Initially it is often simplest to use the identity of the host as a means of identifying an individual species of powdery mildew fungus (See Table 18). A key to the identification of the powdery mildews is described in 'The Powdery Mildews' (Spencer, 1978).

Symptoms. Greyish hyphae grow over the leaf surface producing spores giving a characteristic white powdery appearance (Plate 14d, f). Later, the leaf shrivels, turns brown and drops off. Stems, thorns and buds become white especially in early summer. Sometimes, powdery mildews cause the

Table 18 **Examples of powdery mildews**

Name of fungus	Typical hosts	Example
Erysiphe	herbaceous plants	*Erysiphe asperifoliorum: Myosotis; E. cichoracearum: Aster, Phlox, Stokesia; E. polygoni: Eschscholtzia californica; E. ranunculi: Adonis vernalis, Clematis;*
Sphaerotheca		*E. graminis:* grasses; *Sphaerotheca alchemillae: Alchemilla; Sphaerotheca macularis* var. *fuliginea: Taraxacum* and other Compositae;
Leveillula		*Leveillula taurica:* Compositae;
Oidium		*Oidium cyclaminis* on *Cyclamen;*
Microsphaera	trees, shrubs	*Microsphaera euonymi: Euonymus europeaus; M. euonymi-japonici: E. japonicus; M. alni: Syringa; M. viburni: Viburnum;*
Phyllactinia		*Phyllactinia guttata: Betula;*
Podosphaera		*Podosphaera clandestina* (syn. *P. oxycanthae*): hawthorn; *P. myrtillina: Vaccinium;*

leaves to swell as with *Hypericum* infected by *Erysiphe martii*. Powdery mildew fungi also produces spots on flower petals as with rose powdery mildew (*Sphaerotheca pannosa*). Conidia are rare in *Microsphaera* on *Viburnum* and have never been seen on *Vaccinium* and *Oxycoccus* infected by *Podosphaera* .

Life cycle. Most of the powdery mildews which have been studied in detail affect economically important plants for example *Erysiphe graminis* on cereals, *Podosphaera leucotricha* on apple and *Sphaerotheca pannosa* on rose. These provide the basis for the following account which, nevertheless is applicable to the lesser studied species from ornamentals. Infection by powdery mildew fungi comprises (a) a source of the fungus (primary inoculum), (b) infection and colonisation of the host by mycelium, (c) production and dispersal (secondary inoculum) and (d) survival between seasons. All are dependent on favourable environmental conditions. Infection starts in spring from sexual spores (ascospores) released from cleistothecia, or as vegetative spores (conidia) produced from mycelium which has survived the winter as a colony on a leaf, or enclosed within a bud e.g. *Microsphaera alni* (syn. *M. lonicerae*) on lilac, *Podosphaera leucotricha* on apple and *Sphaerotheca pannosa* on rose. Either type of spore may come from the same plant or from different plants such as weeds, crops or ornamental plants. The sources of infection may be nearby or

a. Damage to tulip leaves by slugs – note slime trails

b. Damage to *Primula* flowers by slugs

c. Eggs of field slug, *Deroceras reticulatus*

d. Garden snail, *Helix aspersa*

e. Banded snail, *Cepaea nemoralis*

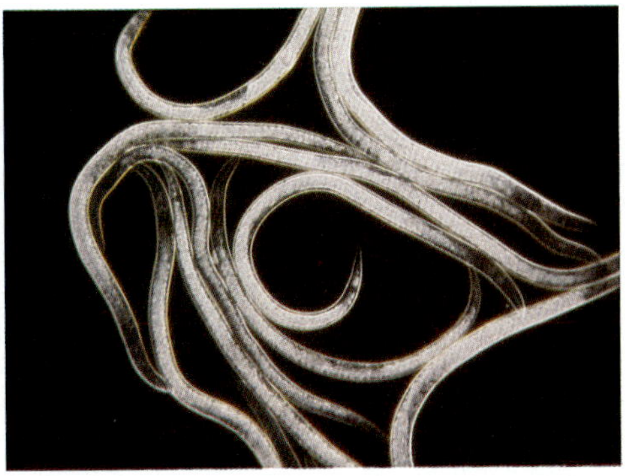

f. Eelworms

a. Downy mildew on *Viola*

b. White blister, *Albugo*, on *Capsella*

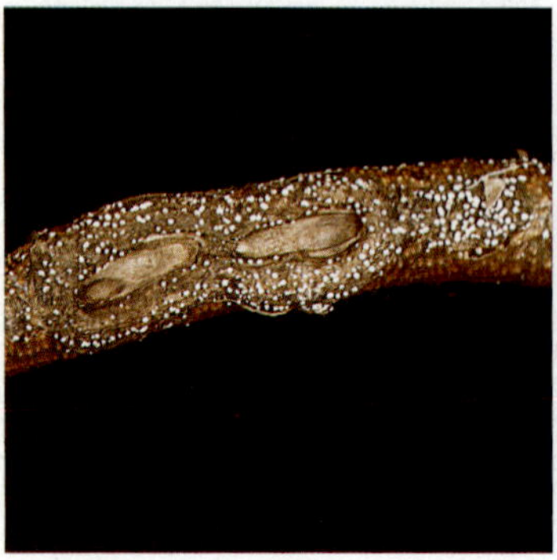

c. Coral spot, *Nectria cinnabarina*

d. Powdery mildew on *Anemone*

e. Soft rot, *Rhizopus*, on *Narcissus* bulb

f. Powdery mildew on *Lamium*

a. *Fusarium oxysporum* on gladiolus; corms shrivel in store

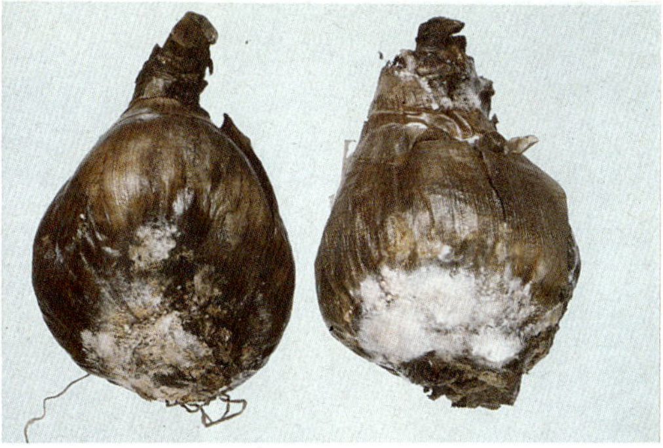

b. *Fusarium* basal rot on *Narcissus* showing pale fungal mycelium

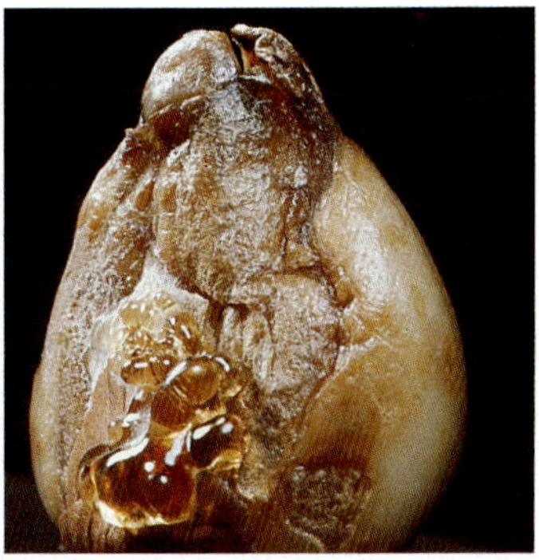

c. *Fusarium* bulb rot on tulip showing presence of gum

d. *Sclerotinia (= Stromatinia) gladioli* on gladiolus

e. *Rhizoctonia* on lily scales

f. White mould, *Sclerotinia sclerotiorum*, showing profuse white mycelium

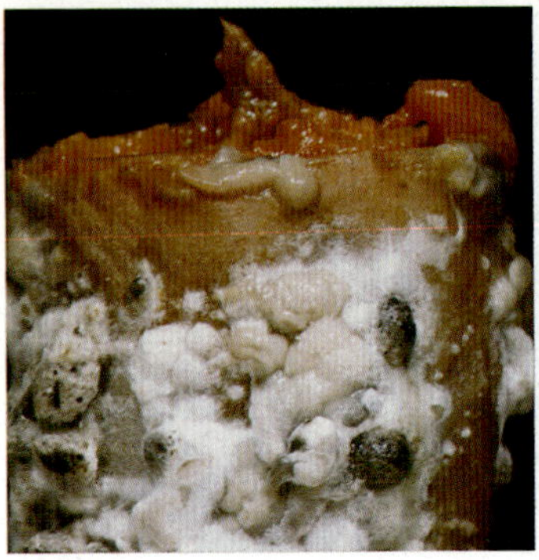
a. White mould sclerotia which later germinate to produce apothecia and ascospores

b. Black rot, *Dumontinia tuberosa*, on *Anemone nemorosa* showing brown apothecia at soil level

c. *Anemone* black rot apothecia which produce ascospores spread infection

d. White rot sclerotia which survive for long periods in soil

e. *Allium* whiterot, *Sclerotium cepivorum*, showing characteristic white mycelium on roots and base of plant

f. Grey mould, *Botryotinia fuckeliana (= Botrytis cinerea)*, killing shoots in *Androsace*

distant. The spores germinate to form hyphae which then form small branches or haustoria which penetrate the outer layer of cells of the host tissue; extensive colonisation of host tissue, as occurs with some of the other groups of fungi, is uncommon. Specialised hyphae called conidiophores develop and produce large (up to 700µm) one-celled vegetative spores arranged singly or in chains. These spores are readily dispersed in air to other parts of the same plant or to different plants and another vegetative cycle begins. Dark, minute fruiting bodies (called cleistothecia) of the teleomorph are produced later in the season on dying leaves and survive the winter. Sometimes the sexual stage (teleomorph) is rarely seen, as in rose powdery mildew (*Sphaerotheca pannosa*), or apparently absent as in *Cyclamen* powdery mildew (*Oidium cyclaminis*).

Powdery mildew fungi are prevalent in dry weather. The conidia are able to germinate in dry conditions but nevertheless require humid conditions for the initial colonisation of the host. In dry weather the humid conditions which are needed occur at night during dew formation.

Since powdery mildew fungi can survive inside buds, infected cuttings are both a source (primary inoculum) (See p.88) and a method of dispersal (secondary inoculum) of powdery mildew fungi. Pruning woody plants in summer removes the apical dominance of the lower buds causing them to open slightly and allowing entry by the fungus and increasing the opportunities for survival over winter. Powdery mildews are not seed-borne.

Powdery mildews do not always have the same distribution as their hosts particularly in alpine regions. For example, *Dryas* escapes attack by *Sphaerotheca volkartii* above 2000 m in the Swiss alps. Similarly powdery mildews have not been reported from Andorra even though susceptible plants grow there. The implication is that alpine plants may be more likely to be attacked in the garden than in their natural environment.

Control. The nature of the life cycle of the powdery mildew give clues to the methods of control. Thus, control measures aim (a) to remove the source of the fungus (primary inoculum), (b) to minimise the opportunities for the fungus to grow and spread to other plants (secondary inoculum) and (c) to minimise survival (See Table 13).

Powdery mildews are sensitive to sulphur, bupirimate, dinonocap, fenarimol and triforine (Table 45). When first used, benzimidazole fungicides (benomyl, thiophanate-methyl) were very effective against powdery mildew fungi. Since then many populations of the fungi have become resistant and are no longer controlled. If benzimidazoles are found to be effective in a particular situation they should be used in alternation with fungicides from a different chemical group in order to reduce the chances of resistance developing. Clearly a fungicide from another chemical group should be used if benzimidazole fungicides fail to give control. All the fungicides are applied as sprays to the leaves, buds or shoots.

Selected powdery mildew fungi which cause important diseases of alpine and other garden plants are described below and in Table 27, Table 28.

Table 19 **Control measures for powdery mildew diseases**

Target	Action
Sources of the fungus	prune woody plants in winter or spring to remove infected buds; remove dead leaves, stems, etc, which help the fungus to overwinter; do not use infected plants for propagation;
Spread to other plants	inspect plants regularly during spring and summer and remove infected plants or plant parts, or spray with a fungicide;
Survival in winter	minimise bud infection in woody plants by not pruning in summer; treat or remove infected plants during autumn and winter thereby minimise movement of fungus to new and susceptible plant tissue – ('green bridge' effect); remove infected shoots and buds in autumn and winter

Erysiphe cichoracearum DC. (anamorph *Oidium erysiphoides* Fr.) is a variable fungus affecting many of the genera in the Compositae, but also *Vinca*, *Antirrhinum*, and *Digitalis*. It causes typical powdery mildew symptoms on any aerial part. The symptoms are similar to those of *Sphaerotheca fuliginea* but the shape of the appendages on the cleistothecia is different. *E. polygoni* DC. ex Saint-Aman affects the Polygonaceae, causing dense white mycelia on leaves and stems, with single or chains of conidia, followed by yellow-brown cleistothecia.

Sphaerotheca fuliginea (Schlect.) Poll. (anamorph *Oidium erysiphoides* Fr.) affects Compositae, Cistacaceae (*Helianthemum*), Cruciferae (*Arabis*), and Scrophulariaceae (*Veronica*). The fungus produces patches of sparse white mycelium with long chains of white conidia. *S. alchemillae* (Grev.) Junell. produces typical white mycelium and conidia on *Alchemilla* leaves, followed by brown cleistothecia in summer.

Fusarium and the vascular wilts

Fusarium and *Verticillium* are the vegetative stages (anamorphs) of a group of fungi which damage a wide range of plants. The sexual stage (teleomorph) is rare or absent therefore the anamorph name is generally used. These fungi belong to the Order Hypocreales. The same Order also contains the anamorph genera *Trichoderma* and *Gliocladium*, many species of which, for example *Trichoderma viride* and *T. harzianum* exert biological control of plant disease fungi.

The structures which protect asci (ascomata), if produced at all, are called cleistothecia (See Table 17, p.111) and are often produced on a crust-like growth of hyphae or **subiculum** or immersed in a fleshy, brightly coloured mass of hyphae called a **stroma** (See Table 17). The fungi attack dead plant tissue (being saprophytic) or parasitise live tissue (being obligately necrotrophic). Many species are able to colonise and kill other fungi and hence have potential for biological control of plant diseases.

Fusarium species produce up to three types of spore: **microconidia**, **macroconidia** and **chlamydospores** (Fig. 17). Microconidia are tiny, spherical and usually have one cell; macroconidia are much larger, long and narrow and characteristically sickle shaped or **fusiform**, and have 3 – 5 cells; chlamydospores are round, have thick cell walls and are produced from hyphae or macroconidia, and help the fungus to survive for long periods in the absence of a host.

Species found in diseased plant tissue include *F. culmorum*, *Gibberella avenacea* R.J. Cook (syn. *Fusarium avenaceum* (Fr.) Sacc., syn. *Fusarium roseum* 'Avenaceum') producing orange mycelium on *Tulipa*, *F. oxysporum* and *Nectria haematococca* (*F. solani*). Most are unspecialized and either affect a wide range of plants or are not pathogenic and are part of the normal or resident soil microflora. However, the latter two species also have **formae speciales** (abbreviated to f.sp.). Formae speciales of *Fusarium* are strains which are restricted to specific hosts even though the mycelium and spores appear similar and often cause a lot of damage.

Figure 17 Types of *Fusarium* spore

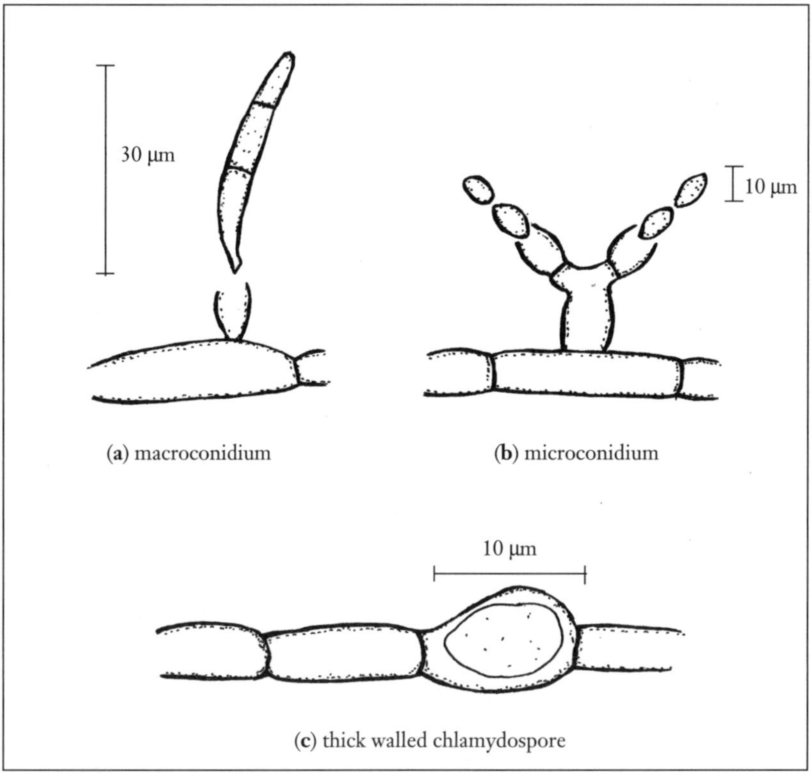

Recommended reading: 'The Genus Fusarium' (Booth, 1971).

There are two possible explanations for the presence of *Fusarium* in diseased plant tissue:

1 *Fusarium* was a direct cause of the symptoms. The *Fusarium* might have been a forma specialis and unlikely to affect other unrelated plants, or it might be one of the unspecialised fusaria capable of attacking other unrelated plant species.

2 The *Fusarium* colonised dead tissue killed for some other reason i.e. the *Fusarium* was not pathogenic. The tissue might have been killed by a forma specialis which was then overrun by a saprophytic *Fusarium*, it might have been killed by physical factors such as drought or damage, or it might have died naturally.

   Even when pathogenic fusaria are present in soil they are not necessarily able to infect the plant. Intense competition by micro-organisms, including non-pathogenic forms of *Fusarium oxysporum*, near the root surface can limit infection. This has lead to the use of non-virulent forms of formae speciales for the biological control of vascular wilts e.g. f.sp. *dianthi*.

The most important species of *Fusarium* that cause diseases of alpine and other garden plants are described below.

***Fusarium oxysporum* Schlect.** is a very variable fungus existing in forms which are of similar appearance but differ in the way they grow in culture. The sexual stage (teleomorph) is unknown. Usually *F. oxysporum* is saprophytic and is often involved in seedling disease. However, a small proportion of strains (formae speciales), the **vascular wilt** fungi, produce toxins, block the vascular tissue, reduce water uptake and cause wilting. Several formae speciales affect bulbs for example *Fusarium oxysporum* f.sp. *narcissi* and *F. oxysporum* f.sp. *cepae* which are restricted to *Narcissus* or *Allium cepa* respectively. Formae speciales were once thought to be limited to a single species of host plant. However, some formae speciales are now recognised as being less specific e.g. f.sp. *gladioli* which affects *Gladiolus*, *Crocus* and *Ixia* of the Iridaceae.

Symptoms. Infection reduces emergence, kills seedlings, stunts growth and rots the roots and bulbs of growing plants, causing premature maturation of the plant and basal rotting in the field and during storage. A whitish cotton wool-like mould sometimes occurs on the scales of the bulb (Plate 16). *F. oxysporum* only affects leaves indirectly by blocking the vascular tissue and restricting water uptake. As a result foliar symptoms are not very distinctive, generally being a yellowing (**chlorosis**) of the leaf tips and a resultant premature senescence (Plate 16).

Infected bulbs often appear healthy when dug from soil, but rot when stored. This gives the impression that the fungus has spread in store. However, there are other explanations. Firstly, the bulb could have been infected when removed from the ground but the symptoms were overlooked. The symptoms would then become more obvious as the disease developed. Secondly, the bulbs may have been healthy but the fungus gained entry from contaminated soil on the outside of the bulb. Seed-borne infection is not an important source of the fungus.

Life cycle. The fungus infects roots then spreads to the vascular system which turns brown. Soft parts of the plant wilt in hot weather because damage to the roots reduces water uptake. Also, changes in host physiology occurring at flowering or fruiting cause 'stress' in the plant and this increases the likelihood of damage. The fungus sometimes enters the plant through wounds created by the emergence of adventitious roots from the base plate. Similarly, wounds caused by eelworms increase infection. However, the various insect larvae which feed on dead tissue have little effect on the disease.

F. oxysporum grows in soil organic matter and dust, and can also be present in cuttings used in vegetative propagation. Survival is by chlamydospores formed in infected plants and their release into soil increases the chances of infection when susceptible plants are grown again in the same area of ground. Subsequently, the fungus is dispersed in soil with plants, on tools, pots, seed boxes, footwear or by wind. Thus the sources of infection and methods of dissemination are typical of soil-borne diseases in general.

Control. Control is difficult because the fungus is contained within the soil or host tissue. Consequently, control measures are based on good horticultural practices such as long rotations, destruction of diseased plants and careful removal of infested soil. In this context long rotation means not planting susceptible plants in land known to be affected by the fungus because the fungus survives for several years. Ideally, planting material such as bulbs should be produced and planted in areas where the pathogen is known to be absent. Clearly the gardener cannot know the source of the bulbs he buys, but any which appear unhealthy should be destroyed and not planted. Dispersal can be reduced by restricting the movement of infested soil sticking to susceptible and non-susceptible plants. If vascular wilts are diagnosed during growth it makes sense to remove and destroy infected plants together with the surrounding soil, taking care not to contaminate other parts of the nursery or garden. If there are too many plants to treat in this way, e.g. bulbs naturalised in grass, it would be best to leave them alone and not to risk disturbing the soil and spreading the fungus to other areas.

Bulbs and corms are often treated in hot water before sale to kill eelworms. *Fusarium* is also partially controlled if formaldehyde is added to the hot water. However, this method of treatment is not available for amateur use (See Chapter 5). Control by fungicides is based on the use of benzimidazole compounds, either as a bulb dip, or as a drench to the base of the plant. However, prolonged use is likely to lead to the development of *Fusarium* strains which are resistant to the chemical and hence not controlled. Soil fumigation reduces *Fusarium* populations but the effect is temporary because the populations re-establish themselves in the presence of susceptible plants. Fumigation is available to professional contractors with the appropriate specialised training but is not available to the amateur gardener.

Formae speciales of *Fusarium oxysporum*

F.sp. *gladioli* (Massey) Snyder & Hansen affects *Gladiolus*, *Crocus*, bulbous *Iris*, *Freesia* and *Ixia* and probably occurs in most of the places where *Gladiolus* and *Iris* are grown. Isolates of the fungus from *Gladiolus* are able to infect *Iris*, but isolates from *Iris* have little effect on *Gladiolus*; isolates from the large-flowered *Gladiolus* cultivars also infect *G. nanus* and *G. colvillei*.

Leaves turn yellow prematurely usually starting from the leaf tips and they may curl or curve. Roots and the base of the corm decay and yellow-brown lesions occur on the corm e.g. of *Crocus* and *Gladiolus*. Later the central core of the corm turns brown, the infected tissue shrinks and hardens or '**mummifies**' leaving concentric ridges; a pale pink mycelium sometimes occurs on the outside of the corm (Plate 15a). The fungus survives in soil for many years and is easily spread by spores to other plants and areas of the nursery or garden.

F.sp. *narcissi* Snyder & Hansen affects varieties of hybrid *Narcissus* and some *Narcissus* species and is responsible for two distinct diseases called ***Fusarium* basal rot** and ***Fusarium* neck rot**. Fusarium basal rot develops from root infection occurring during active growth of the host (Plate 15b). The fungus grows into the base of the bulb and the base of the scales turn brown and become soft. Infected bulbs shrink and harden when dry. Infection occurs at any time when the plant is growing, usually via natural wounds in the base of the bulbs or via roots; most infection occurs in summer when the soils are warm and roots begin to die. Thus, bulbs which are to be moved should be dug before the soil warms up and infection occurs. The above-ground symptoms of basal rot merely reflect the root damage and are not distinctive; they include a yellowing and progressive death of the leaves and stunting of the plant.

Fusarium neck rot results from infection at the base of the flower stalk as the flower dies. The fungus grows into the bulb in June-July and the bulb starts to rot one or two months later. As the rot spreads down into the bulb, the symptoms become indistinguishable from basal rot.

The main source of f.sp. *narcissi* is from infested soil. However, the disease sometimes occurs when *Narcissus* has not been grown before; the reasons for this are not known. Soil sticking to the outside of healthy bulbs can be a source of the fungus; bulbs can be infected but show no symptoms that is to say the infection is **sub-clinical**. A similar situation occurs with f.sp. *gladioli* and f.sp. *tulipae*.

F.sp. *tulipae* Apt is restricted to *Tulipa* and occurs in most areas where tulips are grown. The first signs are small, yellow-brown, slightly sunken specks on the outer scales. The specks enlarge, spread to the inner scales of the bulb and become covered with a pale mauve mycelium (Plate 15c). Infected bulbs turn brown, shrink and mummify; they also produce ethylene gas which damages healthy bulbs. The fungus develops during warm weather and the plant collapses as the base of the bulb and roots are destroyed. Bulbs may appear healthy when dug from the ground but develop symptoms in store. The sources of infection are similar to those for f.sp. *narcissi*.

Resting spores of f.sp. *tulipae* are produced during infection and then released into soil enabling the fungus to survive for several years in the absence of the host. Latent infection, that is infection which has not caused symptoms, or small infections on the outer scale of the bulb which go unnoticed, are also sources of the fungus.

As with f.sp. *narcissi*, control is mostly based on cultural methods such as planting healthy bulbs, avoiding infested ground, and removal and destruction of infected plants. Infection may be reduced by planting bulbs late in the season but this is of no value in subsequent years.

F.sp. *lilii* Imle infects the roots and the base of lily bulbs, and also gains entry via wounds caused by other soil-borne microorganisms.

Several other formae speciales of *F. oxysporum* affect the commercial production of flowers and pot plants e.g. *Fusarium oxysporum* f.sp. *callistephi* (*Callistephus* spp.), f.sp. *chrysanthemi* (chrysanthemum), f.sp. *cyclaminis* (*Cyclamen persicum*), f.sp. *dianthi* (carnation, *Dianthus caryophyllus*).

Other *Fusarium* species

Fusarium culmorum (W.G.Sm.) Sacc. affects seedlings of a large number of plant species, particularly when the plant suffers from water stress. The sexual state (teleomorph) is unknown. Dark-brown lesions develop at the base of the stem in older plants resulting in softening and death of the stem e.g. in *Aster*. The fungus grows on dead plant tissue in soil, forms chlamydospores and survives for long periods. The optimum temperature for growth is 25°C. The fungus is mainly soil-borne but occasionally seed-borne.

Fusarium roseum Schwabe exists in several different forms, is widespread and often involved in damping-off of seedlings of a wide range of plants. The fungus is not very damaging to mature plants but frequently colonises dead tissue.

Nectria haematococca Berk. & Br. usually occurs as the vegetative stage (anamorph) *Fusarium solani* (Mart.) Sacc. It is widespread and causes damping-off, foot rot and stem cankers in a wide range of plants.

Other related fungi

***Nectria cinnabarina* (Tode) Fr.** (anamorph *Tubercularia vulgaris* Tode.) causes the coral spot which is common on dead or dying woody tissue and old canes, pea sticks, etc. (Plate 14). Coral spots are salmon-pink pustules, 1-2 mm across which form on the surface of woody tissue or emerge through bark. The pustules darken in colour with age. Coral spots are produced at most times of the year and initially form vegetative spores at the surface and these are dispersed by rain. In humid conditions in late summer, coral spots produce perithecia (See Table 17, p. 111) which contain the asci and ascospores. Initially, the fungus grows and produces coral spots on dying woody tissue left by pruning or by natural causes. The fungus then uses the dead tissue as a food base from which to invade living tissue and is said to be weakly pathogenic. As a result there is a progressive die back of twigs and branches particularly in weak-growing trees and shrubs such as *Acer japonicum*. Coral spot also affects trees and shrubs whose vigour is reduced by adverse soil conditions such as low soil fertility or lack of moisture. If the fungus grows down a side-branch it can girdle and kill the main branch causing damage out of all proportion to the size of the original infection.

Coral spot is controlled by removing dead twigs from the plant and burning them; old canes, beans sticks etc. should also be burnt. Pruning wounds should be kept to a minimum. As a precaution, wounds can be sprayed or painted with a fungicide of the benzimidazole group but this is unlikely to control deep-seated infections which should be pruned back to healthy tissue; take care to clean the secateurs after use on infected tissue.

Cylindocladium scoparium Morgan affects most parts in a wide range of plants causing damping-off, root rot, stem wilt and die-back, stunting, and leaf spotting. It is particularly damaging to cuttings e.g. *Rhododendron*. Control is based on the use of healthy cuttings and compost and the standard methods of strict hygiene (See Chapter 5). Cuttings can be dipped, sprayed or drenched with benomyl. However, it would be wise to check that the particular plants are not sensitive to the fungicide.

Verticillium dahliae Kleb. affects a wide range of annual and perennial dicotyledonous plants. The sexual stage (teleomorph) is unknown. Originally this fungus was confused with ***Verticillium albo-atrum*** Reinke & Berth. which causes vascular wilt in hops, *Begonia*, *Dahlia* or *Liatris* but *V. dahliae* differs by producing minute sclerotia called microsclerotia.

The symptoms are characteristic of root damage in that soft tissues wilt during the day but often recover at night when the demand for water is less, provided the damage is not too severe. Leaves turn yellow between the veins, the vascular system is stained brown and plant growth is stunted. The fungus produces microsclerotia which are a source infection for plants in following years although not in the same season. The fungus is often present in damaged host tissue in association with other soil-borne pathogens such as *Thanatephorous* (*Rhizoctonia solani*), *Thielaviopsis basicola* and *Alternaria radicina*.

There is little that can be done to control the disease because of the large numbers of microsclerotia which are produced. Treatment of the root system with fungicide is unlikely to give control. Consequently, control is dependent on minimising the opportunities for introducing the fungus into the garden or nursery and its subsequent survival. Accordingly, plants should always be inspected for evidence of root damage; ideally the source of the plants should be known and any which are suspect avoided. Infected plants and roots should be destroyed.

White moulds and grey moulds

White and grey moulds are caused by species of *Sclerotinia* and *Botryotinia* respectively. Both genera belong to the Order Helotiales which is characterised by the production of asci in apothecia (See Table 17, p.111). Do not confuse the name white mould with a different white mould caused by *Ramularia vallisumbrosae* in *Narcissus*. Apothecia are structures (ascomata) which carry the asci and comprise aggregations of hyphae arranged in a cup- or saucer shape, often on top of a stalk (Fig. 16; Plate 15d). The asci are arranged in a layer, the **hymenium**, on the upper surface which is exposed to the air when mature. The sexual ascospores are often discharged in spring. Two other Orders, the Rhytismatales and the Pezizales also contain apothecium-forming fungi. The Rhytismatales include *Rhytisma* which forms tar spots on the leaves of a variety of trees and shrubs, and the Pezzizales contain the truffles and morels which are of culinary value. Neither Order is important in the present context. Families within the Helotiales are distinguished by the type and the method of development of the ascus. Several species are pathogens which cause serious damage to plants for example e.g. *Sclerotinia* (white mould), *Botryotinia* (grey mould) and *Diplocarpon rosae* (black spot of rose).

Sclerotinia and *Botryotinia* have often been confused mainly because of the difficulties in observing the apothecia (See Table 17; Fig. 16) of *Botryotinia*, and because the disease symptoms are similar.

Life cycle. Sclerotia from diseased tissue are released into soil and germinate to produce (a) hyphae which infect plant tissue directly (**myceliogenic germination**), (b) stalked apothecia which then form ascospores (**carpogenic germination**) or (c) vegetative spores. Apothecia are also produced from compact hyphae growing within the host. Ascospores are the primary source of infection in *Sclerotinia sclerotiorum* providing a focus from which the disease spreads to other plants by growth of mycelium along roots. In other species such as *Botryotinia fuckeliana* (syn. *Botrytis cinerea*) sclerotia produce vegetative spores which are a source of primary inoculum (See p.88). Again, primary infection gives rise to infection foci but this time the fungus spreads to other plants by means of similar vegetative spores produced on infected plant tissue. The frequency with which each stage occurs and its timing affects the characteristics of the particular disease. For example ascospores are the only type of infective spore in *Sclerotinia sclerotiorum* and the main source of inoculum in *Botryotinia polyblastis*. Ascospores are less important in *Sclerotinia minor* and *Botryotinia fuckeliana* (syn. *Botrytis cinerea*, grey mould). Furthermore, the production of apothecia, hence the production of ascospores, is often sporadic usually occurring mainly in spring and early summer and clearly this affects the prevalence of the disease.

The appearance of the vegetative spores (conidia) and conidiophores produced by different species are often very similar. Consequently conidiophores are often described as, for example, the *Botrytis*-type (See p.95). When environmental conditions are favourable, vegetative spores are formed in abundance and are readily dispersed to other plants, and the disease rapidly develops into an epidemic.

Control is complicated by the wide host range of some of the species and the capacity of most to colonise dead or dying tissue and subsequently to invade living tissue. Therefore, control is based on a combination of measures aimed at excluding infected planting material such as bulbs from the garden or nursery, treating infected planting material such as bulbs or seed to kill the fungus, protecting healthy tissue e.g. leaves, flowers and cuttings from infection, removing infected plants during growth (roguing) and providing an environment which limits activity of the fungus particularly the production of vegetative spores.

The most important species of white and grey moulds that affect alpine and other garden plants are described below (See also Table 27, Table 28).

Sclerotinia gladioli Drayton (syn. *Stromatinia gladioli* (Drayton) Whetzel) is very common, causing dry rot in *Gladiolus* (Plate 15d) and other members of the Iridaceae, and Liliaceae such as *Crocus*, *Narcissus* and *Galanthus*. The leaves become stunted soon after emergence, turn yellow and die. Tiny sclerotia – seen as black specks – form on the leaves, corm and roots and the corm becomes soft. Hyphae grow from infected corms and bulbs and infect adjacent plants. Infected plants rot releasing sclerotia which then survive in soil for several years. Control measures are based on treating bulbs and corms in hot water before sale, and standard methods of hygiene such as removal and destruction of infected plants together with surrounding soil.

Sclerotinia sclerotiorum (Lib.) de Bary, also named *S. libertiana* or *Whetzelinia sclerotiorum*, is common and affects an extremely wide range of herbaceous plants including *Anemone* and *Eranthis*. The type of symptom depends on the method of infection and the stage of growth of the host. Sclerotia which are close to the host germinate to produce hyphae which infect the stem and lower leaves directly (myceliogenic germination). Plant growth is checked, the plant becomes less vigorous, leaves wilt and ultimately the plant collapses and dies. Infected tissue becomes soft and turns brown. Often there is a profuse growth of whitish mycelium near soil level (Plate 15f) – hence the name white mould – followed by production of sclerotia (Plate 16a); the stem cavities also become filled with mycelium and sclerotia. Sclerotia in soil may also germinate to produce apothecia – this process being described as carpogenic germination – in spring and early summer and ascospores are dispersed by air or rain splash and then infect leaves and flowers. Irrespective of the method of infection, only sclerotia in the upper 5 cm or so of soil are infective. The fungus is most active at 15-20°C although infection can occur at lower temperatures, but then more slowly. Ascospores require a period of 15-24 hours wetness for germination and infection but once the fungus is established within the host, disease progress is less dependent on moisture. Dead or dying tissue is readily colonised and provides a food base from which the fungus invades healthy tissue and produces a progressive rot. The fungus forms large (about 1 cm across) dark sclerotia, those on the inside of the plant being protected from attack by the soil microflora and from high temperatures. Vegetative spores are not produced by this fungus.

Control measures are based on the standard methods of hygiene with particular attention being paid to the removal of dead and dying plant tissue and minimising air humidity. Soil fumigation reduces the numbers of sclerotia but is often ineffective because those which survive produce apothecia and the resulting ascospores are dispersed over a wide area. Benzimidazole fungicides are applied to the base of the plant to reduce infection from germinating sclerotia, or sprayed on leaves and flowers to limit infection by ascospores.

Sclerotinia minor Jagger is similar to *Sclerotinia sclerotiorum* except that the sclerotia are smaller and apothecia are rarely produced. The fungus affects a similarly wide range of herbaceous plants and its activity is also confined to the upper few centimetres of soil. Infection of the host is accompanied by the production of profuse whitish hyphae at soil level, collapse of the stem and lower leaves, and wilting. Sclerotia are released into the soil as the infected tissue decays and survive for about 5 years. Control measures are based on standard methods of hygiene, the application of fungicides to the base of the plant to reduce infection from sclerotia and burial of sclerotia by deep digging to render them ineffective. Soil fumigation is generally more effective than it is with *S. sclerotiorum* because the spore stage is less frequent.

Sclerotium cepivorum Berk. is restricted to the genus *Allium*, and causes white rot. Again the type of symptom is dependent on the stage of plant growth, the environmental conditions, particularly temperature, and the numbers of sclerotia in soil. Symptoms range from pre- and post-emergence seedling death, wilting and yellowing of the outer (older) leaves, stunted growth, and death at any stage of plant growth (Plate 16d). There is no sexual stage and vegetative spores are not produced. Host infection starts from hyphae produced by germinating sclerotia, the hyphae growing through the soil to infect the roots and invade the stem base of the plant. As a result the roots collapse, the bulb decays and the plant is easily dislodged from the soil. Infected bulbs are then a focus for infection of neighbouring healthy plants by growth of hyphae between root systems which often intermingle, or by contact between stem bases. Thus infected plants are found in patches. The base of the plant becomes covered in whitish mycelium (white rot) which then invades the inside of the bulb (Plate 16e). Sclerotia, which are black and similar in size to foxglove seed, form in the mycelium on the outside and inside of the bulb. Sclerotia are released into soil following decay of host tissue and have the potential to survive at least 15 years. However, survival can sometimes be much less, probably because of anaerobic conditions in wet soil or attack by other fungi. Sclerotia are also weakened by sub-lethal temperatures, as may occur during composting, and as a result take longer to germinate or are more readily colonised by the soil microflora and fail to survive. Sclerotial germination is uniquely dependent on various sulphur-containing compounds which exude from the roots of *Allium*. The total amount and proportion of these compounds varies in different species of *Allium* and this affects the amount of sclerotial germination. Species such as *A. aflatunense*, *A. cristophii* and *A. karataviense* produce little stimulatory material hence escape infection and may appear, incorrectly, resistant. Others such as *A. caeruleum*, *A. moly* and *A. sphaerocephalon* are highly stimulatory and hence vulnerable to infection. This difference in response of the host to the pathogen is limited to their effects on sclerotial germination and is not due to tissue resistance. Therefore, it seems likely that non-stimulatory species of *Allium* will become infected if planted near those which are stimulatory. *S. cepivorum* is mainly active at 10-20°C and in moderately moist soil. As a result damage occurs in April-June and September-October but rarely between November-March unless the weather is mild. Activity ceases in hot summers, starting again as temperatures fall in the autumn.

Control measures are based on standard methods of hygiene. As with other soil-borne fungi, particularly those forming resistant sclerotia, it is important to exclude the fungus from the nursery or garden and to minimise the movement of infested soil. Leek seedlings bought for transplanting in the vegetable garden are a common source of the fungus and infection may not be very obvious at this stage. Once introduced into the garden the fungus soon spreads to other areas. Before planting, therefore, leek seedlings should be placed on damp kitchen paper covered with polythene and kept at about 15°C for 3 or 4 days. By this time, infected plants will produce a cotton wool-like growth of mycelium on the roots and shank. If this happens it is best to destroy all the seedlings or return them to the supplier. Infected shallots, onion sets or garlic cloves are another source of infection and any with decay, mycelium or sclerotia should be destroyed. Plants which wilt or turn yellow during growth should be examined and those with white rot removed and destroyed (roguing). The soil surrounding infected plants contains sclerotia therefore it should be removed for about 5 cm around and below and disposed of carefully. The heat generated during composting is easily sufficient to kill sclerotia provided the heap is constructed and insulated properly. However, optimum construction is not always feasible in the garden and whilst sclerotia are weakened by sub-lethal temperatures it would be safer not to put infected plants on the compost heap. Chemical control is based on the application of benzimidazole fungicides to the bulb before planting, or to the base of the bulb during growth. Dicarboximide fungicides such as iprodione and procymidone are also effective but are either not available for amateur use or not sold in the UK. Unfortunately, benzimidazole and dicarboximide fungicides which are used regularly on the same areas of ground breakdown much more rapidly than they do when first used, probably because of changes in the soil microflora. As a result these fungicides become ineffective at controlling soil-borne diseases. Calomel (mercurous chloride) is effective but its use as a fungicide is now illegal. Soil fumigation is effective when sclerotial numbers are low but not otherwise because the remaining sclerotia are still able to initiate infection. A novel method of control is based on the use of materials which stimulate sclerotial germination in the absence of the host causing them to starve and die. Unfortunately, results have been rather variable probably for similar reasons as soil fumigation, that is to say not all sclerotia are eradicated and those that remain are infective. The provision of plenty of space between plants, say about 25 cm, restricts the growth of the fungus to adjacent plants hence prevents infection foci from increasing in size. Finally, sclerotia on infected plants are produced at the soil surface and hence present an easy target for biological control.

Sclerotinia bulborum (Wakker) Rehm is occasionally seen causing black slime in *Hyacinthus* and other bulb-, corm- and rhizome-forming species of the Liliaceae, Ranunculaceae and Iridaceae e.g. *Anemone*, *Crocus*, *Iris* and *Scilla* (Tables 27 and 28). The fungus forms long, thin, dark sclerotia which germinate to produce mycelium which either infects the roots and bulb directly (myceliogenic germination) or produce apothecia (carpogenic germination) above ground in spring which are a source of ascospores. Bulbs are colonised by whitish hyphae and rot from the base upwards followed by the formation of sclerotia inside the bulb.

Control measures are based on the removal and destruction of infected plants together with the surrounding soil.

Dumontinia tuberosa (Hedw.) Kohn) is the most recent (1979) name for the fungus previously known as *Sclerotinia tuberosa* (Hedw.) Fuckel. The fungus causes black rot of corms and rhizomes of *Anemone blanda*, *A. coronaria*, *A. nemorosa*, *A. ranunculoides*, and *Eranthis* (Plate 16b). Sclerotia develop underground on, not inside, the corms and rhizomes, and produce apothecia up to 2 cm diameter in spring. The apothecia form at ground level (Plate 16c) and ascospores germinate to produce hyphae which colonise the rhizome and form more sclerotia.

Botryotinia and Botrytis

Botryotinia is the sexual state of the fungus better known as *Botrytis* in its vegetative (anamorph) state. The name 'Botrytis' is based on the Greek for 'bunch of grapes' which describes the characteristic appearance of the conidiophore and vegetative spores (Fig. 18). As mentioned before, other genera in the Helotiales also form *Botrytis*-like conidiophores and vegetative spores. Much smaller spores called microspores are also produced and these fertilize receptive cells in apothecia prior to the formation of asci and ascospores.

Botrytis exists in four different forms namely vegetative spores, sclerotia, mycelium and ascospores. Vegetative spores are produced in very large numbers and blown to other plants or splashed by rain and give rise to epidemics in humid conditions. Apothecia are thought to be rare but could be overlooked; therefore their role as a source of primary inoculum is uncertain but is probably underestimated. Mycelium is readily dispersed in the form of infected plant tissue, particularly petals, and these initiate new infections when in contact with other healthy or dying tissue. Mycelium is also dispersed in the form of infected planting material such as bulbs, corms etc. and seed. Sclerotia are dispersed mainly with decaying infected plant tissue, on corms and bulbs etc., or with soil. The sclerotia then produce very large numbers of vegetative spores which are dispersed in air and by rain splash in the usual manner. In contrast to *Sclerotinia*, *Botryotinia* sclerotia rarely produces hyphae which infect host tissue directly.

Most damage by *Botrytis* occurs in cool damp conditions favouring the production of vegetative spores. These conditions occur in autumn and cool summers, or in greenhouses at almost any time of the year. Air humidity is closely related to temperature, the lower the temperature the greater the humidity for a given amount of water. About 15 hours at 15°C in saturated air is required for infection and such conditions are quite common. Dead or dying tissue is very readily colonised as is tissue which suffers even a slight amount of frost damage. Because of the importance of humidity on the development of grey mould, the shape of the plant and the spacing between plants has a marked effect on the occurrence of the disease. Plants with compact branching or crowded parts e.g. the petals in flower buds provide humid conditions which are ideal for the fungus. Similarly, plants which are crowded together either in the open or in the greenhouse have a humid microclimate; efficient weed control is relevant in this respect because weeds restrict air movement hence raise the humidity.

Figure 18 *Botryotinia (Botrytis)* spore production by grey mould Fungus

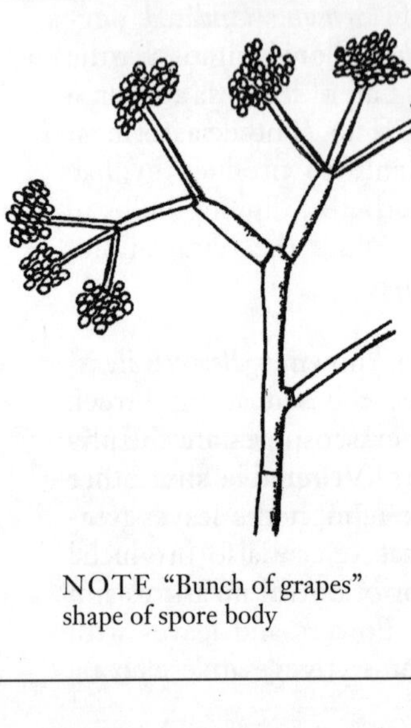

NOTE "Bunch of grapes" shape of spore body

There are many ways of growing plants to avoid infection e.g. good ventilation, generous spacing between pots, strict hygiene and avoidance of the use of excessive fertilizers or overwatering.

Botryotinia fuckeliana (de Bary) Whetzel (syn. *Sclerotinia fuckeliana* (de Bary) Fuckel) is best known in the vegetative state (anamorph) *Botrytis cinerea* Pers.:Fr., causing the ubiquitous grey mould of soft plant tissue (Plate 16f). The most common symptoms are collapse of seedlings and flower buds, and the occurrence of brown spots on leaves and flowers. Infected tissue provides a food base from which the fungus invades healthy tissue resulting in a progressive brown rot and further collapse of tissue. The fungus produces abundant greyish vegetative spores on dead and dying tissue. Vegetative spores are readily dispersed and, given suitably moist conditions, grey mould can quickly develop into an epidemic. The fungus occurs everywhere in the form of spores or mycelium within dead host tissue. Seed-borne infection is a source of seedling collapse probably when seeds have been stored in rather humid conditions. Sclerotia vary in shape and size, 0.5-2 cm being typical, but are not produced very often. They usually give rise to vegetative conidia, similar to those produced on host tissue, and apothecia are thought to be rare.

Control is based on a combination of cultural measures including hygiene, promoting active growth in the host and minimising air humidity. Benzimidazole fungicides applied as sprays may be effective initially but when used routinely result in the selection of resistant strains of the fungus and consequent loss of control. Dicarboximide fungicides such as iprodione are also effective and being from a different chemical group reduce the chance of resistance. However, iprodione is available only to the professional horticulturist and not to the amateur. Other fungicides from different groups are thiram and captan (See Table 45). Immersing the plant, still in its pot, in a bucket of fungicide in late autumm helps prevent susceptible cushion plants such as *Androsace* from rotting.

Botryotinia narcissicola (Greg.) Buchw. (anamorph *Botrytis narcissicola* Kleb. ex Westerd. & van Beyma) causes **'smoulder'** mainly in *Narcissus* but sometimes also in *Galanthus*. Lesions develop on the leaf tip and on one side of the leaf causing the leaf to curve in a similar way to infection by stem and bulb (*Narcissus*) eelworm (Plate 17a; Fig. 11). Dead tissue also occurs on the flower buds and stems or flowers may fail to emerge. The fungal mycelium spreads to the bulb causing the flower stalk and leaves to rot and also to the flowers causing a light brown speckling. Vegetative spores form on dead tissue and infect damaged or dying tissue; the mycelium is then able to invade healthy tissue. Later, sclerotia form on the bulb or in leaves and flower stalks (Plate 17b, c). The disease most often starts from infected bulbs or from sclerotia in soil.

Control is based on the planting of healthy bulbs, dipping bulbs in fungicides such as benzimidazole before planting and the removal and destruction of infected leaves, flowers and bulbs.

Botryotinia polyblastis (Greg.) Buchw. (anamorph *Botrytis polyblastis* Dowson) causes *Narcissus* 'fire'. Fire describes the spreading brown lesions which form on leaves in humid conditions. Ascospores are the primary inoculum, causing brown spots on flowers. Vegetative spores are then produced on the dead and dying flowers and infect the leaves (secondary inoculum). Later, large (1.5 cm long) dark sclerotia form on the leaves and produce apothecia the following spring. Control measures aim to limit the production of vegetative spores on flowers and leaves with fungicide sprays, and to remove infected plants or tissue and sclerotia hence limit the production of primary inoculum.

Botryotinia draytoni (Buddin & Wakef.) (anamorph *Botrytis gladiolorum* Timmermans (syn. *Botrytis gladioli*)) is restricted to *Gladiolus*, causing considerable damage. Brown sunken specks develop on the upper part of the corm in cool conditions (2-13°C) then spread to the rest of the corm producing a spongy brown rot. As a result, the leaves turn yellow and die. Spores are produced on leaf tissue and are splashed or blown to fresh tissue and flowers giving rise to water-soaked spots.

Control measures are based on hygiene chiefly the exclusion of infected corms from the garden and removal and destruction of infected plants. Sprays of captan or chlorthalonil control leaf and petal spot but have little effect on corm infection.

Botrytis tulipae Lind. forms small pale spots on the aerial parts of *Tulipa* and sometimes on *Lilium*. When conditions remain humid the spots spread and join together forming the symptom called 'fire'; spots also form on the bulbs. Sclerotia are produced on bulbs, dying leaves and flower stems. The disease starts from sclerotia in soil or attached to bulbs, or from lesions on the bulbs (Plate 17d). The fungus grows into the leaves and flower stem which turn yellow and wither. Brown spots develop on leaves followed by the production of vegetative spores (Plate 17). The spores are blown or splashed to other parts of the plant or to other plants. Mycelium from the spreading type of lesion grows into the bulb and then to the daughter bulbs. However, these lesions are very small, hence easily overlooked. Consequently, infected bulbs can be planted accidentally.

Other species of *Botryotinia* or *Botrytis* which may be found are *Botrytis convallariae* (Kleb.) Ondrej ex Boer. & Hamers (grey spores and black sclerotia on *Convallaria* leaves, stems and flowers), *Botryotinia convoluta* (Drayton) Whetzel (on *Iris* rhizomes and leaf bases), *B. elliptica* (Berk.) Cooke (*Lilium* leaves, rarely bulbs e.g. *L. longiflorum* and *L. speciosum*), *B. galanthina* Berk. & Br. Sacc. (*Galanthus*; Plate 17e), *Botrytis hyacinthii* Westerd. & van Beyma (*Hyacinthus* leaves, stems, flowers) and *B. paeoniae* (*Paeonia*) (See Tables 27 and 28). All produce the typical *Botrytis* grey mould symptoms as well as sclerotia but apothecia are rare or absent. As before, control measures are based on a combination of exclusion of infected planting material, strict hygiene and control of humidity.

Other Ascomycetes

Thielaviopsis basicola (Berk. & Broome) Ferraris. (syn. *Chalara elegans* Nag Raj & Kendr.) causes 'black root rot' in more than 130 plant species from a wide range of families; it belongs to the Order Ophiostomatales. The fungus attacks the roots of herbaceous plants such as tuberous *Begonia*, or *Viola*, and container-grown shrubs such as *Ilex crenata*, *I. pernyi*, *Pieris japonica*, *Euonymus japonicus aureo-variegatus* and *Buxus sempervirens*. The fungus also affects greenhouse pot plants such as poinsettia (*Euphorbia pulcherrima*), *Primula obconica* and *Cyclamen*, and pansy (*Viola tricolor*) grown for bedding. The symptoms depend on the stage of growth when infection occurs and are not very specific. The plant may be infected but show only mild symptoms. Alternatively, infected plants may lack vigour, have fewer, smaller and later flowers, and senesce prematurely. Sometimes mature plants are killed, particularly if grown from container stock. Infected roots turn dark brown and rot. Dark chlamydospores develop within the roots and can be seen under the microscope or with a hand lens (magnification ×10-40); they comprise 1-3 thin-walled basal cells on top of which are 1-8 dark cells. The fungus also produces pale thin-walled spores called **phialospores** which are probably responsible for the rapid dissemination of the pathogen during the growing season. The fungus is readily isolated and identified by placing small amounts of soil or infected plant tissue onto discs of carrot and incubating in damp conditions and chlamydospores are produced in a few days. *T. basicola* is an example of an organism which is 'out of place'. Normally the fungus survives by saprophytic growth on organic matter in soil or as drought resistant chlamydospores. Hence, the fungus is non-pathogenic and a normal part of the soil microflora even in soils which have never been cultivated. In certain circumstances the balance changes in favour of the fungus and the host plant then succumbs. This balance is linked to environmental conditions which cause stress in the host plant. Stress is a somewhat vague term used to describe unfavourable environmental or biological factors which adversely affect the plant such as unfavourable temperatures, water content of the growing medium, fertilizer imbalance or attack by pests or fungi. For example, the short periods of high temperatures which occur in greenhouses at mid-day in summer are thought to induce stress. Incorrect soil acidity is another form of stress with little black root rot damage occurring at pH 5.6-5.9 but increasing at higher soil pHs. Stress may be more prevalent when plants are grown in small containers because the small amount of growing medium is unable to buffer changes in temperature, moisture, pH and nutrients.

Plants react differently to changes in environmental conditions depending on their inherent physiological make-up and the conditions in which they grow. For example, species adapted to hot dry conditions conserve moisture by quickly closing their stomata in hot dry conditions whereas species adapted to cool, humid conditions, react less readily hence continue to lose water and consequently wilt. It follows that stress is most likely to affect plants grown in conditions to which they are not adapted and this might include alpines plants grown in lowland conditions.

Blue moulds and green moulds

Blue mould fungi belong to the Order Eurotiales (See Table 15, p.96) and include *Penicillium*, the vegetative state (anamorph) of *Eupenicillium*; however many *Penicillium* species do not appear to have a sexual state. The vegetative spores are various shades of blue or green. *Talaromyces* is another sexual state and some species are studied for use in biological control of plant disease.

As with *Botryotinia*, these fungi are usually seen in the vegetative state and the name of the vegetative (anamorph) state is generally used. The name *Penicillium* is derived from the shape of the spores and the vegetative conidiophore which is brush-like or penicillate (Fig. 19).

Penicillium species live mainly on dead organic matter (saprophytic). However, some species invade living plant tissue of bulbs, corms and fruits (obligate necrotroph). Blue and green moulds are very common on oranges and lemons (*Penicillium cyclopium* West. (syn. *P. aurantiogriseum* Dierckx)) and garlic (*P. hirsutum* Dierckx (syn. *P. corymbiferum* West.) and *P. cyclopium*). The asci of the sexual state are contained in cleistothecia. Similar structures which do not contain asci are sometimes formed and are called sclerotia; their function is unknown and it is doubtful if they survive long.

Two species are important to the nurseryman and gardener. *Penicillium gladioli* McCulloch & Thom, the vegetative state of ***Eupenicillium crustaceum*** Ludwig, affects the corms and bulbs of many plants in the Iridaceae and Liliaceae e.g. *Gladiolus*, *Crocus*, *Scilla*, *Iris*, *Montbretia*, and *Cyclamen* (See Tables 27 and 28). The sexual state (teleomorph) is uncommon. Infected corms etc. develop brown sunken lesions several centimetres wide. In cool, moist condition such as occur during storage, the blue or green vegetative spores develop and spread by contact with other corms etc. to start new infections. At temperatures above 20°C light brown pin head-sized sclerotia are produced below the scale leaves. ***Penicillium hirsutum*** Dieckx causes a green mould on Liliaceae such as *Tulipa* and *Ornithagalum*, and on *Crocus* and bulbous *Iris*. Both *Penicillium* species enter the plant via wounds including those made by emerging adventitious roots. Control is by a combination of post harvest heat treatment in air to seal the wounds, reducing humidity in storage to limit the formation of vegetative spores and the avoidance or removal of infected planting material.

Figure 19 Spore production by blue mould fungus, *Penicillium*

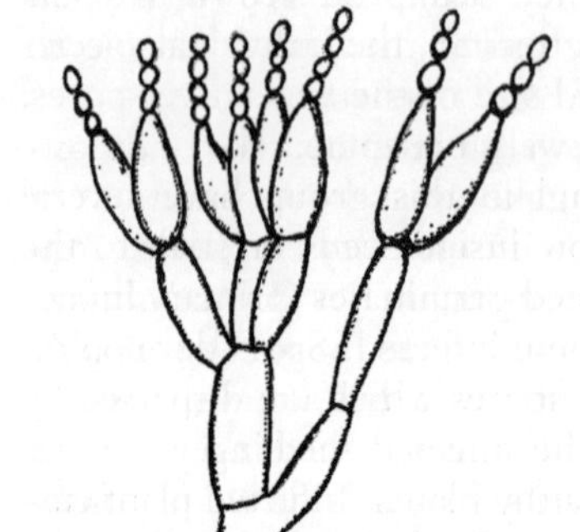

NOTE "Brush-like" sporing bodies

Acremonium and *Aspergillus* also belong to the Eurotiales, but are not blue or green moulds; they are important plant pathogens in warmer climates and are unlikely to occur in the UK, except possibly on bulbs stored at 25-30°C for forcing (e.g. *Aspergillus niger* v. Tiegh).

Rosellinia necatrix Prill (anamorph *Dematophora necatrix* R. Hartig). This fungus belongs to the Sphaeriales most of which have fruiting bodies embedded in a layer of compact dense hyphae (stroma). Most species of *Rosellinia* are saprophytic on wood but *R. necatrix* also parasitises herbaceous plants such *Narcissus*, *Paeonia*, *Viola* and *Cyclamen* (See Tables 27 and 28). The symptoms on aerial parts are those formed indirectly as a result of root infection i.e. loss of vigour, stunting and yellowing of foliage. When a root grows near a fungal strand or infected plant, the fungus produces a profuse mass of white mycelium. The mycelium first grows over the root then infects the root tissue. On woody plants the fungus invades the bark and underlying tissue, the mycelium forming compact 'fingers'. The fungus is able to use the food base to grow through soil to infect neighbouring plants. Fungal strands are broken during cultivation and the fragments act as primary inoculum. Control is based on the removal of primary inoculum (infected plant roots and woody tissue) or soil, or fumigation of soil.

Leaf and stem spots

This large group, the Order Dothideales, contains fungi mostly with dark coloured mycelium, causing spots on leaves, stems and flowers. Many of the fungi are specific to the hosts they attack and are limited to soft tissue such as seedlings and cuttings, or to damaged, weakened or dying tissue. The sexual stage (teleomorph), comprises asci protected in cavities (locules) in a mass of compact, dark, hyphae sometimes including pieces of the host (stroma). Generally, however, it is the vegetative state (anamorph) which is the most common and damaging (Plate 18a). The shapes of the vegetative spores of the different species are distinctive and are used as the basis for identification. First, the fungi are classified on the basis of whether the vegetative spores are protected in a flask-like structure called a **pycnidium**, or whether they are produced on hyphal branches or conidiophores (See Table 20). Second, the individual species are identified on the basis of the shape and size of the vegetative spores, and the numbers and arrangement of cross walls or septae.

The life cycles of the different fungi in this group have several features in common. The fungi often grow inside seeds or stick to the outside i.e. they are seed-borne. Infected seed germinates (primary inoculum) to produce seedlings which also become infected. Spots develop on the leaves and stems producing vegetative spores which are dispersed by rain splash (secondary inoculum). Thus, the infected seedling is a focus from which the fungus spreads to other healthy plants. Infected plant cuttings also act as a source of infection. Later, the fungus grows into the seed or sticks to the outside of the seed thus completing the life cycle. As well as infected seed, the remains of infected plants in soil are a source of primary inoculum. Therefore control methods are based on (a) eliminating the source of the fungus by producing healthy seed, treating seed against infection, eradicating the remains of infected plants, or practising a long rotation so that the fungus dies before planting and (b) minimising secondary spread by removing infection foci or by protecting the remaining plants with a dithiocarbamate fungicide.

Table 20 **Fungi causing leaf spots**

Fungus	Features
Alternaria *Cercospora* *Cladosporium* *Drechslera* *Ramularia*	pale or dark vegetative spores with 1 or more cells produced on single or clumps of conidiophores; spores have transverse cross walls
Aschochyta *Coniothyrium* *Phoma* *Septoria*	vegetative spores protected by pycnidium; pycnospores have 1 or more cells and tranverse cross walls

The fungi causing leaf-spot diseases may be divided into those producing their vegetative spores on hyphal branches and those which produce them in pycnidia. The most important leaf spot fungi that infect alpine and other garden plants are described below and are listed in Tables 20, 27 and 28.

Fungi producing vegetative spores on hyphal branches

Alternaria produces unbranched hyphae (conidiophores) with dark spores with both transverse and longitudinal cross-walls; the spores are produced in chains. Examples are *Alternaria zinniae* in ornamental Compositae, *A. cheiranthus* (infecting *Cheiranthus)*, *A. dianthus* (infecting *Dianthus*) and *A. violae* (infecting *Viola*).

Cladosporium produces branched conidiophores with clustered or single 1- or 2-celled spores. Most species grow on dead plant tissue attacking live tissue only when it is weakened or senescent e.g. *Cladosporium herbarum* (Pers.) Link (teleomorph *Mycosphaerella tassiana*); they also cause sooty mould on leaves (See Page). Apart from accelerating leaf senescence most *Cladosporium* species appear to have little effect on plants. Exceptions are *Cladosporium cucumerinum* which attacks plants in the Cucurbitaceae causing water soaked lesions and scabs on the fruit, and *C. iridis* (teleomorph *Mycosphaerella macrospora* (Kleb) Jørstad) on iris.

Drechslera (syn. *Bipolaris*) (teleomorph *Pyrenophora*) causes yellow streaks on leaves e.g. on bulbous iris followed by the production of dark vegetative spores (*Drechslera iridis* (Oudem) M.B.Ellis).

Mycocentrospora acerinum (R. Hartig) Deighton produces spore-bearing hyphae with broad scars where the multicellular inverted club-shaped spores join. Usually the fungus is limited to seedlings or dying tissue and affects a wide range of plant species including *Campanula* spp., *Aquilegia* spp., *Geum chiloense*, *Myosotis alpestris*, *Omphalodes linifolia*, *Ranunculus asciaticus*, and *Viola cornuta*. Infected tissue contains chains of dark chlamydospores which germinate to produce vegetative spores able to disperse over short distances. This is the same fungus which, in commerce, causes considerable damage in celery and carrot after harvest.

Pycnostysanus azaleae (Peck) Mason produces 1-celled elongate vegetative spores on bunches of hyphae called **coremia**. The fungus affects *Rhododendron* causing the flower buds to shrivel and die (bud blast), and the branches to die back from the tips. The first signs occur in autumn when the flower buds turn brown then greyish. The buds die and become covered in a dark stubby bristles which are the coremia bearing the vegetative spores. The bristly dead buds can remain attached to the bush for several years. The spores are spread by rain splash, possibly also by leafhoppers, to other parts of the bush; damage caused by leafhoppers during feeding helps the fungus to infect the buds. Control measures are based on killing the leafhopper with insecticide, using fungicides before flowering to stop the fungus from spreading to other buds, and removing and destroying infected buds.

Ramularia produces spore-bearing hyphae in clusters through leaf stomata. The fungus produces cylindrical vegetative spores which are usually 2-celled but sometimes 1- and 3-celled and spread to new leaves by rain splash. Often the centre drops out of the leaf spot causing a 'shot hole' symptom. There are a large number of *Ramularia* species each limited to a particular species of host e.g. *Ramularia agrestis* and *R. lactea* on *Viola*, *R. hellebori* on *Helleborus* or *Ramularia primulae* on *Primula*, the latter species particularly when grown under glass.

Sooty moulds. Leaves sometimes become covered in a mat of dark hyphae called sooty mould. Several fungi are involved including *Alternaria alternata*, *Capnobotrys dingleyae* (teleomorph *Metacapnodium*), *Cladosporium cladosporiodes*, *Cladosporium herbarum* (teleomorph *Mycosphaerella tassiana*) and *Trichothecium roseum*. The fungi grow as saprophytes in the sugary 'honey dew' excreted by aphids. (See also Chapter 2) It is not known for certain what effects sooty moulds have on the plant. They are unsightly, and therefore reduce the value of the plant, but otherwise they probably do little harm except for weakening the plant by reducing photosynthesis, or speeding up senescence. Control is best based on prevention by eliminating sources of honey dew, mainly aphids, and making sure that humidity is not excessive. Fungicides kill the fungi but do not dislodge the dark spores and the unsightliness remains.

Vegetative spores produced in pycnidia

Ascochyta produces 2-celled oblong vegetative spores. The teleomorphs are *Didymella* and *Mycosphaerella*. *Ascochyta* attacks living host tissue (obligately necrotrophic) and is often seed-borne. The fungus causes seedling damping off, spots on leaves and stems, and foot rot symptoms at the base of the stem; sometimes the roots are affected. Pycnidia are produced on spots on leaves etc. and the vegetative spores spread by rain splash. When flowers are infected, the fungus grows through the capsule to the seed; seed also becomes contaminated by the fungus sticking to the outside. Infected seed then give rise to infected seedlings which form foci from which the fungus spreads to neighbouring plants. Examples are *Ascochyta clematidina* (wilt and collapse in *Clematis*), *A. primulae* and *A. violae* in *Primula* and *Viola* respectively.

Coniothyrium produces 1-celled vegetative spores. Initially, the pycnidia are embedded in the leaf surface (epidermis) and emerge later. *Coniothyrium* is one of the two fungi causing leaf spot in *Helleborus*, this species being distinguished by its dark hyphae. The fungus causes dark spots on leaves and flowers, and the stems of large species such as *H. corsicus* are weakened and break (Plate 18b). The habit of *Helleborus* provides clues to the life cycle of this fungus. Vegetative spores survive through winter on old leaves and stems. The new leaves and flowers emerge from the centre of the 'root stock' in spring and become contaminated with spores from the old leaves. When the leaf spot is serious it is advisable to remove the old plant parts before the new leaves or flowers emerge. Also, treatment of new growth with fungicides prevents the infections from spreading. *H. orientalis*, *H. niger*, *H. corsicus* and *H. foetidus* are affected, the latter possibly less so than the others.

Coniothyrium minitans, a species which does not attack plants, has long been known for its capacity to parasitise sclerotia hence it has potential for the biological control of plant disease fungi.

Phoma and *Phyllosticta* both produce 1-celled vegetative pycnospores. In the past the two genera of fungi have been differentiated according to the part of the plant they affected, fungi causing stem spot being called *Phoma* and those causing leaf spots, *Phyllosticta*. The distinction is artificial and as a result some species have more than one name. As with other genera in this group, *Phoma* and *Phyllosticta* generally attack damaged, young, weakened or dying tissue and most attack a range of plants (plurivorous). For example, *Phoma exigua* var. *foveata* ('gangrene') causes considerable damage in potatoes but only when the tubers have already been bruised or wounded; it is often sufficient to minimise damage at harvest and then provide conditions for any wounds on the tubers to heal for the disease to be controlled. *Phoma exigua* var. *lilacis* causing damping-off in cuttings of *Syringa*, and *P. hedericola* causes leaf spot in *Hedera* (Plate 18c).

Ramularia vallisumbrosae is included here because it forms pycnidia, in contrast to other *Ramularia* species. The fungus affects *Narcissus* but mainly during large-scale commercial production. Vegetative spores are produced in winter from tiny black sclerotia (microsclerotia) contained in old infected leaves (primary inoculum) and infect newly emerging leaves. Small, sunken yellowish spots develop towards the leaf tips and on flower stalks. The spots enlarge, turn pale brown and in humid weather produce large numbers of white vegetative spores (white mould; but see *Sclerotinia*, p.121) which are the secondary inoculum. In warm, damp weather the fungus spreads rapidly, the leaves die early, and the bulbs are small hence are less likely to flower the following year. The vegetative spores are dispersed by wind or rain splash but cannot survive in dry air. Microsclerotia are produced on dying leaves, overwinter and germinate to produce vegetative spores thus completing the life cycle.

Septoria (teleomorph *Mycosphaerella* or *Leptosphaeria*) produces long thin (filiform) many-celled vegetative spores. There are large numbers of species each restricted to a different species of plant. Examples include *Septoria antirrhini*, *S. dianthi*, *S. drummondii* (infecting *Phlox*), *S. gladioli*, *S. helenii* (infecting *Helenium*), *S. leucanthemi* (infecting *Chrysanthemum maximum*), and *S. paeoniae*. Infected or contaminated seed is a frequent source of these fungi.

Stagonospora curtisii produces 3- or more celled elliptical vegetative pycnospores. It causes a scorch mainly on leaf tips on *Narcissus* and *Galanthus* and mainly in wet seasons. Initial infection is from primary inoculum in dead leaf bases at the neck of the bulb or in infected old leaves. The fungus produces small brown spots on the new leaves which, in wet seasons, spread to the flowers (Plate 18d).

Leaf curl and leaf blister fungi

These fungi belong to the Order Taphrinales. They are a very common cause of deformation, reddening and thickening on leaves of trees in the Rosaceae, particularly almond, peach (e.g. peach leaf curl), nectarine and apricot; attacks are so severe that most of the leaves drop off and this weakens the tree if it happens several years running. *Taphrina* species also cause leaf spots and witches broom symptoms in alder (*Alnus*) and birch (*Betula*). However, this group of fungi is not very importnat in the present context and is not discussed further. The rust fungi also cause galls and witches brooms in woody plants (See p.138).

Basidiomycetes

The Basidiomycetes (Sub-division Basidiomycotina: Table 14) contains about a quarter of all fungal species. Many cause serious plant diseases for example rust fungi and the honey fungus (*Armillaria mellea*), or damage buildings (dry rot: *Serpula lacrimans* (Wulfen: Fr.) Schröter). Basidiomycetes are often found as wefts of white mycelium, or as black 'boot laces' called **rhizomorphs**, under the bark of damp dead wood, as variously coloured mushrooms, toadstool and bracket fungi, or as fairy rings in lawns. The group also includes the **smuts** which produce masses of dark powdery spores, and **mycorrhizae** which colonise plant roots and benefit the host plant by increasing the uptake of nutrients from soil. Some basidiomycetes, such as *Agaricus*, *Boletus* and *Cantharellus*, are good to eat.

Basidiomycetes are considered to be the most advanced, in evolutionary terms, of the fungi. They are characterised by tiny specialised cells called **basidia** (sing. basidium) which produce basidiospores. At its simplest, a basidium comprises a single cell with four finger-like extensions or **sterigmata** (sing. sterigma) each producing a 1-celled **basidiospore** containing a nucleus with one set of chromosomes (Fig. 20). Sometimes fewer than 4 spores are produced – for example the cultivated mushroom has only two basidiospores per basidium. Basidia are produced either directly from hyphae or on a fruiting body called a **basidioma** (plural basidiomata), examples of which are mushrooms and toadstools; basidia can be produced on gills, as in the edible mushroom, or in long narrow tubes called pores as with the birch bracket fungus *Piptoporus betulinus* (Fr.) Karsten (syn. *Polyporus betulinus* Fr.).

Life cycle

There are three distinct stages to the basidiomycete life cycle (Fig. 20). First, a **primary mycelium** is produced from a germinating basidiospore. The mycelium becomes septate and each cell has a single nucleus. Secondly, the contents of compatible hyphae fuse and the resultant **secondary mycelium** contains two nuclei per cell; this mycelium gives rise

Figure 20 Life cycle of a basidomycete fungus

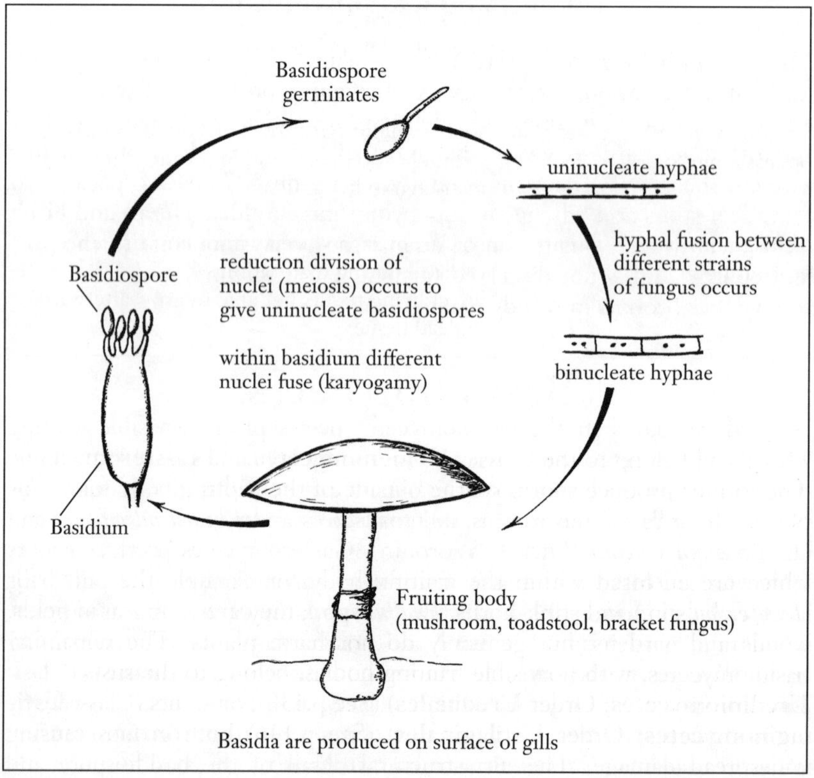

to the third stage, the production of basidia and subsequently the basidiospores. Basidia are usually produced on a fleshy fruiting body or basidioma e.g. mushroom or toadstool.

Asexual reproduction within the basidiomycetes is by conidia produced from basidiospores, by mycelia, by uredospores (See Rusts, p.138), or by fragmentation of hyphae.

Classification

Older classifications are based on the presence or absence and type of fruiting body (See Table 21).

Table 21 **Classification of the Basidiomycetes**

Taxonomic Class	Fruiting body (basidioma)	Characteristics
Hymenomycetes or mushrooms, toadstools and bracket fungi	present	basidiospores not covered during production, or covered for only a short time; affect dead or living tissue
Gasteromycetes or puff balls, earth stars, stinkhorns	present	basidiospores spores generally enclosed at least until maturity; affect dead or living host tissue
Urediniomycetes or rust fungi	absent	spores yellow-red-brown produced in sori within host tissue, erupting during maturation; restricted to living tissue
Ustilaginomycetes or smut fungi	absent	black spores produced within host tissue are released during maturation; infect living tissue, but able to grow afterwards in dead tissue

More than half the basidiomycete species produce visible fruiting bodies and belong to the Classes **Hymenomycetes** and **Gasteromycetes**. The former produce spores on the outside of the fruiting body for example on the gills of mushrooms and toadstools and *Rhododendron* leaf gall (*Exobasidium vaccinii* (Fuckel) Woronin). Gasteromycetes produce spores which are enclosed within the fruiting body for example the puff balls (*Lycoperdon* spp.) and stink-horns (*Phallus* spp.); they are common in fields, woods and gardens, but generally do not harm plants. The remaining basidiomycetes, with no visible fruiting bodies, belong to the rusts (Class: **Urediniomycetes**; Order **Uredinales**) (See p.138), or smuts (Class: **Ustilaginomycetes**; Order **Ustilaginales**) (See p.146) both groups causing widespread damage. The ultrastructural detail of the basidiospore and septum is increasingly used in the classification of the Basidomycetes the revised taxa being (a) **Hemibasidiomycetae** (including the rust fungi), (b) **Holobasidiomycetae**, (c) **Phragmobasidiomycetae** and (d) the **Teliomycetae** (including the smut fungi).

Rusts

There are about 6,000 species of rust fungi affecting a wide variety of herbaceous and woody plants in the nursery or garden, and in the wild. Examples are *Sempervivum* (*Endophyllum sempervivi* de Bary), groundsel (*Senecio vulgaris*) (*Puccinia lagenophorae* Cooke), rose (*Phragmidium tuberculatum* J. Müller) and *Mahonia* (*Cumminsiella mirabilissima* (Peck) Nannf.). Rusts only grow in living plant tissue, that is to say they are obligate biotrophs (See p.83). They rarely kill plants but spoil their appearance, reduce plant growth because there is less leaf tissue for photosynthesis, and reduce flowering and seed production. Some rusts are being studied for the biological control of weeds such as groundsel or bramble. Certain groups of flowering plant particularly the Cruciferae, Cucurbitaceae, or Solanaceae are rarely affected by rusts.

Table 22 **Types of spore produced by basidiomycete rust fungi**

Type of spore (alternative name)	Structure produced from	Function
0: Spermatium (pycniospore)	spermogonium	function as uninucleate gametes which fertilize receptive hyphae
I: Aeciospore (aecidiospore)	aecium (aeciosorus)	1-celled binucleate non-repeating vegetative spore
II: Urediniospore (uredospore)	uredinium (uredosorus)	1-celled binucleate vegetative summer spore which repeats infection (secondary inoculum)
III: Teliospore (teleutospore)	telium (teleutosorus)	2- or more celled resting or winter spore; nuclear fusion occurs in teliospore
IV: Basidiospore (sporidium)	basidium produced on teliospore	reduction division occurs in basidium to produce 1-celled uninucleate homokaryotic spores

Table 23 **Rusts with alternate hosts**

Name of rust fungus	Spermogonia (0) and aecia (I)	Uredinia (II) and telia (III)
Chrysomyxa ledi var. *rhododendri*	*Picea* spp.	*Rhododendron* spp.
C. pirolata; *C. woroninii*		*Pyrola* spp. *Ledum* spp.
Coleosporium tussilaginis (sometimes split into formae speciales)		*Aster, Campanula, Solidago, Ranunculus*
Cronartium comptoniae		*Myrica gale*
C. flaccidum	*Pinus* spp.	*Gentiana, Nemesia, Paeonia, Pedicularis, Tropaeolum*
C. ribicola		*Ribes* spp.
Gymnosporangium spp.	*Crataegus, Malus, Pyrus, Sorbus*	*Juniperus* spp.
Melamspora allii-populina	*Arum, Allium*	*Populus* spp.
M. epitea var. *epitea*	*Orchids, Euonymus*	*Salix* spp.
Melampsorella caryophyllaceae	*Abies* spp.	*Arenaria, Cerastium, Stellaria*
Melampsoridium betulinum	*Larix* spp.	*Betula* spp.
Milesina spp.	*Abies* spp.	*Ferns*
Ochrospora ariae	*Anemone nemorosa*	*Sorbus* spp.
Puccinia graminis	*Berberis, Mahonia*	cereals and wide range of grasses
P. hordei	*Ornithagalum, Leopoldia*	barley
P. iridis	nettle	*Iris* spp.
P. recondita formae speciales	*Anchusa, Ranunculus, Thalictrum*	cereals and wide range of grasses
P. sessilis	*Arum, Convallaria, Dactylorhiza, Gymnadenia*	*Phalaris arundinacea*

Table 24 **Rusts with alternate hosts (contd.)**

Name of rust fungus	Spermogonia (0) and aecia (I)	Uredinia (II) and telia (III)
Pucciniastrum spp.	*Abies, Picea, Tsuga* spp.	wide range of flowering plants including orchids
Pucciniastrum epilobii	*Abies* spp.	*Epilobium, Fuchsia* spp.
Tranzschelia discolour	*Anemone coronaria, A. ranunculoides*	wild and cultivated *Prunus* spp.
Uromyces dianthi	*Euphorbia* spp.	*Dianthus, Gypsophila, Lychnis, Saponaria, Silene*
U. pisi-sativi	*Euphorbia cyparissius*	*Astragalus* and other Leguminosae

Life cycle

Spores germinate on leaf surfaces producing hyphae which grow towards stomata. The hyphae enter the stomata, grow between the leaf cells and produce minute branches called **haustoria** which invade the plant cells to obtain nutrients. The life cycle is complicated by having up to five different types of spore. The five states are concerned with fertilisation, initiation of colonies on the host after winter or other adverse conditions, and rapid dispersal; they are described as 0-IV (See Table 22: the alternative technical terms are included in parenthesis).

Rusts which produce all five types of spore on one species of plant are called **autoecious**. Others need two different species of host for completion of the life cycle and are called **heteroecious**. Heteroecious rusts form summer vegetative urediniospores and winter sexual teliospores on the **primary host**, whereas spermogonia and vegetative aeciospores are formed on the second or **alternate host**. Examples are described in Tables 23 and 24. Aeciospores and urediniospores are dispersed by wind and are capable of initiating infection at long distances from the original source. Aeciospores of heteroecious rusts do not re-infect the original host, and therefore the primary host is essential for completion of the life cycle. This distinction is important because the presence of a heteroecious rust may originate from a totally different species of plant. As a result, control measures may not be needed where the garden plant is the alternate host. For example, *Euphorbia* is the alternate host for the pea rust fungus which only completes the life cycle on the pea; control measures for the *Euphorbia* stage are not really necessary. However, those growing the primary host as a crop, rather than the garden plant may not agree! Thus, *Berberis* is the alternate host to black stem rust of wheat; whilst the rust does not spread on *Berberis*, its removal is one method of reducing primary infection of wheat hence of delaying disease epidemics in a major food crop (See Chapter 5).

Rusts with all five spore states are called **macrocyclic** an example being the groundsel rust. It follows that a rust can be macrocyclic and autoecious, for example *Mahonia* rust, or macrocyclic and heteroecious e.g. *Coleosporium solidaginis* on *Solidago* (Fig. 21).

Some rust fungi do not have the aecial or uredinial stages and consequently they are called **microcyclic**; because of their shortened life cycle, microcyclic rusts are autoecious. The missing stages of microcyclic rusts may yet to be discovered or, alternatively, they may have been lost during evolution.

The need for an alternate host to complete and repeat a life cycle is both an advantage and a disadvantage to the fungus. The advantage is that the fungus is not dependent on a single species of plant to complete the life cycle; the disadvantage is that the fungus cannot reproduce sexually without the presence of the alternate host.

Symptoms

Rusts affect soft tissue such as leaves, petioles, flower bracts and rhizomes (Plate 18); they also affect woody tissue in flowering trees and shrubs, and conifers. As the name indicates, rusts are recogniseable from their rusty yellow-brown colour which is derived from the spores. The sori which

Figure 21 Life cycle of a rust fungi may be on one or two host species

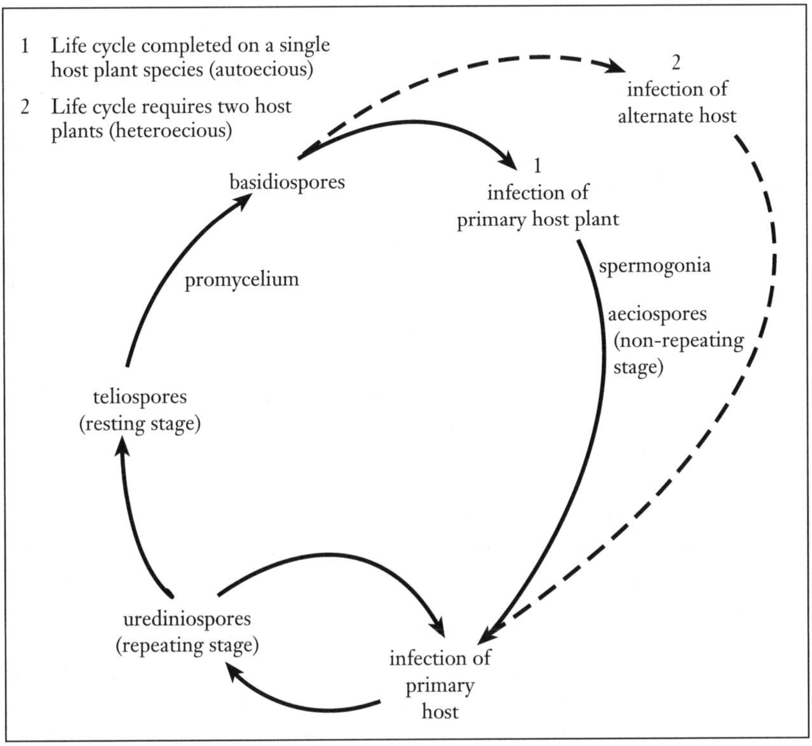

contain the spores may be extremely abundant making the leaf appear brown, for example birch rust *Melampsoridium betulinum* (Pers.) Kleb. In general, aecia tend to be clustered in groups on the host, and for this reason are called 'cluster cups', whereas uredinia and telia are more scattered. Also, aeciospores tend to be pale, often orange to yellow, whereas urediniospores and teliospores are straw-coloured or pale to dark brown. However, rusts are white if the basidiospores are abundant and obvious, as in Chrysanthemum white rust. The collar or peridium which surrounds the aecium or telium is often distinctive either in colour, for example being white in *Puccinia graminis* and yellow in *Cumminsiella mirabilissima*, or in structure, the margins being smooth or ragged. The position of the sori on the leaf is a useful character particularly that of uredinia and telia which are sometimes limited to one surface or the other; aecia, on the other hand, are usually produced on the lower leaf surface.

Infection of soft tissue initially gives rise to a pale green spot which later turns various shades of yellow, red or brown and becomes powdery; sometimes the spots are tinged with red as with the *Mahonia* and bramble rusts. Spots indicate the presence of sori either on the upper or lower leaf surfaces. Long, narrow leaves, such as conifer needles or grass, develop yellow or red-brown bands. The mycelia from aeciospores or urediniospores can invade the host, become systemic and perennial, and distort growth as in *Anemone* infected by *Tranzschelia*. Rust-infected twigs of conifers or flowering trees and shrubs are often swollen, and develop galls or cankers which persist for years; host growth is sometimes stimulated to produce groups of short branches called witches brooms.

Ferns also have sori which produce brown spores but, of course, their function is totally different. They are superficially like rusts but there should be no difficulty distinguishing them. Fern sori are produced in distinctive regular patterns on the lower leaf surface along the leaf veins; the spores of some fern species are produced within a leaf which is rolled inwards for protection (e.g. *Crytogramma*, *Osmunda*). The sori of many fern species are protected by green or brown flaps of tissue called **indusia** (sing. indusium) and these are highly distinctive for a particular species; some ferns such as *Polypodium* do not possess indusia but then the sori are very much larger than those of rusts.

Control

Rusts are limited to the main host plant species, and possibly their close relatives, therefore the presence of a 'rusty' plant in the garden does not necessarily mean that control measures are needed. Rose rust (*Phagmidium*) or *Mahonia* rust (*Cumminsiella*) are two common rusts which are unlikely to spread to alpine plants in different genera. However, some rusts clearly do pose a threat to alpines. Rusts spoil the appearance of infected plants and reduce growth. Therefore rusts should definitely be controlled on susceptible show plants, propagation stock, and plants for sale. At other times, control measures are of doubtful value.

Control measures are aimed at (a) eliminating the sources of infection, outside or inside the garden, which have not started to develop (the primary inoculum), (b) eliminating sources of infection which are already spreading to healthy plants (the secondary inoculum), and (c) reducing survival of the fungus when the weather is unfavourable, or susceptible plants are dormant or absent. Summarising, the rust disease cycle starts from teliospores, basidiospores or aeciospores, or from plants infected by the mycelial stage of the fungus (systemic infection); urediniospores spread the fungus from infected to healthy plants thus starting a disease epidemic (secondary inoculum); and teliospores or winter spores survive adverse weather, or periods when susceptible hosts are absent. Infection occurs from spring to autumn in the open garden, or all the year round in glasshouses when there is a constant supply of urediniospores and susceptible host tissue – the 'green bridge' effect. As the weather improves in spring, teliospores surviving from the previous autumn on dead plants, seeds or in soil start a new infection cycle. The initiation, spread and survival in rusts follow similar principles to other plant diseases (See p.84).

Many rust diseases are known from the damage caused to food crops. Many species of alpine are uncommon, or recently introduced to cultivation, and it is quite likely that there may be no information about the rusts which affect them; information from closely related species or genera is all that is available in these circumstances.

The different types of control measure are described below:

Exclusion of infection. Species of *Salix*, *Populus*, *Abies*, *Juniperus*, *Picea* or *Pinus* are alternate hosts for several rust diseases (See Table 23). When these hosts are abundant in areas around the garden, and are infected, it is preferable to select garden plants which do not become cross-infected, thereby avoiding the disease. In theory the infected alternate host could be removed; in reality this is hardly practicable especially if someone else's property is involved. However, rust-infected cankers and galls on trees and shrubs within the garden are sources of spore inoculum and they should be pruned to stop them spreading to other plants. Naturally, it is best not to purchase plants showing signs of infection, nor to give or accept them as gifts; do not plant infected vegetative propagating material such as diseased corms. Furthermore, only healthy stock plants should be used for propagation. Whenever possible remove infected leaves and flowers and burn them.

Many rusts are not present in the UK but occur in Europe and other parts of the world. Often they affect commercially important plants and hence pose a threat to UK agriculture, horticulture and forestry. Also, rusts affect alpine plants in their natural habitat. It is highly desirable that these diseases are not brought into the UK, therefore quarantine regulations should be scrupulously observed (See Chapter 6).

Spread of infection. Rusts spread only when there is a source of infection, a supply of susceptible plants, and environmental conditions are favourable. It follows that attention to one factor is sufficient to stop disease spread. The removal of infected plants checks disease spread. Alternatively, healthy plants, particularly valuable show plants or propagating stock, can be removed from the source of infection (See Chapter 6). Disease spread can also be controlled with fungicides. In common with other diseases, prompt treatment, before infection becomes severe, improves the chances of successful control. Rusts are controlled by maneb or mancozeb (protectant action), triforine (protectant, curative, and locally systemic action), propiconozole (protectant, curative and systemic action), myclobutanil (protectant, curative and systemic action) or sulphur (protectant action).

Food crops, particularly cereals, are protected from rust diseases by breeding resistant varieties; these act by slowing the rate of development of disease epidemics. However, no varieties of alpine plants have been bred with resistance to disease (See Chapter 5 for information on resistant varieties).

Survival. Rusts survive as teliospores on infected dead plant tissue, or as mycelium in herbaceous perennial plants, corms, rhizomes, or woody plants. Ideally, infected plant tissue should be removed before teliospores are produced, and infected dead plants, leaves etc. destroyed.

Rust species

Individual rusts are described below and in Tables 23, 27 and 28.

Puccinia and Uromyces are closely related being distinguished on the basis of the teliospore which has two cells in *Puccinia* and one cell in *Uromyces* (Fig. 22). They are both very common and have large numbers of species adapted to particular hosts; the life cycles cover the whole range from microcyclic, to heteroecious and macrocyclic. In agriculture, *Puccinia* is generally more important on cereals and grasses whereas *Uromyces* is more often found on Leguminosae.

Pucciniastrum is heteroecious and macrocyclic producing spermogonia and aecia on *Abies*, *Picea* or *Tsuga*, and uredinia and telia on flowering plants including Orchidaceae. *P. vaccinii* (Winter) Jørst produces yellow-red uredinia on the undersides of *Vaccinium* leaves and other Ericaceae; aecia are not found, and telia are rarely produced in the UK.

Chrysomyxa is autoecious, heteroecious and macrocyclic, or microcyclic. Yellow telia form within yellow bands on *Picea* leaves (needles) and break through the epidermis the following spring. Basidiospores are produced from teliospores and infect the same host species if autoecious, or the alternate host if heteroecious. *Chrysomyxa ledi* de Bary occurs in northern Europe and produces aecia with a white collar (peridium) on *Picea* leaves; var. *rhododendri* produces telia on yellow bands on *Rhododendron* leaves and var. *ledi* produces similar symptoms on *Ledum*.

Coleosporium is heteroecious and macrocyclic producing spermogonia and aecia in silvery blisters on *Pinus*; yellow-orange uredinia and orange-red telia are produced on the lower leaf surface in Campanulaceae, Compositeae and Ranunuclaceae. *Coleosporium campanulae* (Pers.) Lév. affects *Campanula*; *C. solidaginis* (Schwein.) Thümen affects *Aster* and *Solidago*

a. *Narcissus* smoulder, *Botryotinia narcissicola*, on leaf

b. *Narcissus* smoulder on bulb

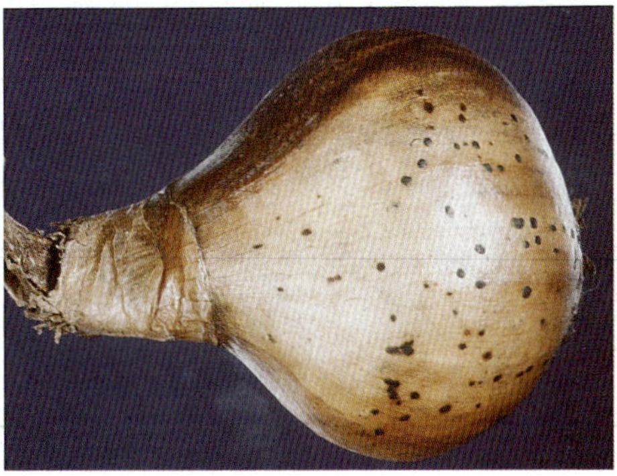

c. Sclerotia of *Narcissus* smoulder fungus

d. Tulip fire, *Botrytis tulipae*, showing leaf scorch and spotting

e. *Botryotinia galanthina* on *Galanthus* showing grey spores at soil level; black sclerotia develop on flower stem

f. Tulip fire showing spores on emerging shoot

a. Spots and scorch affecting both sides of *Rhododendron* leaf

b. *Coniothyrium* causing scorch on *Helleborus*

c. Leaf spot on *Hedera*

d. Red spot, *Stagonospora curtisii*, on *Hymenocallis*

e. Spores of *Hypericum* rust, *Melampsora hypericorum*, on leaf underside

Examples of primary and secondary infection; stunting and mosaic symptoms caused by virus infection

a. *Chenopodium amaranticolor* infected with arabis mosaic virus showing primary necrotic lesions on innoculated leaves

b. Healthy and narcissus yellow stripe infected narcissus plants (Courtesy A A Brunt)

c. Healthy and narcissus yellow stripe infected bulbs (Courtesy A A Brunt)

d. Marrow infected with cucumber mosaic virus

e. Iris infected with iris severe mosaic virus (Courtesy A A Brunt)

f. *Narcissus pseudonarcissus* infected with narcissus yellow stripe virus (Courtesy A A Brunt)

Examples of chlorotic and ringspot leaf symptoms

a. Veinal chlorosis caused by turnip mosaic virus in a mustard leaf

b. Potato showing chlorosis caused by arabis mosaic virus

c. Chlorotic veins in elderberry caused by arabis mosaic virus

d. Vein clearing in cauliflower caused by turnip mosaic virus

e. Necrotic ringspots in *Nicotiana clevelandii* caused by turnip mosaic virus

f. Chlorotic ringspots in *Primula* caused by cucumber mosaic and Monocotyledineae; *C. tussilaginis* (Pers.) Berk. affects *Campanula*, *Rhinanthus* and *Senecio*.

Cronartium is heteroecious and macrocyclic. Aecia cause yellow spotting of *Pinus* leaves (needles), and the mycelium is perennial and kills the ends of twigs. The disease causes considerable losses in European, Canadian and north American forests. Pale yellow uredinia and yellow-red telia are produced on the lower leaf surfaces of herbaceous plants including alpines and herbaceous plants such as *Impatiens*, *Nemesia*, *Paeonia*, *Pedicularis*, *Schizanthus*, *Tropaeolum*, *Verbena* and possibly *Gentiana* (*Cronartium flaccidum* (Alb. & Schwein.) Winter).

Endophyllum sempervivi de Bary is autoecious and microcyclic on *Sempervivum*. Yellow-brown aecia-like teliospores are produced below the leaf epidermis; uredinia are probably not produced.

Gymnosporangium is heteroecious and macrocyclic producing aecia on woody Rosaceae such as *Crataegus* species (hawthorn), *Chaenomeles*, *Cotoneaster*, *Pyrus* or *Sorbus*. The uredinial and telial stages are perennial in Cupressaceae, particularly *Juniperus*, causing witches brooms and galls, and killing the ends of twigs, e.g. *Gymnosporangium* species (See Table 27).

Melampsora is heteroecious and macrocyclic, autoecious or microcyclic. Aecia, often orange-coloured, usually affect herbaceous flowering plants (Plate 18e) including orchids, whereas uredinia and telia are produced on poplar or willow (See Table 27).

Phragmidium is autoecious and macrocyclic on woody Rosaceae such as raspberry (*Phragmidium rubi-idaei* (DC.) Karsten), rose (*P. mucronatum*

Figure 22 Differences in the resting spores (teliospores) of rust fungi

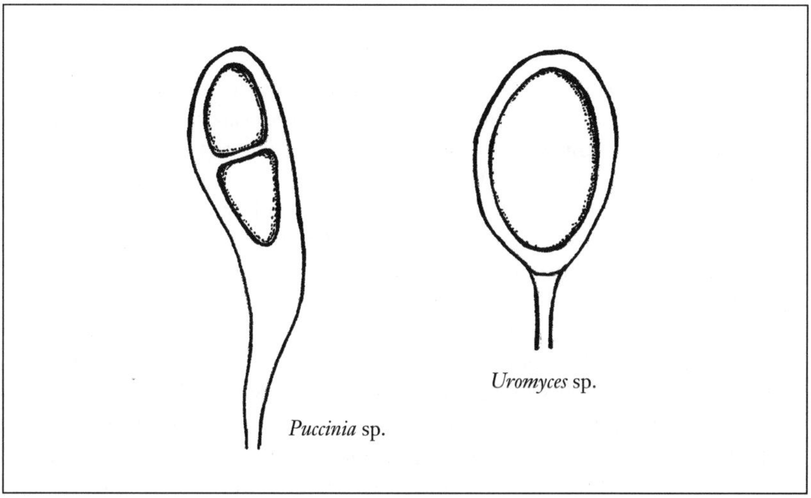

(Pers.) Schlect., *P. tuberculatum* Müller) or blackberry (*P. violaceum* (Schultz) Winter). Infected plants are stunted and have violet-spotted leaves which die early. Black sticky teliospores, with up to 10 cells, survive winter and the basidiospores infect emerging leaves in spring (See Table 27).

Tranzschelia is heteroecious and macrocyclic producing aecia on Ranunculaceae and the other stages on Rosaceae, or autoecious on Ranunculaceae.

Some other rusts

Cumminsiella mirabilissima (Peck) Nannf. is autoecious and macrocyclic on *Berberis* and *Mahonia*, causing red spots on leaves. The *Cumminsiella* aecium has a yellow collar (peridium) which distinguishes it from the less common *Puccinia graminis* which has a white peridium.

Melampsoridium betulinum (Fr.) Kleb. often affects birch (*Betula*) in late summer. The fungus is heteroecious and macrocyclic producing masses of yellow powdery uredinia on yellow spots, and dark telia on the lower leaf surface; aecia are produced on *Larix* leaves (needles) but the disease persists without alternation between hosts.

Ochropsora ariae (Fuckel) Ramsb. (anamorph *Aecidium anemones* Pers.) is heteroecious and macrocyclic, and produces spermogonia and aecia on the leaves and sepals of *Anemone nemorosa*, and uredinia and dark telia on *Malus*, *Pyrus* and *Sorbus* causing yellow spots which become tinged with red later in the season. The fungus also survives as mycelium in rhizomes, each year producing aecia on the leaves. In the past the aecia of this fungus have been named as *Tranzschelia anemones*.

Smuts

Smuts, of which there are nearly 1000 species, belong to the Class Ustilaginomycetes, Order Ustilaginales and are very common on Gramineae. The smuts are usually grouped with the rusts, but this does not mean that the two groups are closely related.

Smuts initially attack living tissue but later also live on dying tissue. Infected plants produce masses of powdery spores, which are usually dark – hence the name smut. The spores germinate at low temperatures (5-15°C) and damage often occurs in the cooler months of the year. The spores are blown for short distances and fall to the ground where they generally survive for several years; however, some smut species produce spores which survive for only a few days. One group, the **anther smuts**, has spores which are carried between plants by insects as they visit flowers. **Loose smuts** arise from mycelium already within the plant which then invades the flowers and large numbers of seeds become infected by mycelium. **Covered smuts** infect individual ovaries and hence are limited to a few seeds and the spores replace the seed within the seed wall. The spores are released when the seed coat is broken and contaminate the outside of large numbers of seed but leaving the embryo free of infection; This difference in the role of spores between loose and covered smuts obviously affects the choice of control method (See below).

The powdery spores produced by smuts are teliospores (See also Rusts, p.138), also called **ustilospores** or 'brand spores'. Each ustilospore has a thin inner wall and a thicker outer wall, the latter being patterned with tiny spines or ridges which are useful in identification. Ustilospores produce basidiospores which infect leaves or seedlings; a secondary mycelium is produced in the plant which invades underground stems and buds, colonises dividing (meristematic) tissue and thereby becomes systemic and perennial in the plant. A large number of smut species colonise flowers and infect the young ovary, producing spores in place of seeds. When infection is systemic in the host, the mycelium grows into the young flowering shoot and most of the flowers become infected.

Individual smut species are usually restricted to a single host or to their close relatives; unlike the rusts, there is no alternation of hosts.

Symptoms

Smuts rarely kill plants but distort leaves, reduce growth, spoil flowers and ruin the seeds. Infection causes blisters to form on soft tissue such as leaves, petioles, flower bracts and rhizomes, roots and corms; often the blisters follow the direction of veins and hence are long and narrow as in *Iris* and *Colchicum*. The blisters burst, releasing masses of powdery spores which are usually dark brown or purplish as in anther smut of campion (*Silene*) and onion smut; however some species of *Entyloma* have yellow or pale brown spores. The presence of smut spores on the surface of seeds or within the seeds is very characteristic of smuts. Woody tissue is not affected.

Life cycle

The basic life cycle comprises the standard stages of cell fusion (plasmogamy), and nuclear fusion (karyogamy) followed by reduction division (meiosis). Basidiospores, sometimes called **sporidia**, are produced from ustilospores and contain a single haploid nucleus; they germinate to produce a primary mycelium, also with one nucleus per cell, which then infects the host. Sometimes basidiospores produce additional, secondary, basidiospores, which also infect the host. Hyphae of compatible mating types fuse (plasmogamy) within the infected host to produce a binucleate or dikaryotic secondary mycelium; alternatively, dikaryotisation takes place by fusion between compatible basidiospores or between a basidiospore and a compatible hypha. It is the secondary mycelium which forms the greater part of the life cycle of smuts. The secondary mycelium grows extensively within the host eventually producing smut balls comprising groups of ustilospores often of characteristic appearance. The secondary mycelium produces vegetative spores (conidia, also called sporidia), usually whitish in colour, which start new infections on the same or on different host plants; *Primula* smut (*Urocystis primulicola*) is an example.

Nuclear fusion (karyogamy) and reduction division (meiosis) take place when teliospores germinate, the precise timing of the two processes varying between smut species. However, the end result is that several basidiospores are produced, contrasting with the four basidiospores produced by rusts. Most smuts are heterothallic and bipolar so that half the basidiospores contain nuclei of one mating type **A**, and half contain nuclei with the **a** mating type.

Control

Covered smuts are easier to control because the spores are confined to the outside of the seed; the seeds are usually treated with a contact fungicide, or with a systemic fungicide which also has contact action, to kill the spores. Loose smuts infect the inside of seeds; therefore infection is killed by dipping the seed in hot water or by treatment with a systemic fungicide usually of the oxathiin (carboxin) or benzimidazole (benomyl) group. Fungicides which contain mercury, such as calomel, are now banned in the UK. Both types of treatments have been developed mainly for cereals. Clearly there is a risk that they may damage the seed, especially if the seed is small. As result these methods are either not readily available to the gardener, or are not recommended because too little is known about the particular species of plants involved. Probably the safest action is to remove infected host tissue, particularly flowers, as soon as possible after infection is seen, taking care not to disperse the spores; the infected plant material should be burnt. When infection is suspected in the whole plant – for instance when smut blisters are found on underground stems, or perennial plants have swollen, distorted shoots which produce flowers with smut blisters – they should preferably be destroyed; they should never be used for propagation.

Individual smuts are described in Tables 27 and 28.

Other basidiomycetes

Rhizoctonia and *Rhizoctonia*-like fungi

These two groups of fungi are responsible for killing seed, for pre- and post emergence damping-off in seedlings, stem rots in growing plants and decay in cuttings during propagation; some are responsible for web-blight in *Azalea* (*Rhododendron*). Different forms live on dead plant tissue, or they infect living plants and either kill them or, in contrast, assist in the uptake of nutrients – particularly with orchids.

Originally there was considerable confusion over the identity of this group of fungi, mainly because of similarities in the appearance of hyphae, and the difficulties in producing the basidiospore stage. We now know that there are three main groups based on the numbers of nuclei per cell and the form of the sexual stage. Isolates in the first group have three or more nuclei per cell, and a sexual state named *Thanatephorus* Donk, those in the second group have two nuclei per cell, and a sexual state named *Ceratobasidium* Rogers, and isolates in the third group also have several nuclei per cell, and the sexual state is called

Waitea Warcup & Talbot (See Table 25). The groups are further subdivided on the basis of the capacity to fuse (anastomose) with each other in culture. Isolates which fuse are said to belong to the same **anastomosis group**, abbreviated to AG, whereas isolates in different AGs do not fuse. *Rhizoctonia solani* Kühn, the vegetative state of *Thanatephorus cucumeris* (Frank) Donk has, at the time of writing, nine AGs of which four are important in the present context (Table 25). Similarly, *Ceratobasidium* has fifteen *Ceratobasidium* **anastomosis group**s, or CAGs. CAG 3 and CAG 7 cause web blights in *Azalea* (*Rhododendron*) but since they require temperatures of 24-27°C they are confined to warm climates, particularly the southern states of the USA. The *Waitea* group is not important in ornamental horticulture.

Rhizoctonia solani infects seeds either when they are still on the plant – for example if splashed with soil, or in the soil after sowing. The seeds rot and provide the fungus with a food base from which to spread to neighbouring seedlings causing pre-emergence damping-off. Infection can continue at any time until seedlings are past the susceptible juvenile stage. The damping-off symptoms are somewhat similar to those of *Pythium*; however, *Rhizoctonia* usually attacks at soil level and grows downwards into the roots whereas *Pythium* infects root tips and grows upwards. The pale brown colour and greater width of *Rhizoctonia* hyphae (x 10 hand lens is useful) help to distinguish them from the pale thin hyphae of *Pythium*. In contrast to infection by *Pythium*, mature as well as young tissue is attacked causing cankers or **wirestem** symptoms on the hypocotyl or stem. An example is the 'neck' rot in *Gladiolus* plants, either from soil or from infected corms, which then spreads down into the corm. Leaves in contact with soil may also become infected, the disease spreading along the leaf petiole to the stem which is girdled and collapses. *Lilium* scales are affected in a similar manner (Plate 15e). The fungus is a serious problem in vegetative propagation usually attacking the stem at the surface of the rooting medium but leaving the roots intact. (*Rhizoctonia* is also responsible for 'black scab' on potato tubers, which is very

Table 25 **Diseases caused by *Thanatephorus* (*Rhizoctonia*)**

Anastomosis group	Host range	Symptom
1	Leguminosae, Graminae	seed and hypocotyl rots, aerial and web blight
2	Chenopodiacae, Cruciferae, Graminae	root rot of conifers, canker on root crops
3	Solanaceae, Graminae	stem canker of potato, root rot in barley, seed rot
4	Chenopodiaceae, Leguminosae, Solanaceae	seed, hypocotyl rots

common and recognised by the presence of flat black sclerotia.)

Infection is best controlled by a combination of good hygiene – clean seed trays, pots, etc., avoiding seed from diseased flowers and avoiding overwatering. Fungicides are also effective, for example benomyl, iprodione, mancozeb, maneb or thiram, dusted onto seeds, or applied either as a dip to the base of cuttings or watered on the cuttings afterwards. As with all pesticide treatments it is essential to follow the manufacturers Recommendations regarding suitability, safety, and the possibility of damage to plants.

Rhizoctonia tuliparum (Kleb.) Whetzel & Arthur (syn. *Sclerotium tuliparum*) infects *Tulip* and *Iris* bulbs and is very different from *R. solani*. Infection starts from sclerotia in soil in winter, the stem being affected first followed by the bulbs. The rot is initially greyish and later turns brown. Control is based on hygiene and sanitation – infected bulbs should not be planted, and contaminated soil should be avoided.

Honey fungus

Honey fungus or *Armillaria mellea* (Vahl ex Fr.) Kummer attacks tree or shrub roots in gardens, parks and woodland. Another name for this fungus, *Armillariella mellea* (Vahl ex Fr.) Karst., is no longer used. As generally understood, *A. mellea* comprises several species which differ in their aggressiveness, the hosts they attack, their reaction in culture, and their soil requirements. The name *A. mellea*, as used in an up-to-date sense, refers to the honey fungus which occurs in alkaline soil and attacks a wide range of healthy broad-leaved shrubs and trees, and conifers which have been damaged or stressed in some way (Table 26). In contrast, *A. ostoyae* occurs in acid soil and is able to attack conifers which are healthy. Both fungi are widespread.

There are two distinct types of damage: infected shrubs and trees either slowly decline in vigour, or they collapse rapidly, particularly in dry weather. The bark at the base of the plant becomes loose and a whitish weft of mycelium grows upwards from the roots between the wood and the bark. Black strands called rhizomorphs, which look like boot-laces, develop on the roots and below the bark. The branches die because infected roots cannot supply sufficient water. Later, brown or honey-coloured toadstools develop in clumps on the base of the plant. Rotten roots or stumps contain black lines, specialised structures called **pseudosclerotia**, which protect the hyphae and ensure survival. Plants killed by weak species of honey fungus, such as *A. bulbosa*, often sprout again from the base, whereas plants killed by *A. mellea* do not recover.

A. mellea survives as mycelia in the black lines (pseudosclerotia) in rotten roots, etc., or as rhizomorphs on pieces of woody root, trunks or stumps. Rhizomorphs of the aggressive species (See Table 26) produce mycelium which enters the root and spreads up the roots system to soil level and above, and forms whitish 'fans' just below the bark; black rhizomorphs are also produced. The rhizomorphs grow through the soil, using the dead wood as a food base, until another host is located, and the cycle of infection and spread starts again. Spores produced on the toadstools seem to play little part in the life cycle.

Armillaria species fall into two distinct groups, one comprising aggressive parasites (e.g. *A. mellea*, *A. ostoyae*) which can kill healthy plants, the second comprising weak parasites (*A. borealis*, *A. bulbosa* and *A. cepaestipes*) which only attack plants which have been damaged, for example by pruning or grazing by animals, or weakened, for example by drought, water logging, frost, soil compaction, crowding, or insect or fungal attack. These weak *Armillaria* species colonise roots but remain inactive until the plant is stressed. Then they rapidly colonise the root system, using it as a food base from which to spread to neighbouring plants. Spread can be as mycelium growing along roots or as rhzimorphs growing through soil. Hence the infection starts from one plant, then spreads outwards.

The key factor to control is the removal of the infected stump and woody roots to deprive the fungus of its food base. Ideally the soil should be removed from a hole about 0.5 m in depth and 1 m across, and passed through a 2.5 cm sieve (a sieve is cheaply made from wire mesh stretched over a wood frame). It also pays to provide the plant with good growing conditions and thereby minimise stress. Chemicals are of doubtful value chiefly because of the difficulties in ensuring adequate contact between chemical and fungus. In the future, it seems likely that control measures will be based on the idea of using chemicals to weaken the rhizomorphs and hence make them susceptible to attack by organisms already present in soil.

Table 26 **Honey fungus species on shrubs and trees**

Armillaria species	Hosts attacked	Type of attack	State of host
A. borealis	insufficient information	weak	stressed, damaged
A. bulbosa	mostly broad-leaved	weak	stressed, damaged
A. cepaestipes	insufficient information	weak	stressed, damaged
A. mellea	mostly broad-leaved	aggressive	healthy
	conifers	weak	stressed, damaged
A. obscura	mostly conifers	aggressive	healthy
A. ostoyae	conifers, mainly pine	aggressive	healthy

BACTERIA

Bacteria belong to the Prokaryotae which differ from the Eukaryotae – the organisms described so far up to now – by their smaller size, absence of nuclear membrane, absence of organelles such as mitochondria, genetic information carried on a single strand of DNA (rather than on chromosomes), thinner cell walls and simple flagellae. Some forms of bacteria produce capsules or spores which are highly resistant to extremes of temperature or moisture, and survive on the outside of seed or in dry soil.

Individual bacteria are very small and cannot be seen with the naked eye. They can divide about once an hour and hence have an enormous potential for increase. Some bacteria have flagellae and are motile, although they move only minute distances. As with the fungi, some bacteria live on decaying plant tissue whereas others have more specific requirements and may be restricted to a single host plant species or cultivar.

Some bacterial species affect the soft tissue of almost any host plant species e.g. *Erwinia caratovora* subsp. *carotovora*. Some only gain entry through natural openings such as stomata, lenticels, hydathodes, the cut surface in plant cuttings, or if wounded for example by eelworms. Others only infect particular host plant species or varieties and cannot spread between different host plant species; examples are some species of *Erwinia*, *Pseudomonas* and *Xanthomonas*. All types of plant pathogenic bacteria require moist or wet conditions in order to multiply and spread; they are called opportunistic when they cause damage only when the host is wounded. Infected vegetative plant material such as bulbs, corms, etc., or cuttings are all sources of plant pathogenic bacteria; bacteria can also be carried by true seed.

In contrast to the plant pathogenic bacteria, some types of bacteria are extremely beneficial to the host plant, notably those which fix nitrogen and contribute to the nutrition of the host plant. There is also a group called the rhizobacteria which colonise roots and enhance the growth of the host, or protect the roots against soil-borne disease fungi.

Classification and nomenclature

Bacteria were first classified by their shape and appearance of the cell, flagellum, spore, etc. in much the same way as the fungi. This was unsatisfactory because bacteria often look the same but have totally different nutrient requirements for growth and are adapted to different plants. The biochemical basis for these differences is exploited and has given rise to standard tests for identification. One such test is the LOPAT test used in the identification of plant pathogenic bacteria; LOPAT is an acronym derived from the initial letters of a series of five different cultural and chemical tests. Information from biochemical tests can be supplemented by knowledge of the host range. This is not entirely satisfactory because of the likelihood that the host range is incompletely known. This lead to the development of a system for identifying bacteria as **pathovars** based on their reaction to a defined range of plant host species.

Symptoms

Once infected the host tissue often dies and becomes brown. If wet, the dead tissue collapses and rots; if dry it becomes becomes necrotic. Spots are common on leaves because the bacteria can enter through stomata, and hydathodes. The spot may be rather angular if a vein limits further development e.g. *Pseudomonas syringae* pv. *syringae* on lilac; or it may be surrounded by a yellow circle or halo, caused by the outward diffusion of bacterial toxins e.g. *Pseudomonas syringae* pv. *phaseolicola* on bean. The original pathogen is often followed by different bacteria which live on the dying tissue but which are not pathogenic, and produce leaf spots. In dry weather the centre of the spot drops away causing a 'shot hole' symptom; this is quite commonly seen on *Prunus* trees but note that several leaf spot fungi also cause shot hole symptoms.

Once inside the plant the bacteria multiply and spread in the intercellular spaces. This causes the plant to wilt, for example if the vascular system is blocked; or the symptoms may be limited to a slight stunting. Fireblight, caused by *Erwinia amylovora*, enters the flowers and then spreads to the shoots, infects the shoot tip, and rapidly colonises the parenchyma and collenchyma; the shoot tip withers and dies as infection progresses down the shoot.

Several types of bacteria upset the balance of hormones in the plant causing the tissue to proliferate and form galls or cankers. Examples include root nodules caused by nitrogen fixing bacteria, and crown gall caused by *Agrobacterium*. Cankers are produced on woody tissue and are perennial; bacterial activity frequently slows down in cold weather, renewing as the weather becomes warmer the following year – sometimes causing a bacterial ooze.

Control

The most practicable control measures are based on a combination of hygiene and sanitation. In situations where bacteria may be a problem, e.g. in large scale propagation by cuttings, care should be taken to use only healthy plant material and to disinfect knives in household bleach (1:100 dilution, 500-1000 ppm available chlorine) at regular intervals, to minimise the risk of spreading the bacteria. For similar reasons, powder formulations of rooting hormone are preferable to liquid formulations. Infected tubers and rhizomes can sometimes be saved by cutting away the diseased tissue.

Bacterial spread on leaves or flowers may be checked by sprays containing copper compounds, but deep-seated infection is unlikely to be controlled because of the difficulties of penetration of the spray.

Individual species of bacteria which may occur are described below.

Agrobacterium tumefaciens produces roundish galls on the underground and aerial plant parts of a very wide range of hosts.

Corynebacterium fascians (syn. *Rhodoccocus fascians*) causes the peculiar flattening of stems of a wide range of host plant species but does little damage otherwise.

Erwinia amylovora causes fireblight, recognized initially by the death of twigs, later whole branches. The bacterium infects flowers and then spreads to other soft tissue by rain splash or insects, and eventually forms cankers on wood tissue; bacteria from the cankers then provide a source of bacteria in future years. The disease is common on Rosaceae such as *Cotoneaster*, *Crataegus*, *Pyracantha* and *Stransvaesia*.

Erwinia caratovora subsp. *carotovora* causes a wilt and crown rot of *Primula* and a soft rot in *Arum* and *Iris* rhizomes.

Pseudomonas caryophylli and *Erwinia chrysanthemi* pv. *dianthicola* causes wilt in carnation (*Dianthus caryophyllus*). The bacterium is transmitted by infected cuttings, or in irrigation water draining from infected stock plants. It is unlikely to be a problem and then only in large-scale propagation and is unlikely to affect the alpine gardener.

Pseudomonas gladioli exists as several pathovars but they become a problem only in storage and then only at high temperatures.

Pseudomonas syringae pv. *syringae* is said to cause leaf spots on *Syringa*, pv. *delphinii* on *Delphinium*.

Xanthomonas campestris pv. *hyacinthi* causes 'yellow disease' of *Hyacinthus orientalis*, which results in the development of yellow streaks inside the bulb. Infected bulbs may not flower.

In summary, bacteria are unlikely to cause problems for the horticulturalists except possibly during propagation by bulbs, corms, etc., or cuttings when they are easily distributed.

Recommended Reading 'Methods for the diagnosis of bacterial disease in plants.' (Lelliott & Stead, 1987)

Table 27 **Selected fungal pathogens**

FUNGUS	PLANT	PART AFFECTED	SYMPTOM	SEASON
Albugo candida	Cruciferae incl. *Arabis*, *Cardamine*, *Matthiola*	above ground parts	distortion, powdery white pustules	spring-autumn
Alternaria cheiranthi	*Cheiranthu*	living leaf, stem	red-brown spot	spring-autumn
A. dianthi	*Dianthus* incl. *D. caryophyllus*, *D. barbatus*	living leaf, stem	purple-brown spot, yellow edge girdling canker, death	summer
A. violae	*Viola*	living leaf	pale brown zonate spot	summer
Aschochyta primulae	*Primula vulgaris*	living leaf	large, white spot, yellow edge	late summer
A. vincae	*Vinca major*, *V. minor*	living leaf	large, pale brown spot, dark edge	spring
A. violae	*Viola odorata* and cultivated spp.	living leaf	white-brown spot, 'shot hole'	spring-autumn
Bremia lactucae	wide range of Compositae	living leaf	yellow spot, white felty growth, tissue death	all
Bremiella megasperma	*Viola*			
Botryotinia convoluta	rhizomatous *Iris*	rhizome	black, convoluted sclerotia	all
B. draytoni (=*Botrytis gladiolorum*)	*Gladiolus*	corm, living leaf flower	brown sunken specks on corm and hard rot leaf yellow and wilt, flower spot	all
B. fuckeliana (=*Botrytis cinerea*)	wide range of herbaceous species	any soft tissue	brown spot on leaf or flower; 'grey mould' brown rot on cuttings, seedling collapse	all
B. narcissicola	*Narcissus*, *Galanthus*	living leaf, bulb, flower	collapse, rot ('smoulder'), poor flowering	spring-summer
B. polyblastis	*Narcissus* incl. *N. pseudonarcissus*	living leaf, flower	spreading yellow-brown blotch ('fire')	spring
Botrytis elliptica	*Lilium*	living leaf, flower shoot	brown spot	spring-summer
B. cinerea (see *Botryotinia fuckeliana*)		–	–	–
B. galanthina	*Galanthus*	bulb; shoot; flower	bulb rot, sclerotia; brown spot, collapse	spring
B. hyacinthi	*Lilium regale*, *Muscari*, *Hyacinthus*	bulb	spreading brown lesion ('fire')	spring
B. paeoniae	*Paeonia*	living leaf, stem	wilt, brown spot; sclerotia (1 mm)	spring
B. tulipae	*Tulipa*, *Lilium*	soft tissue	spreading brown lesion ('fire')	spring
Cainiella johansonii	*Dryas*	living petiole	small brown spot	summer
Cercoseptoria handelii	*Rhododendron*	living leaf	brown-purple spot, dark purple edge	summer
Cercosporella primulae	*Primula vulgaris*	living leaf	brown spot, grey centre	summer

Table 27 (continued) **Selected fungal pathogens**

FUNGUS	PLANT	PART AFFECTED	SYMPTOM	SEASON
Cercospora violae	*Viola* e.g. *V. canina*, *V. riviniana*	living leaf	grey-brown spot	summer
Chalara elegans (see *Thielaviopsis basicola*)		–	–	–
Chrysomyxa rhododendri	*Rhododendron* (alternate host=*Picea*)	lower surface of living leaf	orange-red rust spot	summer
Cladosporium orchidis	*Dactylorhiza*	living leaf	large, dark spot	summer
Coleosporium tussilaginis	*Pinus nigra*, *P. sylvestris*, Compositae	living leaf	yellow rust spot	spring
	Campanula rotundifolia, *Euphrasia*, *Rhinanthus*	living leaf	yellow to orange-red rust spot	summer
Colletotrichum malvarum	*Malva*, *Lavatera*	stem	brown spot	summer
C. trichellum	*Hedera*	living or dead leaf	brown dark-edged spot (0.1 mm)	all
Coniothyrium hellebori	*Helleborus* e.g. *H. viridis*	leaf, stem, flower	spot, streak, stem collapse	spring
Corticium rolfsii	wide range of herbaceous species	stem, root, bulb	white hyphae, orange sclerotia	warm temps only
Cryptocline paradoxa	*Hedera*	living leaf	orange-yellow spot	summer
Cumminsiella mirabilissima	*Mahonia*	living leaf	red rust spot	all
Dendryphion nanum	Cruciferae, Umbeliferae	living leaf	black mould	summer
Dennisiella babingtonii	*Rhododendron* and other evergreens	living leaf	sooty mould	all
Diaporthe eumorpha	*Vinca major*, *V. minor*	living stem	blackening, dark spot 0.2-0.5 mm	summer
Didymella ligulicola	*Chrysanthemum* (ray blight)	leaf, stem, bud, flower	brown blotch, black spot	summer
Dothidea puccinioides	*Daphne*, *Ulex*	dead branch	black spot <5 mm	all
Drechslera iridis	*Iris* (ink disease)	living, dying leaf	brown oval spot or black streak	summer
Dumontinia tuberosa (=*Sclerotinia tuberosa*)	*Anemone* e.g. *A. nemorosa*, *A. blanda*	rhizome	brown apothecia with long stalk	summer-autumn
Ectostroma iridis	*Iris pseudacorus*	living leaf	black spot, yellow halo	summer
Entyloma eryngii	*Eryngium*	living leaf	pale brown raised spot <5 mm	autumn
E. fergussoni	*Myosotis*	living leaf	pale brown spot	mid-summer
Erysiphe aquilegiae	*Aquilegia*, *Caltha*	living leaf	white powdery mildew	summer
E. asperifoliorum	Boraginaceae incl. *Myosotis*, *Cynoglossum*	living leaf	white powdery mildew	summer
E. cichoracearum	Compositae incl. *Aster*, *Centaurea*, *Phlox*	living leaf	white powdery mildew	summer

Table 27 (continued) **Selected fungal pathogens**

FUNGUS	PLANT	PART AFFECTED	SYMPTOM	SEASON
E. cruciferarum	Cruciferae incl. *Cheiranthus*	living leaf	white powdery mildew	summer
E. galeopsidis	*Lamium*	living leaf	white powdery mildew	summer
E. hyperici	*Hypericum*	living leaf	white powdery mildew	summer
E. knautiae	*Knautia*	living leaf	white powdery mildew	summer
E. ranunculi	*Adonis vernalis*, *Delphinium*, *Ranunculus*	living leaf	white powdery mildew	summer
E. trifolii	*Cytisus*, *Trifolium*	living leaf	white powdery mildew	summer
E. verbasci	*Verbascum* e.g. *V. nigrum*, *V. thaspus*	living leaf	white powdery mildew	summer
Eupenicillium crustaceum	Iridaceae incl. *Crocus*, *Gladiolus*	stored corms	blue-green powdery mould	autumm-spring
Exobasidium vaccinii	*Rhododendron*, *Vaccinium*	living leaf	thickening and distortion, powdery white	summer
Fusarium culmorum	wide range of herbaceous species	seedlings	collapse, damping-off	all
Fusarium oxysporum				
f.sp. *cyclaminis*	*Cyclamen*	corm	low vigour, pink rot	summer
f.sp. *dianthi*	*Dianthus*	stem	lesion spreading from leaf base to shoots on one side of plant; stunting wilt	summer
f.sp. *gladioli*	*Gladiolus*, *Iris*, *Crocus*	corm; living leaf	corm dry rot; wilt	summer
f.sp. *lilii*	*Lilium* (*Fusarium* scale rot)	bulb; living leaf	scale dry rot; wilt	summer
f.sp. *narcissi*	*Narcissus*	bulb, root; living leaf	bulb and root rot; leaf tip die-back	early summer
f.sp. *tulipae*	*Tulipa*		bulb and root rot; leaf tip die-back	early summer
Gemmamyces piceae	*Picea engelmannii*, *P. pungens* var. *glauca*	bud swelling, distortion	June-December	
Gloeosporium rhododendri	*Rhododendron*	leaf	brown purple-edged spot	all
Gymnosporangium cornutum	*Juniperus communis*, *Sorbus*	living leaf or stem	orange-brown spot	spring
Haplobasidion thalictri	*Aquilegia*, *Thalictrum*	living leaf	brown purple-edged spot	summer
Helicobasidium brebbissonii (=*H. purpureum*, =*Rhizoctonia crocorum*)	wide range of herbaceous species incl. *Viola*, *Crocus*	underground parts	purple specks on surface	all

Table 27 (continued) **Selected fungal pathogens**

FUNGUS	PLANT	PART AFFECTED	SYMPTOM	SEASON
Herpotrichia juniperi	*Juniperus*	living leaf or branch	black specks	all
Heterosphaeria (Heteropatella) antirrhini	*Antirrhinum* e.g. *A. majus*, *A. orontium*	living leaf	small dark spot; 'shot hole'	summer
Isothea rhytismoides	*Dryas*	living leaf	red-black spot <5mm	summer
Leptosphaerulina myrtillina	*Vaccinium*	living leaf, stem	brown purple-edged spot	autumn
Leveillula taurica	Compositae	living leaf, stem	white powdery mildew	summer
Lophodermella conjuncta	*Pinus* e.g. *P. nigra*, *P. sylvestris*	living leaf	discolouring; apothecia	spring-summer
Macrophoma falconeri	*Rhododendron falconeri*	edge of living leaf	large red-brown spot	autumn
Marssonina daphnes	*Daphne mezereum*	dying leaf	brown spot	autumn
Melampsora epitea	*Orchidaceae*	living leaf	orange rust	summer
M. euphorbiae	*Euphorbia*	living leaf	brown rust	summer
M. hypericorum	*Hypericum*	living leaf	orange red-brown rust	spring-summer
Melampsorella caryophyllacearum	*Cerastium* e.g. *C. tomentosum*	living leaf	orange-yellow rust	summer
Melampsoridium betulinum	*Betula*		yellow rust	autumn
Microsphaera berberidis	*Berberis thunbergii*, *B. vulgaris*, *Mahonia*	living leaf	white powdery mildew	summer
M. euonymi-japonici	*Euonymus japonicus*	living leaf	white powdery mildew	summer
M. mytillina	*Vaccinium*	living leaf	white powdery mildew	summer
M. viburni	*Viburnum opulus*	living leaf	white powdery mildew	summer
Monochaetia karstenii	*Rhododendron*	living leaf	white or brown spot	autumn
Mycocentrospora acerina	*Aquilegia*, *Campanula*, *Geum*, *Myosotis*, *Omphalodes*, *Ranunculus*, *Viola*	root, living leaf	root collapse; white spot, dark spores on leaf	summer
Mycosphaerella brunneola	*Convallaria majalis*	living leaf, flower stalk	white spot	spring
M. dianthi	*Dianthus barbatus*, *D. caryophyllus*	living leaf, inflorescence	spot, collapse	summer
M. buxicola	*Buxus*	living leaf	white spot, brown edge	spring
M. hedericola	*Hedera*	living leaf	white spot, brown edge	summer
M. macrospora	*Iris*, *Gladiolus*	living or dying leaf	oval brown spot	summer-autumn

Table 27 (continued) **Selected fungal pathogens**

FUNGUS	PLANT	PART AFFECTED	SYMPTOM	SEASON
M. rhododendri	*Rhododendron*	living or dead leaf	dark spot	spring
Myrothecium roridum	*Antirrhinum*, *Viola* e.g. *V. tricolor*	living leaf, stem	pale brown spot, 'shot hole'	early summer
Nectria cinnabarina	wide range of woody species e.g. *Acer*	dead twig, wounds	salmon-coloured pustules	all
Ochropsora ariae	*Anemone nemorosa*, *Sorbus*	living leaf	yellow-red rust	all
Ovulinia azaleae	*Rhododendron*	flower	brown spot	summer
Penicillium corymbiferum	*Gladiolus*, *Iris*, *Hyacinthus*	bulb, corm	blue-green powdery mould	all
Peronospora agrestis	*Veronica*	seedling, living leaf, flower	yellow-brown or purple spot	spring-summer
P. anemones	*Anemone coronaria*, *A. globosa*			
P. antirrhini	*Antirrhinum majus*, *A. orontium*			
P. arborescens	*Meconopsis betonicifolia*, *M. simplicifolia*			
P. conglomerata	*Geranium* e.g. *G. molle*, *G. pusillum*			
P. dentariae	*Cardamine* e.g. *C. pratense*,*C. amara*			
P. destructor	*Allium*			
P. dianthi	*Dianthus chinensis*			
P. dianthicola	*Dianthus caryophyllus*			
P. erodii	*Erodium*			
P. euphorbiae	*Euphorbia*			
P. ficariae	*Anemone* e.g. *A. nemorosa*, *Ranunculus*			
P. galligena	*Allysum saxatile*			
P. gei	*Geum*			
P. grisea	Shrubby *Hebe* (=*Veronica*) species			
P. lamii	*Lamium*			
P. leptoclada	*Helianthemum*			
P. myosotidis	*Myosotis* e.g. *M. arvensis*, *M. rampsissima*			
P. oerteliana	*Primula* e.g. *P. veris*, *P. vulgaris*			
P. parasitica	Cruciferae incl. *Aubretia*, *Cheiranthus*, *Dionysia*, *Iberis*, *Matthiola*			

Table 27 (continued) **Selected fungal pathogens**

FUNGUS	PLANT	PART AFFECTED	SYMPTOM	SEASON
P. pulveracea	*Helleborus niger*			
P. radii	*Chrysanthemum* e.g. *C. segetum*			
P. ranunculi	*Ranunculus*			
P. verbasci	*Verbascum* e.g. *V. nigrum*, *V. thaspus*	seedling, living leaf, flower	yellow-brown or purple spot	
P. violacea	*Knautia*			
P. violae	*Viola calcarata*, *V. cornuta*, *V. tricolor*, *V. wittrockiana*			spring-summer
Phialophora asteris	*Aster*	living stem	yellow leaf, brown blotch, wilt	summer
P. cinerescens	*Dianthus caryophyllus*		reddish leaf, vascular browning	
Phacidium infestans	*Pinus sylvestris*	living leaf	grey spot	summer
Phoma exigua var. *exigua*	wide range of herbaceous species	dying leaf, stem	black speck	summer-autumn
P. exigua var. *lilacis*	*Syringa*	seedling	collapse, damping-off	all
P. hedericola	*Hedera*	living leaf	white brown-edged spot	all
Phomatospora gelatinospora	*Rhododendron*	dead, attached leaf	clusters of dark specks	spring
Phomopsis caryophylli	*Dianthus* e.g. *D. barbatus*, *D. caryophyllus*	living leaf	white patch turning black	summer
P. juniperovora	*Juniperus*	living leaf or twig	collapse, die-back	summer
Phyllosticta primulicola	*Primula*	leaf	brown spot	spring-summer
Physalospora vitis-idaeae	*Vaccinium vitis-idaea*	living leaf	dark specks	autumn
Phytophthora cactorum	>100 species incl. *Erica*, *Lilium*, *Primula*			
P. cinnamomi	>1000 species, many conifers			
P. cryptogea	*Tulipa* and many conifers			
P. erythroseptica	*Tulipa*			
P. fragariae	*Dryas*, *Geum*, *Potentilla*	root, crown, stem	root and crown rot, poor growth	all
P. porri	*Allium*, *Campanula*, *Dianthus*, *Gladiolus*			
P. primulae	*Primula*			
P. verrucosa	*Primula*			
Plasmodiophora brassica	Cruciferae incl. *Cheiranthus*	root, underground stem	swelling, distortion, low vigour	all

Table 27 (continued) **Selected fungal pathogens**

FUNGUS	PLANT	PART AFFECTED	SYMPTOM	SEASON
Plasmopara halstedii	wide range of Compositae	living leaf	pale spot, tissue collapse	spring-summer
P. pygmaea	*Anemone nemorosa*			
Podosphaera myrtillina	*Vaccinium myrtilis*	living leaf	white powdery mildew	summer
Puccinia allii	*Allium*	living leaf, petiole, stem	yellow-orange-brown spots swelling, witches broom	mostly summer
P. antirrhini	*Antirrhinum majus*			
P. arenariae	Caryophyllaceae incl. *Arenaria*, *Dianthus* *Gypsophila*, *Silene*, *Lychnis*			
P. bistortae	*Polygonum bistortae*			
P. buxi	*Buxus*			
P. calcitrapae	Compositae incl. *Centaurea*, *Carlina*			
P. calthae; *P. calthicola*	*Caltha*			
P. cnici-oleracei	Compositae incl. *Achillea*, *Aster*			
P. campanulae	*Campanula* e.g. *C. rotundifolia*; *Jasione*			
P. fergussonii	*Viola*			
P. gentianae	*Gentiana* e.g. *G. verna*, *G. acaulis*			
P. hieracii	Compositae incl. *Hieracium*, *Centaurea*			
P. hordei	*Ornithagalum*			
P. iridis	*Iris* e.g. *I. foetidissima*			
P. liliacearum	*Ornithagalum*			
P. malvacearum	*Althaea*, *Lavatera*, *Malva*			
P. menthae	Labiateae incl. *Calamintha*, *Mentha*, *Origanum*			
P. oxalidis	*Oxalis*			
P. primulae	*Primula vulgaris*			
P. recondita	Ranuculaceae, Boraginaceae incl. *Anchusa*			
P. saxifragae	*Saxifraga stellaris*, *S. umbrosa*			
P. sessilis	*Arum*, *Convallaria*, *Dactylorhiza*			

Table 27 (continued) **Selected fungal pathogens**

FUNGUS	PLANT	PART AFFECTED	SYMPTOM	SEASON
P. schoeteri	*Narcissus* e.g. *N. jonquila*, *N. pseudonarcissus*			
P. sessilis	*Arum*, *Galanthus*, *Narcissus*, *Sternbergia*			
P. thymi	*Origanum*, *Thymus*	living leaf, petiole, stem	yellow-orange-brown spots	mostly summer
P. veronicae	*Veronica*		swelling, witches broom	
P. vincae	*Vinca*			
P. violae	*Viola* e.g. *V. cornuta*, *V. lutea*, *V. odorata*			
Pucciniastrum vaccinii	*Vaccinium*	living leaf	yellow-red rust spot	summer
Pycnostysanus azaleae	*Rhododendron*	living leaf, twig	brown-silvery spiny buds, shoot die-back	spring-summer
Pythium oligandrum	*Viola* (stem rot)			
P. ultimum	*Hyacinthus*, *Tulipa*	root, bulb, stem	collapse, rot	spring-summer
P. mammilatum	*Viola*			
Ramularia ajugae	*Ajuga reptans*			
R. agrestis	*Viola* e.g. *V. tricolor*			
R. ari	*Arum maculatum*			
R. asteris	*Aster*			
R. bellunensis	*Chrysanthemum frutescens*			
R. calthae	*Caltha*			
R. cardamines	*Cardamine* e.g. *C. flexuosa*, *C. pratensis*	living leaf	pale grey-pink,	summer
R. centaureae	*Centaurea* e.g. *C. nigra*, *C. scabiosa*		reddish-brown or brown	
R. centranthi	*Centranthus ruber*		dark-edged spot 1-15 mm diam.;	
R. gei	*Geum*		'shot hole'	
R. doronici	*Doronicum*			
R. geranii	*Geranium* e.g. *G. pratense*			
R. hellebori	*Helleborus* e.g. *H. foetidus*, *H. viridis*			
R. knautiae	*Knautia*			
R. lactea	*Viola* e.g. *V. odorata*			

Table 27 (continued) **Selected fungal pathogens**

FUNGUS	PLANT	PART AFFECTED	SYMPTOM	SEASON
R. lamiicola *R. lysimachiarum* *R. macrospora* *R. primulae* *R. sambucina* *R. vallisumbrosae* *R. variabilis*	*Lamium* *Lysimachia* *Campanula* *Primula* e.g. *P. veris*, *P. vulgaris* *Sambucus* *Narcissus* e.g. *N. pseudonarcissus* *Digitalis*	living leaf	pale grey-pink, reddish-brown or brown dark-edged spot 1-15 mm diam.; 'shot hole'	summer
Rhizoctonia solani (see *Thanatephorus cucumeris*)		–	–	–
Rhizoctonia tuliparum	*Tulipa*	stem, bulb	grey-brown rot	spring
Rosellinia necatrix	wide range of herbaceous species incl. *Narcissus*, *Paeonia*	root	white fungal growth	spring-summer
Sclerotinia bulborum	*Crocus*, *Hyacinthus*, *Scilla*, *Muscari* rhizomatous *Iris*, *Chionodoxa*	bulb, corm, rhizome	black slime	all
S. gladioli (=*Stromatinia gladioli*)	*Crocus*, *Gladiolus*, *Montbretia*	root; corm	root rot; dry rot	all
S. minor	wide range of herbaceous species	stem at soil level	white mould, stem collapse, black sclerotia	summer
S. sclerotiorum	wide range of herbaceous species	stem, living leaf, flower	white mould, stem collapse, brown spot, black sclerotia, apothecia	spring-autumn
S. tuberosa (=*Dumontinia tuberosa*)	*Anemone*	rhizome	tissue collapse, apothecia	spring-summer
Sclerotium cepivorum	*Allium* e.g. *A. cristophii*	root, bulb, leaf	leaf wilt, yellowing, root rot, white mould, black sclerotia	spring-autumn
Septoria anemones *S. armeriae* *S. azaleae* *S. chamaecysti*	*Anemone nemorosa* *Armeria* *Rhododendron* *Helianthemum*	corm, stem, living leaf	pale, grey-yellow-brown spot up to 15 mm diam., sometimes with dark, coloured edge	spring-summer

Table 27 (continued) **Selected fungal pathogens**

FUNGUS	PLANT	PART AFFECTED	SYMPTOM	SEASON
S. chrysanthemella	*Chrysanthemum*			
S. chrysanthemi				
S. clematidis	*Clematis*			
*S. cornicola**	*Cornus sanguinea*			
S. dianthi	*Dianthus* incl. *D. barbatus*, *D. caryophyllus*			
S. euonymi	*Euonymus japonicus*			
S. ficariae	*Ranunculus ficaria*			
S. gladioli	*Gladiolus*	corm, stem, living leaf	pale, grey-yellow-brown spot up to 15 mm diam., sometimes with dark, coloured edge	spring-summer
S. hederae	*Hedera*			
S. hyperici	*Hypericum*			
S. lamii	*Lamium*			
S. lavendulae	*Lavendula*			
S. leucanthemi	*Chrysanthemum*			
S. lysimachiae	*Lysimachia* e.g. *L. nummularia*			
S. obesa	*Chrysanthemum*			
S. scabiosicola	*Knautia*			
Sphaerotheca alchemillae	Rosaceae incl. *Alchemilla*, *Geum*			
S. erigontis-canadensis	*Erigeron*			
S. euphorbiae	*Euphorbia peplus*			
S. fugax	*Geranium*	living leaf	white powdery mildew	summer
S. fuliginea	*Veronica*, Compositae			
S. fusca	*Doronicum*			
S. volkartii	*Dryas*			
Stagonospora curtisii	*Narcissus*, *Galanthus*	living leaf, flower	large brown spot ('scorch')	spring-summer
Sydowia polyspora	*Juniperus*, *Pinus*	living leaf	dead leaf remains attached	summer
Synchytrium anemones	*Anemone nemorosa*	living leaf	minute black gall	spring-summer
Taphrina betulina	*Betula*	living leaf, stem	small, pale leaf on witches' broom	mid-summer

Table 27 (continued) **Selected fungal pathogens**

FUNGUS	PLANT	PART AFFECTED	SYMPTOM	SEASON
Trematosphaeria heterospora	*Iris*	rhizome	black specks	all
Thanatephorus cucumeris (=*Rhizoctonia solani*)	wide range of species with soft tissue incl. *Azalea*, *Primula*, *Viola*	soft stem (e.g. cuttings), root, stem	seedling rot, brown stem rot, weak growth; black root;	all all
Thielaviopsis basicola	wide range of herbaceous and woody species incl. *Ilex*, *Viola*	root	plant death	all
Trachyspora intrusa	*Alchemilla*	living leaf, rhizome	erect pale leaf with orange rust	mid-summer
Tranzschelia anemones	*Anemone nemorosa*,	living leaf	brown rust spot	spring-summer
T. discolor	*Anemone coronaria*	living leaf	brown rust spot	spring-summer
Urocystis anemones	*Anemone nemorosa*, *A. pulsatilla*, *Ranunculus*, *Trollius*			
U. colchici	*Colchicum*	corm, root stock, living leaf	blisters filled with dark spores	mainly spring also autumn-winter
U. eranthidis	*Eranthis*			
U. floccosa	*Helleborus*			
U. gladiolicola	*Gladiolus*			
U. violae	*Viola* e.g. *V. odorata*			
Uromyces armeriae	*Armeria*			
U. dianthi	*Dianthus* e.g. *D. barbatus*, *D. caryophyllus*			
U. erythronii	*Erythronium dens-canis*			
U. gageae	*Gagea*			
U. gentianae	*Gentianella amarella*	living leaf, stem	orange or red-brown rust spot	spring-summer
U. geranii	*Geranium* e.g. *G. pratense*, *G. sylvaticum*			
U. muscari	*Endymion non-scriptus*, *E. hispanicus*, *Muscari polyanthum*			
U. pisi-sativi	*Cytisus*, *Genista*, *Euphorbia cyparissias*			
Ustilago flosculorum	*Knautia*			
U. heufleri	*Erythronium oreaganum*	anther, ovary	pale, dark or purple powdery spores	spring-autumn
U. ornithogali	*Gagea lutea*			

Table 27 (continued) **Selected fungal pathogens**

FUNGUS	PLANT	PART AFFECTED	SYMPTOM	SEASON
U. scabiosae	*Knautia*	anther, ovary	pale, dark or purple powdery spores	spring-autumn
U. vaillantii	*Chionodoxa*, *Muscari botryoides*, *Scilla*			
U. violacea	Caryophyllaceae incl. *Cerastium*, *Dianthus*, *Lychnis*, *Silene*, *Gypsophila*			
Venturia geranii	*Geranium* e.g. *G. sylvaticum*	living leaf	dark-brown spot	autumn-spring
Verticillium dahliae	wide range of herbaceous or woody species	root	root and stem collapse; leaf wilt	mainly summer
Wettsteinina dryadis	*Dryas*	living leaf	brown spot	mid-summer

Table 28 **Fungal diseases in host order**

PLANT	SYMPTOM	FUNGUS
Amaryllidaceae		
Allium	root and bulb rot; leaf yellow, plant stunted; white mycelium, small black sclerotia at soil level	*Sclerotium cepivorum*
	leaf withers from tip downwards; yellow spot on leaf	*Peronospora destructor*
	reddish rust spot on living leaf in summer	*Puccinia allii*
Galanthus	leaf and bulb rot, grey mould; black sclerotia	*Botrytis galanthina*
	yellow leaf, tip die-back and rot; bulb rot ('smoulder')	*Botryotinia narcissicola*
	brown blotch on leaf and leaf tip die-back; brown spot on flower ('scorch')	*Stagonospora curtisii*
Narcissus	yellow leaf, brown tip and rot, bulb rot ('smoulder') brown spot on flower; apothecia on dead leaves in spring	*Botryotinia narcissicola*
	yellow blotch on living leaf ('fire'); brown spot on flower in spring; large black sclerotia on dead leaves; apothecia in spring	*Botryotinia polyblastis*
	i) bulb base and scales rot ('basal rot'); ii) base of flower stalk rots then bulb ('neck rot'); leaf tip die-back	*Fusarium oxysporum* f.sp. *narcissi*
	purplish rust spot on living leaf	*Puccinia schoeteri*
	elongate yellow-brown spot on living leaf	*Ramularia vallisumbrosae*
	root rot with white mould	*Rosellinia necatrix*
	large brown blotch on leaf and leaf tip die-back; brown spot on flower ('scorch')	*Stagonospora curtisii*
Apocynaceae		
Vinca	dark specks (sclerotia) on dry outer scale	*Stromatinia narcissi*
	large brown spot, dark edge on living leaf in spring	*Ascochyta vincae*
	blackening and dark specks (perithecium) on stem	*Diaporthe eumorpha*
	brown rust spot on living leaf	*Puccinia vincae*

Table 28 (continued)

PLANT	SYMPTOM	FUNGUS
Boraginaceae		
Anchusa	orange rust spot on living leaf in late summer	*Puccinia recondita*
Cynoglossum	white powdery mildew on living leaf	*Erysiphe asperifoliorum*
Myosotis	pale spot, brown spores on living leaf in early summer	*Entyloma fergussoni*
	white powdery mildew on living leaf	*Erysiphe asperifoliorum*
	yellow spot, downy mildew on living leaf	*Peronospora myositidis*
Campanulaceae		
Campanula	yellow to orange-red rust spot on living leaf	*Coleosporium tussilaginis*
	crown rot in summer	*Phytophthora porri*
	red-brown rust spot on living leaf	*Puccinia campanulae*
	brown spot 3-15 mm diam. on living leaf in summer	*Ramularia macrospora*
Jasione	red-brown rust spot on living leaf	*Puccinia campanulae*
Caryophyllaceae		
Arenaria (+ other genera)	grey-brown rust spot on living leaf	*Puccinia arenariae*
Cerastium	orange-yellow rust spot on living leaf in summer	*Melampsorella caryophyllacearum*
	purple powdery spores in anthers	*Ustilago violacea*
Dianthus	yellow spot, purple edge on living leaf; stem killed	*Alternaria dianthi*
	death of leaf base spreading up shoots on one side of plant; plant stunted and wilted	*Fusarium oxysporum* f.sp. *dianthi*
	red-mottled leaf, vascular browning, wilt	*Phialophora cinerescens*
	white patches on stem and flower stalk	*Phomopsis caryophylli*
	pale spot, red edge on living leaf and flower shoot	*Mycosphaerella dianthi*
	brown rust spot on living leaf	*Puccinia arenariae*
	yellow spot, purple edge, 5 mm diam. on older leaf	*Septoria dianthi*
Gypsophila	grey-brown rust spot on living leaf in summer	*Uromyces dianthi*

Table 28 (continued)

PLANT	SYMPTOM	FUNGUS
Lychnis	purple powdery spores in anthers	*Ustilago violacea*
Silene	brown rust spot on living leaf	*Puccinia arenariae*
	purple powdery spores in anthers plant may be stunted	*Ustilago violacea*
Compositae		
Affecting several genera	dark brown specks (sori) on brown spot on living leaf	*Puccinia cnici-oleracei*
	small yellow spot on living leaf, tissue collapse in spring or late summer	*Bremia lactucae*
	yellow to orange-red rust spot on living leaf	*Coleosporium tussilaginis*
	white powdery mildew on living leaf	*Erysiphe cichoracearum*
	brown rust on yellow spot on living leaf	*Puccinia hieracii*
	white powdery mildew on living leaf in autumn	*Sphaerotheca fuliginea*
Achillea	dark brown specks (sori) on brown spot on living leaf	*Puccinia cnici-oleracei*
Aster	white powdery mildew on living leaf in summer	*Erysiphe cichoracearum*
	similar to Phialophora in Dianthus	*Phialophora asteris*
	brown rust on yellow spot on living leaf	*Puccinia cnici-oleracei*
	white-pink spot on senescent leaf in summer	*Ramularia asteris*
Carlina	brown rust on yellow spot on living leaf in summer	*Puccinia calcitrapae*
Centaurea	white powdery mildew on living leaf in summer	*Erysiphe cichoracearum*
	brown rust on yellow spot on living leaf in summer	*Puccinia calcitrapae*, *P.hieracii*
	greyish spot 5 mm diam. on living leaf in summer	*Ramularia centaureae*
Chrysanthemum	brown blotch, black spot on leaf, stem, bud, flower	*Didymella ligulicola*
	downy mildew on living leaf and flower; brown spot	*Peronospora radii*
	brown spot, dark edge on living leaf in summer	*Ramularia bellunensis*
	pale to dark spot, dark edge on living leaf	*Septoria chrysanthemella*, *S. chrysanthemi*,
	pale spot, dark edge on living leaf, 'shot hole'	*Septoria leucanthemi*
	large brown blotch on living leaf	*Septoria obesa*

Table 28 (continued)

PLANT	SYMPTOM	FUNGUS
Doronicum	pale brown spot on living leaf in summer	*Ramularia doronici*
	white powdery mildew on living leaf in summer	*Sphaerotheca fusca*
Erigeron	white powdery mildew on living leaf in summer	*Sphaerotheca erigerontis-canadensis*
Eryngium	yellow raised spot on living leaf	*Entyloma eryngii*
Hieraceum	brown rust on red-yellow spot on living leaf	*Puccinia hieracii*
Knautia/Scabiosa	white powdery mildew on living leaf	*Erysiphe knautiae*
	yellow spot, downy mildew on living leaf in summer	*Peronospora violacea*
	dark spot <5 mm, on living leaf in summer	*Ramularia knautiae*
	pale spot, purple edge on living leaf	*Septoria scabiosicola*
	powdery black spores in anthers	*Ustilago flosculorum*
	pale-brown spores in anthers	*Ustilago scabiosae*
Cruciferae		
Affecting several genera incl. Arabis, Cardamine, Cheiranthus, Iberis, Matthiola	dense white powdery mould on any above-ground part	*Albugo candida*
	white powdery mildew on living leaf	*Erysiphe cruciferarum*
	seedlings killed; yellow spot on living leaf with white mould on lower surface; plant may be distorted	*Peronospora parasitica*
	swollen roots, 'club root', 'finger and toe' disease	*Plasmodiophora brassicae*
Alyssum	yellow spot and downy mildew on lead; seedling rot	*Peronospora galligena*
Cheiranthus	large yellow spot on living leaf or stem; stem wilt	*Alternaria cheiranthi*
Ericeae		
Calluna and Ericacea	young roots rot, hence leaf yellows and stem dies-back	*Phytophthora cinnamomi*
Rhododendron/azalea	brown-purple spot, dark purple edge on living leaf	*Cercoseptoria handelii*
	orange-red rust spot on living leaf	*Chrysomyxa rhododendri*
	sooty mould on living leaf (also other ever-greens)	*Dennisiella babingtonii*
	thick, distorted living leaf; powdery white covering	*Exobasidium vaccinii*

Table 28 (continued)

PLANT	SYMPTOM	FUNGUS
Ericeae (continued)	large brown spot, purple edge on living leaf	*Gloeosporium rhododendri*
Calluna and Ericacea	large red-brown spot on edge of living leaf in autumn	*Macrophoma falconeri*
Rhododendron/azalea	whitish-brown spot on living leaf in autumn	*Monochaetia karstenii*
	dark spot on living or dead leaf	*Mycosphaerella rhododendri*
	brown spot on flower; black sclerotia in autumn	*Ovulinia azaleae*
	clusters of dark specks on dead attached leaf in spring	*Phomatospora gelatinospora*
	clusters of dark spikes (perithecia) on dead, silvery buds in spring and summer; twig die-back	*Pycnostysanus azaleae*
	yellow brown scorch from tip of living leaf in summer	*Septoria azaleae*
Vaccinium	thick, distorted living leaf; powdery white covering	*Exobasidium vaccinii*
	brown spot, purple edge on living stem or leaf in autumn	*Leptosphaerulina myrtillina*
	dark specks (perithecia) on living leaf in autumn	*Physalospora vitis-idaeae*
	whitish powdery mildew on living leaf in summer	*Podosphaera myrtillina*
	yellow-red rust on living leaf in summer	*Pucciniastrum vaccinii*
Euphorbiaceae		
Euphorbia	brown rust spot on living leaf and stem in summer	*Melampsora euphorbia*
	yellow-brown spot on living leaf in summer	*Peronospora euphorbiae*
	white powdery mildew on living leaf in summer	*Sphaerotheca euphorbiae*
	orange-brown rust spot on living leaf in summer	*Uromyces pisi-sativi*
Geraniaceae		
Erodium	yellow-brown spot, downy mildew on living leaf	*Peronospora erodii*
Geranium	brown spot, downy mildew on living leaf	*Peronospora conglomerata*
	brown spot on living leaf	*Ramularia geranii*
	white powdery mildew on living leaf in summer	*Sphaerotheca fugax*
	orange-brown rust spot on living leaf	*Uromyces geranii*
	dark brown spot on living leaf in autumn-spring	*Venturia geranii*

Table 28 (continued)

PLANT	SYMPTOM	FUNGUS
Gentianaceae		
Gentiana	brown rust spot on living leaf in summer	*Puccinia gentianae*
Gentianella	pale brown rust spot on living leaf in summer	*Uromyces gentianae*
Iridaceae		
Crocus	blue-green mould on corm; corm rot	*Eupenicillium crustaceum*
	yellow leaf; corm rot	*Fusarium oxysporum* f.sp. *gladioli*
	roots covered in purple hyphae and minute purple specks	*Helicobasidium brebissonii*
	bulb rot with large black sclerotia	*Sclerotinia bulborum*
Gladiolus	shoot yellows and dies; black flecks (sclerotia) on corm	*Sclerotinia gladioli*
	small, sunken spot on upper corm; corm rot; yellow leaf	*Botryotinia draytoni*
	blue-green mould on corm; corm rot	*Eupenicillium crustaceum*
	corm rot; leaf tip yellow spreading down	*Fusarium oxysporum* f.sp. *gladioli*
	blotch on corm	*Mycosphaerella macrospora*
	blue-green mould on corm; corm rot	*Penicillium corymbiferum*
	shoot yellow and dies; black flecks (sclerotia) on corm	*Sclerotinia gladioli*
	pale spot, purplish edge on older leaf; dark spot on corm; corm mummifies	*Septoria gladioli*
	blister on leaf and corm with dark powdery spores	*Urocystis gladiolicola*
Iris	corm rot, yellow, wilted leaf; black sclerotia on rhizome	*Botryotinia convoluta*
	yellow streak turning brown then black on living leaf spreading to bulb (ink disease)	*Drechslera iridis*
	black specks on living leaf and on brown elongate spot, yellow edge in summer	*Ectostroma iridis*
	corm rot; leaf tip yellow spreading down; leaf curved	*Fusarium oxysporum* f.sp. *gladioli*
	blotch on rhizome (AE check CMI 435)	*Mycosphaerella macrospora*
	blue-green mould on corm, corm rot	*Penicillium corymbiferum*

Table 28 (continued)

PLANT	SYMPTOM	FUNGUS
Iris	red brown rust spot on living leaf	*Puccinia iridis*
	bulb rot with large (5-20 mm) black sclerotia	*Sclerotinia bulborum*
Labiatae		
Ajuga reptans	pale brown spot, purplish edge on living leaf	*Ramularia ajugae*
Calamintha	elongate stem, pale brown rust on living leaf	*Puccinia menthae*
Lamium	white powdery mildew on living leaf	*Erysiphe galeopsidis*
	brown spot on living leaf, purplish mould	*Peronospora lamii*
	pale brown spot, dark edge on living leaf in summer	*Ramularia lamiicola*
	white or brown spot, red edge on living leaf	*Septoria lamii*
Lavandula	young roots rot, hence leaf yellows and stem dies-back	*Phytophthora cinnamomi*
	white spot, purple edge	*Septoria lavandulae*
Origanum	elongate stem, pale brown rust on living leaf	*Puccinia menthae, P. thymi*
Thymus	witches broom	*Puccinia thymi*
Liliaceae		
Affecting several genera	root and bulb/scale rot	*Pythium ultimum*
Chionodoxa	bulb rot with large (5-20 mm) black sclerotia	*Sclerotinia bulborum*
Colchicum	anthers filled with dark powdery spores	*Ustilago vaillantii*
	black blister on living leaf and corm	*Urocystis colchici*
Convallaria	brown rust spot on living leaf in spring	*Uromyces colchici*
	brown spot on living leaf	*Mycosphaerella brunneola*
Endymion (see Scilla)	brown rust spot on living leaf	*Puccinia sessilis*
Erythronium	brown rust spot on living leaf in spring-summer	*Uromyces erythronii*
	black blister with powdery spores	*Ustilago heufleri*
Gagea	brown rust spot on living leaf in spring	*Uromyces gageae*
	black blister on living leaf and flower stalk	*Ustilago ornithogali*

Table 28 (continued)

PLANT	SYMPTOM	FUNGUS
Hyacinthus	spreading brwon lesions on leaves ('fire')	*Botrytis hyacinthi*
	blue-green powdery mould on bulb; bulb rot	*Penicillium corymbiferum*
	bulb rot with large (5-20 mm) black sclerotia	*Sclerotinia bulborum*
	root and bulb rot	*Pythium ultimum*
Lilium	brown spot, yellow edge; bud, stem rot; black sclerotia	*Botrytis elliptica*
	yellow-grey spots on leaf ('fire') spreading to bulb	*Botrytis tulipae*
	bulb scale rot	*Fusarium oxysporum* f.sp. *lilii*
	root and bulb rot	*Phytophthora cactorum*
Muscari	spreading brown lesions on leaves ('fire')	*Botrytis hyacinthi*
	bulb rot with large (5-20 mm) black sclerotia	*Sclerotinia bulborum*
	yellow rust spot on living leaves in spring and summer	*Uromyces muscari*
	anthers filled with dark powdery spores	*Ustilago vaillantii*
Scilla/Endymion	yellow rust spot on living leaf in spring	*Uromyces muscari*
	bulb rot with large (5-20 mm) black sclerotia	*Sclerotinia bulborum*
	anthers filled with dark powdery spores	*Ustilago vaillantii*
Tulipa	yellow-grey spots on leaf ('fire') spreading to bulb	*Botrytis tulipae*
	yellow sunken fleck on outer bulb scale; rot starts at base of bulb; plant collapses	*Fusarium oxysporum* f.sp. *tulipae*
	root and bulb rot	*Phytophthora cryptogea*
	shoots fail to emerge, grey-dark brown patches on bulb, black sclerotia (5 mm) near top of bulb	*Rhizoctonia (Sclerotium) tuliparum*
Oleaceae		
Syringa	root rot, unthrifty growth	*Phytophthora cactorum*
Orchidaceae		
Dactylorhiza	large, dark spot on living leaf	*Cladosporium orchidis*

Table 28 (continued)

PLANT	SYMPTOM	FUNGUS
Paeoniaceae		
Paeonia	grey-brown lesion on stem at soil level; black sclerotia young shoots wilt	*Botrytis paeoniae*
	white mould on roots, stems rot at soil level	*Rosellinia necatrix*
Papillionaceae		
Cytisus	white powdery mildew on living leaf	*Erysiphe trifolii*
	orange-brown rust spot on living leaf	*Uromyces pisi-sativi*
Plumbaginaceae		
Armeria	brown spot 5-10 mm, purple edge on living leaf	*Septoria armeriae*
	brown rust on living leaf in spring and early summer	*Uromyces armeriae*
Primulaceae		
Primula	large white spot, yellow edge on living leaf in autumn	*Ascochyta primulae*
	brown spot, grey centre on living leaf	*Cercosporella primulae*
	yellow spot, downy mildew on living leaf in summer	*Peronospora oerteliana*
	brown spot on living leaf in spring-autumn	*Phyllosticta primulicola*
	root and stem rot	{ *Phytophthora cactorum*, *P. primulae* *P. verrucosa*
	yellow spot, with brown rust on living leaf in summer	*Puccinia primulae*
	pale brown spot or 'shot holes' on living leaf in summer	*Ramularia primulae*
Cyclamen	blue-green mould on corm; corm rot	*Eupenicillium crustaceum*
Lysimachia	yellow-brown spot 10 mm diam. on living leaf	*Ramularia lysimachiarum*
	small brown spot dark edge on living leaf	*Septoria lysimachiae*
Ranunculaceae		
Anemone	yellow-red rust spot on living leaf and sepal; leaf pale and narrow	*Ochropsora ariae*

Table 28 (continued)

PLANT	SYMPTOM	FUNGUS
Anemone	yellow spot, downy mildew on living leaf	{ *Peronospora ficariae*, *P. ranunculi*
		Plasmopara pygmaea
	mycelium on rhizome and rot; apothečia in autumn	*Dumontinia (Sclerotinia) tuberosa*
	pale spot, brown edge on living leaf in summer	*Septoria anemones*
	minute black gall on leaf and flower in spring-summer	*Synchytrium anemones*
	brown rust spot on living leaf in spring-summer	*Tranzschelia anemones*, *T. discolor*
	blisters filled with black powdery spores on living leaf	*Urocystis anemones*
	white powdery mildew on living leaf in summer	*Erysiphe aquilegiae*
Aquilegia	pale brown spot purple edge on living leaf	*Haplobasidion thalictri*
	white powdery mildew on living leaf	*Erysiphe aquilegiae*
Caltha	brown rust spot on living leaf in summer	*Puccinia calthae*, *P. calthicola*
	pale spot, brown edge <5 mm diam	*Ramularia calthae*
Delphinium	white powdery mildew on living leaf in summer	*Erysiphe ranunculi*
Eranthis	blisters filled with black powdery spores on living leaf	*Urocystis eranthidis*
Helleborus	spot on leaf, stem, flower, spring onwards; stem break	*Coniothyrium hellebori*
	pale spot, dark edge on living leaf	*Ramularia hellebori*
	blister filled with dark powdery spores on living leaf	*Urocystis floccosa*
Ranunculus	white powdery mildew on living leaf in summer	*Erysiphe ranunculi*
	yellow spot, downy mildew on living leaf	*Peronospora ficariae*, *P. ranunculi*
	pale spot, brown edge on living leaf in mid-summer	*Septoria ficariae*
	blisters filled with dark powdery spores on living leaf	*Urocystis anemones*
Thalictrum	pale brown spot purple edge on living leaf	*Haplobasidion thalictri*
Rosaceae		
Alchemilla	white powdery mildew on living leaf	*Sphaerotheca alchemillae*
	erect pale leaf with orange rust in spring-summer	*Trachyspora intrusa*
Dryas	dark specks (perithecia) on living petiole in summer	*Cainiella johansonii*

Examples of necrotic, deformity and reddening leaf symptoms

a. Augusta disease in tulip where the necrosis is caused by the soil-borne tobacco necrosis virus (Courtesy A A Brunt)

b. Necrotic lesions caused by turnip mosaic virus on external leaves of white cabbage

c. 'Wart-like' outgrowths (enations) caused by strawberry latent ringspot on cucumber leaves

d. Healthy and distorted, 'strap-like' leaves of dwarf bean infected with bean common mosaic virus

e. Reddening symptoms caused by beet western yellows virus in honesty

f. Reddening symptoms caused by beet western yellows virus in cauliflower

Examples of petal-break symptoms

a. Petal-break (syn. Flower-break) caused by turnip mosaic virus in *Aubretia deltoidea* (Courtesy John Roberts)

b. In *Viola* caused by cucumber mosaic virus

c. In *Cyclamen* caused by cucumber mosaic virus (Courtesy A A Brunt)

d. In *Narcissus* caused by narcissus yellow stripe virus (Courtesy A A Brunt)

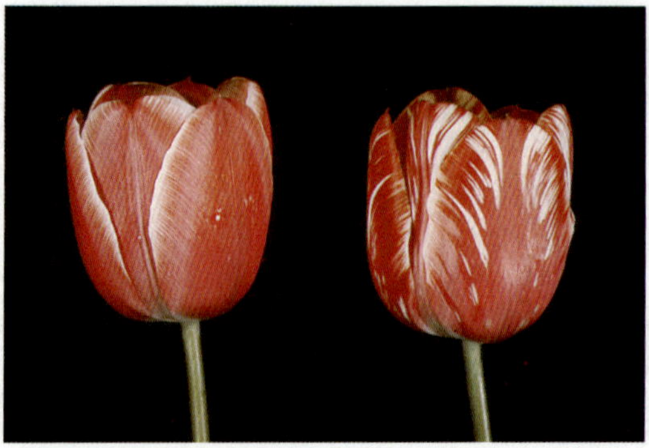

e. In tulip caused by tulip-breaking virus

f. In *Iris* caused by iris severe mosaic virus

An example of virus symptoms on seed and of leaf disorders caused by herbicide sprays, chemical deficiency and genetic variegation

a. Brown stains on broadbean *(Vicia faba)* seeds caused by broadbean strain (syn. Evesham strain) virus

b. Leaf chlorosis caused by spraying of herbicide

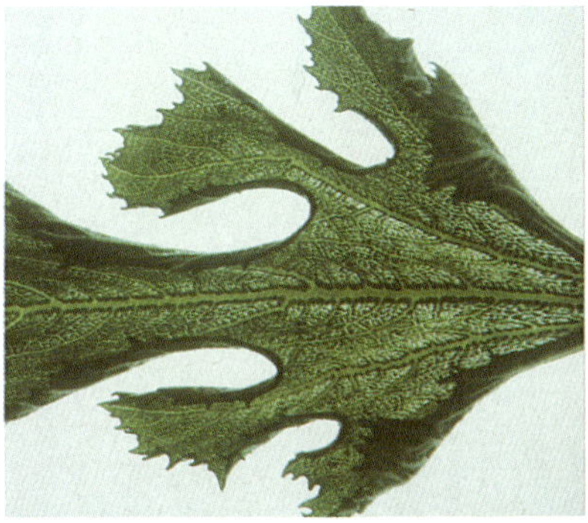

c. Leaf deformity and veinal chlorosis in courgette caused by hormone drift

d. Chlorosis in cauliflower leaf caused by magnesium deficiency

e. A natural chlorotic vein variegation in *Arum maculatum*

f. Natural chlorotic variegation in privet

a. Virus infected *Primula allionii* plant with latent symptoms, note the relatively small flowers and the leaves showing through the poor flower canopy

b. A virus-free plant of the *P. allionii* hybrid 'Ethyl Barker' showing large flowers with few leaf gaps

Table 28 (continued)

PLANT	SYMPTOM	FUNGUS
Dryas	dark red spot 5 mm on living leaf	*Isothea rhytismoides*
	whitish powdery mildew on living leaf in summer	*Sphaerotheca volkartii*
	dark specks on living leaf in early summer	*Stomiopeltis dryadis*
Geum	yellow spot and downy mildew on living leaf in summer	*Peronospora gei*
	pale brown spot, reddish edge 5 mm diam. in summer	*Ramularia gei*
	white powdery mildew on living leaf in summer	*Sphaerotheca alchemillae*
Helianthemum	yellow spot, downy mildew on older living leaf	*Peronospora leptoclada*
	pale brown spot, dark edge on living leaf	*Septoria chamaecysti*
Scrophulariaceae		
Antirrhinum	small spot dark spot on living leaf; 'shot hole'	*Heterosphaeria (Heteropatella) antirrhini*
	pale spot on living leaf in summer; 'shot hole'	*Myrothecium roridum*
	yellow spot, downy mildew on living leaf	*Peronospora antirrhini*
	yellow to orange-red spot on any above-ground part	*Puccinia antirrhini*
Digitalis	dark brown spot on living leaf	*Ramularia variabilis*
Euphrasia	yellow rust spot on living leaf in summer	*Coleosporium tussilaginis*
Verbascum	white powdery mildew on living leaf	*Erysiphe verbasci*
Veronica	yellow spot, pale purple spores on living leaf	*Peronospora agrestis, P. grisea*
	brown rust spot on living leaf in summer	*Puccinia veronicae*
	whitish powdery mildew on living leaf in summer	*Sphaerotheca fuliginea*
Thymelaeaceae		
Daphne	brown spot on older leaf	*Marssonina daphnes*
Violaceae		
Viola	pale brown spot on living leaf	*Alternaria violae*
	brown spot on living leaf, 'shot hole'	*Ascochyta violae*

Table 28 (continued)

PLANT	SYMPTOM	FUNGUS
Viola	grey-brown spot on living leaf in summer	*Cercospora violae*
	weak growth, black roots; death of plant	*Thielaviopsis basicola*
	roots covered in purple hyphae and minute purple specks	*Helicobasidium brebissonii*
	dark brown root; seedling death; white spot on leaf	*Mycocentrospora acerina*
	pale spot on living leaf in summer; 'shot hole'	*Myrothecium roridum*
	yellow spot, purplish spores on living leaf	*Peronospora violae*
	large yellow spot, brown rust on living leaf	*Puccinia fergussonii P. violae check*
	root rot, seedling death; stem rot	*Pythium oligandrum*
	pale spot, dark edge in autumn	*Ramularia agrestis, R. lactea*
	blister filled with dark spores on leaf or rootstock	*Urocystis violae*

CHAPTER FOUR

Virus diseases

GENERAL INFORMATION

Unlike diseases caused by fungi where the gardener can usually see the fungal fruiting body or spore mass with the naked eye or hand-lens, viruses are far too small to be seen without considerable magnification. They are in fact, one of the smallest of all living organisms (See Fig. 23) and can only be seen with an electron microscope at magnifications approximately 20-40,000 × life size.

The symptoms we see and recognise in plants in the garden or alpine house as virus diseases, are the effects of the virus infection on the plant tissues, rather than the virus itself.

Virus diseases also differ from fungal or bacterial diseases in that they cannot be treated and cured by chemicals which might kill or reduce the effects of the disease organism. Once a plant becomes infected by a virus, under normal circumstances the infection will remain in the plant for the rest of its life. This, of course, is of great importance to the gardener or nurseryman with plants that are vegetatively propagated. For once an individual clone becomes infected by virus, all cuttings, or other vegetative propagules, taken from the infected parent plant will also be infected. Only by the use of advanced and complex laboratory techniques, which will be described later in Chapter 5, can a virus be eradicated from an infected plant.

Because virus diseases are difficult to identify and their symptoms may be confused with other plant disorders such as chemical damage and genetic abnormalities, they are an enigma to most growers. Although some gardeners and nurserymen may recognise the symptoms of some of the more obvious and common virus diseases, few know how to handle or avoid such infections.

The intention of this chapter is to introduce the reader to viruses, the symptoms caused by viruses, the mechanisms by which they are transmitted and to the control measures that may be used to avoid or reduce their effects. Because of their small size the techniques and equipment required to study viruses are usually complicated and expensive. Consequently, most of the studies relating to viruses and virus diseases have been carried out with economically important commercial crops and little work has been done directly on virus diseases of rock plants or other plants of interest to the alpine gardener. It is necessary to refer to examples of virus diseases that infect crops such as vegetables, fruits and larger flowers in order to describe the nature of viruses and their symptoms. It should be emphasized, however, that most of the symptoms described are likely to have occurred in rock plants, but may not have been attributed to virus infection because no one has carried out the studies necessary to identify the cause.

What is a Virus?

A virus is one of the simplest of living organisms. It consists of one or more nucleic acid molecules (the **genome**) which carries the genetic information necessary for the virus's multiplication, and this is surrounded by a protective protein coat or shell (called the **capsid**) (See Fig. 25). The nucleic acid of most plant viruses is composed of **ribonucleic acid (RNA)**, but a few have **deoxyribonucleic (DNA)** genomes.

A virus is a complete (obligate) parasite and is only able to multiply after it has entered the cells of the host plant. Once inside a suitable host, the virus is able to take over and control the cell's synthesising machinery to provide the protein and other chemicals necessary for its own multiplication. In some virus infections the effects upon the host cells are so severe as to cause their death, a reaction that is observed externally as browning or blackening symptoms which is referred to as necrosis. Such reactions may

Figure 23 The size of the virus particles in relation to the plant cell and other pathogenic agents

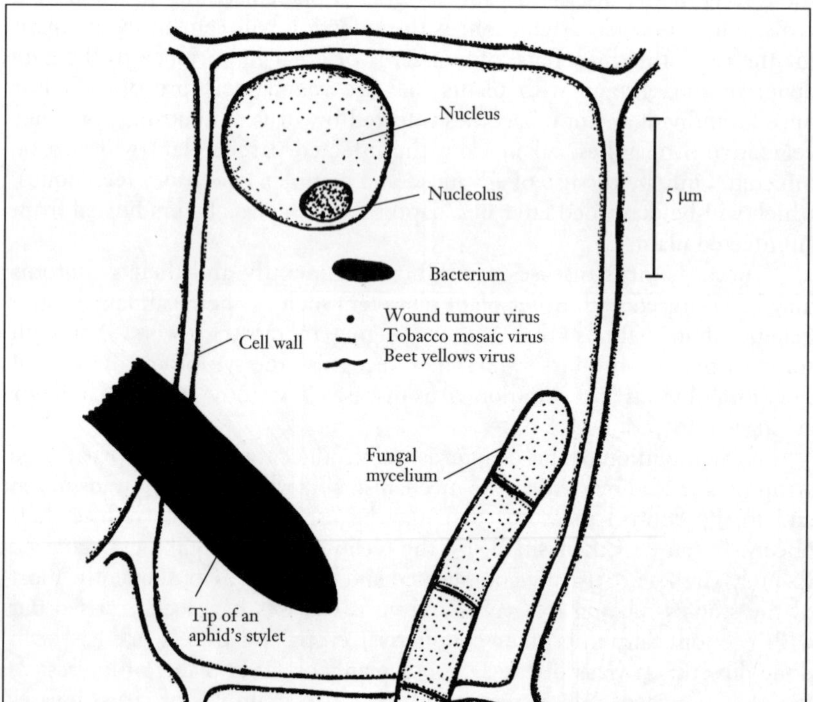

Figure 24 Electron micrographs of various types of virus particles (Courtesy C M Clay (a) Long flexuous rods of beet yellows virus, magnification bar = 200 nm; (b) Flexuous rods of turnip mosaic virus, magnification bar = 200 nm; (c) Bullet shaped particles of the Rhabdovirus broccoli necrotic yellows virus, magnification bar = 100 nm; (d) Spherical particles of cucumber mosaic virus, magnification bar = 100 nm; (e) Spherical and elongated particles of alfalfa mosaic virus, magnification bar = 50 nm; (f) Short and long rod shaped particles of tobacco rattle virus, magnification bar = 200 nm; (g) Large spherical particles of cauliflower mosaic virus, magnification bar = 50 nm; (h) Straight rod shaped particles of tobacco mosaic virus showing the central axial canal, magnification bar = 100 nm; (i) The twin geminate particles of maize streak virus, magnification bar = 100 nm; (j) Hexagonal shaped particles of arabis mosaic virus.
Note: some empty particles, magnification bar = 100 nm.

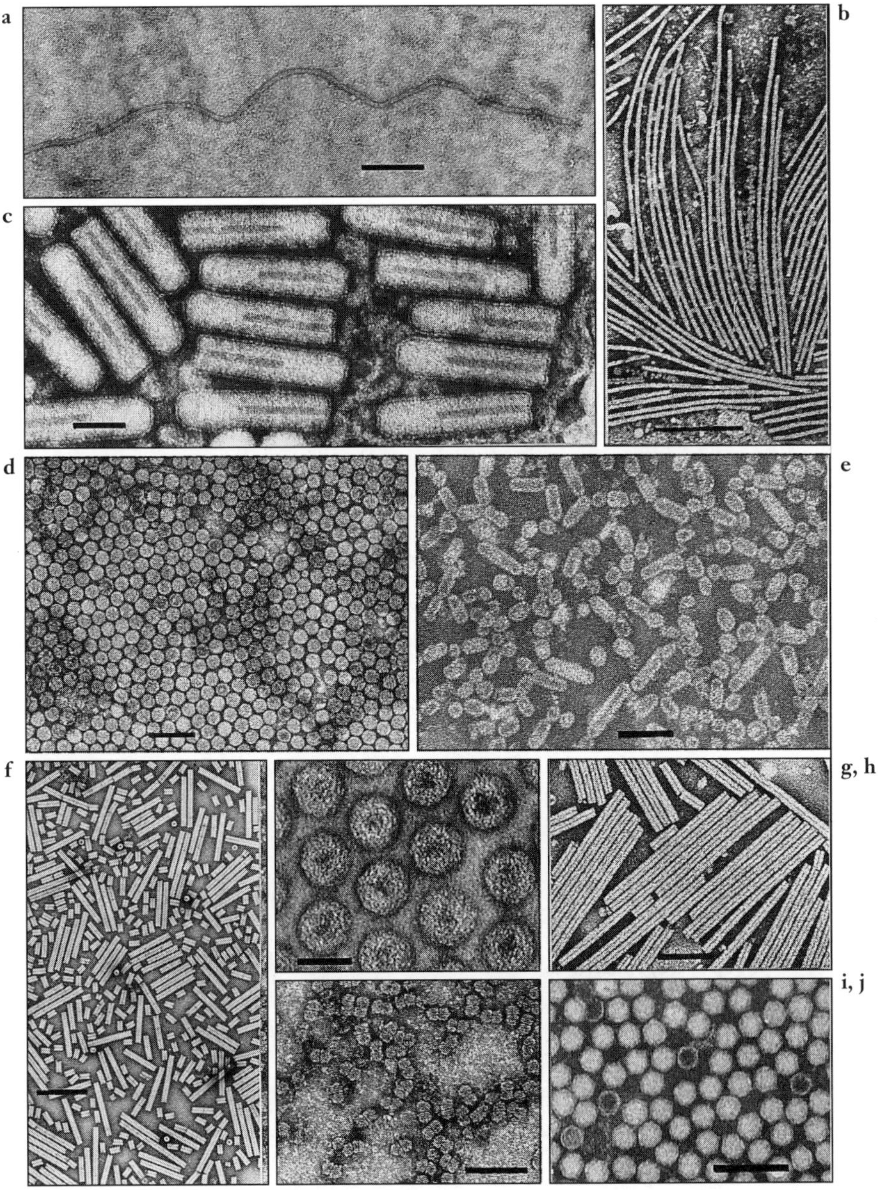

kill a plant quickly. In other infections the virus may only attack the chloroplasts which give the plant its green colour, resulting in chlorotic (yellowing) symptoms. Other viruses may infect the cells of the vascular (transporting) system, causing the plant to be short of food, water and essential chemical elements, especially at the growing point and leaf margins. The most subtle viruses, however, multiply rapidly within the cells of the plant, but have little observable effect upon them. In such cases, external visual symptoms may be negligible or absent and the infection is said to be **latent**.

Morphology of the Virus Particle

Plant viruses may be spherical or hexagonal in shape (See Fig. 24) and measure from 15 to 85 nanometres (nm) (1 nanometer is one millionth of a millimetre) in diameter and in this form they are composed of a spherical protein shell which protects the nucleic acid which is attached to the inner surface of the protein (See Fig. 25). Other plant viruses are rod-shaped and vary from viruses with short, rigid rods measuring 100 to 200 nm in length × 15 nm in width, to very long flexuous rods measuring more than 2000 nm in length × 13 nm in width (See Fig. 24). In many rod-shaped viruses the protective protein sub-units are arranged in a spiral (helical) around a central canal, with the nucleic acid attached in a long spiral strand to the inner surface of the protein (See Fig. 25). A few viruses are bullet-shaped (bacilliform) and measure about 250-350 nm in length and 75-90 nm in width (See Fig. 24). The small size of viruses may be emphasized by the calculation that 30,000 particles of a typical spherical virus such as cucumber mosaic virus (measuring 30 nm in diameter) could be laid end to end across a 1 mm wide pin head. Alternatively, 166,000 particles of the rod-shaped tobacco mosaic virus (measuring 300 nm in length) could be laid end to end along a match.

Figure 25 Diagrams of the arrangement of protein sub-units and ribonucleic acid in a spherical and rod-shaped virus particle

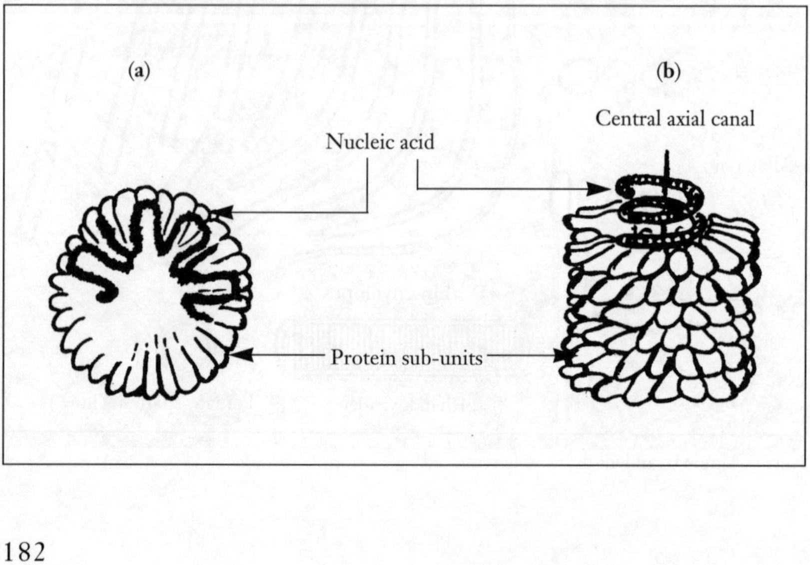

The shape and size of a virus is very important in helping to identify a particular infection and can usually be quickly determined by examining particles in squashed fragments of an infected leaf or other tissue, in the electron microscope.

Plant Virus Names

Plant viruses are named after the disease symptom they cause in their host. For example, one of the first virus diseases to be recognised was the mosaic

Figure 26 Plant virus groups and families

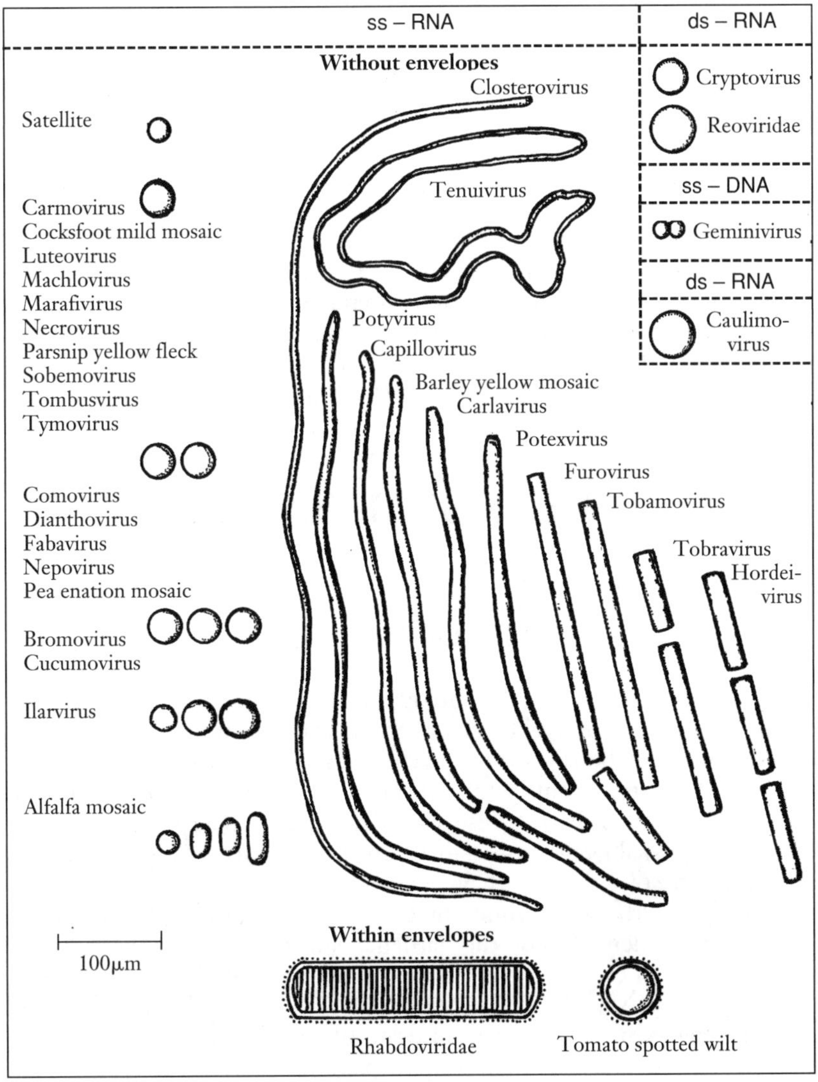

Key: ss, single stranded; ds, double stranded

disease of tobacco, which was called **tobacco mosaic virus**, other examples which are familiar to most gardeners are the mosaic diseases of cucumber called **cucumber mosaic virus** and of cauliflower called **cauliflower mosaic virus**. In any written communication concerning viruses the full name is normally used the first time it appears in the text, but then it is shortened to its initial letters e.g. **TMV** (**t**obacco **m**osaic **v**irus) and **CMV** (**c**ucumber **m**osaic **v**irus). Because cucumber and cauliflower mosaic viruses have the same initial letters, cauliflower mosaic virus is usually shortened to **CaMV**.

Thus, a virus is named after the host plant in which it was first found, irrespective of the economic importance of that host. An example is **arabis mosaic virus** (AMV) which is named after the *Arabis* species from which it was first isolated, even though **AMV** causes important diseases in many commercial crops including, *Narcissus*, strawberry and raspberry, and is of no economic importance in *Arabis*.

The naming of plant viruses has to be approved by an official international committee, and the viruses are arranged in **Groups** based on such characteristics as particle morphology, the type and quantity of the nucleic acid and their natural method of transmission. Individual virus groups are frequently named after the **type** (typical) virus of the group. For example the group containing tobacco mosaic virus is called the **tobamovirus** group, the name being derived from **toba**cco **mo**saic.

At present there are 37 plant virus groups (See Fig. 26) but this number changes regularly as new viruses are found and described, and more information is obtained about existing, unclassified viruses, which allows them to be placed in a group.

VIRUS SYMPTOMS

Introduction

It was emphasised in the Morphology of the Virus Particle (p.182) that symptoms are the observable effects that a virus has on the growth, development and metabolism of an infected host plant. In the early days of plant virology, symptoms were extremely important for they were the means by which a virus disease was identified. Today, there are many techniques available that assist in diagnosis, but viruses are still named after the type of symptom they cause in the diseased plant (See p.183) and very often the field symptoms caused by a virus give an immediate clue as to its identity. For the gardener and grower, however, disease symptoms are of course, the most important aspect of any virus infection. The nature and severity of the symptoms will determine the economic importance of a particular virus, in terms of yield loss, reduced quality or the necessity for a prize-winning alpine plant to be destroyed.

When a virus infects a susceptible plant it begins to multiply in the host's cells. This process alters the metabolism of the infected cells which in turn causes biochemical and physiological changes within the plant. The virus symptoms that are described in this section are the results of the abnormal metabolism that the virus causes in the host's tissues. These changes may be macroscopic and clearly visible on the external surface of the plant's organs, or there may be internal changes that may only be seen within the tissues if they are examined in a light or electron microscope.

It should be emphasised that a virus is unlikely to cause just one symptom in an infected plant. Usually, virus infections result in more than one type of symptom and frequently they cause a sequence of symptoms as the disease spreads throughout the plant. For example, visible infection may start with mosaic symptoms (See p.186) and leaf puckering near the apical growing point of the plant. This may be followed by the development of necrotic symptoms with overall stunted growth and dwarfing, and in extreme cases death may follow as necrosis spreads throughout the plant.

If more than one type of symptom occurs in a diseased plant the symptoms are called a **syndrome**. Sometimes a plant may be infected by more than one virus or other type of disease such as a fungus and the combined effects of the two diseases may be greater than the effect of a single disease. These cumulative symptoms are referred to as **synergism** or a **synergistic** effect.

In the following sections the main external, visible symptoms that may be seen in virus infected plants are described, together with the main factors that can influence or govern the expression of these symptoms. Further information on plant virus symptoms and more detailed information on the symptoms that may occur internally within the tissues and cells of virus infected plants may be obtained from books by Smith (1972), Bos (1978) and Walkey (1991a).

The Main External Symptoms

The visible effects of virus diseases occur as two basic types of symptom, those resulting from **primary infection** in the inoculated cells of the host plant, and those caused by **secondary** or **systemic infection** after the virus has moved from the sites of primary inoculation into the remainder of the plant (see Plate 19). It is the secondary systemic symptoms that are of most concern to the gardener or grower.

(a) Primary infection

Unlike fungal plant diseases, viruses are normally only able to enter the cells of a host plant through a wound. This most frequently occurs in nature when an insect vector (See p.201), such as an aphid, lands on the surface of a leaf and starts to feed by probing into the leaf cells with its mouthparts (**stylet**) (Fig. 7). Some viruses may also enter the leaf cells through broken epidermal hairs, or through small abrasions in the epidermal layer of cells (See Fig. 27a, b) caused by infected and healthy leaves rubbing together as they are blown in the wind. In the research laboratory most viruses are transmitted experimentally by dusting the leaf surface with a fine abrasive such as carborundum, and then rubbing the surface with virus-infected sap (See p.197).

The symptoms that develop at the sites of primary infection are known as **local** symptoms and often take the form of distinct areas of diseased cells called **local lesions** (See Plate 19a). The lesions may vary in size from pin-points to large patches and may be chlorotic through loss of chlorophyll, or necrotic, which is often the case as the cells die. In some virus/host infections, the virus is unable to spread in the plant beyond the site of primary infection and the local lesions are the only symptoms seen. Usually, however, the virus is not confined to the site of primary infection, but spreads from this initial site by cell to cell movement within the leaf until it eventually reaches the vascular system. Once in the vascular system, spread may be rapid throughout the plant and the virus may cause secondary, systemic symptoms at various sites. The most important of these symptom types are described below.

(b) Secondary or systemic infection

Stunting and dwarfing

Most virus infection will result in some degree of stunting of the infected plant (See Plate 19) and it is the symptom most likely to be found in combination with any of the other systemic symptoms described in this section. Sometimes, unless healthy and infected plants are grown side by side, it is difficult to observe the reduced growth and it may not be as dramatic as other systemic symptoms. In terms of reduced growth and yield, however, stunting symptoms can be very important to the commercial grower or to the keen alpine exhibitor.

Growth may be evenly reduced throughout the plant or the stunting may be confined to specific parts or organs. Stunting may also occur in the root system of an infected plant, but this symptom may be easily overlooked when the diseased plant is examined.

Mosaic

A number of symptoms occur, in which the infection causes some areas of the leaf or organ to become discoloured, while other areas remain normal. These symptoms are called mosaics. The infected areas are usually pale green or yellow (**chlorotic**) due to loss, or reduced production of chlorophyll, while the adjacent area remains a healthy green. The shape and pattern of mosaic symptoms may vary considerably (See Plate 19). When the discoloured areas of leaf are rounded, the symptoms may be referred to as a mottle, and chlorotic flecking, spotting or blotching may also occur. The leaves of brassicas infected with cauliflower mosaic virus develop distinctive light and dark green bands and in infected monocotyledonous plants, the mosaic symptoms develop on the leaves as light and dark green striping or streaking (See Plate 19). Mosaic symptoms may also occur on the stems (See Plate 19) or fruits of infected plants as is the case with marrows infected with cucumber mosaic virus.

Chlorosis

Some virus infections cause the whole leaf to become chlorotic due to reduced chlorophyll production and break down of the chloroplasts. Chlorosis is the main symptom associated with the economically-important 'yellowing' viruses, beet yellows and barley yellow dwarf (See Plate 20).

The symptoms of chlorosis generally start between the leaf veins and spread throughout the leaf. In some infections the chlorosis may be confined to the cells along the veins and the symptoms are then referred to as **veinal chlorosis** or **vein yellowing** (See Plate 20). A variation on this type of symptom is called **vein clearing**, in which the cells adjacent to the veins become translucent (See Plate 20).

Ringspotting and line patterns

Ringspotting is a common symptom of some viruses. In such infections the diseased area is restricted to a distinct ring or broken ring of infected cells (See Plate 20e, f). Occasionally the pattern may be extended to form a line across the leaf or fruit. The infected cells may become chlorotic or necrotic and sometimes concentric rings of diseased cells may develop (See Plate 20). Ringspotting symptoms usually occur on the leaves of infected plants, but may also occur on stems, fruits and pods.

Necrosis

The occurrence of primary necrotic local lesions has been described earlier in this section, but in addition to these, many other types of necrotic symptoms may occur in the systemically-infected leaves as infected cells die.

Systemic necrosis may occur in the form of small or large lesions, as in cabbage infected with turnip mosaic virus (See Plate 21b), or the necrosis may spread into the vascular system causing the stem and root tips to become necrotic eventually leading to death of the plant. This may happen with some varieties of dwarf French bean infected with bean common mosaic virus. In some infections necrosis may occur in the fruits and seeds of the infected plant (See Plate 23a).

Leaf and stem deformity

Some viruses cause distortion of the leaf blade, which may become reduced in surface area, twisted or strap-like. Dwarf beans infected with bean common mosaic virus often develop this type of symptom (See Plate 21d), as can tomato infected with some strains of cucumber mosaic virus. The abnormal growth is the result of an upset in the hormone balance within the leaf caused by the virus within the cells. The symptoms are, therefore, almost exactly the same as those caused by certain hormone weed killer sprays, and care must be taken in diagnosing these infections to be sure that such sprays were not the cause.

Enations or tumours

Other virus infections may be characterised by tumour-like outgrowths on the leaves or roots. Outgrowths on the leaves appear like 'warts' on the upper or lower leaf surface and are normally called **enations** (See Plate 21c). These growths are caused by abnormal cell proliferation resulting from virus-induced changes in hormone concentrations in the leaf (Bos, 1978). Such enations are common in peas infected with pea enation mosaic virus.

One virus, wound tumour virus, causes round, wart-like **tumours** on both the stems and roots of clover plants.

Petal or flower 'break'

One of the commonest virus symptoms seen by the alpine gardener, is a virus-induced colour 'break' symptom in the petals of infected plants. Such symptoms have been known in tulips for many centuries and were once greatly prized by Dutch tulip growers. The symptom in tulips is caused by tulip-breaking virus infection (See Plate 22e), but this type of symptom is also common in cyclamen and violas infected with cucumber mosaic virus (Plate 22b, c), wallflowers infected with turnip mosaic virus, narcissus infected with narcissus yellow stripe virus (Plate 22d) and gladioli infected with bean yellow mosaic virus. The 'break' symptoms may take the form of streaks, flecking or sectoring of the petal tissues with a colour different from the normal. Pink cyclamens and purple violas may be streaked white, because the break-colour usually results from loss of the overlying anthocyanin pigments causing the underlying colours to be exposed.

In addition to colour-break symptoms, the flowers of infected plants are frequently stunted and deformed and may be fewer in number than on healthy plants.

Fruit, seed and pollen abnormalities

Mosaic, ringspotting and necrotic symptoms are also frequent on fruits and seeds produced by infected plants (See Plate 23), but infection may affect these structures in various other ways. Fewer fruits may be expected from infected plants and these may be smaller, mis-shapen or their texture changed. For example, plums infected with prune dwarf virus yield less fruit, and the fruits of marrow infected with cucumber mosaic or zucchini yellow mosaic viruses are very stunted and mis-shapen. Similarly, peppers infected with tobacco mosaic virus produce distorted fruits and apples infected with apple rough skin or apple star- cracking viruses have abnormal skin textures.

Mother plants infected with virus may produce abnormally low quantities of seed. This frequently occurs in lettuce infected with lettuce mosaic virus, where the virus causes many of the flowers to abort. In some cases the virus is transmitted through the seed of the infected mother plant, resulting in the germination and vigour of the infected seed being significantly impaired.

Virus infection often causes the pollen of infected plants to be sterile, or its viability reduced. Often the rate of germination of the infected pollen is low and the length of the pollen tube shorter than that of healthy pollen, resulting in poor pollination and fertilisation.

Non-virus symptoms

There are several types of virus-like symptoms that commonly occur in garden plants but which have no association with virus infection. Certain hormone herbicides can induce leaf distortion symptoms that are more or less indistinguishable from the symptoms caused by certain viruses. Other herbicides and agrochemicals can cause chlorosis-type symptoms on leaves which are similar to the virus-induced mosaic and chlorosis symptoms described above (See Plate 23). Only experience and knowledge of what chemicals have been used in the vicinity of the injured plant, will enable the gardener to make a correct diagnosis of the problem.

It must also be remembered that certain plants have genetically controlled natural variegation, that results in chlorotic and dark-green banding that is unconnected with virus infection (See Plates 23e, f). Variegated privet and ivy are common examples of such horticulturally desirable plants (See Plate 23g). Often, however, it is difficult to distinguish such variegation from virus infection; as is the case with 'variegated' *Abutilon*, where the mosaic is caused by virus infection and may be grafted onto a green leaved plant. In the laboratory, however, it is possible to distinguish genetic from virus-induced variegation by testing for the presence of virus particles in such plants.

Latent Infection

Often viruses can infect a plant and multiply within it without causing visible external symptoms. This type of infection is called **latent infection** and the phenomenon is known as **latency**. It is frequent in naturally-infected wild plants including many common garden weeds. Cucumber mosaic virus for instance, often infects chickweed, *Stellaria media*, without causing symptoms. The infected chickweed then provides an overwintering host for the virus so that a reservoir of virus exists in the garden ready to infect garden and glasshouse plants the following season. Various perennial shrubs such as privet, honeysuckle and *Daphne* may also act as reservoirs of CMV in the same way yet show negligible symptoms themselves.

Latent virus infection is usually due to the host plant having a high level of tolerance to the virus concerned. In wild plants latency has probably evolved as a result of natural selection over a long period of time, so that only the most vigorous, tolerant plants have survived. In horticulture, man has often unwittingly selected for latent viruses in cultivated crops, and this is especially true for vegetatively propagated crops such as rhubarb and garlic which have been grown vegetatively for centuries. In these crops, virus-infected clones can be quite high yielding, and in some instances their yield may be as high as from virus-free clones.

It is quite probable that the alpine gardener likewise has selected vigorous clones with a high level of tolerance to virus, resulting in some plants being infected with virus without the gardener being aware. An example of such latency is seen in some named varieties of *Primula allionii* and its hybrids, where reasonably good flowering is obtained even though the clone can be shown to be virus-infected (Walkey, 1991b) (See Plate 24).

Although in some ways tolerant plants with latent infection are useful in the garden, gardeners must be aware that such plants may often be of poorer quality and be less vigorous than uninfected, healthy plants. Small reductions in quality may not be observed and would only be detected if growth comparisons were made by growing healthy and virus infected plants side by side. The greatest problem with such latent infection is, however, the danger that the virus carried latently in the plant, could be transmitted to a neighbouring healthy plant that is not tolerant to the particular virus. This could easily happen in the alpine house with an aphid-transmitted virus (See p.202).

Factors that Influence Symptom Expression

A number of factors may effect the development and severity of symptoms in virus-infected plants. The most important of these are the genetic composition of the host plant and the virus, the age of the host plant at the time of infection and environmental conditions before and after infection.

Genetic and host factors

The genetic composition of the virus and the host plant will govern whether infection actually occurs, and the severity of the symptoms produced. The occurrence of plants tolerant to virus infection has been discussed in the previous section. The degree of susceptibility or resistance of all plants is under genetic control and dependent on the genes a particular plant possesses (See Chapter 5). Furthermore, the genetic composition of different varieties of the same plant species govern whether or not a particular virus strain can infect a particular host plant, and the severity of the attack. Consequently, some varieties of a plant species are highly susceptible to a particular virus or an individual strain of that virus, while other varieties are only mildly susceptible or completely resistant to the same virus strain. Such genetic variation is the basis of resistance breeding, in which individual plants are deliberately selected by the plant breeder to develop varieties that are resistant to infection by virus or other diseases (See Chapter 5).

Besides its genetic composition, the age of the host plant at the time of virus infection is an important factor in determining the severity of virus symptoms. Usually, the younger the plant, the greater its susceptibility to virus infection. Often old plants are relatively resistant to infection. The probable reason for this is that the virus is entirely dependent upon cells of the host plant for its multiplication, and in older leaves the metabolism and movement of foods and essential chemicals (**assimilates**) is slower than in younger leaves.

Environmental and nutritional factors

Environmental factors that favour rapid plant growth such as high temperature and high light intensities, will reduce virus symptoms. Conversely, maximum virus symptoms can be expected in winter at low temperatures and under low light intensities. This is very noticeable when cultivating viruses under experimental glasshouse conditions, where optimal temperatures for virus multiplication are between 18 and 25°C. When temperatures rise above 26°C, symptoms in virus-infected plants are drastically reduced, a factor that makes refrigeration-cooling an essential requirement for satisfactory glasshouse experimentation with viruses in tropical countries or in temperate countries in summer.

The effect of host plant nutrition upon virus symptoms may be variable, sometimes nutritional conditions that favour plant growth may also favour increased host susceptibility to virus infection. For example, high nitrogen levels have been shown to increase the susceptibility of marrow seedlings to cucumber mosaic virus infection. In contrast, with certain other host/virus infections, high nitrogen levels have been reported to mask symptoms.

VIRUS DISEASES KNOWN TO INFECT ALPINE PLANTS

Introduction

The lack of information relating to virus diseases of alpine plants has been discussed in the introduction to plant viruses (See p.179). The absence of research on the virus diseases of alpine plants and of other non-commercial flower species is not surprising, however, for the costs of operating plant virology research laboratories are very high and the number of plant virologists in any one country limited. Consequently, the resources of such laboratories must be directed towards economically-important food crops or other high value crops, where the introduction of successful disease control measures can result in substantial savings.

Nevertheless, the information that is available on viruses of commercially-important flower crops, such as bulbs and carnations, is likely to be directly relevant to related alpine-garden species in these groups. Likewise, much of the information gained as a result of virus studies on vegetables and other crops, is of relevance to the alpine-gardener. Occasionally, an individual virus research worker may be interested enough in alpine plants to carry out studies on them. The information currently available on virus diseases of alpine-plants is presented in this section.

The reader must consider all the virus symptom types that have been outlined in the chapter on diagnosis and described in detail in Section 4.2 and relate these to the disease problem that may occur in his or her own plants. If it is decided that the problem encountered could be caused by a virus, then it is important to consider the appropriate control measure that might be taken to eradicate the diseases which are described in Chapters 5 and 6.

Viruses Reported from Alpine Plants

Viruses that have been isolated and identified from infected alpine-garden plants or other closely-related species, are shown together with a summary of symptoms in Tables 29 and 30. The non-bulbous species listed in Table 29 are a diverse mixture of species from eleven different families and they demonstrate the type of virus infection that is likely to be a problem in the alpine-garden. As would be expected, the commonly-occurring, aphid-transmitted viruses are a major problem (See p.202). This is clearly illustrated by the widespread occurrence of cucumber mosaic virus (CMV), a virus with a very wide host range in monocotyledonous and dicotyledonous flowering plants. CMV commonly infects a range of perennial garden species that provide reservoirs of the virus (Table 31) and it is readily transmitted by a number of aphid vectors including the common greenfly, the peach-potato aphid (*Myzus persicae*; see also Chapter 2). CMV causes severe symptoms in a number of alpine-garden and alpine-house species and is especially common and severe in *Viola*, *Campanula* and various genera of *Primulaceae*. Infected plants belonging to these groups develop leaf mottle, leaf distortion and flower-break petal symptoms (Plates 22 and 27). This virus is particularly widespread in alpine *Primula* hybrids that are vegetatively propagated. The leaf symptoms are most obvious on the older, more mature leaves after flowering in the late spring and summer. Besides, the genus *Primula* itself, other dwarf genera of the *Primulaceae* may be affected by CMV and species of *Cyclamen* appear to be quite susceptible. Flower-break symptoms in their petals are particularly obvious symptoms (Plate 22), but the leaves of infected plants may be twisted, stunted and grow very slowly. The author has observed virus symptoms in *Cyclamen cyprium* and *C. persicum*.

Table 29 **Viruses reported to infect rock plants and other closely related species other than bulbs**

HOST SPECIES	VIRUSES	SYMPTOM TYPE[a]	METHOD OF TRANSMISSION[b]
Boraginaceae			
Anchusa sp.	Cucumber mosaic	M	A (n-p)
Campanulaceae			
Campanula allionii	Cucumber mosaic	M, D, Fb	A (n-p)
C. pyramidalis	Tomato spotted wilt	N, D, S	T (p)
Lobelia cardinalis	Cucumber mosaic	M, D	A (n-p)
Cruciferae			
Aubretia deltoides	Turnip mosaic	M, S, Fb	A (n-p)
Cheiranthus cheiri (Wallflower)	Turnip mosaic	M, S, Fb	A (n-p)
Mattiola incana (Stock)	Cauliflower mosaic	S, M	A (n-p)
	Turnip mosaic	M, S, Fb	A (n-p)
Fumariaceae			
Dicentra spectablis	Tobacco rattle	C, M	E
Geraniaceae			
Geranium carolinianum (Cranesbill)	Cucumber mosaic	S, M	A (n-p)
Leguminosae			
Lupinus angustifolius (Lupin)	Cucumber mosaic	D, N	A (n-p)
Portulacaceae			
Lewisia heckneri	Cucumber mosaic	M	A (n-p)
Primulaceae			
Cyclamen sp.	Cucumber mosaic	D, Fb	A (n-p)
Primula sp.	Cucumber mosaic	S, M, Fb	A (n-p)
	Unidentified potyvirus	M, S	A (n-p)
	Tomato spotted wilt	M, D, S	T (p)
	Tobacco necrosis	N	F
Ranunculaceae			
Aquilegia sp.	Cucumber mosaic	M, N, S	A (p)
Delphinium sp.	Cucumber mosaic	M, C, S	A (n-p)
	Tomato spotted wilt	N, D, S	T (p)
Scrophulariaceae			
Antirrhinum majus	Tobacco ringspot	N	E
Calceolaria sp.	Tomato spotted wilt	N, D, S	T (p)
Penstemon sp.	Cucumber mosaic	M, S	A (n-p)

Table 29 (continued) **Viruses reported to infect rock plants and other closely related species other than bulbs**

HOST SPECIES	VIRUSES	SYMPTOM TYPE[a]	METHOD OF TRANSMISSION[b]
Thymelaeceae			
Daphne mezereum	Cucumber mosaic	M	A (n-p)
Violaceae			
Viola tricolor var. *hortensis* (Pansy)	Beet curly-top[c]	D, C	L (p)
	Cucumber mosaic	Fb, M, S	A (n-p)
	Viola mottle[d]	Fb, M, S	O
V. cornuta	Beet curly-top[c]	D, C	L (p)
	Cucumber mosaic	Fb, C, M	A (n-p)

Key
[a] C, chlorosis; D, leaf distortion; Fb, flower-break; M, mosaic or mottle; N, necrosis; S, stunting
[b] A, aphid-transmitted; E, eelworm-transmitted; F, fungus-transmitted: L, leafhopper-transmitted; T, thrips-transmitted; n-p, non-persistent transmission; p, persistent transmission; O, not known
[c] Only found in the USA
[d] Only found in Northern Italy

Aphid-transmitted viruses frequently cause important diseases of bulb species, with CMV again infecting species in most bulb genera (Table 30). The majority of other aphid-transmitted bulb viruses are much more specific in their host range and usually only infect one bulb genus. Of the aphid-transmitted viruses that infect *Narcissus*, narcissus yellow stripe virus causes severe symptoms on leaves and stems. These take the form of intense light and dark-green streaks (Plate 19f). The virus also induces flower-break and stunting symptoms in the flowers (Plate 22d) and bulb size is greatly reduced. Iris severe mosaic virus causes a similar distinct mosaic streaking symptom on the leaves and stems of infected plants, stunting and flower-break symptoms in the flower (Plate 22f). Tulip breaking virus infects tulips and lily species causing flower-break symptoms (Plate 22e). Bean yellow mosaic virus is very common in *Gladiolus* and also infects some other dicotyledonous garden plants including sweet peas and lupins.

Turnip mosaic virus (TuMV) is another common aphid-transmitted virus affecting garden plants. It frequently infects wallflower, stocks and *Aubretia*, in which it causes leaf mottling and flower-break symptoms in the petals (Plate 22a). Unlike CMV which has a wide host range, TuMV is mainly found in plants of the family *Cruciferae*. Its effect on members of the genus *Draba* has not been reported.

The soil-borne viruses transmitted by eelworms and fungi (See p.205 and p.207) also cause important diseases of bulbous and non-bulbous species (Tables 29 and 30). Both these vectors are destroyed if the soil is heat sterilised, so the use of sterilised soil for the germination and growing of seedlings is an important control measure for this type of virus. The eelworm-transmitted **Nepoviruses**, arabis mosaic, tomato blackring and tobacco rattle are important viruses of *Narcissus* and *Tulipa* species, and the fungal-transmitted, tobacco necrosis virus, causes the particularly serious Augusta disease in tulip (Plate 21a).

Table 30 **Viruses reported to infect bulb species**

HOST SPECIES	VIRUSES	SYMPTOM TYPE[a]	METHOD OF TRANSMISSION[b]
Amaryllidaceae			
Narcissus spp.	Arabis mosaic	L	E
	Cucumber mosaic	M	A (n-p)
	Narcissus degeneration	C, N	A (n-p)
	Narcissus latent	L	A (n-p)
	Narcissus late yellows	N, C, M	A (n-p)
	Narcissus mosaic	M	O
	Narcissus tip necrosis	N	O
	Narcissus white streak	N	A (n-p)
	Narcissus yellow stripe	C, M, D, Fb	A (n-p)
	Raspberry ringspot	L	E
	Strawberry latent ringspot	L	E
	Tomato blackring	L	E
	Tobacco rattle	C	E
	Tobacco ringspot	L	E
Iridaceae			
Gladiolus spp.	Bean yellow mosaic	M	A (n-p)
	Tobacco rattle	D	E
	Tomato ringspot	S	E
Iris spp.	Broad bean wilt	L	A (n-p)
	Iris fulva mosaic	M, D	A (n-p)[c]
	Iris mild mosaic	M	A (n-p)
	Iris severe mosaic	M, Fb	A (n-p)
Crocus vernus	Iris severe mosaic	M, Fb	A (n-p)
Liliaceae			
Lilium spp.	Cucumber mosaic	M	A (n-p)
	Lily symptomless	L	A (n-p)
	Lily virus x	LM	Sp
	Tulip breaking	M, Fb	A (n-p)
	Tulip virus x	M, N, Fb	O
Tulipa spp.	Cucumber mosaic	C, N, D, S	A (n-p)
	Tomato blackring	C, N, D	E
	Tobacco necrosis	N, D, S	F
	Tobacco rattle	N	E
	Tulip breaking	M, Fb	A (n-p)

Key
[a] C, chlorosis; D, leaf distortion; Fb, flower-break; L, latent infection; M, mosaic or mottle; N, necrosis; S, stunting
[b] A, aphid-transmitted; E, eelworm-transmitted; F, fungus-transmitted; Sp, mechanically transmitted by sap; O, no known transmission method; n-p, non-persistent transmission
[c] Only found in the USA

Table 29 shows that tomato spotted wilt virus (TSWV) has been reported in a number of alpineplants, in which it causes severe necrotic symptoms. Most of these reports were associated with a particular outbreak of the disease in the 1950's and since that date TSWV does not seem to have occurred regularly or to have been widespread in alpine plants. In 1989 and 1990, however, severe outbreaks of TSWV were reported in ornamental, glasshouse-grown flower crops on the continent of Europe and in the United Kingdom. These outbreaks have been asso-

Table 31 **Common garden plants that act as virus reservoirs**

HOST SPECIES	VIRUSES	SYMPTOM TYPE[a]	METHOD OF TRANSMISSION[b]
Brassica oleraceae var. *italica*[c] (broccoli)	Beet western yellows Cauliflower mosaic Turnip mosaic	R, S M, S M, N, S	A (p) A (n-p) A (n-p)
Buddleia davidii	Cucumber mosaic	M, L	A (n-p)
Daphne spp.	Cucumber mosaic	M	A (n-p)
Forsythia viridissima	Arabis mosaic	C	E
Gladiolus sp.	Bean yellow mosaic	M, S	A (n-p)
Laburnum anagyroides (Golden Chain)	Arabis mosaic	C	E
Liqustrum vulgare (Privet)	Arabis mosaic	M	E
Lunaria annua (honesty)	Beet western yellow	R, S	A (p)
Magnolia sp.	Cucumber mosaic	M, D	A (n-p)
Rheum rhaponticum (Rhubarb)	Arabis mosaic Cherry leaf roll Cucumber mosaic Strawberry latent ringspot Turnip mosaic	M M L L M	E E A (n-p) E A (n-p)
Rubus ideaeus (Raspberry)	Arabis mosaic	C, S	E
Sambucus nigra (Elder)	Arabis mosaic	C, M	E
Vinca minor (Periwinkle)	Cucumber mosaic	M, S, Fb	A (n-p)

Key

[a] C, chlorosis; D, leaf distortion; Fb, flower-break; M, mosaic or mottle; R, reddening; S, stunting

[b] A, aphid-transmitted; E, eelworm-transmitted; n-p, non-persistent transmission; p, persistent transmission

[c] Other brassicas including Brussels sprout, cabbage, cauliflower, swede and turnip may also be reservoirs of BWYV, CaMV and TuMV.

ciated with the importation and spread in Europe of the Western Flower Thrips (*Frankliniella occidentalis*). This vector of TSWV was until recently only found in the Americas (See also Chapter 2).

The disease outbreaks in 1990 included severe attacks on glasshouse *Primulas*, and the possible transmission of TSWV by the thrips vector to rock plants within the protected environment of the alpine house cannot be ruled out if the spread of the vector continues (See Chapter 5 for control measures).

As far as Britain and Europe are concerned, beet curly-top virus is not a problem. The virus occurs widely in California and in the Pacific states of Western America as far east as the Rocky Mountain divide. East of the divide the virus only occurs in restricted areas of Southern Colorado, western Texas and New Mexico. The importance of the various carnation viruses that infect sweet william and pinks (Table 32) on alpine *Dianthus* species and varieties is not known. It seems likely, however, that the aphid-borne carnation viruses do infect some alpine garden plants..

Table 32 **Viruses of *Dianthus***

HOST SPECIES	VIRUSES	SYMPTOM TYPE[a]	METHOD OF TRANSMISSION[b]
Dianthus barbatus	Carnation latent	L	A (n-p)
(Sweet William)	Carnation vein mottle	M	A (n-p)
Dianthus caryophyllus	Carnation etched ring	N	A (s-p)
(Pink)	Carnation latent	L	A (n-p)
	Carnation mottle	M	Sp
	Carnation necrotic fleck	N	A (s-p)
	Carnation ringspot	R	E
	Carnation vein mottle	M	A (n-p)

[a] L, symptomless infection; M, mosaic or mottle; N, necrosis; R, ringspots
[b] A, aphid-transmitted; E, eelworm-transmitted; Sp, mechanically-transmitted by sap; n-p, non-persistent transmission; s-p, semi-persistent transmission

THE TRANSMISSION OF PLANT VIRUSES

Introduction

It is essential for the gardener to know how different viruses are transmitted in nature, for unless the mode of transmission is known and understood, it is difficult or impossible to develop control measures to avoid infections. Under natural conditions a plant virus is a complete (**obligate**) parasite and reliant upon the host plant for its survival. It must therefore spread from time to time from one susceptible host to another in order to survive. If the virus is infecting an annual or short-lived plant then trans-

Figure 27 Scanning electron micrographs of the surface of a tobacco leaf before and after sap inoculation. (a) An untreated leaf showing intact hairs and epidermis.

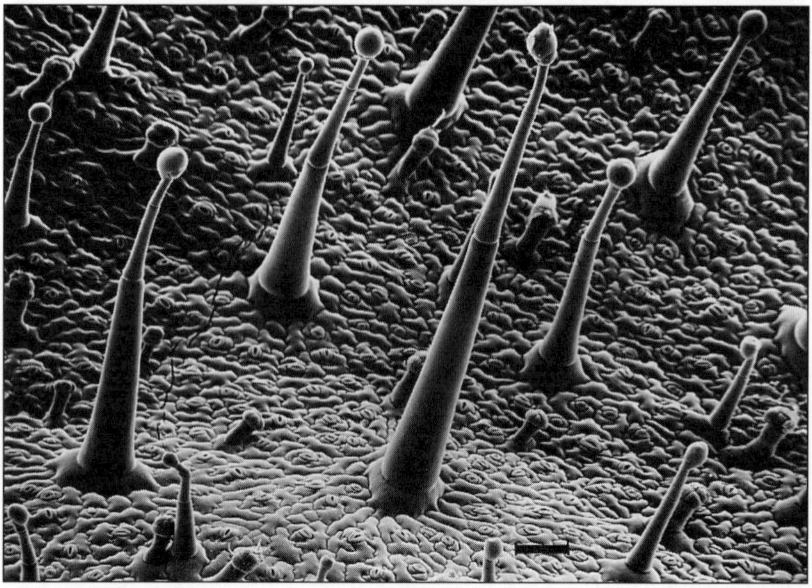

(b) The broken hairs following sap inoculation. The particles of the carborundum abrasive may be clearly seen, magnification bar = 0.1mm

(courtsey of M. J. W. Webb)

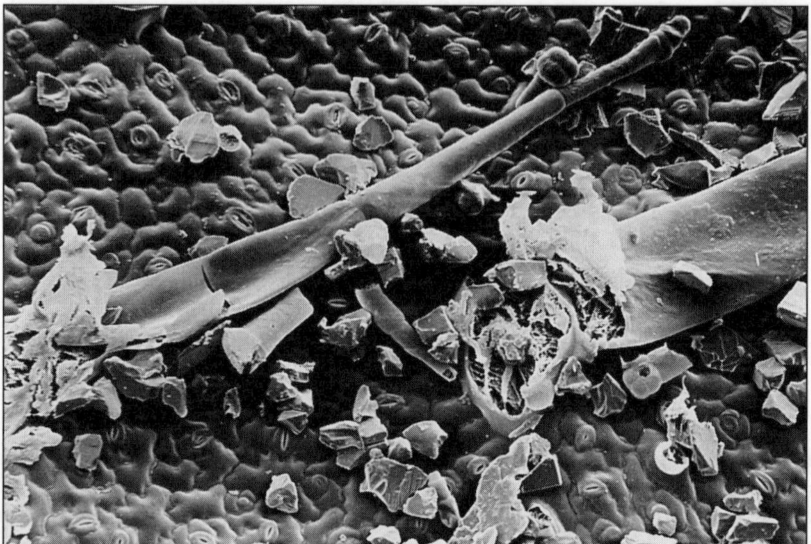

missions must be quite frequent, whereas if it is infecting a tree or other long-lived plant, then less frequent transmissions are necessary.

Since no plant virus is able to penetrate the surface (**cuticle**) of the leaf of its host and establish infection by its own processes, infection can only be initiated by the virus entering the tissues through a wound. For many viruses this is achieved through another organism, which carries the virus from an infected to a healthy plant when it feeds. The organism carrying the virus is referred to as a **vector**. With some viruses the entry process may be avoided altogether, as the virus is transmitted in the seed or pollen of the infected mother plant, and with others, infected, vegetative propagules may transmit the virus from the mother plant to the new, young plant.

In the laboratory, mechanical transmission is used as the main method of transmitting viruses. In this process, sap from an infected plant is rubbed onto the leaf surface of a healthy plant, that has been dusted with a fine abrasive powder such as carborundum (See Fig. 27). The wounds caused by the abrasive to the leaf hairs and surface cells (**cuticle** and **epidermis**) as the sap is rubbed onto the leaf (See Fig. 27), allows the virus particles to enter the cells beneath the leaf surface.

Many viruses have only one normal method of natural transmission, but others have more. Lettuce mosaic virus for instance is transmitted by aphids and is also seed-transmitted. One or both methods of transmission may be important in the outbreaks and spread of a particular virus disease. The development and spread of a disease is referred to as its **epidemiology**.

In the remainder of this section the various types of plant virus transmission will be discussed and several of these processes are of direct importance to the alpine gardener and nurseryman.

Mechanical Transmission

Although mechanical transmission is the principal method of transmitting plant viruses experimentally, the transmission of viruses in the field by natural mechanical damage to the plant tissues is relatively rare and probably of only minor economic importance. Usually it occurs only with very stable viruses that multiply to high concentrations in the host plant. Potato virus X is an example of such a virus and it may be transmitted from infected to healthy plants when their leaves rub together in a wind. Perhaps of more relevance to the gardener and grower, however, is tobacco mosaic virus (TMV). This virus causes a severe disease in tomatoes and will also infect a range of other plant species. It is very persistent in plant debris in glasshouse soils and on glasshouse structures that have been in contact with the leaves of infected plants. Transmission occurs when the roots of young seedlings grow through the soil. As they penetrate between the soil particles abrasions may occur in their surface cells which allow the virus particles to enter. TMV is also readily transmitted by contaminated hands and tools as young healthy seedlings are pricked out or transplanted.

The most probable way in which the alpine gardener or grower will mechanically transmit a virus, however, is while taking cuttings or other types of propagules from an infected plant. If the hands, knife or other tool that is being used become contaminated with sap from an infected parent plant, it is quite likely for the virus to be transmitted to a healthy cutting that is subsequently handled. The importance of using sterilised tools and clean hands for taking cuttings has been clearly demonstrated in experiments with pink (*Dianthus allwoodii*) cuttings (Abdul Magid, 1981). As much as 36% infection occurred with carnation ringspot virus, if a sterilised knife was passed once through an infected shoot prior to it being used to remove a cutting from a healthy plant. However cuttings remained healthy if a sterilised knife was used directly. The results of these experiments with a number of other carnation virus are shown in Table 33.

Table 33 **Effect of unsterilised knives on the virus status of (*Dianthus allwoodii*) cuttings**

Virus	Incidence of transmission in cuttings taken by					
	Unsterilised Knife		Flame sterilised Knife		Unsterilised Hands	
Carnation etched ring	2/36[a]	(6)[b]	0/36	(0)	0/38	(0)
Carnation latent	7/36	(19)	0/36	(0)	3/38	(8)
Carnation ringspot	13/36	(36)	0/36	(0)	5/38	(13)
Carnation vein mottle	4/36	(11)	0/36	(0)	2/28	(5)

[a] Number of plants infected/number of cuttings taken
[b] Percentage infection

(data from Abdul Magid, 1981)

Transmission by Grafting

The technique of grafting is an ancient horticultural practice in which a union is established between the cut tissues of two different plants. There are many ways in which a graft may be established (Garner, 1958) and one of the most common is the union between the shoot portion of one plant, referred to as the **scion** and the root bearing portion of another, called the **stock** (Fig. 28). If either the scion or the stock is infected, then the virus will probably pass from the infected portion to the healthy one and establish infection.

Virus infection through grafting is particularly important to the grower and alpine gardener, as many conifers and dwarf shrubs are propagated by this method. The nurseryman must be particularly vigilant that the stock plants and root-stocks used for grafting are free from virus infection.

Transmission by Insects

Of all types of vectors, insects are by far the most important, both in terms of the number of different types of viruses transmitted and the economic importance of the diseases concerned. Of 381 animal species reported to transmit plant viruses, approximately 94% belong to the phylum *Arthropoda* and 6% to the phylum *Nematoda* (the eelworms), and of the arthropod vectors approximately 99% are insects (Harris, 1981).

The majority of all insect vectors (over 70%) of plant viruses belong to the order *Hemiptera*, and the aphids (family *Aphididae*) are the most important vectors of this group (See also Chapter 2 on plant bugs). The leafhoppers (*Cicadellidae*), planthoppers (*Delphacidae*), treehoppers (*Membracidae*), whiteflies (*Aleyrodidae*) and mealy bugs (*Pseudococcidae*) are also vectors and members of this insect order. There are examples of plant virus vectors in other insect groups, but only the beetles (*Coleoptera*) are economically important.

In general, viruses that are transmitted by vectors in one of the above groups are not transmitted by a vector from another group, and the type of vector is a useful diagnostic feature when trying to identity a virus.

Figure 28 Techniques for graft transmission. (**a**) *Wedge graft*; (**b**) *Sliced approach graft* in which two components have been sliced to expose the cambium; (**c**) *Tongued approach graft* in which surface contact is increased by an additional cut downwards on the one component and upwards on the other

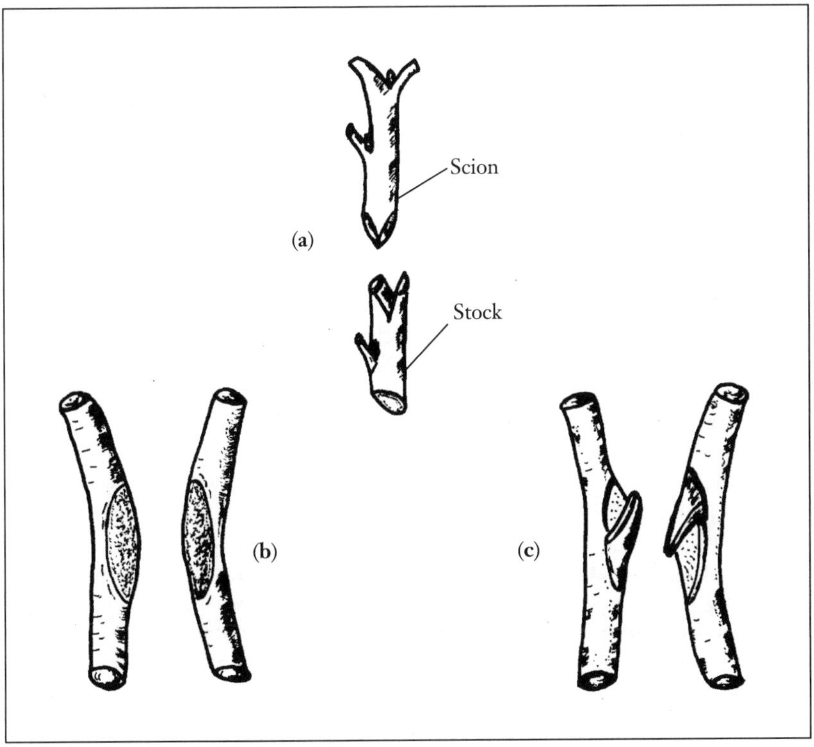

Aphid transmission

As far as the alpine gardener and grower in temperate regions is concerned, aphids are the most important insect vector (Plate 2) and the majority of common viruses that are likely to be encountered in the alpine-house or rock-garden will be aphid-transmitted (Table 34). Aphid transmission of plant viruses is divided into three basic types, **non-persistent**, **semi-persistent** and **persistent**. Sometimes the non-persistent manner of transmission is referred to as **stylet-borne** and the persistent as **circulative**. Both sets of terms may be encountered in the literature and it is important that the grower understands the basic characteristics of each type of transmission, so that appropriate measures can be taken to control viruses transmitted by either type (Chapter 5).

Table 34 **Examples of some common garden viruses that are transmitted by aphids**

Virus	Aphid vector	Type of transmission
Alfalfa mosaic	Various spp.	non-persistent
Bean yellow mosaic	*Acyrthosiphon pisum**	non-persistent
Cauliflower mosaic	*Brevicoryne brassicae**	non-persistent
Cucumber mosaic	Various spp.	non-persistent
Iris severe mosaic	*Myzus persicae**	non-persistent
Lettuce mosaic	*M. persicae**	non-persistent
Narcissus yellow stripe	*Aphis fabae**	non-persistent
Tulip breaking	*M. persicae**	non-persistent
Turnip mosaic	*M. persicae**	non-persistent
Beet western yellows	*M. persicae**	persistent
Pea enation mosaic	*Aphis pisum**	persistent

* principle but not the only aphid vector

Non-persistent transmission. Viruses transmitted in a non-persistent way are of considerable economic importance and are far more numerous than those transmitted by aphids in a semi-persistent or persistent manner. Non-persistent transmission is characterised by the following features.

(a) The virus is acquired by the insect after feeding on the infected plant for a very short time (referred to as the **acquisition feeding time**), often only a few seconds or minutes are necessary.

(b) The virus is transmitted to a healthy plant immediately the insect transfers from an infected plant and inserts its stylet (referred to as the **inoculation feeding period**).

(c) The insect rapidly looses the ability to transmit the virus after leaving the infected plant (usually within a few hours).

(d) Non-persistent viruses are carried on or near the mouthparts of the insect and do not multiply within the insect.

The process of non-persistent virus transmission, results from contamination of the mouthparts with virus as the insect feeds. Because non-persistent viruses can be acquired and transmitted by the aphid vector during feeding probes as short as ten seconds, it is thought that the virus is taken from, and inoculated into, the outermost layer (**epidermis**) of leaf cells.

Persistent transmission. Viruses which are transmitted in a persistent (circulative) way have the following characteristics.

(a) A long acquisition feeding period with transmissions being most efficient following acquisition periods of six to twenty-four hours.

(b) A time lapse, referred to as the **latent period**, of twelve hours or more may occur following the time the insect starts feeding on the infected leaf, and the time when the vector is able to transmit the virus to a healthy plant.

(c) Once the insect has acquired the virus it retains the ability to transmit it for at least a week, but often much longer, and sometimes for the remainder of its life.

(d) The ability to transmit the virus is retained through the moult of the insect.

Viruses which are transmitted in a persistent way can be divided into two further categories, those which do not multiply within the insect and those which do. Persistent viruses which do not multiply in the insect are thought to enter the gut with sap from an infected plant as the insect feeds. The virus then passes through the gut wall into the insects' **haemocoel** (blood) and circulates to the salivary glands. From here it is transmitted in the saliva as the vector feeds.

If a persistent virus multiplies within the insect vector it is said to be **propagative**. Propagative viruses may be transmitted through the eggs of the infected vector to its offspring, a virus movement that is called **transovarial** transmission. Persistent viruses are usually located in or close to the phloem cells of the vascular system of the infected host plant. Because this location is more specific and deeper within the plant compared with the epidermal cell location of non-persistent viruses, viruses transmitted in a persistent manner have a more specific relationship with their vector than non-persistent viruses. Individual non-persistently transmitted viruses are often transmitted by a number of aphid species, but a persistently transmitted virus may have only one specific aphid vector. The feeding characteristics of this specific vector would be such, that it probes deeply into the vascular system of the leaf to feed for relatively long periods of time.

Viruses which are transmitted in a semi-persistent manner are intermediate between non-persistent and persistent in the mechanism of their transmission. Basically they are non-persistent in that they do not circulate within the insect, but the vector may retain the ability to transmit them for three or four days.

Although the terms non-persistent, semi-persistent and persistent originate from studies with aphid vectors, they are often applicable to other types of insect vector.

Other insect vectors

Whiteflies (*Aleyrodidae*) are very important vectors of plant viruses in subtropical and tropical regions, but of less importance to the alpine gardener and grower in temperate countries. In tropical areas, they transmit viruses that are of major economic importance in food and other crops (Table 35) such as beans, cassava, cucurbits, tobacco and cotton, in countries such as India, Africa, Indonesia and Central America. The major

Table 35 **Examples of economically important viruses that are transmitted by other insects**

Virus	Vector type	Type of transmission
Beet curly top	*Circulifer tenellus* (leafhopper)	persistent
Potato yellow dwarf	*Agallia constricta* (leafhopper)	persistent
Rice tungro	*Nephotettix cincticeps* (leafhopper)	semi-persistent
Maize mosaic	*Peregrinus maidis* (planthopper)	persistent
Cassava mosaic	*Bemisia tabaci* (Whitefly)	–[a]
Cotton leaf-curl	*B. tabaci* (Whitefly)	–
Tobacco leaf-curl	*B. tabaci* (Whitefly)	–
Cowpea mosaic	*Cerotoma trifurcata* (beetle)	persistent
Southern bean mosaic	*C. trifurcata* (beetle)	persistent
Squash mosaic	*Diabrotica longicornis* (beetle)	–
Cacao swollen shoot	*Planococcoides njalensis* (mealy bug)	semi-persistent
Tomato spotted wilt	*Frankliniella occidentalis* (thrips)	persistent
Wheat streak mosaic	*Aceria tulipae* (mite[b])	persistent

[a] Information not available
[b] Belongs to the class *Arachnida*

vector is a whitefly called *Bemisia tabaci* which is widespread in many tropical areas and which, unfortunately, has recently been discovered in certain glasshouses in Britain (See also Chapter 2).

Similarly, the closely-related leafhoppers (*Cicadellidae*), planthoppers (*Delphacidae*) and treehoppers (*Membracidae*), are also important vectors of plant viruses in the tropics and sub-tropics, but are not important vectors in more temperate regions. At least thirty different viruses have been reported to be transmitted by a range of over thirty leafhopper species, including some which cause major diseases of rice, maize and beet, while planthoppers are responsible for transmitting two important virus diseases of maize (Table 35).

Beetles have been found to transmit about forty-five different plant viruses and usually, viruses that are beetle transmitted have no other vector. Most beetle vectors belong to the families *Chrysomelidae* and *Curculionidae*, and at least seventy-four species of beetle are known to be virus vectors. There are no beetle-transmitted viruses that are known to infect alpine garden plants, but two viruses, broadbean strain (syn. Evesham strain) and broadbean true mosaic are fairly common diseases of broadbean and could occur in the garden. They are transmitted by beetles whose feeding damage is frequently observed as semi-circular bites removed from the outer margins of the leaf. The biting mouthparts of beetles contrast with the sucking mouthparts of aphids, leafhoppers and whitefly vectors.

Mealy bugs (*Pseudococcidae*) are also only of interest in the tropics where the most important virus they transmit is cocoa swollen shoot. This virus is economically devastating in the West African cocoa crop. Only one virus is known to be transmitted by thrips (*Thysanoptera*) and until recently this was thought to be of no economic importance. The severe outbreaks of TSWV in Europe in 1989 and 1990 (See p.196) transmitted by the thrips *Frankliniella occidentalis*, however, may result in the importance of this group of vectors being re-evaluated.

Eriophyid mites (belonging to the class *Arachnida*) are known to transmit several important viruses of wheat and ryegrass in temperate climates, but they are not known to transmit any virus that is of interest to the alpine gardener or grower. Recent studies have suggested, however, that some garlic viruses may be mite transmitted. If this is the case then mite vectors may be responsible for the transmission of some ornamental bulb viruses, which could be of importance in the alpine garden. Mite vectors are extremely small and can easily be overlooked on infested plant material unless a hand-lens is used for examination.

Transmission by Eelworms (Nematodes)

Soil-inhibiting eelworms (nematodes) belonging to the phylum *Nematoda* are another important group of virus vectors. The eelworms which transmit plant viruses are free-living in the soil and are just visible to the naked

Table 36 **Examples of some common viruses that are eelworm transmitted**

Virus group	Virus	Vector	Particle shape
Nepovirus	Arabis mosaic	*Xiphinema diversicaudatum*	spherical
	Cherry leaf roll	*X. coxi, X. diversicaudatum*	spherical
	Raspberry ringspot	*Longidorus elongatus*	spherical
	Strawberry latent ringspot	*X. diversicaudatum*	spherical
	Tobacco ringspot	*X. americanum*	spherical
	Tomato blackring	*L. attenuatus, L. elongatus*	spherical
	Tomato ringspot	*X. americanum*	spherical
Tobravirus	Pea early browning	*Paratrichodorus, Trichodorus* spp.	tubular
	Tobacco rattle	*Paratrichodorus, Trichodorus* spp.	tubular

eye as transparent small 'worms'. The eelworm vectors include species from the genera *Xiphinema*, *Longidorus*, *Trichodorus* and *Paratrichodorus* (Tables 12, p.73) and several viruses transmitted by *Xiphinema* and *Longidorus* species are common in gardens and likely to be of importance to the alpine gardener and nurseryman.

Eelworms have probing mouthparts consisting of a single stylet (spear). The spear is hollow and connected to the foregut by muscles (Fig. 8). These allow the spear to be thrust forward to penetrate the root cells during feeding (See Plate 13f). As eelworms feed, the virus-laden plant material is sucked into the eelworm's gut where the virus contaminates the lining of the foregut and spear. When the vector moves and starts feeding on the roots of a healthy plant, the virus passes together with secreted saliva into the root cells.

The viruses transmitted by eelworms are divided into two distinct groups, the **tobraviruses** which have short rod-shaped particles typified by tobacco rattle virus from which the group derives its name, and the **nepoviruses** whose type member is tobacco ringspot virus, which have spherical particles (Fig. 24). Tobacco rattle virus is transmitted by *Trichodorus* and *Paratrichodorus* eelworms which prefer sandy soils. The virus has a wide host range which includes ornamental bulbs (including narcissus; See Table 30), potato and lettuce, and common garden weeds such as chickweed (*Stellaria media*) and *Viola tricolor*.

A number of nepoviruses including, tobacco ringspot, arabis mosaic, raspberry ringspot and strawberry latent ringspot viruses have been shown to infect bulbs such as *Narcissus* (See p.195). These viruses also have a wide host range among weeds, shrubs and hedgerow plants, which allow them to survive in a particular garden or field when the crop plant is not present.

In addition to being able to survive in infected weed and shrub species, nepo-and tobraviruses are often seed-transmitted in weeds, a factor which is very important in their epidemiology and survival. Infected seeds may be scattered at random throughout a field, with each infected plant providing a focus for additional virus spread. Spread within the soil is slow, however, and can only occur over short distances as the eelworm moves through the soil. Consequently, plants infected with eelworm-transmitted viruses are generally confined to relatively small and distinct patches within the crop, or to areas adjacent to the hedgerows where the virus can maintain itself in hedgerow plants.

Spread of these viruses over longer distances may occur through dispersal of infected seed stocks, movement of eelworm-contaminated soil on the wheels of vehicles or garden and farm implements, or in the soil surrounding the roots of transplanted plants.

Fungus Transmitted Viruses

There are a number of viruses that are transmitted by soil inhabiting fungi (Table 37). One of the most important of these is lettuce big vein virus which is a major disease of lettuce throughout temperate regions of the world. Another, tobacco necrosis virus, causes the Augusta disease of tulip which could be a problem for the alpine gardener (Plate 21).

Figure 29 Diagram of a generalized life cycle of *Olpidium*, a fungal vector

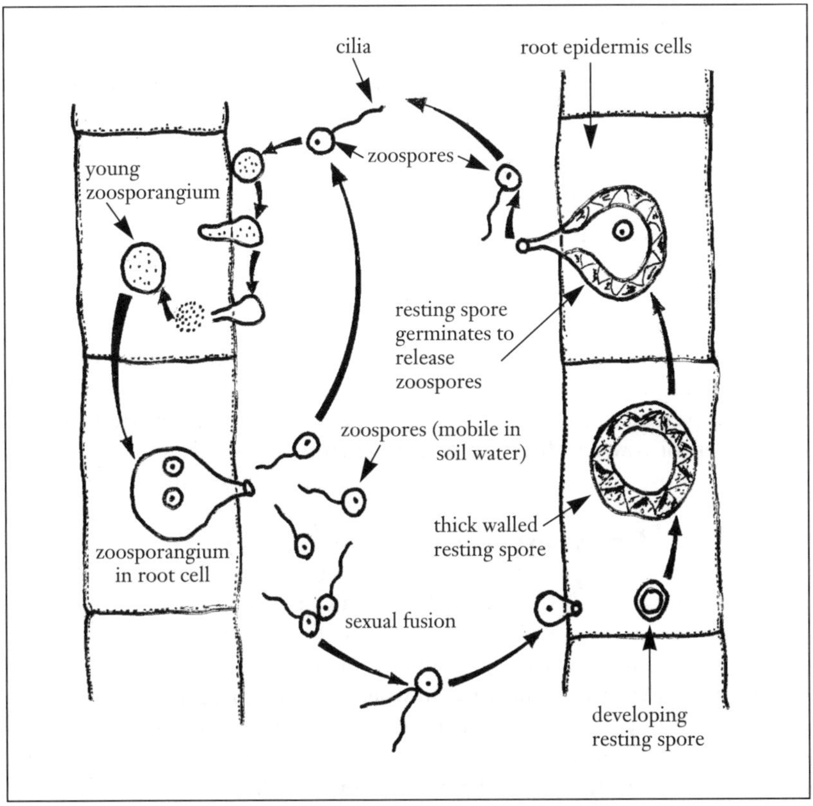

Table 37 **Examples of some viruses that are fungus transmitted**

Virus	Vector	Particle shape
Cucumber necrosis	*Olpidium cucurbitacearum*	spherical
Lettuce big vein	*O. brassicae*	rod
Potato mop top	*Spongospora subterranea*	straight rod
Tobacco necrosis	*O. brassicae*	spherical
Wheat mosaic	*Polymyxa graminis*	straight rod
Wheat spindle streak mosaic	*P. graminis*	filamentous rod

The fungal vectors are *Olpidium* spp. (*Chytridiales*) and *Polymyxa* or *Spongospora* spp. (*Plasmodiophorales*). To understand the mechanism of virus transmission by these fungi, it is essential that the life-cycle of the vector-fungus is fully understood. The fungus *Olpidium brassicae*, the vector of tobacco necrosis virus, infects cells close to the surface of the root (**epidermal cells**) and produces spore-forming bodies in these cells called **zoosporangia** (See Fig 29). These produce exit tubes through which mobile **zoospores**, which swim by means of flagella (called **cilia**), are liberated into the soil water surrounding the root. The zoospores may do one of two things. Firstly, they may swim through the soil water and attach themselves to the surface of another root and produce thin-walled zoospore cysts. These cysts produce an infection canal after about two hours, which penetrates the wall of the root cell. After a further two or three days, the contents of the zoospore passes into the cell and forms a body which develops into another zoosporangia. This in turn produces more zoospores to repeat the cycle.

Alternatively, the liberated zoospores may fuse in pairs to form a 'seed' (called a **zygote**) which penetrates the root cells and produces a thick-walled resting sporangium. The resting spores are resistant to drying and can remain viable in decaying plant debris in the soil for long periods. Eventually they germinate to produce new zoosporangia and zoospores.

Viruses transmitted by fungi can either be transmitted by the virus particles being carried on the surface of the mobile zoospores or by the virus being carried within the fungal resting spore and then transmitted by the zoospores when the resting spore germinates.

Transmission Through Seed and Pollen

Several virus diseases of economic importance are seed-transmitted (Table 38) but it is not known if any of them are of importance to the alpine specialist. In view of the wide range of plant species in which viruses are transmitted by seed, however, it is probable that some alpine plants may carry virus in their seed. This may be particularly true for cucumber

a. Yellow water trap

b. Sticky insect trap

c. Adult seven spot ladybirds, *Coccinella septempunctata* feeding on aphids

d. Larva and pupa of ladybird, *Coccinella septempunctata*

e. Eggs of ladybird, *Coccinella septempunctata*

f. Large white butterfly caterpillar parasitised by the wasp, *Apanteles glomeratus*

a. Adult green lacewing, *Chrysopa carnea*

b. Eggs of lacewing, *Chrysopa carnea*

c. Larva of lacewing, *Chrysopa carnea*, feeding on aphids

d. Larva of hoverfly feeding on aphids

e. Scales of glasshouse whitefly; parasitised ones are black

f. Adult chalcid wasp, *Encarsia formosa*, emerging from parasitised glasshouse whitefly pupa

a. Close up of virus-free flowers of *P. allionii* hybrid 'Beatrice Wooster'

b. Virus-infected *Primula* 'Beatrice Wooster' (Courtesy Harry Smith Collection)

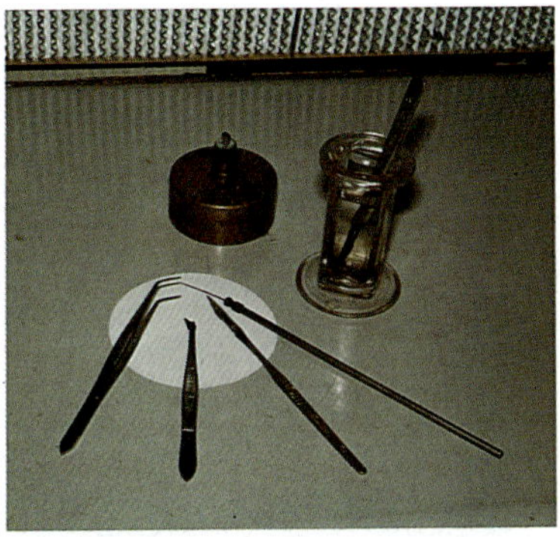

c. Tools required for removing explants for meristem-tip culture

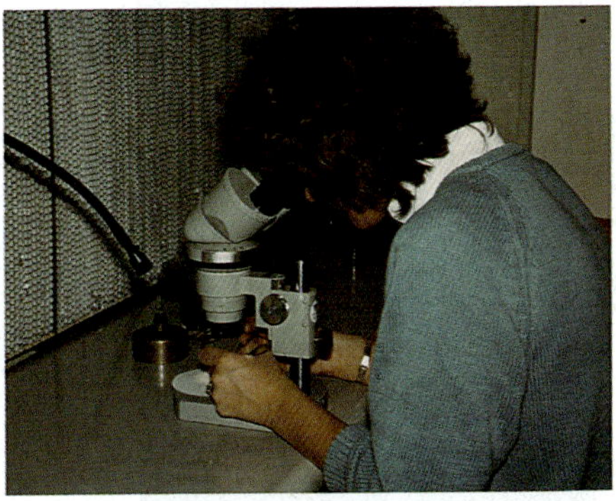

d. Using a binocular microscope in a sterile air-flow bench to dissect the meristem-tip from the shoot bud

e. Meristem-tip cultures growing under daylight fluorescence tubes in a culture room

f. Equipment required for sap inoculating a virus to a test plant

Various stages in the regeneration of a *Primula* plantlet by meristem-tip culture

a. Small meristem-tip established in culture tube

b. Tip may be made to proliferate many shoots on media containing high cytokinin and low auxin (IAA) concentrations

c. A rooted *Primula* plantlet ready for transfer to soil

d. The transferred plantlet in a peat 'jiffy pot'

e. Plastic seed-trays used to harden the plantlets before transfer to open air

f. A culture tube contaminated by fungus infection

Table 38 **Examples of common viruses that are seed-transmitted**

Virus	Host species	Percentage seed infected	Pollen transmitted
Transmitted on seed-coat			
Tobacco mosaic	tomato	2-94	–
Transmitted in embryo			
Alfalfa mosaic	alfalfa	10-55	+
Arabis mosaic	*Chenopodium album*	80-100	–
	tomato	1-2	–
Bean common mosaic	dwarf bean	18-76	+
Broad bean true mosaic	broad bean	15	–
Cucumber mosaic	chickweed	21-40	–
Lettuce mosaic	lettuce	1-14	+
Pea seed-borne	pea	<90	–
Soybean mosaic[a]	soybean	50	–
Squash mosaic[a]	melon	6-20	–

[a] These viruses are common in sub-tropical and tropical regions

mosaic virus which has been reported to infect a large number of alpine species (See p.192) and is known to be seed-transmitted in some species.

Virus transmission through the seed of an infected mother plant plays a major role in both the transmission and survival of a number of virus diseases. Seed transmission is also important in the establishment of a virus disease in a garden or field crop. Firstly, it enables infection to occur at the earliest possible time in the development of a young seedling, a factor that often governs the severity of a virus disease in a particular plant (See p.186); and secondly, infected seed results in diseased, individual seedlings being scattered widely through a field crop, where each seedling can provide a reservoir of virus for subsequent secondary spread. This is a very important factor if the particular virus is also aphid-transmitted. For example, lettuce mosaic virus (LMV) is both seed and aphid-transmitted and if commercial lettuce seed is infected with LMV even at a rate as low as 0.1%, subsequent spread by aphids in the field can result in disease epidemics. Secondary spread can be particularly severe if successive lettuce sowings are grown side by side allowing infected aphids to move rapidly to healthy young seedlings.

A similar example of a seed and aphid-transmitted virus occurring in the garden and in the nursery is cucumber mosaic virus (CMV). CMV commonly infects weed species such as chickweed (*Stellaria media*), and not only can it overwinter in the garden or nursery in this plant, but it is also seed-transmitted in it. Consequently new chickweed seedlings that germinate in spring and summer, may contain a reservoir of the virus even though the young infected chickweed shows no virus symptoms. The virus is then transmitted by aphids to various garden plants, including *Primula*, *Viola* and *Campanula* spp. to name but a few. Furthermore, weed seeds, such as those of chickweed, can remain viable in the soil for many years, allowing the long term persistence of the virus even during the temporary absence of a susceptible garden plant.

Besides the importance of seed transmission in the local spread and survival of certain viruses, seed transmission is also extremely important in the movement of viruses between countries. With this possibility in mind alpine gardeners who donate seed to the seed distributions of the various alpine garden societies, should be especially vigilant that they don not collect and donate seed from plants that display any symptoms of a virus or other disease.

A few viruses, such as the very stable and infectious tobacco mosaic virus (TMV) in tomato, are transmitted externally in or on the seed coat (**testa**). Transmission to the seedlings occurs when the cotyledon pushes its way out through the TMV-contaminated testa, or when the seedlings are handled during transplanting. This type of external virus contamination of the seed coat can be eliminated by treating the seeds with strong acid or tri-sodium phosphate solution to sterilise the surface of the seed.

In contrast to this superficial type of seed transmission, most seed-transmitted viruses enter the embryo of the seed during its development. This type of seed transmission is the most important as it cannot be eradicated from the seed. When the embryo type of seed transmission occurs, the percentage of seed infected may vary from 1 to more than 90%, depending on the particular virus and host plant concerned (Table 38).

In addition, viruses which are seed-transmitted in one host species may not be seed-transmitted in another. Other factors, such as the age of the plant at the time of infection may also determine whether seed transmission occurs and the amount of seed transmission. Temperature also has a marked effect upon seed transmission, with high temperature usually lowering the rate of transmission.

The major question relating to seed transmission that puzzles plant virologists, however, is why are some viruses able to enter the embryos of their host plant and be seed-transmitted and others not? Many theories have been advanced to answer this question, but the complete explanation is still not known.

Even when viruses are not transmitted in the seed, virus infection of the mother-plant often results in reduced seed production and loss of seed vigour. This results in low viability and slow germination and poor vigour in the young seedling.

The female gametes of a healthy plant may also become infected by the plant being pollinated by virus-infected pollen. The virus enters the ovule via the infected pollen grain. In addition, infected pollen can result in poor pollination and fertility (See p.219).

Table 39 **Common garden weeds that may be reservoirs of virus**

HOST SPECIES	VIRUS[a]	METHOD OF TRANSMISSION[b]
Boraginaceae		
Myosotis arvensis (forget-me-not)	AMV*, TBRV*, TRV	E
Caprifoliaceae		
Sambucus racemosa (elder)	CLRV	E
Caryophyllaceae		
Cerastium holosteoides (mouse-ear)	CMV*	A (n-p)
Stellaria media (chickweed)	AMV*, RRSV*, SLRV* TBRV*	E
	BWYV	A (p)
	CMV*	A (n-p)
Spergula marginata (sand-spurrey)	CMV*	A (n-p)
Chenopodiaceae		
Chenopodium album (fat hen)	AMV*	E
Commelinaceae		
Commelina nudiflora	CMV	A (n-p)
Compositae		
Anthemis cotula (stinking mayweed)	BWYV	A (n-p)
Galinsoga parviflora	CMV	A (n-p)
Matricaria maritima (scentless mayweed)	BWYV	A (p)
	CMV*	A (n-p)
Senecio vulgaris (groundsel)	AMV*, SLRV*, TBRV* TRSV*, TRV*	E
	BWYV	A (p)
	CMV	A (n-p)
Sonchus oleraceus (sowthistle)	BWYV	A (p)
	CMV	A (n-p)
Taraxacum officinale (dandelion)	CRLV, TRSV*	E
	BWYV	A (p)
Cruciferae		
Alliaria petiolata (garlic mustard)	BWYV	A (p)
Capsella bursa-pastoris (shepherds purse)	AMV*, RRSV*, SLRV* TBRV*, BWYV, TRV*	E
	BWYV	A (p)
	CMV	A (n-p)
Coronopus didymus (lesser swinecress)	BWYV	A (p)
Sinapsis alba (white mustard)	BWYV	A (p)
Thlaspi arvense (field penny-cress)	BWYV	A (p)
Cucurbitaceae		
Bryonia dioica (white bryony)	BWYV	A (p)
Labiatae		
Lamium album (white dead nettle)	BWYV	A (p)
	CMV	A (n-p)
Lamium amplexicaule (henbit)	AMV*, SLRV*, TBRV*, TRV*	E

Table 39 (continued) **Common garden weeds that may be reservoirs of virus**

HOST SPECIES	VIRUS[a]	METHOD OF TRANSMISSION[b]
Lamium purpureum (red deadnettle)	BWYV	A (p)
	CMV*	A (n-p)
Leguminosae		
Trifolium dubium (trefoil)	BWYV	A (p)
Trifolium repens (white clover)	BWYV	A (p)
Malvaceae		
Malva sylvestris (mallow)	CMV	A (n-p)
Onagraceae		
Epilobium montanum (broad-leaved willow-herb)	BWYV	A (p)
Plantaginaceae		
Plantago major (greater plantain)	AMV*	E
	BWYV	A (p)
	CMV	A (n-p)
Polygonaceae		
Polygonum convolvulvus (black bindweed)	BWYV	A (p)
	TBRV	E
Polygonum persicaria (persicaria)	AMV*	E
Rumex obtusifolius (broad-leaved dock)	CLRV	E
	TuMV	A (n-p)
Primulaceae		
Anagallis arvensis (scarlet pimpernel)	BWYV	A (p)
Rubiaceae		
Galium aparine (goosegrass)	BWYV	A (p)
Scrophulariaceae		
Veronica agrestis (field speedwell)	TBRV	E
Veronica persica (Buxbaum's speedwell)	BWYV	A (p)
	CMV	A (n-p)
Urticaceae		
Urtica urens (annual nettle)	CMV	A (n-p)
Violaceae		
Viola arvensis (field pansy)	BWYV	A (p)
	TRV	E
Viola tricolor (wild pansy)	CLRV	E
	CMV	A (n-p)

* This virus is seed-borne in this host.

[a] Key to virus identification AMV, arabis mosaic; BWYV, beet western yellows; CLRV, cherry leaf roll; CMV, cucumber mosaic; CRLV, cherry raspleaf; RRSV, raspberry ringspot; SLRV, strawberry latent ringspot; TRV, tobacco rattle; TRSV, tobacco ringspot; TBRV, tomato blackring; TuMV, turnip mosaic.

[b] Key to mode of transmission: E, eelworm-transmitted, A, aphid transmitted; p, persistent transmission; n-p, non-persistent transmission

Transmission by Vegetative Propagation

Vegetative propagation is widely used for the multiplication of many horticultural crops including many plants of interest to the alpine gardener. The importance of vegetative propagation in the transmission of viruses has already been mentioned (See p.179), for if a mother-plant is infected with virus the majority of the vegetative propagules will also be infected. This is the case with any kind of propagule, whether it be a cutting, tuber, runner, sucker or bulb.

Consequently, vegetative propagation is a very efficient method of virus spread, without the problem for the virus of having to enter and establish infection in a healthy plant.

In nature, virus spread through vegetative propagules may be expected to occur over short distances by natural scattering of infected propagules such as tubers, but man has been responsible for the long distance and often worldwide movement of many viruses by this means.

Although, in general, virus infection within the plant cannot be cured by chemical or other treatments, complex procedures do exist whereby viruses can be eradicated from valuable infected clonal plant material. These procedures are described and discussed in Section 5.5.

CHAPTER FIVE

Control

There are really two main approaches to tackling pest and disease problems. The first is to prevent problems from starting at all; the second is to eliminate or reduce an existing infestation. Together they constitute control measures the general principles of which are described below. More specific details of these measures are provided in the chapters describing individual pests and diseases.

CULTURAL METHODS OF CONTROL

This chapter describes cultural practices to prevent pest or disease problems from starting or, failing that, from getting out of hand. The basis of all these practices is attention to good hygiene and sanitation. This aspect is frequently mentioned in this book particularly as there may be no other control measures available for certain pests and diseases.

It is important to understand the biology and life histories of pests and diseases, their interrelationships, and the effects of the environment on them i.e. their **ecology** because this helps to understand the nature of the problems they cause. Plant pathologists frequently refer to the epidemiology of a disease – which means the development, dispersal and amount of disease and this information is needed to decide when and how to control these problems. The identification of pests and diseases has been discussed earlier in the book (Chapters 2, 3 & 4). We stress that it is not possible to choose the appropriate method of prevention or control unless you accurately identify the cause of the problem whether it be a pest, fungus or some other factor. It is not difficult to recognise most common pests and to learn which are harmful and which are beneficial, but it is surprising how many people confuse hover flies with wasps, or can't tell a ladybird larva from a Colorado potato beetle grub or a vine weevil from a ground beetle. Diseases caused by bacteria and fungi are more difficult to identify partly because the causal organisms are much smaller and also because many cause similar symptoms on plants. Identification usually depends on isolating the disease organism and growing it in culture. Nevertheless the major groups of bacteria and fungi and the diseases they cause can be recognised and this is often sufficient for choosing the appropriate control measures. The identification of a virus disease usually requires even more specialist knowledge and often eradication of the diseased plant is the only viable option to control its spread.

Diseases caused by pests, bacteria, fungi or viruses are much easier to control if treated at an early stage and clearly this saves time and trouble. By checking plants regularly for the first signs of attack, causes can be identified and treated promptly. The various cultural methods that may be used to prevent or control pests and diseases are described below.

Weeds and other plants as sources of harmful organisms. Weeds, perennial herbaceous plants, trees and shrubs are major sources of certain pests, fungi and viruses of alpine plants. For example, once certain perennial shrubs are infected by virus they remain infective throughout their life and are subsequently a perennial source of infection for other plants. Annual weeds such as chickweed (*Stellaria media*) which grow during winter provide an opportunity for aphids and viruses to survive. Consequently the viruses can be readily transmitted from these weeds to ornamental plants in the spring. The remains of plants killed by fungi and left in the ground can be a source of new infection months or even years later. This is particularly true of diseases caused by fungi forming persistent survival structures such as sclerotia (*Botryotinia*, *Helicobasidium*, *Sclerotinia*, *Sclerotium*, *Thanetephorus*) or chlamydospores (*Thielaviopsis*, *Fusarium* – See Chapter 3). It follows, that you must be aware of these sources of infection with a view to removing them from the garden. Some garden plants and weeds which often act as reservoirs of viruses are listed in Tables 31 and 39. Note the importance of these plants as reservoirs of cucumber mosaic virus (CMV) and arabis mosaic virus (AMV), the two viruses which occur most frequently in bulbs and other plants (Tables 29 and 30). Since CMV is readily transmitted by aphids commonly found in the garden, it may be necessary to consider removing CMV-infected shrubs from the garden. Unfortunately, the decision to remove infected shrubs is not an easy one, because the symptoms of virus-infection are often minor or **latent** in the shrubs. The dilemma is whether to uproot a well-established shrub or risk infection of susceptible alpine plants by CMV, especially since neighbouring gardens may also contain CMV-infected shrubs. Fortunately, the threat posed by AMV is less serious because the eelworms which transmit the virus usually remain close to the roots of the infected shrub. It is unlikely that AMV will spread far provided you avoid placing alpine plants close to AMV-infected shrubs or do not remove soil from the vicinity for use elsewhere (Chapter 4).

Because of their potential danger as reservoirs of insects, viruses and some fungi, annual weeds such as chickweed, or perennial weeds such as dock (*Rumex obtusifolius*) should be removed at regular intervals by hand or hoe, or with chemical weedkillers. It is particularly important to remove chickweed before it produces seed, because CMV is transmitted to seedlings via the seed (Chapter 4).

Beet western yellows virus (BWYV) is a relatively 'new' virus which is rapidly becoming established in crops and weeds in Britain. A strain of BWYV which infects lettuce and various brassica crops is now widespread in Britain, Europe and the USA, infecting commercial vegetable crops and a wide range of weed species (Table 39). It causes severe yellowing of the older outer leaves in lettuce and reddening of the leaf margins in some brassicas (Plate 21). The symptoms in weeds and other hosts are similar, with either chlorosis or reddening of the older leaves developing. The colour depends on whether or not the host species has the red-coloured anthocyanin chemical present in the leaves. The reddening symptoms of BWYV are frequently seen in gardens in cauliflower, calabrese and honesty (*Lunaria annua*) (Plate 21). There have been no reports to date of BWYV infecting alpine plants, but the recent spread of the virus, together with its wide host range, makes their infection almost inevitable.

Cutworms can be harboured by a wide range of weed species from where they migrate to ornamental plants. Removal of weeds reduces damage from cutworms provided it is done before the adult moths have laid their eggs.

Removal of infected plants (roguing). As well as removing plants which are reservoirs of pests and diseases, it is important to remove plants which become infected during growth. The process of removing individual, infected plants is referred to as 'roguing' and is often used in commercial crops to prevent the spread of pests and diseases. In the garden, CMV frequently infects marrows, cucumbers and violas (Chapter 4) and the plants should be removed and destroyed as soon as symptoms appear. CMV-infected plants remain infective when pulled from the ground and should not be placed on top of the compost heap where aphids can continue feeding. Infected plants should be burnt promptly or sealed in a polythene bag and disposed of with the household waste. Bulbs which develop abnormal leaf growth should be removed and destroyed as they are usually infected with narcissus bulb flies or narcissus eelworm. Plants which have been attacked by high populations of aphids or other pests may never recover and are also best removed and destroyed.

Some fungal diseases can be controlled in a similar manner. Infection by the *Allium* white rot fungus (*Sclerotium cepivorum*) starts from sclerotia in soil then grows to neighbouring plants by contact between roots and stem bases (Plates 16d, e). This explains the characteristic patchy occurrence of white rot disease. If left, infected plants produce large numbers of sclerotia which greatly increases the chances of infection in future years. The disease usually shows as wilting and yellowing of the outer leaves. Such plants, together with the adhering soil and sclerotia, should be removed with a trowel, transferred to a polythene bag and burnt or removed with household waste. Other soil-borne diseases can be treated in this manner e.g. *Sclerotinia*, *Helicobasidium*. Aerial diseases can be controlled by removing infected leaves before they produce spores. Dead and yellowing leaves with grey mould (*Botryotinia fuckeliana* (*Botrytis cinerea*)) should be removed as soon as possible to minimise spore production. *Coniothyrium hellebori* causing spotting on leaves and flowers is partly controlled by removing infected old leaves before emergence of the healthy new leaves (Plate 18b). This stops the spores from the previous season's leaves transferring to new growth. Powdery mildews, rusts and smuts are easily recognised and prompt removal and destruction of diseased tissue helps to stop them spreading to other plants.

Eradication of 'volunteer' plants. Plants surviving from a previous season's crop are called 'volunteers' and are potential reservoirs for viruses, fungi and certain pests. For example potato tubers left in the ground produce shoots the following spring. The new shoots are often a source of virus for transmission by aphids or of spores of the potato blight fungus *Phytophthora infestans* to infect new susceptible crops which may be some distance away. As a precaution, volunteer plants should be removed and destroyed. Similarly, the overwintered stumps of old cabbage, Brussels sprouts or other brassica plant should be removed and destroyed because they are sources of turnip mosaic virus (TuMV) or cauliflower mosaic virus (CaMV) as well as the cabbage aphid which transmits both viruses in spring.

Modification of planting procedures. Another practice which causes serious problems from pests and diseases in commercial crops, is the year round cultivation of similar crops. This is common in tropical and subtropical areas where crops overlap during the season. The problem also occurs in northern Europe with *Allium* species (onions and leeks) and brassicas. Overwintered crops overlap in spring with newly emerged or planted seedlings and this provides a 'green bridge' for viruses, eelworms and fungi to spread to the new crop. The problem is reduced by making sure that there is a short break between old and new crops. The epidemics of leek yellow stripe virus in leeks which occurred in the Netherlands in the early 1970s were controlled by introducing a short break between consecutive leek crops. Similar breaks have been used to control celery mosaic virus in celery in California, USA.

When spring plantings of brassicas overlap with overwintered crops of broccoli or cabbage, turnip mosaic virus and cauliflower mosaic viruses can increase rapidly and become a threat to alpine crucifers. A break between crops of two to three weeks is sufficient to avoid the problem.

Cultivation in isolated areas. Diseases can often be avoided by growing crops away from the sources of infection as with the production of virus-free potato 'seed' tubers and virus-free strawberry runners. There are certification schemes whereby legislation ensures that the disease-free parent plants are grown only in areas remote from other potato or strawberry crops and private gardens.

The same principle can be effective in the garden even though only short distances are involved. For example, it would be unwise to place a virus-free *Primula* next to other primula plants which are likely to be infected by virus. The new virus-free *Primula* should be isolated by either placing it in another part of the garden, or by removing the old plants.

It follows that new plants, whose health status is not known, should be isolated or quarantined for several weeks at least, before placing them in the alpine-house. This procedure has already been recommended when checking for insect pests (Chapter 2) and fungi (Chapter 3).

Virus-free seed. Viruses can be transmitted via the seed produced on infected plants (See Chapter 4). Therefore seed should only be obtained from reliable sources ensuring, as far as possible, that it is free of virus. However, to put the matter in perspective, only about one third of plant viruses are transmitted by seed and then not in all the host species they infect.

When seed transmission does occur it can be serious, especially if aphid-transmission occurs as well (See Chapter 4). Very small amounts of seed transmission are sufficient to provide scattered, infected plants, from which aphids transmit viruses to other plants and start an epidemic. The very low rate of 0.1% seed infection by lettuce mosaic virus (LMV) is sufficient to cause an outbreak of the virus in lettuce. Other examples of viruses which are both seed- and aphid-transmitted and important in commerce are bean common mosaic virus in dwarf beans (*Phaseolus vulgaris*) and alfalfa mosaic virus in alfalfa (*Medicago sativa*).

Unfortunately, it is not known which viruses are transmitted by the seeds of alpine plants and which are not. Without this knowledge it would be wise to adopt a safety first policy and avoid collecting seed from plants which are suspected of being infected. Clearly, it is essential that seed from plant suspected of being infected by viruses is not given to seed-exchange programmes or other gardeners. Even if the seed does not carry virus, germination is likely to be poor and the resulting plants of low vigour (See Chapter 4).

Virus-free planting material. This is very important to the alpine gardener and nurseryman because many popular plant varieties are propagated vegetatively. Vegetatively propagated or cloned plants present special problems because once infected with virus there is no easy method of curing them. The eradication of virus from an infected plant is achieved only by the complicated process of meristem-tip culture, heat- or chemotherapy or a combination of these procedures (Chapter 5). Because of the time and cost of eradicating virus from infected clones only the most desirable clones are likely to be treated. It is desirable that healthy and virus-free material of the more popular clones, particularly the older, named *Primula* hybrids, should be available. The difference in vigour and quality between infected and healthy plants of these hybrids is often very great (Plate 24). Furthermore, a healthy plant would not be a source of virus infection for other plants.

It is also highly desirable that only virus-free stocks of plants should be propagated and distributed. Hopefully some propagators will adopt the techniques required for producing virus-free clones and make available healthy clones of the popular, old varieties of alpine plants. The possibility of individuals or groups carrying out virus eradication programmes is discussed in Chapter 5.

Infected vegetatively propagated planting material also provides a means by which pests and diseases spread between countries. Most 'advanced countries' have import and quarantine regulations aimed at controlling the entry of diseases and pests of plants and excluding specific virus diseases and/or their vectors (See Chapter 6). Such schemes are expensive to establish and administer and their effectiveness is frequently restricted by economic and political considerations. Nevertheless, the enforcement of such regulations is essential if the spread of harmful viruses, bacteria, fungi and pests is to be minimised world-wide. If gardeners and growers in different countries wish to exchange vegetatively propagated material it is possible that this could be done with young virus-free plants raised by tissue culture (See p.255). Only healthy planting material would be distributed and such plants would readily meet the various plant health (phytosanitary) requirements for international exchange.

Avoidance of the virus vector. One of the control measures described earlier (Chapter 4) was to grow susceptible plants in areas where the virus is absent, for example the production of virus-free 'seed' potatoes. A similar procedure can be used to avoid the vector of a virus. This is the other main reason why most British 'seed' potatoes are produced in Scotland. The climate there is unfavourable for aphids in the spring and, as a result, the spread of potato viruses is negligible.

This suggests that gardeners and growers in Scotland, and hilly, windy areas of Britain probably don't have to contend with aphid-transmitted viruses. Elsewhere, however, the aphid vectors are likely to be present. Aphid vectors can be excluded from small areas by covering a garden frame with nylon gauze of suitably fine mesh to exclude aphids. In this way virus-free plants can be kept healthy. Nylon mesh is routinely used to exclude aphids and other insects from commercial greenhouses in which virus-free stock plants are grown. The frame could be completely covered with gauze or could have a glass top and gauze sides. Alternatively, the alpine house can be made insect-proof by covering the vents with gauze and by fitting a gauze-covered second door. Such aphid-proofing should be seriously considered by professional nurserymen at least for some of their alpine houses and certainly where primulas are propagated.

Viruses transmitted by soil-borne eelworms and fungi can be controlled by the use of compost prepared from sterilised soil (See Chapter 4).

Cross-protection against viruses. Infection by a mild strain of certain viruses protects the plant against subsequent infections by severe strains of the same virus. This phenomenon is called **cross-protection**. There may be some loss of vigour following infection with a mild strain of virus but the extensive damage caused by the severe strain is avoided.

Cross-protection was widely used in the 1970's to protect tomato crops against the effects of tobacco mosaic virus (TMV). Mild strains of TMV were produced by mutagenesis in the laboratory and used to inoculate tomato seedlings. This method has also been used to protect citrus crops against citrus tristeza virus and courgettes against zucchini yellow mosaic virus. Cross-protection probably occurs naturally. Some garlic plants which are naturally infected with virus still produce as high a yield as virus-free plants of the same variety. If, however the virus-free plants are re-infected with different, severe, strains of virus the yield is dramatically reduced and much lower than the yield of plants naturally infected with mild virus strains.

It seems likely that natural cross-protection has occurred with some alpine primulas. For example, certain clones of some varieties show only very mild symptoms of virus and grow reasonably well year after year. Other clones of the same variety, initially virus-free, deteriorate rapidly and show severe symptoms of virus infection. One explanation is that the mild virus strains in the former clones cross-protect them against the more severe strains. Over the years, the mildly infected clones of vegetatively propagated alpines may have been selected unknowingly because they were more vigorous. Clones infected with severe virus stains would have been discarded or died.

Pest traps. Sometimes it is possible to determine whether pests are present or to identify peaks of pest activity by using traps. The pests are seen in the traps before becoming noticeable on the plant. Most traps use a chemical or specific colour to attract the pest together with a mechanism of killing them. For example, many aphids, whiteflies and true flies are strongly attracted by a yellow colour – as shown by the large numbers of aphids on cars of this colour. Insect traps can be bought at garden centres or you can prepare your own. A suitable water trap consists of a flat-bottomed plastic dish 20 cm in diameter and 6 cm deep which is painted fluorescent yellow (obtainable from Dane & Co Ltd., Sugar House Lane, London E15 2QN) (Plate 25). The trap is half-filled with water containing a drop of washing-up liquid in which the pests drown; you can also include a Campden tablet (as used in wine-making) to stop the insects rotting and producing a putrefying mess. The trap should be examined regularly and the insects identified. The water should be replenished or replaced as necessary. This type of trap is most suitable for the greenhouse. Unfortunately, if used in the open garden or on the nursery they also catch beneficial insects such as hover flies and butterflies. Another version of the yellow trap uses glue to catch and kill the insects. The sticky trap consists of a sheet of card or plastic (obtainable from Corruplast Ltd., Correx House, Madleaze Industrial Estate, Bristol Road, Gloucester, GL1 5SG) 15 cm × 20 cm and a few mm thick, painted yellow and coated with the sticky material (Biological Control Systems, Treforest Industrial Estate, Pontypridd, Mid-Glamorgan, CF37 5SV) (Plate 25). Sticky traps also catch spiders, hover-flies and other beneficial insects and small animals so, as before, are best confined to the greenhouse. Traps are mainly used to monitor the presence and abundance of insect pests and any resulting reduction in populations is a bonus. Sticky traps have developed from 'fly papers' used for hanging in kitchens. The fly papers contained insecticide and have now been withdrawn because they proved to be toxic to humans.

Traps for catching mammals such as moles, mice, rabbits and voles are particularly effective in greenhouses, frames and sheds. However, they should be used and stored carefully to avoid killing other animals or birds, or injuring children.

Exclusion of pests. Barriers are useful for excluding cats, dogs, rabbits and birds. To exclude rabbits, a wire netting fence should be installed round the garden or part of the garden with the base buried at least 30 cm deep. Frames can be covered to keep out birds and rabbits and wire mesh (mesh size 1 cm) placed at the bottom of the frame or buried to keep out voles and field mice. Fine netting as described earlier for protecting virus-free plants against aphids, woven fabrics and polythene are becoming more popular for the exclusion of insects from the seed bed and frames. Some synthetic materials used for nets will last for up to five years and should be removed carefully, cleaned and dried and stored in a dry place out of sunlight. In the garden, black cotton thread can be 'woven' to protect special crocus, primulas etc. from birds. Avoid nylon thread which takes a long time to break down and becomes tangled in birds feathers; for similar reasons make sure that all unwanted cotton thread is cleared away after use.

Mulches are also used to deter some pests in Israel and the USA, and reflective aluminium-coated or grey or white plastic sheets are used to repel aphids, whiteflies and other insects which transmit viruses. Again they probably have limited use in the garden but they might help protect plants in the propagating frame or plunge bed.

Table 40 **Species available for biological control and pests controlled.**

BIOLOGICAL CONTROL SPECIES	PEST CONTROLLED
Amblyseius cucumeris	Thrips
Aphidius matricariae	Aphids
Aphidoletes aphidimyza	Aphids
Bacillus thuringiensis	Caterpillars
Chrysopa carnea	Aphids and thrips
Cryptolaemus montrouzieri	Mealy bugs
Dacnusa sibirica	Leafminers
Diglyphus isaea	Leafminers
Encarsia formosa	Whiteflies
Heterorhabditis sp.	Vine weevils
Leptomastix/Leptomastidea	Mealy bugs
Metaphycus helvolus	Scale insects
Phytoseiulus persimilis	Red spider mites
Praon volucre	Aphids
Steinernema feltiae	Vine weevils
Verticillium lecanii	Aphids

BIOLOGICAL CONTROL

All living organisms have natural enemies and, in the wild, these exert a considerable influence on their prey and may limit the build-up of populations of harmful species. Thus, most pests have parasites or predators which help to keep their numbers in check. The use of this phenomenon in crop protection is what we call classical biological control, although over the years biological control has sometimes been used as an umbrella term to include most non-chemical methods of suppressing pests and diseases as well; here we will use the term in its strict sense. In the absence of their natural enemies pests can reach devastating numbers which may lead to crop loss. For example, certain sub-tropical pests have been imported into temperate regions and they have found an ideal niche in glasshouses or polytunnels. In the absence of natural enemies these pests have run riot – good examples include red spider mites, glasshouse and tobacco whiteflies and western flower thrips in glasshouses and polytunnels in Britain and northern Europe. Similarly, many of the most severe pests in north America originated in Europe. In other cases pests have developed resistance to the insecticides which are used to control them yet their natural enemies are killed by these chemicals. Where these insecticides are still used the pests survive and, in the absence of their natural enemies, they build-up to even greater populations than if there were no chemicals applied at all. Such a situation occurred in the control of red spider mite in glasshouses and with onion fly some years ago and more recently with western flower thrips.

The remarkable benefits of natural enemies has stimulated man to harness their use in crop protection. This has led to extensive research on parasites and predators of pests leading to their identification, evaluation of their potential as biological control organisms and their introduction into problem areas. The idea of harnessing these organisms is not a new one and one of the earliest records goes back to the 13th century when the Chinese placed ants' nests in citrus and litchi trees to control fruit pests. One of the first records in European horticulture dates back to Louden's (1850) recommendation for growers to keep toads in the mushroom house to eat ants, other insects and worms; we don't know how many growers took up this idea! A significant milestone in the history of biological control in horticulture occurred when Dr Fox-Wilson, who worked as the entomologist at the Royal Horticultural Society's Garden during the period between the two world wars, found glasshouse whitefly being parasitised by the native wasp *Encarsia partenopea*. This parasite was actually reared, maintained and released to RHS members but soon lost favour, probably because it failed to operate in hot summer conditions. A new era began when Mr Speyer, an entomologist working at the Cheshunt Research Station (the fore-runner of the Glasshouse Crops Research Institute, which is now part of Horticulture Research International) was asked to examine some blackened whitefly scales on foliage in a tomato-grower's glasshouse. These turned out to be scales parasitised by the sub-tropical insect, *Encarsia formosa*, the minute wasp which is now widely used to control glasshouse whitefly in many parts of the world. Mr Speyer developed methods of mass-rearing these parasites which culminated in the production of one and a half million wasps in 1935 which were distributed to many different countries. The production of parasites continued until 1949 when the advent of the new generation of potent synthetic insecticides, the organo-chlorines such as DDT, aldrin and dieldrin, offered growers a panacea for all their pest problems and so the use of biological control agents lost favour. It was not until the discovery of new races of red spider mite which could resist first the organo-chlorine compounds, and later, the organo-phosphorus insecticides which led to a total breakdown in the pest's control, that interest in biological control was re-kindled. At our Institute, methods for the rearing, maintenance and release of a range of parasites and predators to control several important glasshouse crop pests have been developed since the 1960s and have attracted the horticulture industry's attention. Today many of these biological control agents are used by amateurs and commercial growers to protect their crops and it is now an established crop protection measure and gaining in importance.

The potential of biological control agents is quite clearly enormous and we have really only exploited the 'tip of the iceberg' when it comes to studying natural enemies and their affects on pests. It is not just the pests which has attracted the attention of biologists but also diseases; thus methods for controlling plant diseases using biological agents has also received a great deal of attention. Attempts have been made to develop a biological control system for the suppression of the silver leaf disease of plum. An antagonistic fungus, *Trichoderma viridis* was introduced into the infected tree by driving wooden plugs containing the fungal inoculum into the bark. Whilst showing initial promise, subsequent results have been variable.

To be a promising candidate for use in biological control, a parasite or predator or pathogen must possess certain qualities. Ideally it should be;

1. **Easily bred or cultured** so that large numbers can be produced for release in troubled areas.
2. **Specific in its action**. It is no use rearing and releasing a parasite or predator which devastates beneficial and harmless organisms as well as pest species. This would become a pest or disease in its own right.
3. **A species which does not attack the crop plant as well as the target pest or disease**. If it attacked the crop this would be self-defeating and would cause more harm than good.
4. **An organism which can operate successfully under the conditions which normally prevail where the crop is grown**. Thus the parasitic wasp *Encarsia partenopea*, mentioned above, was abandoned for glasshouse whitefly control because it did not operate efficiently in the hot conditions in glasshouses in the summer months. Interest in this species has been renewed recently with the view to controlling cabbage whitefly which lives outdoors in temperate regions.
5. **A species which can find its prey easily or locate the disease pathogen**, and for all agents they should be capable of breeding rapidly to keep up or overtake the development of the prey or pathogen species.

The timing of the release of biological control agents is critical. These agents do not take immediate action like a chemical spray, they build up slowly and gradually consume the prey. They must therefore be introduced early on in the infestation of plants otherwise they will not keep up with the build-up of the pest or disease. So it is imperative to monitor pest problems. In commerce it has sometimes been found necessary to introduce the pest itself – something that takes some courage, but this is to ensure that the correct balance between predator or parasite and prey is achieved right at the beginning of the season. This is not necessary for the amateur who can usually act quickly in what is most often a small growing area and release natural enemies to control a pest outbreak.

Natural enemies can be encouraged in the garden or on the nursery by strictly limiting the use of insecticides – no widespread spraying of large areas. They can also be encouraged by growing plants attractive to them. For example, hover flies, whose larvae are important predators, are attracted to the flowers of the ornamental bindweed *Convolvulus tricolor*, buck wheat, *Fagopyrum esculentum*, rose of Sharon, *Hypericum calycinum*, and certain Eryngiums (e.g. *Eryngium tripartitum*). Some gardeners collect ladybirds and release them on aphid-infested plants and this proves to be useful even although some of the ladybirds will scurry off.

Specific details about biological control organisms, their availability and use are provided in the following chapter, Natural Enemies of Pests. The organisms presently available for controlling pests are listed in Table 40 and suppliers in Table 41.

Natural enemies of pests

The populations of most parasites and predators are governed by the size of the population of their prey and effective control tends to lag behind the rapid growth of the pest or disease. Therefore, in most cases considerable damage is done to plants before the natural enemies have suppressed the pest or disease. Another problem is that in the garden and on the nursery there is little control over most of the factors which govern the fluctations in both pest and predator. In the greenhouse or polytunnel conditions can be more effectively controlled so that parasites and predators are provided with favourable conditions. It is worth mentioning that most pesticides are just as lethal to parasites and predators as they are to pests. The more important parasites and predators are briefly outlined below;

Insects

Mirids or Capsids (Family Miridae, Order Hemiptera)

These bugs are equipped with mouthparts which are modified to form a slender, jointed beak (**proboscis**) which can either be used to pierce plant tissues (certain mirids are important plant pests – See Chapter 2) or to spear and suck up the juices of their prey. The adults have two pairs of wings, the fore pair are hardened and helped to protect the membraneous hind wings (Plate 1). These insects have an incomplete metamorphosis the life stages including egg, nymphs and adults. An important predatory species is the black-kneed capsid, *Blepharidopterus angulatus* (Fall.). Both nymphs and adults feed on red spider mites in particular but also aphids, leafhoppers, thrips and caterpillars. This capsid is particularly important in orchards. Several other species are common in gardens.

Anthocorid bugs (Family Anthocoridae, Order Hemiptera)

These bugs are related to mirids and have similar piercing mouthparts. Several species occur commonly in gardens and they will even give the gardener a painful stab. Important species include *Anthocoris nemorum* (L.) and *Anthocoris nemoralis* (Fab.). Once more both nymphs and adults are predatory and will attack aphids, scale insects, suckers, mirids, caterpillars, midges, weevils and mites. One of the most active anthocorids, an *Orius* species, can be reared in large numbers and is due to be marketed as a biological control agent soon.

Dragonflies (Order Odonata)

These insects are familiar to most gardeners and can be seen darting to and fro particularly near ponds in their hawking for prey. In their juvenile stages in ponds and streams and as adults they eat other insects. The adults feed on flies, mosquitoes, beetles and sometimes wasps or sawflies. Most prey are caught on the wing.

Lacewings (Order Neuroptera)

There are three families of lacewings which include important predatory species. The most familiar species are probably the green lacewings particularly *Chrysopa carnea* Steph. (Plate 26) which is commonly seen on windows or indoors searching for somewhere to hibernate. These insects lay their eggs on long stalks on leaves (Plate 26). It is the larva of the lacewing which is a valuable predator and its jaws are curved to form hollow callipers which are used to hold, pierce and suck up the body contents of the prey (Plate 26). A single larva of *C. carnea* will consume about 400 aphids in 15 days. Lacewing larvae also consume adelgids, suckers, leafhoppers and red spider mites. Mass-rearing methods and larval releases techniques have been worked out for two species of lacewings but in trials on cucumber crops infested with the cotton aphid neither species established a breeding colony in the glasshouse and therefore repeated releases were required. These experiments eventually achieved control of the aphids. Three companies produce lacewings commercially (Table 2).

Table 41 **Suppliers of biological control agents**

BIOLOGICAL CONTROL SUPPLIER	**PEST** OR **DISEASE** (see key below)																
	1	**2**	**3**	**4**	**5**	**6**	**7**	**8**	**9**	**10**	**11**	**12**	**13**	**14**	**15**	**16**	**17**
Agricultural Genetics Co Ltd, MicroBio Division, 126 Science Park, Milton Road, Cambridge, CB4 4FZ										●					●		
Applied Horticulture, a division of Fargro Ltd., Toddington Lane, Littlehampton, West Sussex, BN17 6LP	●	●	●	●	●	●	●	●	●	●		●	●				●
Biological Crop Protection Ltd, Occupation Road, Wye, Ashford, Kent	●	●	●	●		●	●	●	●	●		●	●		●		●
Brinkman Biological Control, Spur Road, Quarry Lane, Chichester, West Sussex, PO19 2RP	●	●	●	●		●	●	●	●		●	●	●				●
English Woodlands Ltd, Graffham, Petworth, West Sussex, GU28 0LR	●	●	●	●		●			●		●	●	●	●			●
Koppert (UK) Ltd, 1 Wadhurst Business Park, Faircrouch Lane, Wadhurst, East Sussex, TN5 6PT	●	●	●	●	●	●	●	●	●	●	●	●	●		●	●	●
Natural Pest Control, Yapton Road, Barnham, Bognor Regis, West Sussex, PO22 0BQ	●	●	●		●	●	●	●	●				●				

KEY TO NUMBERS
1 Amblyseius cucumeris
2 Aphidius matricariae
3 Aphidoletes aphidimyza
4 Bacillus thuringiensis
5 Chrysopa carnea
6 Cryptolaemus montrouzieri
7 Dacnusa sibirica
8 Diglyphus isaea
9 Encarsia formosa
10 Heterorhabditis sp.
11 Leptomastix/Leptomastidea
12 Metaphycus helvolus
13 Phytoseiulus persimilis
14 Praon volucre
15 Steinernema feltiae
16 Verticillium lecanii
17 Sticky traps

Beetles (Order Coleoptera)

There are a large number of extremely useful parasitic and predatory beetles many of which are common in gardens and on nurseries. The more important species are described below;

Ladybirds (Family Coccinellidae)

These brightly coloured beetles are probably the most familiar of all insects to gardeners and commercial growers and their predatory behaviour is legendary. There are about 40 species in Britain the most familiar being the seven spot ladybird, *Coccinella septempunctata* L., with its red wing cases bearing seven black spots (Plate 25c). Both adult and larva (Plate 25) are predatory and eat large numbers of aphids, scale insects, mealybugs, thrips and mites. One seven spot larva can eat 400 peach-potato aphids in 35 days. Ladybirds over-winter as adults often in large groups. All gardeners and nurserymen should learn to identify the stages of the ladybird's life cycle including the eggs which are elongate, bright orange-yellow and deposited on end in clusters on plant foliage or surrounding objects such as stones (Plate 25c). The pupae (chrysalids) (Plate 25d) are commonly mistaken for Colorado potato beetles. Mass-rearing of common species of ladybirds is extremely difficult and laborious and there are no commercial producers of these valuable predators.

However, one particular success story concerns the use of the predatory coccinellid, *Cryptolaemus montrouzieri* Mulsant, for the control of mealybugs on citrus and under glass. In the USA 30 million beetles are reared annually for control of these pests. In its development a single beetle larva may consume up to 250 mealybugs. These ladybirds are also widely available in Britain for use in glasshouses (See Table 41).

Ground beetles (Family Carabidae) and **Rove beetles** (Family Staphylinidae)

There are many different species of ground and rove beetle in the garden and on the nursery, some of them like the black ground beetle, *Pterostichus melanarius* (Illiger), are very familiar to growers. Most of the species are predatory and are equipped with powerful jaws. They are mainly nocturnal in activity but are frequently observed when plants, stones and debris are disturbed. Both adults and larvae feed on other insects taking eggs, larvae, pupae and adults. The violet ground beetle, *Carabus violaceus* L., also consumes slugs and there is considerable interest in the rearing of beetles for use in slug control. As far as we know there are no commercial suppliers of these predatory beetles.

Parasitic wasps (Order Hymenoptera)

This important group of insects contains many different species widely used in biological control.

Ichneumon flies (Family Ichneumonidae) are mainly parasites of butterflies and moths. The adults are characterised by having very long antennae, legs and **ovipositor** (egg-laying organ). This ovipositor is used to locate and insert an egg into the prey's body, the larva living as an internal parasite. None of these ichneumons is reared on a commercial basis for biological control.

Braconids (Family Braconidae) are smaller insects but extremely important internal parasites particularly of butterflies, moths and also aphids. One species, *Aphidius matricarius* Hal., is reared by commercial companies for aphid control in glasshouses (Table 41). This species causes the body of the aphid to form the dry papery 'mummy' which is easily recognised and commonly displays a perfectly round hole through which the adult parasite has escaped. Many gardeners will be familiar with the species, *Apanteles glomeratus* (L.) which commonly parasitises the large white butterfly. The larvae of this parasite are gregarious and after emerging from the body of the fully-grown caterpillar they pupate in a mass of yellow cocoons (Plate 25f). Three other braconids, *Dacnusa sibirica* Telenga, *Diglyphus isaea* and *Opius pallipes* Wesmael, are valuable internal parasites of leaf-miners, the adult female insect locating the leaf-miner larva with her ovipositor and laying an egg inside the host within the leaf. Certain of these species of braconid are reared commercially for biological control in glasshouses and have even been shown to be effective against the recently introduced south American leaf miner *Liriomyza huidobrensis* (Table 41).

Chalcids (Family Chalcidae) are very tiny insects and very valuable parasites and include the glasshouse whitefly parasite *Encarsia formosa* Gahan, which is probably the most widely used biological control insect throughout the world. The adult wasp which is only 0.6 mm long has a yellow abdomen and black head and thorax. It is attracted to its host by the odours given off by the whitefly honeydew. Adults feed on the honeydew and on body fluids of the parasitised whitefly scales. Each female lays its eggs singly, parasitising about 50-100 scales. The larval wasp feeds within the scale which turns black half way through the wasp's development (Plate 26e). The wasp pupates within the scale and finally emerges through a hole in the body of the scale (Plate 26f). Males of this wasp are rare and most reproduction takes place parthenogenetically. This parasitic wasp also attacks the tobacco whitefly, *Bemisia tabaci* (Gennadius), which is becoming a pest of ornamental plants in glasshouses in Britain and a very severe pest of a wide range of crops in sub-tropical regions of the world.

Another important parasite is *Trichogramma* which feeds on butterflies and moths. This parasite has been the subject of considerable research but is not yet available commercially.

Predatory wasps (Family Vespidae)

Several species of common wasp are predators of insects in gardens and fields. This comes as a surprise to many people who only think of wasps as being a nuisance. The adult wasps feed on nectar and other sweet materials but the young are fed almost entirely on flies, spiders and other small prey. Some specialists even recommend setting up nest boxes for wasps to encourage these species in gardens but sited well away from the house.

Predatory and Parasitic flies (Order Diptera)

Many species of true fly are important predators or parasites of insects and mites in the garden. Amongst the most important predators of insects and mites are hover flies (Family Syrphidae) which resemble small bees or wasps with their bright yellow and black coloration. A few species of this group are pests like the bulb flies (See Chapter 2), while others are saprophytic but many have larvae which feed on aphids and other small insects. Adult insects are expert fliers and pollinate flowers. The minute eggs which are pale yellow or white are laid on leaves. The larva which emerges from these eggs has no legs or head and has a tapered soft body typical of many maggots (Plate 26d). The anterior end has two mouth hooks with which the larva lacerates its prey. Body fluids are then sucked up (Plate 26d). The life cycle is completed when the larva pupates. Certain hover fly larvae have been recorded as eating 600 peach-potato aphids in their 3-week life and as females may lay up to 150 eggs, it is clear these insects have great potential for biological control. Hover flies can be encouraged in gardens by establishing plants which produce flowers with abundant nectar and pollen as a source of food for the adults.

Flies in several other families are predatory; these include the robber or assassin flies (Family Asilidae), stiletto flies (Family Therevidae), phorids (Family Phoridae) and chloropids (Family Chloropidae). One Family, the Sciomyzidae, includes species which feed on slugs and snails. The Family Cecidomyiidae, gall midges, includes several predators and one species, *Aphidoletes aphidimyza* (Rondani), is mass-reared and sold commercially (Tables 40 and 41). The adult midge is only 2 mm long and feeds mainly on honeydew. These insects are active at night and search out a leaf infested with aphids on which they lay their eggs. Each female will lay about 100 eggs. The larva is only 2-3 mm long when fully grown and is a typical maggot. The midges are introduced into glasshouses as pupae held in damp sand which are distributed amongst the crop. In the presence of aphids the midges breed successfully and will even overwinter and re-infest the glasshouse in the following season. It is the larva which kills the aphids and each one consumes up to 30 prey. These predators operate at low densities and will disperse widely in the crop to mop-up aphid infestations. However, there is still a need to improve rearing and release technology for this predator.

Most of the flies belong to the Family Tachinidae are parasitic and their larvae live as internal parasites in an extremely wide range of hosts including earthworms, snails, centipedes, woodlice, grasshoppers, beetles, moths and plant bugs. Eggs are laid on or near the host and the larvae penetrate the skin and develop at the expense of the host. When fully-grown the larva either pupates within the host or leaves the body and pupates in the soil. The pupa is barrel-shaped. The life cycle is complete when the adult insect emerges.

Mites

Although most growers think of mites as pests there are several groups which are important predators, particularly in the Family Phytoseiidae. Three valuable species are mentioned here. *Typhlodromus pyri* Scheuten, is abundant in orchards, woodlands and in shrubs and herbaceous plants. It is an important predator of gall mites and spider mites. *Typhlodromus* mites over-winter as adults and in spring become active and lay their eggs on plants often close to colonies of their prey. The young mites pass through one larval and two nymphal stages before becoming adult in about 2 weeks. There are 3 or 4 generations each year. All active stages except larvae feed on spider mites. The great advantage of these mites is that they will stay on the plant and feed on a variety of other mite pest species rather than being highly specific and flying away as do many insects.

The red spider mite predator, *Phtoseiulus persimilis* Athias-Henriot, is important for biological control of red spider mite in glasshouses and outdoors. It is sold widely in Europe and north America. It was first obtained in 1959 from Chile. Adult mites are yellowish-orange in colour and similar to the red spider mite in size (about 0.6 mm long) but have a pear-shaped body. The tiny eggs and larvae are translucent. The young and adults are very active in their search of prey. At optimum temperatures females lay about 4 eggs a day and eat about 30 mite eggs and 24 young mites. At 20°C the predator population increases 300-fold in 30 days. Above 30°C the predators do not thrive. The predatory mites are sold on leaf material or in shaker canisters for scattering on mite-infested plants. These predators disperse widely and only feed on the spider mites. However, the colonies quickly die in the absence of prey and therefore have to be re-introduced each season. In recent seasons *Phytoseiulus* has been used effectively outdoors in Britain and parts of Europe and north America to control red spider mite on soft fruit crops. This eperience would suggest that effective control of mites on outdoor ornamentals such as alpines may be possible in warm, dry seasons.

Another predatory mite now mass-reared commercially is *Amblyseius mackenziei* which is used for the biological control of thrips in glasshouses. These are pear-shaped, pale, whitish-brown and very active mites. They are smaller and more flattened than *Phytoseiulus* and lay smaller white eggs. A great advantage of *Amblyseius* is that it can survive in the absence of its main prey, the thrips, and turn to spider mites as a source of food. Unfortunately it is very susceptible to most pesticides and therefore great care is needed when treating other pests. Both predatory mites can co-exist although they will feed on each other to a small extent. *Amblyseius* is very cheap and easy to rear and is now used extensively in commerce. Suppliers of predatory mites are provided in Table 41.

Centipedes (Order Myriapoda)

Most gardeners are familiar with centipedes but, as certain species closely resemble millipedes, they are frequently destroyed by mistake. It is therefore important to learn to distinguish the two. The colour plates will help the reader to make the correct identification (Plate 10).

Centipedes are elongate predatory arthropods. The head bears antennae and three pairs of mouth appendages – toothed mandibles which cut up food and filamentous maxillae and leg-like palps which handle prey. Most species have eyes. The first segment of the body has formidable poisonous claws with which the prey is captured and killed. Each body segment has one pair of legs (as opposed to the two pairs per segment in millipedes) and a spiracle (respiratory opening) on each side of the body.

They are similar to millipedes, symphylids and woodlice in lacking an impervious cuticular wax layer. They are therefore mainly confined to damp habitats such as soils crevices and under stones, fallen leaves and the bark of trees. Many are subterranean and most are nocturnal. If they are disturbed in day time for example, by moving a pile of pots or seed trays, they scurry away and seek shelter.

Eggs are laid in spring and summer and the adults exhibit various degrees of parental care. The young grow through a series of moults and some species may not reach maturity until 3 years old.

Centipedes are primarily carnivorous but certain of the *Geophilus* species sometimes feed on plants and damage crops. The food is usually a variety of small soil-inhabiting creatures. However, larger sub-tropical and tropical species feed on insects, worms, mice, frogs, toads and even small birds. Prey are located with the aid of sensory hairs.

Two of the commonest centipede species observed in the garden are *Geophilus* spp. (Plate 10) and *Lithobius forficatus* (L.) (Plate 10). *Lithobius forficatus* lives for up to 5 or 6 years and feeds on worms, slugs, woodlice and insects.

Nematodes

From time to time parasitic nematodes appear in gardens in vast numbers. Mermithid worms which parasitise a range of insects species leave their haunts 1 m below ground on warm summer days after rain and crawl up the stems of plants writhing about in large glistening masses (Plate 13f). Later they descend into the soil and move in search of new hosts to parasitise. Several mermithid worms are being studied as potential biological control agents for pests of field crops. The biggest problem is in developing strains of worms which can operate in a range of conditions in field soils during the growing season.

Certain insect-parasitic nematodes, particularly species of *Heterorhabditis* and *Steinernema* carry a bacterium which infects and kills insects. This bacterium is released after the nematode has entered the host and within 48 hours kills the insect. The nematode then eats the contents of its host, completes its life cycle and produces thousands of larvae which disperse from the remains of the insect. These nematodes are mass-reared in the laboratory and marketed as 'Nemasys'. One product contains *Steinernema bibionis* and is used against black vine weevil on cyclamen, another preparation contains a strain of *Heterorhabditis* which controls vine weevil on nursery stock and strawberries. Nemasys is supplied in the form of a gel which is then suspended in water and applied as a drench or spray. The benefits of using these nematodes is that they only attack certain insects and they are harmless to humans, pets and most wildlife.

Spiders

All true spiders are predators. There is increasing evidence that spiders play a major role in controlling many pests, particularly small insects and mites in gardens and fields. However, there is no commercial exploitation of spiders for biological control.

Amphibians and reptiles

Frogs, toads, newts and slow worms are important predators of many invertebrates including a wide range of insects, mites and slugs. Unfortunately these animals do not discriminate between pests and beneficial insects. However, there is no doubt that the fact they consume slugs is extremely beneficial.

Mammals

Hedgehogs are insectivorous mammals which consume large numbers of invertebrates. Like amphibians and reptiles they do not discrminate between beneficial and harmful species and so they consume predatory as well as pest insects.

Micro-organisms

Fungi. In the wild, plants and animals are exposed to fungal pathogens from time to time and occasionally whole populations of certain insects and other invertebrates or even plants can be wiped out by disease epidemics. For example, root fly populations are sometimes decimated by the fungus *Empusa muscae* when conditions are humid and warm in the the summer months. The case of Dutch elm disease is one in which a fungal pathogen is transmitted by an insect and has had devastating effects. One of the reasons why these epidemics are comparatively rare is because the conditions under which most epidemics occcur are extremely critical and quite rare. They tend to occur sporadically and rarely help in crop protection. Some succcess has been achieved in using these fungi for biological control of pests in glasshouses and polytunnels where climatic conditions can be controlled to favour the pathogen. Research at Horticulture Research International paved the way for the development of the fungus, *Verticillium lecanii* (See Tables 40 and 41) for the control of whiteflies and aphids on glasshouse crops. Another fungus, *Metarhizium anisopliae*, is being investigated with the view to controlling the vine weevil and other pests.

Bacteria. *Bacillus thuringiensis* has been available for many years for controlling caterpillars and other insect pests. It is Approved for use by organic gardeners and represents an alternative to synthetic insecticides. In this case it is a protein produced by the bacterium which results in severe food poisoning and the eventual death of the insect. These proteins are harmless to man and most other animals and are biodegradable. So far a range of different strains of *Bacillus thuringiensis* have been identified which are effective against many different insects and new strains are being bred using genetic engineering techniques. Certain soil bacteria are being investigated which have an antagonistic effect on *Verticillium* wilt of strawberry.

Viruses. Studies of the use of viruses that infect insects as potential biological control agents have concentrated on fruit and forest pests such as gypsy moth, *Lymantria dispar* (L.) and the codling moth *Cydia pomonella* (L.). These viruses have been shown to be very effective but there is still considerable concern over the effects of the release of these micro-organisms into the environment at large.

Further reading: 'Biological Pest Control, the Glasshouse Experience' (Hussey & Scopes, 1985); 'Green Growers Guide, the World Directory of Agro-Biologicals' (Linsansky, 1990).

RESISTANT VARIETIES

Introduction

Recently there has been a move away from the use of chemical methods to control pests and diseases to alternative safer methods. When used correctly chemical pesticides are thought to be safe but nevertheless they are inherently toxic and some have undesirable effects in the environment. This has led to increased efforts to use plant resistance as a control method and already resistant varieties are available in many crops. Consequently, plant breeders are looking for plants with resistance to pests and diseases, using them for breeding and then selecting resistant offspring.

In nature, most plants resist attack from most pests and diseases, but we have seen how certain animals and microorganisms have devastating effects on plants. However, a close look at a particular species, variety or population of plants shows that it possesses considerable genetic variation for resisting attack – in other words plants have different amounts of resistance. Any programme of selection or breeding is based on the existence of this genetic variation between individual plants and its response to a particular pest or disease in its environment. Fortunately, variations in resistance exist in many plant species and can be exploited and there are many examples of resistance providing long-lasting answers to pest and disease problems. The cost of growing a resistant variety is the same as growing a susceptible one and savings are made by not having to use expensive control measures such as chemicals. Resistant varieties are particularly useful for controlling viruses that are transmitted by aphid vectors in a non-persistent manner. Viruses transmitted in this way are not controlled by killing the aphids e.g. with insecticides (See Chapter 4). Resistant varieties are also useful when a pest or disease has developed resistance to a pesticide or where chemical control is too expensive.

Resistant plants cost little to grow but it takes many years to identify resistance and then to combine it with the necessary agronomic characteristics required in a particular crop. The value of a resistant cultivar with low yield or poor flower quality would be questionable but provided the genes controlling pest or disease resistance and the undesirable agronomic features are not genetically linked, the breeder, given time, should be able to produce a resistant cultivar with good agronomic characteristics.

To be able to breed a resistant variety it is necessary to acquire a sound knowledge of the pest or disease concerned. Procedures for handling the pest or disease must be understood and reliable methods must be developed for the assessment of symptoms in the glasshouse or field. The breeder must also be aware of other pest or disease problems associated with the particular species being bred and also the main desirable agronomic characteristics, so that all these requirements are present in the finished variety. It is hardly surprising, therefore, that alpine plants have not been bred for resistance to pests or diseases. Of course many species of alpine plant have been bred for horticultural qualities such as flower size and colour, and plant habit. It is also likely that individual hybrids might also have been selected, unknowingly, with resistance to pests and diseases. Individuals that grew weakly, were abnormal or were susceptible to infection, would almost certainly have died or been thrown away, thereby unconsciously selecting for resistance. Occasionally, varietal resistance is reported in a particular species or genus as in the case of eelworm attack on saxifrage varieties (See Chapter 2).

It is not beyond the scope of the amateur or nurseryman to select new varieties with resistance to such common viruses as CMV. The remainder of this Chapter describes the various techniques involved in breeding for resistance in the context of the procedures that might be used by an enthusiastic amateur.

Definition of terms

There is considerable confusion over the different terms used for describing resistance to pests and diseases. The main terms are defined here according to common and accepted usage (Table 42).

Susceptibility. A plant is susceptible if a disease readily infects and multiplies on or within it or a pest readily colonises and feeds on it. Susceptibility can be considered to be the opposite of **resistance** and low or high degrees of susceptibility are recognised. High susceptibility and low resistance are considered to be synonymous.

Immunity. A plant is immune if it cannot be infected by a specific disease. With pests it implies the failure to colonise the plant even though the pest visits and 'examines' the plant. It follows that immune plants are **non-hosts**. The reasons why plants are immune are not fully understood.

The term immunity has also been commonly used to describe a plant response to virus infection, where a virus is unable to infect a particular variety, although it can infect other varieties of the same species. However, it is difficult to be sure that no virus at all has entered the symptomless variety because a virus might be confined to one or two cells

Table 42 **The meaning of resistance terms in relation to host symptoms and virus multiplication or pest numbers**

Term	Host symptoms	Virus multiplication	Pest numbers
Susceptibility	+++	+++	+++
Immunity (non-host)	–	–	–
Resistance (low susceptibility)	±	±	±
Tolerance	±	++ to +++	++ to +++

– no symptoms, virus or pest, +++ strong symptoms, high virus concentration or high pest numbers

Based on Walkey (1991a)

at the point of inoculation. The term '**extreme resistance** ' is most appropriate for this type of response. Use of 'immunity' should be restricted to the 'non-host' situation where none of the varieties of a particular species can be infected.

Resistance. A plant is **resistant** if it is able to suppress or slow down the multiplication of a pest or pathogen, or the development of symptoms. Resistance is the opposite of susceptibility, and is divided into **extreme** or high, **moderate**, and **low** or **partial resistance**, depending upon its effect. In general a resistant plant develops few if any symptoms and multiplication of a pest or disease is minimal (Table 42).

An individual plant of a particular species may resist attack, while the other plants of that species are susceptible. It is this natural variability that has been used in breeding for resistance. Such resistance may result from various genetically-inherited characters of the plant. For example, a pathogen may be unable to establish infection in the leaf of a particular plant because the outer layer of leaf cells (epidermis and cuticle) is too thick or because the epidermal hairs are too hard or profuse. Such morphological characters also confer resistance to pests. Alternatively, natural chemicals in the plant may reduce the multiplication or movement of a fungal disease within the host plant or influence the development of a pest.

Tolerance is a host response that results in negligible or mild symptoms, even though the plant is infected and contains normal amounts of the pathogen (Table 42). Often 'tolerance' is used wrongly to describe a host response when the symptoms are small because the amounts of virus in a plant are small; this would be more correctly described as resistance, as defined above. With pests, tolerance indicates the ability of the plant to support an infestation without the yield, appearance or marketable value being affected.

Field resistance occurs when a plant remains healthy in the natural conditions in the field but succumbs to the disease in experimental conditions. Often field resistance occurs because the numbers of infective units or inoculum are small (See Chapter 3).

Durable resistance describes long-lasting resistance. It does not mean that the resistance is effective against all strains of a pest or disease, but that the resistance is effective for many years. Sometimes durable resistance in a particular variety is overcome by a new variant of the pest or disease (a race, biotype or pathotype) and the resistance is said to have 'broken down'. However, this is not true for it is the control that has 'broken down'. The variety concerned has not lost its resistance to the original pest or pathogen, but rather it does not possess resistance capable of combating the new variant of the pest or disease.

Two specific terms used to describe the basis of resistance to pests are:
Antixenosis or non-preference resistance. The plant has an adverse effect on the behaviour of the pest i.e. it is unattractive (or less preferred) for egg-laying or feeding. Insects crawl or fly away from these type of plants.

Antibiosis. The plant has an adverse effect on the growth, reproduction or survival of the pest.

Plant breeding terms

It is beyond the scope of this book to describe the detailed genetics and techniques required when breeding for resistance. (Readers should consult "**Flower** and **Vegetable Plant Breeding**" by L. Watts, 1980) for a detailed presentation of this subject. However the essential terms that will be encountered in plant breeding are described here.

Within the cells of any living organism including plants, **chromosomes** control the characteristics of a particular individual. The chromosomes are small rod-shaped structures and are located in a special part of the plant cell called the **nucleus**. Chromosomes consist of a single long molecule of DNA associated with proteins and carry the genes of the organism. Each plant species is characterised by a set number of chromosomes in each cell; for example, the primrose (*Primula vulgaris*) has 22 chromosomes, whereas the wallflower (*Cheiranthus*) has 14. Each chromosome has **genes** which control the activities of the cell and consequently of the whole organism. Although chromosomes can be counted using a microscope, the numbers of genes possessed by an organism is unknown: there are too many and they are too small to be seen even with an electron microscope.

Resistance or any other character, may be controlled by a single gene (**monogenic inheritance/monogenic resistance**) or by many genes (**polygenic inheritance/polygenic resistance**). These genes may be **major** genes which have a large effect, or **minor** genes which have a small effect. Classification of major and minor genes is subjective however and the individual breeder judges the relative size of the effects.

Each gene has two parts called **alleles** and each part is present in the same position on each of a pair of chromosomes. Each allele produces a similar or a different response in the expression of a character depending on the allele's strength i.e. the allele is **dominant** or **recessive**. When the allele is dominant its expression masks the expression of the recessive allele when they occur together. For example, if resistance or susceptibility to a pest or disease in a particular plant is controlled by a single, major

Figure 30(a) Example of the inheritance of a resistance gene that is controlled by a single, major gene with dominant expression

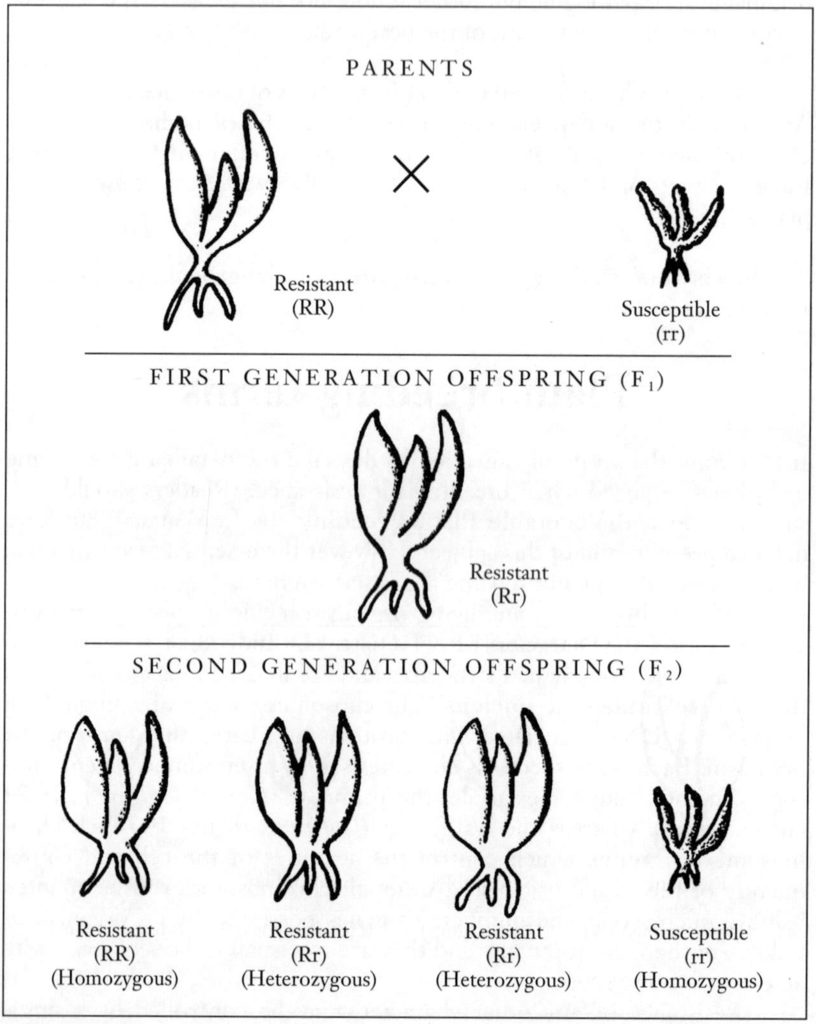

gene which is expressed in a dominant way, the pattern of its inheritance is as shown in Fig 30a. When the resistant parent (possessing the alleles RR) is crossed with the susceptible parent (possessing the alleles rr), because each of the two alleles possessed by an individual segregate separately during reproduction, every individual that results from this cross in the first generation offspring (called the F_1 generation) carries the alleles Rr. Since the allele for resistance (R) is dominant, the effects of the susceptible allele (r) will be masked. In the next generation of offspring (called the F_2 generation), however, the alleles will segregate so that the offspring possess the alleles (RR), (Rr), (Rr), or (rr). This results in a ratio of three resistant plants to 1 susceptible plant in this particular generation. The plant carrying the two identical dominant resistance alleles

Figure 30(b) Example of the inheritance of a resistance gene that is controlled by a single, major gene with recessive expression

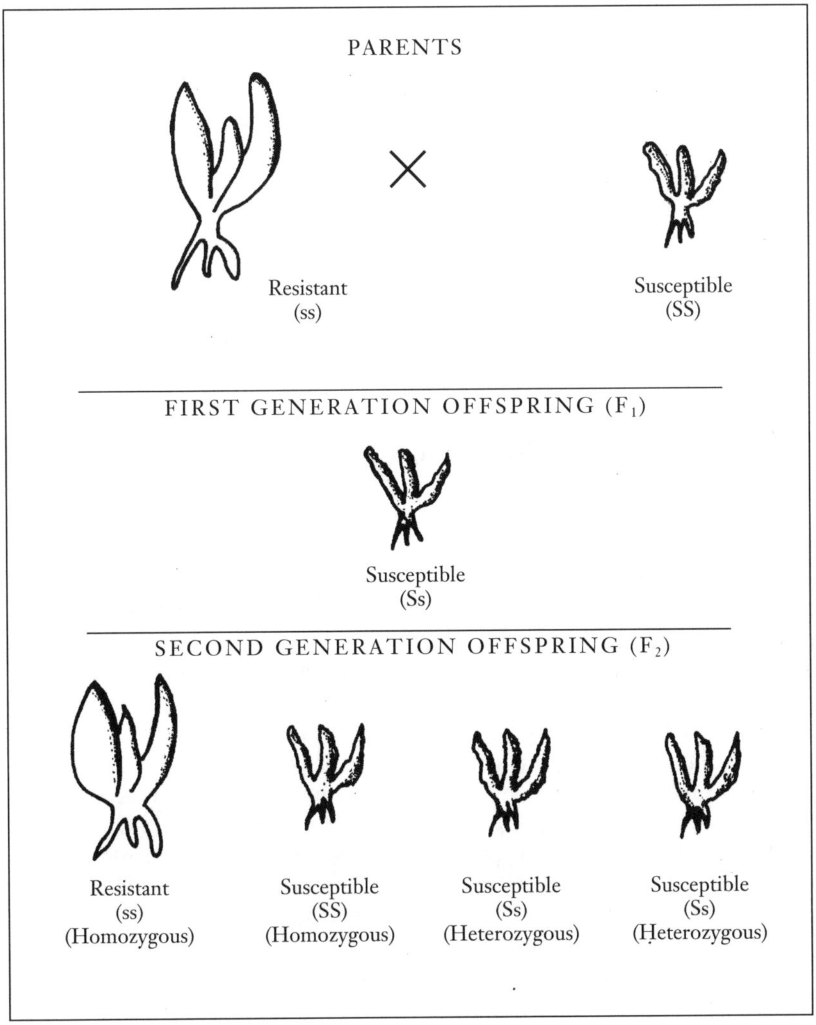

(RR) is said to be **homozygous** for resistance, and the plant possessing the two identical recessive alleles (rr) is homozygous for susceptibility. In contrast, the two plants which carry one dominant allele and one recessive alle (Rr) are said to be **heterozygous**. In this example when the resistance is dominant, the breeder must proceed beyond the F_2 generation of offspring, in order to separate the individuals which are homozygous for the resistance gene from those that are heterozygous for resistance. Subsequent generations are called F_3, F_4 etc. Finally, the breeder produces genetically stable offspring which are all homozygous (RR) for resistance.

If, however, resistance is controlled by a single, major recessive gene, the pattern of inheritance is as in Fig. 30b. When the resistant parent (possessing the alleles ss) is crossed with a susceptible parent (SS), the F_1 offspring will all carry the alleles Ss and will be susceptible. At this stage the recessive resistance allele in the heterozygous generation is being masked by the dominant allele for susceptibility. In the next generation (F_2) the alleles will have again segregated in a 3:1 ratio, but this time there will be only one resistant (ss) to three susceptible plants (SS, Ss, Ss). One group of the susceptible plants is homozygous for susceptibility (SS) and the other two groups heterozygous for susceptibility (Ss). Significantly, the group of resistant plants will be homozygous for resistance (ss) so that the breeder is able to identify the resistant individuals in the F_2 generation, which is not possible if the resistance is dominant (See Fig. 30a). Consequently, major, recessive genes are easier to select than dominant genes, but any single, major gene is usually easier to work with than several genes (polygenic) which have an additive effect on resistance. Finally, once the breeder has selected an individual with the necessary resistance, the plant can be maintained and multiplied by vegetative propagation without additional selection, irrespective of the heterozygous nature of the genotype.

Sources of resistance

The first step in any resistance breeding programme, is to identify plants possessing a high degree of resistance to a particular virus, disease or pest. Sometimes sufficient resistance can be found in an existing variety. This might be a popular variety that has been grown for many years and is known to be resistant, even when other varieties of the same species grown under identical conditions, succumb to attack. Such resistance can be used immediately for combining with other horticultural characters that are present in other susceptible varieties of the particular species. Provided the characters concerned are inherited in a straightforward manner, and especially if they are controlled by a single, major gene, the production of the new cross should be relatively rapid, and the main horticultural characteristics of both parents are likely to be acceptable to the grower. This type of material would be the most suitable as a source of resistance for hybridising and producing resistant alpine plant varieties. Parental material with resistance to cucumber mosaic virus or aphid attack might be looked for amongst existing *Viola* and *Primula* varieties. In other species, however, no sources of resistance to a particular pest or disease may be known and it becomes necessary to test a wide range of varieties and different wild forms of a species to identify a source of resistance. This is done by challenging them with the particular pest or disease concerned in a process called **screening**. Lines, also called **accessions** for screening can be obtained from commercial seed companies, nurserymen, botanical gene banks, botanic gardens or may be collected in the wild. If, during screening, varieties or individuals are identified as being resistant, and provided they are horticulturally acceptable, it may be sufficient to grow this plant material as a replacement for susceptible varieties without the need for breeding or additional selection.

If only one or two resistant lines are identified, however, they will probably not provide sufficient horticultural variation. It is then necessary to use the resistant lines as parents in a breeding programme, hence to generate a wider range of varieties possessing both resistance and the diverse horticultural features required by the grower.

Screening methods

The method used to challenge a range of plants depends on the particular pest or disease concerned. For example, if resistance is required for a soil-borne, eelworm-transmitted virus such as arabis mosaic virus, the simplest procedure would be to grow the test plants in soil which was known to be infested with virus-carrying eelworms. This could be done in pots or in field soil. Similarly, plants could be challenged with an aphid-transmitted virus such as cucumber mosaic virus by growing them outside in close proximity to plants known to be infected with CMV and relying on natural spread of the virus by the aphids. Many successful resistance screening programmes have been carried out in the field in this way.

Reliance on natural infestations is, however, uncertain. This is especially true with insect vectors such as aphids, whose presence depends on the prevailing weather. In warm climates high populations of aphids can be expected annually. However, in cool climates such as in Britain and other parts of northern Europe and north America, aphid infestations are sporadic and may be negligible in some seasons. Many of the test plants would 'escape' the attentions of the pest. Consequently, dependence on natural sources of pests or diseases is not a reliable method of screening in temperate climates. It is more satisfactory to challenge the plants by infesting them with a pest or mechanically inoculating each individual plant with the disease organism (Plate 27f).

Screening against a virus such as CMV (cucumber mosaic virus), is straightforward. A standard strain of the virus could be propagated and maintained initially by inoculating marrow seedlings which are very susceptible to CMV infection. An inoculum of virus and sap could then be prepared by grinding, in a pestle and mortar, the leaves of infected marrow seedlings in a weak phosphate buffer solution, then filtering the sap through a piece of butter muslin (Chapter 6). The infective sap is then rubbed onto the carborundum-dusted leaf surfaces of the plants to be tested using a finger. Afterwards the CMV culture could be kept for later use by deep freezing or by drying infected leaves over calcium chloride.

To reactivate the CMV after storage, the infected leaf would be ground in a little phosphate buffer solution and rubbed onto a small marrow seedling previously dusted with the carborundum abrasive (Chapter 6). To test a range of plants against pests or fungal and bacterial diseases involves rearing pests and culturing disease organisms which is quite specialised and may not always be practical for the amateur enthusiast.

It is important that the plants to be screened should be of a uniform age and stage of development, and that each plant is inoculated with a similar amount of inoculum or infested with the same number of pests. Preliminary tests should be carried out to determine the optimum growth stage at which the test plants should be inoculated for the best symptom development. In addition, it would be advisable to include a variety in the screening test which is known to be highly susceptible to the pest or disease, and in which a uniform response can be expected in order to check the pest or pathogen infectivity.

In any resistance breeding programme the main objective is to distinguish the resistant from the susceptible plants. This is quite easy for some pest and disease/host reactions, which produce obvious, clear cut symptoms. However, symptoms are not always so distinctive and susceptible plants show a graded response from severe, moderate, to mild or no symptoms. It then becomes necessary to measure or estimate the severity of symptoms and to develop a reliable method of selecting resistant plants in successive tests. The response to pests can also be graded, but in addition it is necessary to record/count the numbers of pests or the amount of damage.

The system of grading or scoring is subjective and will depend on colony size or extent of damage by pests or the type of symptom a particular pathogen/host reaction produces. Often a system based on a O (no symptoms) to 5 (severe symptoms) scale is satisfactory (See Table 43). Using such a system the breeder might decide to select only the plants

Table 43 **An example of a scoring system for measuring resistance to cucumber mosaic virus in letuce**

Symptom grade	Description of symptom
0	no symptoms on leaves
1	very mild mosaic (or mottle) symptoms on at least one leaf
2	distinct mosaic symptoms on one or more leaves
3	distinct mosaic or chlorotic symptoms on most leaves
4	intense mosaic or chlorotic symptoms on at least half the leaves
5	intense mosaic or chlorotic symptoms on all leaves

Based on Walkey *et al* (1985)

that have a 0 score for breeding, but if the majority of plants scored 4 or 5 and no 0's were recorded, plants with scores of 1 or 2 might be selected. A more comprehensive coverage of resistance screening procedures is given in 'Applied Plant Virology' (Walkey, 1991a) and in 'Breeding Plants Resistant to Insects' (Maxwell & Jennings, 1980).

CHEMICAL CONTROL

Introduction

Chemical control of pests and diseases is brought about by the use of pesticides. The dictionary definition of a pesticide is a 'substance used to destroy pests' and is derived from the words 'pest' and '-cide' the latter being derived from the latin, caedere, to kill. In current usage the word pesticide is a generic term which includes all chemicals used to destroy pests, diseases and weeds. The chemicals are classified on the basis of the particular pest or disease against which they are targeted – hence insecticide, fungicide, acaricides, aphicide, nematicide, etc.

The use of pesticides dates back many centuries to when primitive tribes tipped their arrows with the extracts of plants for the purpose of poisoning their prey. A number of plant extracts e.g. rotenone (Derris) are still in use today and new ones are being discovered – see chapter on naturally occurring pesticides. Sulphur was used as a fumigant in 1000 BC, the Romans used extracts from hellebore to control mice and rats and in AD 900 the Chinese were using arsenic to control pests. In the late nineteenth century the dye Paris green (a mixture of copper, arsenic and acetates) was found to kill insects and its use launched a new era in the deliberate application of toxic substances for pest control. This and other highly poisonous substances such as lead arsenate and copper sulphate were widely used pesticides until the Second World War. From the Second World War until the 1960s, persistent organochlorines were used extensively and some crop protection experts believed certain pests would be eliminated. However, pests began developing resistance to these chemicals and this problem, together with the realisation that there were serious residue problems associated with these compounds, brought their use to an end. Only one or two organochlorines are still approved for use.

The carbamate, organophosphorus and synthetic pyrethroid chemicals have replaced the organochlorine pesticides and are much less persistent but may be more acutely toxic. These three groups of compounds and naturally occurring pesticides are the main chemicals used to protect crops.

Confusion exists among gardeners and professional nurserymen over the naming of pesticides. Each product has two names, a **proprietry or brand or trade name** which is usually a Registered Trade Mark; this identifies the manufacturer. It may also represent a series of closely related products even though the active ingredients may change from time to time. The second name on all Approved Products is the name of the **active ingredient**, which is an internationally agreed chemical name. This name indicates to the user the main purpose and use of the product. Thus Derris Dust is the trade name given to a product which contains the active ingredient rotenone used in the control of many pests. The chemical names of the active ingredients are the ones used in this book. Different manufacturers may sell a product containing the same active ingredient. Indeed, the most widely-used active ingredients are likely to be manufactured by all the large agrochemical companies each one assigning its own brand name to the pesticide.

A new pesticide is costly to develop and so it is not surprising that agrochemical companies concentrate on markets which will provide them with a satisfactory return on their investment. For every new product on the market, about 10,000 other candidate substances will have been examined and subjected to the long process involving exhaustive tests of toxicology and environmental effects and the complicated registration procedures.

In the United Kingdom and in many other countries the agrochemical industry has collaborated with the Government for many years over safety standards and regulations. In Britain this led to the establishment of the Pesticides Safety Precaution Scheme and the Agricultural Chemicals Approval Scheme. These were consolidated by the Government under the Food and Environment Protection Act 1985.

Pesticide regulations

It is only right and proper that the Government should control pesticide use. Under the Food and Environment Protection Act 1985, the Government introduced strict controls for all aspects of the supply, storage and use of pesticides in the UK. These controls have been specified in the Control of Pesticides Regulations 1986. All products classified as pesticides and intended for use on farms, nurseries, gardens or in the home must be registered specifically for these uses. Suppliers of pesticides must submit their products for Approval of the label and must obtain a Registered Number. The Ministry of Agriculture, Fisheries and Food (MAFF) issues numbers for farm and garden products while the Health and Safety Executive (HSE) issue numbers for products used in and around the home. Under these regulations, products must be used in accordance with the label instructions and it is a criminal offence to use them other than for the purposes specified.

It is no longer permissible (1991) for pesticides registered for professional use in agriculture, horticulture or forestry to be used in the garden. It is also against the law for any Approved pesticide to be supplied in any but the original container. Thus the amateur gardener may no longer legally obtain for their own use small quantities of any pesticide which was supplied to a nurseryman or garden centre in an Approved container.

Before Official Approval is granted for a formulation intended for home or garden use, it must be shown that:
1) it can be applied safely without the use of special protective clothing;
2) it presents no hazards to children, pests or wildlife which might be inadvertently exposed to it;
3) surplus pesticide can be disposed of safely through normal household waste disposal systems.

Precautions for the safe use of pesticides must appear on the product label. If the instructions are strictly followed, it should be possible to apply the pesticide safely.

The Minister for Agriculture has emphasised that criminal proceedings will be taken against anyone – manufacturer, retailer or user – who infringes the regulations.

Thus the owners of chemicals which have now been banned from use are breaking the law by keeping or using them – examples include chlordane, DDT, dieldrin and aldrin.

Precautions with pesticides

When using any toxic compound it is essential to take sensible precautions. For the great majority of pesticides for use in the garden and home the precautions are largely common sense. All gardeners and growers should limit the quantity of pesticide purchased to the amount which they believe will be used in the current season. Products deteriorate rapidly and buying large amounts can be wasteful as well as presenting disposal problems.

Before use:
1. Store in a safe place out of reach of children and away from food.
2. Keep the pesticide in the original container, tightly closed. Never decant products into other containers for storage.
3. If the label has been lost from a container or the label is no longer readable, dispose of the pesticide (see below).

During use:
1. Do not breathe in spray mist, dust or fumes.
2. Keep pesticides off skin; wash off any splashes with running water.
3. Wash hands and exposed skin after use.
4. Keep pesticides away from food, drink and pet foods.
5. Avoid drift onto other plants and prevent any pesticide getting into ponds and water courses either directly or indirectly via run-off.
6. Keep all pesticides away from children, pets, ponds etc.
7. Do not let pets enter treated areas until sprays have dried. Make sure pets don't eat the foliage of treated plants by fencing off the area.

After use:
1. Dispose of all surplus spray solutions as diluted pesticides rapidly degenerate. You may also forget what was prepared when you come to use the sprayer again.

2. Wash out empty pesticide containers thoroughly and dispose of them safely.
3. Empty sachets completely and dispose of them safely.
4. Do not re-use empty pesticide containers.
5. Wash out spraying equipment thoroughly before and after use. Even small quantities of herbicide could cause severe problems if they were used subsequently with insecticides or fungicides. Ideally, separate sprayers should be used for herbicides.
6. Surplus spray solutions may safely be disposed of on a patch of bare soil not intended for planting for 12 months or on a gravel or porous-surfaced path. Never dispose of pesticides close to ponds, water courses, ditches and marshy areas. You should never pour pesticides down drains or through a boundary fence or hedge.
7. Solid pesticides (< 50 g) should be left in their containers with the lid firmly closed and placed in the dustbin. Glass containers require additional protection. If you have substantial quantities (> 50 g) of banned or unwanted chemicals contact your local county council amenity waste disposal office for guidance.

Phytotoxicity

Some pesticides, applied under certain conditions can damage (scorch) the foliage, flowers or other parts of a plant – that is they are **phyto (plant) toxic**. Product labels frequently list the species of plant which are damaged by application of the chemical. However, you can imagine that few alpine species or other garden plant have been screened for phytotoxic effects. When such information is lacking, you will have to experiment for yourself. Clearly it would be foolish to spray a show specimen if other plants of the same species were available for a trial run. Alternatively, test out a small part of a plant first and leave for a few days because effects may be delayed in appearance. If there are no undesirable effects you can treat the remainder of the plant. Always record the results of these tests for future reference and at all times adhere to the label recommendations.

Range of Products

The gardener has available between 350 and 400 pesticides for use in controlling pests, diseases and weeds. The professional nurseryman or grower can choose from more than 1000 products. About 2400 garden centres and nurseries as well as the high street stores sell products to gardeners while growers obtain supplies either directly from chemical company representatives or from wholesalers and consultants. The UK market sales for garden and household pesticides was worth £22 million in 1990 made up of herbicides £9 million, herbicides plus fertilisers £5.1 million, insecticides £7.2 million and fungicides £1.1 million

Selecting the most appropriate chemical for controlling a pest or disease presents difficulties because of what appears to be a bewildering

Table 44

CHEMICAL CONTROL	**PEST** (see key below)															
	1	**2**	**3**	**4**	**5**	**6**	**7**	**8**	**9**	**10**	**11**	**12**	**13**	**14**	**15**	**16**
Aluminium sulphate																
Bacillus thuringiensis					●											
Bioallethrin			●		●										●	●
Borax		●														
Bromophos	●					●							●			
Butoxycarboxim			●													
Carbaryl		●				●							●			
Cresylic acid			●												●	
Cypermethrin		●														
Diazinon		●				●	●						●			
Dichlorvos			●									●				
Dimethoate			●							●					●	
Fatty acids			●												●	
Fenitrothion			●		●									●		
Gamma HCH		●	●	●	●	●		●	●		●	●	●			
Heptenophos			●													
Malathion			●				●									
Metaldehyde																
Methiocarb													●			
Permethrin		●	●		●			●		●	●			●	●	●
Phoxim		●														
Pirimicarb			●													
Pirimiphos-methyl		●	●	●	●	●		●	●		●	●	●	●		
Pyrethrum		●	●		●											
Resmethrin					●											
Rotenone (Derris)			●		●				●							
Quassia			●		●											
Tetramethrin		●	●					●								
	1	**2**	**3**	**4**	**5**	**6**	**7**	**8**	**9**	**10**	**11**	**12**	**13**	**14**	**15**	**16**

PESTS KEY TO NUMBERS

1 Adelgids
2 Ants
3 Aphids
4 Bulb flies
5 Caterpillars
6 Chafer grubs
7 Collembola
8 Earwigs
9 Flea beetles
10 Froghoppers
11 Leafhoppers
12 Leaf miners
13 Leather jackets
14 Lily beetles
15 Mealy bugs
16 Midges

Table 44

CHEMICAL CONTROL	PEST (see key below)															
	17	18	19	20	21	22	23	24	25	26	27	28	29	30	31	32
Aluminium sulphate										●						
Bacillus thuringiensis																
Bioallethrin					●							●		●		●
Borax																
Bromophos															●	
Butoxycarboxim			●	●	●	●						●				
Carbaryl																
Cresylic acid								●								
Cypermethrin																
Diazinon													●		●	●
Dichlorvos					●				●					●		
Dimethoate		●			●							●		●		
Fatty acids					●			●				●		●		
Fenitrothion		●														
Gamma HCH		●							●		●	●	●		●	●
Heptenophos																
Malathion		●			●			●	●			●				
Metaldehyde										●						
Methiocarb	●									●						●
Permethrin		●			●			●					●	●		●
Phoxim												●				
Pirimicarb																
Pirimiphos-methyl		●			●		●	●				●	●	●		
Pyrethrum		●			●									●		
Resmethrin																
Rotenone (Derris)		●			●											
Quassia																
Tetramethrin																●
	17	18	19	20	21	22	23	24	25	26	27	28	29	30	31	32

PESTS KEY TO NUMBERS

17 Millipedes
18 Mirids
19 Mites – acarid
20 – bulb
21 – spider
22 – tarsonemid
23 Sawflies
24 Scale insects
25 Sciarids
26 Slugs
27 Symphylids
28 Thrips
29 Weevils
30 Whiteflies
31 Wireworms
32 Woodlice

array of products. Amateurs and professionals need to consult an expert in the subject of crop protection or refer to up-to-date texts on chemical control (See Chapter 6). Advice is now available at some garden centres but even these nurserymen sometimes find it difficult to select appropriate products which are available for use in particular situations. Pesticides available to the gardener for control of pests are listed in Table 44.

A wider range of chemicals is available to the professional grower than to the amateur for several reasons. For example, certain compounds require the use of specialised protective clothing and equipment. Compounds may require specific storage conditions and disposal procedures which would not be available to the amateur. However, the main difference is that certain compounds have to be applied by appropriately trained and licensed operators who hold a Users Certificate.

Types of pesticide

Pesticides are classified on the basis of their mode of action : Those applied to pests act as:

1) Contact poisons. These pesticides come into contact with a pest either by penetrating the body in the form of a fumigant or by landing on the body and penetrating the skin.
2) Stomach poisons. These pesticides are swallowed when the pest eats the plant and poison the animal. These pesticides are applied to the foliage or roots of the plant.
3) Systemic pesticides. These substances are applied to the foliage or roots of growing plants, and are translocated to all growing parts of the plant. Pests which suck the sap or eat the tissues will be poisoned, whereas pollinators and other beneficial insects landing on the plants are unlikely to be affected.

Fungicides act by coming into contact with the fungus on the surface of the root or foliage but can also work systemically. Fungicides are often applied before infection, the deposit of chemical protecting the plant from infection (See Chapter 3).

Pesticides are available in the following range of formulations:

Dusts and powders. These products are difficult to apply precisely and are mainly used against soil pests and diseases.

Granules. These formulations are also mainly used for soil-borne problems and are generally less hazardous to use than dusts particularly as they can be applied more precisely around plants.

Liquids. The majority of products are formulated as liquids or wettable powders for distribution and use as sprays and drenches. Some products are sold as aerosols and directly applied to plants. Under CEC law warning symbols appear on products which are toxic or hazardous (Table 45). Chemicals used by the gardener may carry the 'harmful', 'irritant' or 'oxidising' labels. These symbols draw your attention to precautions which must be taken when handling pesticides.

Naturally-occurring pesticides

A few plants contain substances that kill pests. Examples include:

1. Rotenone is extracted from two plants – the leguminous barbasco (*Lonchocarpus* spp.) plant from Peru and the related tuba (*Derris elliptica*) plant of Malaysia which is usually known just as derris; rotenone is harmless to man and other mammals.
2. Pyrethrum is obtained from the flowers of a chrysanthemum species *Chrysanthemum cinerarifolium*. This compound is remarkable for its quick knock-down effect on insects.
3. Nicotine obtained from the wild tobacco plant is a narcotic drug that is poisonous in large doses. This compound is no longer Approved for garden use because it is too dangerous.
4. Azatin (Azadirachtin) produced by the neem tree (*Azadirachta indica*) has been used as a natural pesticide for many years. This compound has attracted considerable attention as new methods have been developed for extracting the pure active substance from the kernel of the fruit. It is now available commercially.
5. Dandelions produce polyphenols which are known to protect crops from the soil-borne fungus *Fusarium*. The dandelion extracts also withhold iron from *Fusarium* by binding it to cichoric acid and encourage the growth of beneficial soil organisms that compete with *Fusarium* and hinder infections.
6. Extracts from garlic are being investigated as potential insecticides to control whiteflies and red spider mites.
7. Pepper dust is sold commercially as a repellent particularly for cats.

Many of these naturally-occurring pesticides are Approved for use by The Organic Growers Association. This Approval does not mean that the gardener can abandon the precautions and recommendations applied to synthetic pesticides. For example rotenone is highly toxic to fish, frogs and toads and nicotine, which was available to the amateur until quite recently, is highly toxic to man and animals. It is also now forbidden for gardeners or growers to prepare their own concoctions of chemicals or extracts.

Effective use of pesticides

Pesticides are expensive and because they are toxic substances should only be used as a last resort. Cultural and biological methods should always be the first choice if they are effective against the pest or disease. However, there is no doubt that when used correctly pesticides are highly effective and may offer the most reliable method of control. They are particularly useful for protecting precious or rare alpines and specimens grown for show where pest- and disease-free plants are essential.

Successful pest and disease control depends on the use of the right formulation of the right chemical at the most appropriate time so always read and follow the directions for use on the product label.

Use only the recommended dose. Never add extra concentrate for good measure – this is wasteful and will seldom improve effectiveness and it may cause damage.

When diluting pesticides only mix up enough chemical for the job in hand. Always wear eye protection and rubber gloves (not cotton) when handling concentrated materials. Never suck up concentrates with a pipette or tube.

Never mix garden chemicals together unless there is a recommendation to do so on the product label or leaflet.

Timing is extremely important. Keep a close watch on plants, identify problems then treat early. If an infestation develops rapidly it will be much more difficult to control and may destroy the plant. Some pests and pathogens require repeated applications of chemical. In the case of whiteflies some stages are more susceptible than others to insecticides and so several sprays may be required to kill all insects as they grow to maturity. Do not spray in bright sunshine as occasionally plants can be scorched under these conditions. Try to spray when the foliage is dry and there is no wind. Soil pesticides are usually best applied at planting or seed sowing to protect plants from attack.

It is best to spray plants late in the day when few bees and other beneficial insects are on the wing. Wherever possible try to avoid spraying open flowers to protect beneficial insects which may be gathering pollen and nectar.

When using pesticide aerosols it is important to follow the directions carefully. Application from too close a range or at too heavy a rate can seriously damage plants. Visible wetting of the foliage with aerosol sprays is neither desirable nor necessary.

Take special note of the interval between spraying and handling which should be observed before touching plants that have been treated with pesticides.

Always use high quality sprayers and check that they are in good working condition. One very good reason for using pesticides sparingly and for using an integrated approach (a combination of several control measures) is the distinct possibility that the pest or disease may develop resistance to the chemical. Worldwide about 450 common pest species such as the peach-potato aphid, glasshouse whitefly and red spider mite have developed resistance to specific pesticides. In 1948, only 12 insect species were resistant to pesticides. Resistance to a pest is a characteristic of a population not of individuals. There is genetic variation within all populations of pests and disease and some strains will exhibit a natural tolerance to a particular chemical, probably because they have the ability to detoxify the pesticide by enzyme activity. These strains survive an application of a chemical and, in the absence of their susceptible brethren which are killed, they build up a resistant population. Resistance is most common in species which have a rapid development rate – many generations in a short period of time. The answer to the problem of pesticide resistance is to develop an integrated programme of pest control utilising every possible cultural and biological measure as well as ringing the

Table 45 **Fungicides and their uses on garden plants**

FUNGICIDE	USE (A/P)	ACTION	TARGET
Benzimidazole			
carbendazim	a, p	s, pr, c	*Botrytis*, *Fusarium*, powdery
benomyl	a, p		mildews, *Thielaviopsis*,
			Fusarium, *Botrytis*
thiabendazole	p	s, pr, c	*Penicillium*
thiophanate methyl	a, p	s, pr, c	clubroot
Copper			
copper oxychloride	a, p	pr	broad spectrum: downy mildew,
cheshunt compound	a, p	pr	damping-off
Dicarboximide			
captan	a, p	pr	*Botrytis* (seed dressing)
iprodione	p	pr, e	*Botrytis*, *Fusarium*, *Alternaria*
Dithiocarbamate			
maneb	p	pr	*Alternaria*, down mildew,
			powdery mildew, *Fusarium*;
			downy mildew, rust
mancozeb	p	pr	*Fusarium*, *Septoria*,
thiram	a, p	pr	damping-off, *Botrytis*, *Fusarium*
Imidazole			
imazalil	p	s, pr	powdery mildew;
prochloraz	p	s, e	broad spectrum
Morpholine			
dodemorph	p	s	powdery mildew
Phenylsulfamide			
dichlofluanid	p	pr	*Fusarium*, *Botrytis*
Pyrimidine			
bupirimate	a, p	s, pr, e	leaf spot, powdery mildew, rust
Thiazole			
etridiazole	p	pr	*Phytophthora*, *Pythium*
Triazole			
propiconazole	p	s, pr, c	powdery mildew, rust, *Septoria*;
			Ramularia, *Alternaria*
Other groups			
myclobutanil	p	pr, c	powdery mildew, rust;
quintozene	p	pr	*Fusarium*, *Sclerotinia*, *Botrytis*,
			Rhizoctonia
sulphur	a, p	pr	broad spectrum: powdery mildew;
tecnazene	p	pr	*Botrytis*

Use: a – by amateurs, b – professional horticulturalists; Action: c – curative, e – eradicant, pr – protective, s – systemic

Table 46 **Fungicides for control of specific plant disease fungi**

FUNGUS	FUNGICIDE
Fusarium	benomyl, carbendazim, iprodione, mancozeb, maneb, prochloraz, quintozene, thiabendazole, thiophanate-methyl, thiram
Penicillium	benomyl, carbendazim
Verticillium	thiophanate-methyl
Sclerotinia	benomyl, carbendazim, iprodione, quintozene
Botryotinia (syn. *Botrytis*)	benomyl, captan, carbendazim, iprodione, thiophanate-methyl, thiram
Powdery mildew	bupirimate, carbendazim, myclobutanil, propiconazole, sulphur, triforine
Rhizoctonia	benomyl, carbendazim, iprodione, mancozeb, maneb thiabendazole, thiophanate-methyl, thiram, quintozene
Rust, smut	mancozeb, myclobutanil, propiconazole, triforine
Downy mildew	mancozeb, maneb, propamocarb hydrochloride, copper compounds
Phytophthora	copper compounds, etridiazole, fosetyl-aluminium, furalaxyl, propamacarb hydrochloride
Pythium	copper compounds, thiram, etridiazole, furalaxyl, propamacarb hydrochloride
Clubroot	thiophanate-methyl
Damping-off	maneb, etridiazole, furalaxyl, propamacarb hydrochloride, thiabendazole, thiram, captan, copper, quintozene, benomyl

changes by using different types of pesticides. This approach reduces selection pressure on a pest or disease from a single pesticide.

Chemical control of virus vectors

In general, insecticides are more effective in controlling viruses that are transmitted by vectors in a persistent, rather than in a non-persistent manner (See Chapter 4). The vector of a non-persistent virus will eventually be killed after feeding on a plant that has been sprayed with a systemic insecticide. It will, however, not be killed quickly enough to prevent the virus from being transmitted, for the vector will acquire the virus after a few seconds feeding on an infected plant and is able to transmit it within seconds of starting to feed on a healthy plant. It is also possible that chemical treatments may in fact, agitate the vector and stimulate it to move around and probe more frequently than it would normally do on an untreated plant. Spraying may, therefore, result in a greater number of plants becoming infected if a non-persistent virus is involved, than if the plants were left unsprayed. Even contact insecticide sprays which are formulated to kill the insect very quickly, usually do not act quickly enough to prevent a non-persistent virus from being transmitted. Consequently, it is generally considered to be a waste of time and money to try and prevent the transmission of non-persistent viruses by spraying to kill the vector.

In the case of persistent viruses, however, where the insect may need many hours of feeding to acquire the virus and many hours to transmit it to a healthy plant (See Chapter 4), systemic insecticidal sprays can be an effective control measure. Therefore, it is essential the grower knows which type of insect transmission has to be controlled, before deciding to use a chemical spray. In addition to the effectiveness of spraying to control insect vectors, the question of the cost of spraying has also to be considered because most chemical sprays are very expensive.

Finally, it should be mentioned that although insecticidal sprays may fail to control virus transmission, their use on certain alpine plants which are highly susceptible to aphid feeding damage, may be a necessity, particularly in the alpine-house.

Nematode and Fungal Vectors

Certain nematode-transmitted viruses may persist for relatively long periods in their nematode vector and the use of chemicals (called **nematicides**) to control the eelworm, may be the only effective measure for their control. The problem with most nematicide treatments, however, is that it is difficult to achieve a 100% kill of the vector, because nematodes frequently occur at considerable depths in the soil and may therefore be beyond, or at the fringe of, effective nematicide penetration. Nevertheless, if a gardener or grower does have an area of ground which he knows contains eelworms, chemical fumigation of the contaminated soil is a possibility. It should be noted, however, that two of the most effective nematicides, DD (dichloropropane-dichloropropene) and methyl bromide are both highly toxic chemicals and can only be applied by a professional soil fumigation expert.

Methyl bromide can also be effective as a soil fumigant to kill the resting spores or mobile zoospores of fungal vectors such as *Olpidium brassicae*. Again, however, because of the cost of the treatment, it would only be sensible to use the treatment for relatively small areas of infected soil. Another fungicide, dazomet, has been successfully used to treat the soil to control Augusta disease in tulips which is caused by tobacco necrosis virus and vectored by *O. brassicae*.

Further reading: 'Directory of Garden Chemicals' (Anon, 1986); 'Garden Chemicals. A Guide to their Safe and Effective Use' (Anon, 1991a); 'Pesticides 1991. Pesticides Approved under the Control of Pesticides Regulations 1986 ' (Anon, 1991b).

PRODUCTION OF VIRUS-FREE PLANTS

The importance to the alpine gardener of growing virus-free planting material has already been mentioned in Chapter 5. Once clones of vegetatively propagated plants have become infected with virus, under normal conditions, they will remain diseased for the remainder of their life. Every time the diseased plant is propagated, the virus is passed onto its

Figure 31 Scheme for the production of virus-free plants (based on Walkey, 1991)

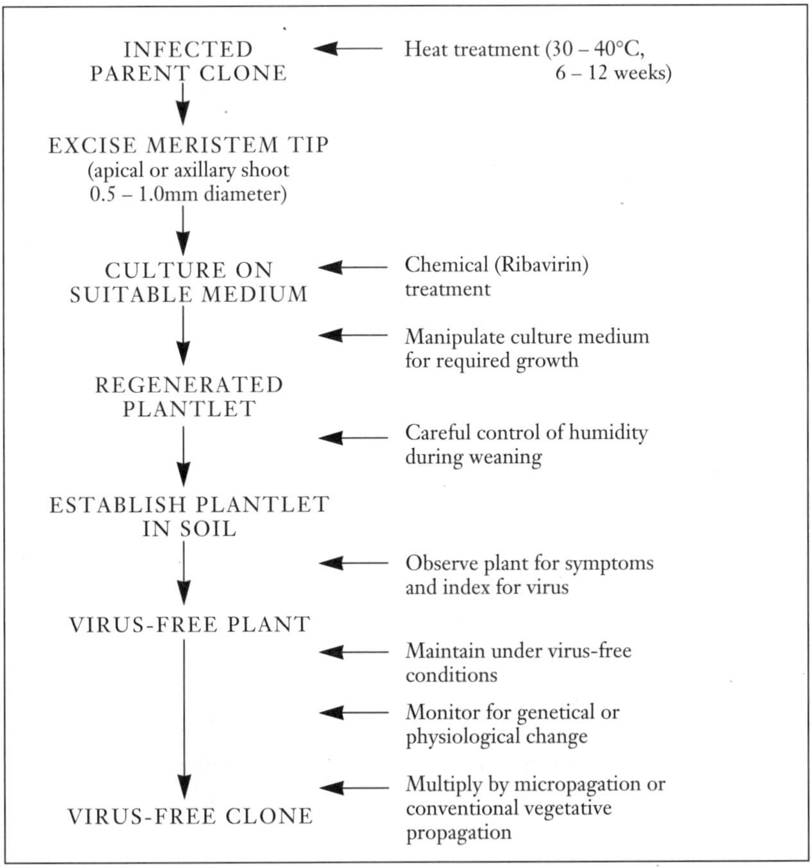

offspring via the cutting, tuber or bulb or by whatever type of vegetative propagule that is being used. Often virus-infected propagules have been so widely distributed that a particular clone may be almost totally infected, and frequently this is the case with some old, popular varieties such as with some clones of *Primula* (See Plate 27a and b).

Fortunately, it is possible with laboratory tissue culture techniques to eradicate virus from such infected clones. These techniques involve the culture of the growing point of the plant shoot under sterile conditions on a specially prepared nutrient medium. The process is commonly referred to as **meristem-tip** culture. Often it is necessary to combine the tissue culture treatments with heat (**thermotherapy**) or chemical (**chemotherapy**) treatments, in order to obtain successful virus eradication.

Figure 32 The regeneration of a plant (such as a *Primula* hybrid) by aseptic tissue culture of a meristem-tip explant

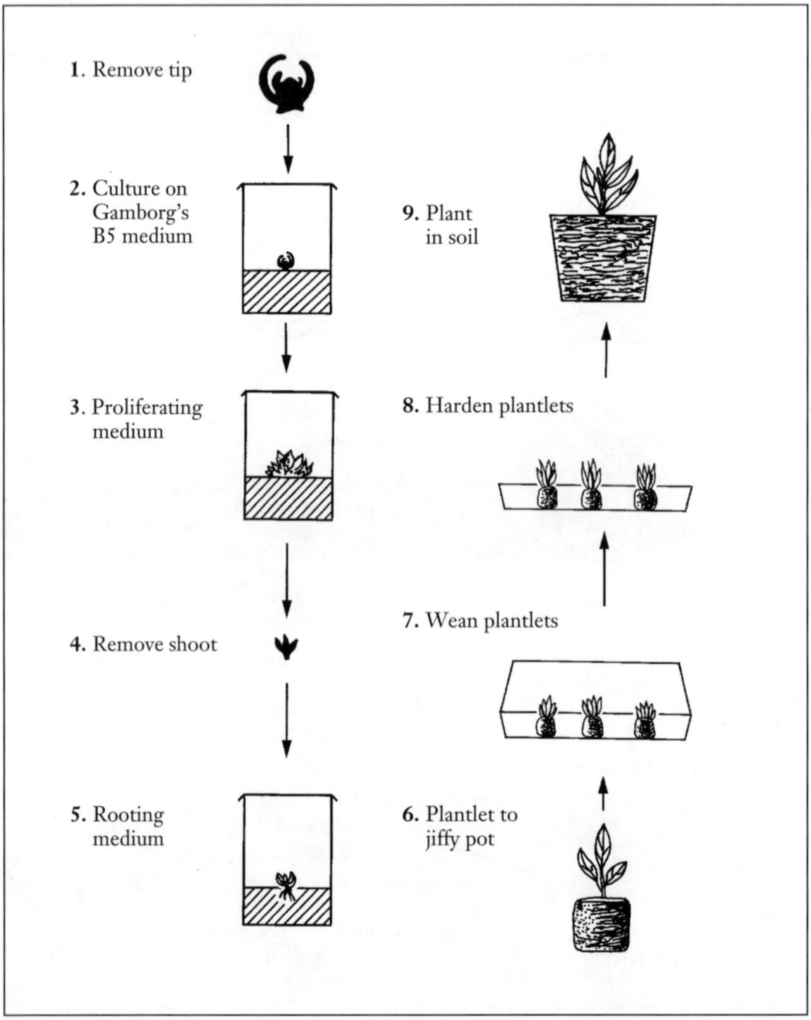

A scheme for the production of virus-free plants by these procedures is shown in Fig. 31. In this chapter the techniques and mechanisms by which viruses can be eradicated in tissue culture systems are discussed. In Chapter 6, detailed practical information is given which will enable the enthusiastic rock-garden specialist to carry out a virus eradication project.

Meristem-tip Culture

Using a binocular microscope under sterile conditions (See Plate 27), the **meristem tip** is removed from the bud of an infected plant and grown on a sterile nutrient medium to produce a rooted plantlet which is finally transferred and estabished in a soil compost (See Fig. 32). The practical details for aseptically isolating the explant and the preparation of a suitable nutrient medium for its growth are described in Chapter 6.2. Most culture media used today are based on Murashige and Skoog's (1962) or Gamborg's B5 medium (1975) and are available commercially in ready-to-use sachets. Basically the medium consists of a range of mineral salts, a source of sugar (usually sucrose), a growth promoting auxin such as indoleacetic acid, a cytokinin such as kinetin and a number of vitamins of which pyridoxine HCl, thiamine HCl, nicotinic acid and inositol are the most important (See Table 47). The nutrient solution is normally adjusted to pH 5.7, after which agar is added to make a gel at a concentration of

Table 47 **Ingredients of a culture medium[c] used for meristem-tip culture**

MINERAL SALTS[b]	(mg/l)	ORGANIC INGREDIENTS	
NH_4NO_3	1650		
KNO_3	1900	Sucrose	30g/l
$CaCl_22H_2O$	440	Indoleacetic acid	8 mg/l
$MgSO_47H_2O$	370	Kinetin	2.56 mg/l
KH_2PO_2	170		
Na_2-EDTA	37[a]	Pyridoxin HCl	0.5 mg/l
FeSO47H_2O	28[a]	Thiamine HCl	0.1 mg/l
H_3BO_3	6.2	Nicotinic acid	0.1 mg/l
$MnSO_44H_2O$	22.3	Myo-Inositol	100 mg/l
$ZnSO_44H_2O$	8.6	Agar (Oxoid No 3)	9 g/l
KI	0.83		
$Na_2MoO_42H_2O$	0.25		
$CuSO_45H_2O$	0.025		
$CoCl_26H_2O$	0.025		

[a] 5 ml/l of a stock solution containing 5.57g $FeSO_4.7H_2O$ and 7.45g Na_2-EDTA per litre of distilled water

[b] The mineral salts may be purchased as a commercially prepared package (see Section 4.7). The medium should be adjusted to pH 5.7 before the addition of agar. The agar may be omitted and a filter-paper bridge used to support the culture

[c] Medium based on Murashige and Skoog (1962)

Figure 33 Diagram of a bud showing the meristem-tip region that is usually removed as the explant for tissue culture

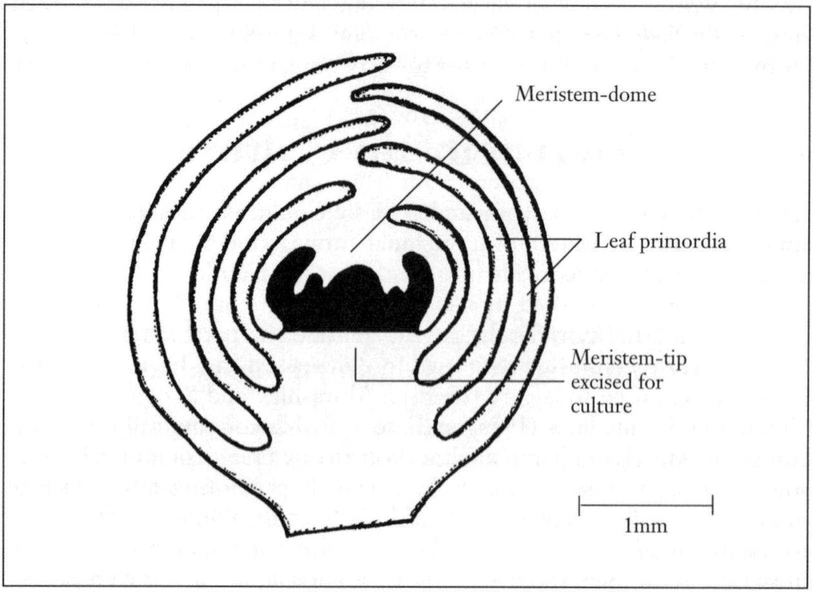

about 0.9% (See Chapter 6). Sometimes the agar, which is used as a support medium for the meristem-tip culture, is omitted, and a filter paper bridge is used to support the culture. After preparation, the culture medium and the vessel in which it is contained is sterilised by autoclaving and then stored in a refrigerator at 4°C until used.

The explant. Numerous terms have been used to describe the explant tissue cut from the shoot-bud for culture. These have included bud-tip, axillary-bud, shoot-apex, meristem-tip, meristem or simply tip culture. Unfortunately, these terms do not accurately describe the exact nature of the explant that is taken for culture. The cells at the actual growing point of a bud are called the meristem dome, and these alone cannot be successfully cultured to regenerate a plantlet. For successful culture and regeneration to occur, the minimum amount of explant taken must consist of the meristematic dome of cells plus at least one or more leaf primordia (young leaves) and should measure between 0.5 mm and 1 mm in diameter (See Fig. 33). These days, however, most people use the term **meristem-tip** to describe this explant.

In addition to being cultured to produce virus-free plants, meristem-tip explants may also be the starting tissue for the rapid clonal propagation of plants, a technique that is being increasingly used for multiplying alpines and other garden plants. It should be emphasized, however, that when meristem-tips are cultured to eradicate virus from an infected parent plant, in contrast to its use for plant propagation, it is only necessary for one healthy plantlet to be produced for the procedure to be successful. The plant can then be multiplied by conventional propagation or by rapid tissue culture multiplication, as required.

Besides using meristem-tip explants as the starting tissue for plant regeneration, it is possible to use other plant tissues such as callus developed from older tissues in the stem or leaf, reproductive tissues such as ovaries and anthers, or even individual plant cells, but these alternative tissues will frequently result in plantlets that are genetically different from the parent plant (Walkey, 1991b). Plants derived directly from meristem-tips, however, are usually genetically stable and their characteristics are identical to the parent plant from which they were grown. The genetical stability of the plant material following tissue culture is most important, for the object of any clonal propagation is to produce offspring with characteristics identical to the parent plant.

Factors controlling the eradication of virus from meristem-tips during tissue culture

Meristem-tip culture was first used for virus-free plant production in France by Morel and Martin to eradicate virus from dahlias (1952) and potatoes (1955). The early workers in the field tended to believe that viruses did not enter the meristematic cells of the shoot-bud, and they assumed that all plantlets regenerated by meristem-tip culture would be virus-free. Sometimes this assumption was correct, but in some virus/host infections the virus did enter the meristem and the tip-culture process did not produce virus-free plants. Unfortunately, some nurserymen propagating orchids by this technique, inadvertently sold material as virus-free when it was still infected. This initially resulted in plants produced by meristem-tip culture having a bad reputation in the orchid industry, but with more research it was soon realized that virus was not always eliminated by tip culture and post-cultural virus-testing procedures were introduced to overcome this problem. Today, it is well known that some viruses invade the meristem tissues of the bud to varying degrees and others do not (Walkey & Webb, 1970). The entry of the virus into the meristem is dependent on the type of virus and the host species concerned. One of the main factors that governs the loss of virus by meristem-tip culture, is the size of the tip that is removed for culture. Tips varying from 0.1 mm to 2 mm in diameter have been cultivated into plantlets, but most workers have used tips measuring between 0.3 mm and 1.5 mm in diameter. As a general rule, the proportion of virus-free plantlets regenerated, is inversely proportional to the size of the tip taken for culture. Unfortunately, however, the smaller the tip taken the greater are the difficulties in getting it to grow and regenerate. Consequently, it is often necessary to take a somewhat larger explant, with an increased possibility of it being virus infected. Nevertheless, in some virus/host infections it is possible to excise a tip small enough to be free of the virus, but big enough to be regenerated into a healthy plantlet (See Fig. 34a).

In other virus/host infections, viruses can be eradicated from cultured meristem-tips even when the tips that are cut actually contain virus (See Fig. 34b). In this situation the virus is inactivated 'in-vivo' during the tissue culture process. The reasons why the virus is inactivated during tissue culture are not known, but the inactivation is more likely to occur if the tissues contain a low concentration of virus than a high one, at the time when the explant is taken. One possible explanation for this "in vivo" virus inactivation is that the auxins and other growth promoting chemicals in the culture nutrient solution, stimulate a resistance mechanism in the cells of the host plant against the virus.

In many virus/host infections, however, the virus is present in the meristem in high concentrations and it is impossible to excise a tip small enough to avoid the virus or to allow 'in vivo' virus inactivation during tissue culture (See Fig. 34c). Fortunately, it is still possible to produce virus-free plants from such infected plants by using heat treatment (**thermotherapy**) or chemical treatment (**chemotherapy**), combined with meristem-tip culture (See Chapter 6).

Meristem-tips for culture may be cut either from an apical, a terminal or an axillary bud (the bud in the axil of a side shoot), but the position of the bud on the infected plant may influence the concentration of virus it contains. There is evidence in some virus/host infections that buds high on the stem contain a lower concentration of virus than buds lower down. The reason for this difference is not known, although it has been suggested that it may be related to the auxin gradient in a shoot, which is high at the top and lower towards the stem's base.

Examples of vegetatively propagated rock plants that have been freed of virus by the author using meristem-tip culture alone, are shown in Table 48.

Figure 34 Diagram showing virus invasion of the meristem-tip in relation to virus eradication by tissue culture and thermotherapy

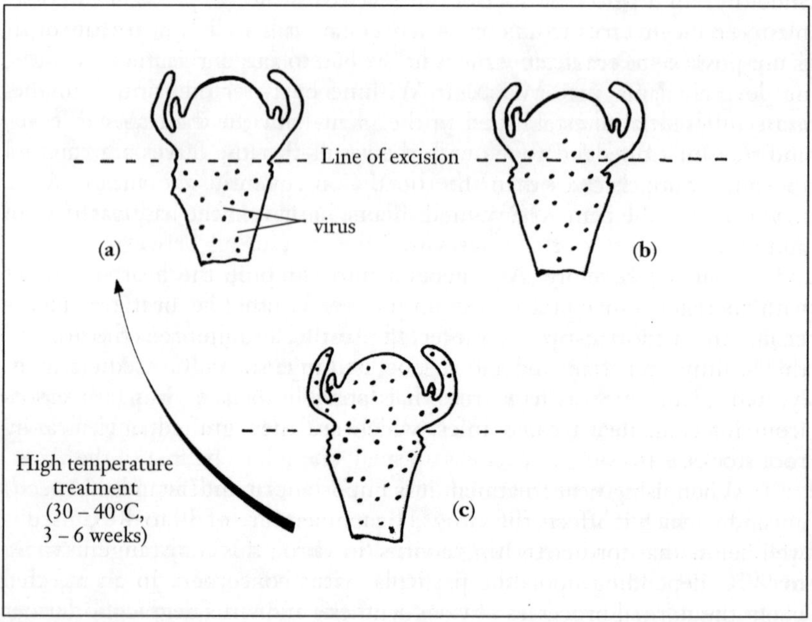

Table 48 **Examples of vegetatively-propagated rock plants that have been freed of virus by meristem-tip culture**

Amaryllidaceae		
Narcissus spp.		
Iridaceae		
Iris spp.		
Liliaceae		
Lilium spp		
Tulipa spp.		
Primulaceae		
Primula	cv.	Beatrice Wooster (*P. allionii* × *P.* 'Linda Pope')
	cv.	Bewerley White (*P.* × *pubescens*)
	cv.	Barbara Barker (*P.* 'Linda Pope' × [*P.* × *pubescens*, 'Zuleika Dobson'])
	cv.	Ethel Barker (*P. allionii* × *P. hirsuta*)
	cv.	Faldonside (*P.* × *pubescens*)
	cv.	'Pritchard's Variety' (*P. marginata*)

Thermotherapy

High temperature treatment has been widely used in the production of virus-free plants (Nyland and Goheen, 1969). The treatments generally involve the infected plant or an infected organ (such as a potato tuber), being grown in hot air in a temperature controlled cabinet at between 30 and 40°C for a period of six to twelve weeks. Although it has been possible to eradicate virus from a complete potato tuber by heat treatment, it is not possible to eradicate virus from a whole plant by this method, without severely damaging or killing it. Within a heat-treated plant, a temperature differential is established in the plant between the exposed leaves and the soil-embedded roots, with the result that the leaves are exposed to higher temperatures than the roots. Consequently, the virus may be inactivated in the plant's leaves and shoots, but not in the base of the stem and roots.

Usually, therefore, it is necessary to combine the heat treatment with meristem-tip culture to eradicate the virus. The heat treatments enable the meristem-tip of an infected plant to become free of virus, and this healthy tip is removed and regenerated in tissue culture. Alternatively, with plants such as fruit trees, it is possible to take virus-free shoots from infected, heat-treated trees, which are then grafted onto healthy root stocks.

When using heat treatment it is important to understand the mechanism by which it affects the virus. The temperature of 30 to 40°C used is well below that for inactivating a virus 'in vitro'; this may range from 45 to 90°C depending upon the particular virus concerned. In an infected plant, the normal processes of virus synthesis and virus degradation occur simultaneously, but at high temperatures (usually above 32°C) virus replication stops, but the breakdown of virus continues within the cells. Consequently, since heat-treatment temperatures of 30 to 40°C are sufficiently high to block virus replication, eventually the newly formed plant tissues around the bud's meristem growing point will be free of virus. The meristem-tip can then be removed for culture and regeneration (See Fig. 34c). The length of the heat treatment period required before a virus is absent from the newly formed tissues if an infected plant, will vary with different virus/host infections, but usually it is from 3 to 10 weeks. It should be remembered however that the older parts of the plant will remain infected, so that when the heat-treatment is ended and the plant is grown again at a lower temperature the virus will start to multiply again and invade the tissues near the bud meristem. So the tips must be excised immediately the heat-treated plants are taken from the high temperature chambers.

Temperature treatments of 30 to 40°C are often close to the high temperature limit at which a plant can survive, although the highest temperature for survival does vary between plant species. Studies have been made therefore, to determine the best methods of applying the high temperature treatments, in order to obtain maximum plant survival and virus eradication. Some plants respond better to high temperatures, if they are subjected initially to a preconditioning treatment at a lower temperature than the one finally used. For example, garlic plants will survive if they are kept at 30°C for 1 week, followed by 2 weeks at 36°C, before transfer to 38°C for a further 2 weeks, but they are killed if transferred directly from 20° to 38°C (Walkey *et al.*, 1987). Also, alternating periods of high and low temperature treatments may be better than a continuous high temperature for plant survival, and may be equally effective in blocking virus multiplication. Diurnal treatments of 40°C (for eight hours) plus 22°C (for sixteen hours), or 22°C (for four hours) plus 36°C (for 20 hours), have for example, been found to be preferable to continuous high temperature treatment for the eradication of cucumber mosaic virus in tobacco (Walkey & Freeman, 1977). Each plant species, however, has a different optimal temperature requirement for virus eradication and this temperature must be determined when a species is being treated for the first time.

Examples of viruses that have been eradicated from infected vegetatively propagated plants by a combination of high temperature and meristem-tip culture are given in Table 49.

Chemotherapy

It has been mentioned earlier, that virus infection cannot be eradicated directly from a plant by chemical treatments in the same way that fungicides and bactericides can be used to cure fungal and bacterial diseases. Many attempts have been made to find chemicals that will control viruses infecting plants and although some chemicals have been found that may suppress virus symptoms or virus multiplication in a complete plant, few, if any, will eradicate virus (Tomlinson, 1982). Also, some proven antiviral chemicals are unsuitable for use on crop plants, because of their phytoxicity and cost.

Table 49 **Species that have been freed of viruses by a combination of meristem-tip culture and thermotherapy or by tip culture alone**[b]

HOST	VIRUSES ERADICATED	TEMPERATURE TREATMENT
Chrysanthemum morifolium	Virus B, vein mottle, greenflower, aspermy	35-38°C (4-37wk)
Cymbidium spp.	Mosaic	–[a]
Dahlia spp.	Mosaic	–
Daphne odora	Daphne S	–
Dianthus barbatus	Ringspot, mottle, latent	–
Dianthus caryophyllus (carnation)	Ringspot, mottle, latent, streak, vein-mottle	35-40°C (3-15wk)
Forsythia x *intermedia*	Unspecified	–
Freesia spp.	Mosaic, bean yellow mosaic	–
Geranium spp.	Tomato ringspot	–
Gladiolus spp.	Unspecified	–
Hydrangea hortensia	Ringspot	–
Hyacinthus orientalis (hyacinth)	Mosaic, lily symptomless	–
Iris spp.	Latent, mosaic	–
Lavendula spp. (lavender)	Dieback	–
Lilium spp.	Cucumber mosaic, lily symptomless	–
Narcissus tazetta (daffodil)	Arabis mosaic, degeneration	–
Nerine spp.	Latent, unspecified	–
Ranunculus asiaticus	Tobacco rattle, cucumber mosaic	–

[a] No heat treatment used
[b] See Quak (1977) and Walkey (1991a) for reference to these studies

There are some antiviral chemicals, however, which act by blocking virus multiplication in the cells of the infected plant. The most effective of these found to date is ribavirin (1,2,4-triazole-3-carboxamide, sold under the trade name of Virazole). If this is added to the tissue culture medium at concentrations in the order of 25 to 100 mg/l, it will block the multiplication of virus in the cells of the meristem-tip of the virus infected shoot being cultured. This will allow the young cells to divide in a virus-free condition, even though the older tissues of the culture remain infected. Eventually, the meristem-tip can be re-cut from the ribavirin-treated culture in a virus-free condition and subsequently regenerated in its healthy condition on a culture medium without ribavirin (Simpkins *et al.*, 1981). In effect, the eradication mechanism of the action of ribavirin is similar to that of high temperature, in that it blocks the multiplication of virus, allowing new tissues to develop without virus at the shoot apex, but it does not inactivate existing virus.

The use of chemotherapy combined with meristem-tip culture is particularly useful for virus eradication when high temperature treatments

Figure 35 A scheme for producing virus-free plants by using a meristem-tip culture combined with chemotherapy

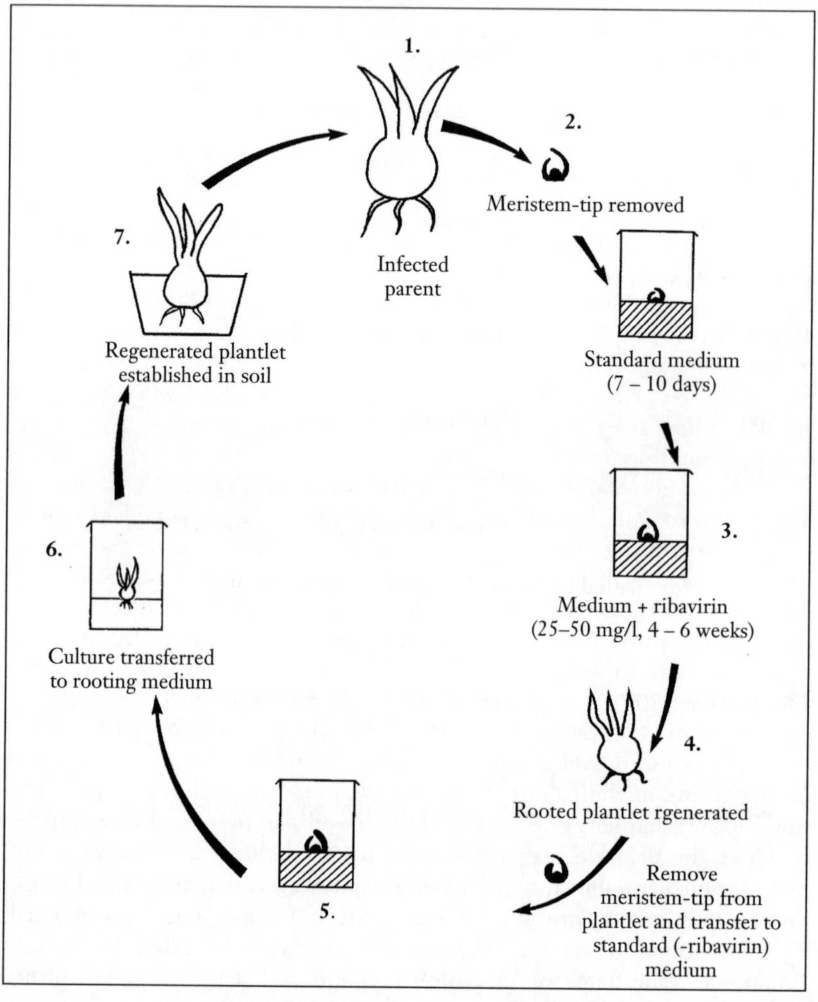

fail to block the replication of a particular virus or when the infected host plant is very susceptible to high temperature treatments. A scheme for producing virus-free plants by a combination of meristem-tip culture and ribavirin treatment is given in Fig. 35.

Tissue Culture Procedures

For normal culture, meristem-tips should be grown at a reasonably constant temperature between 22 to 25°C with a daylength of 16 hours. Illumination may be provided by daylight fluorescent tubes, sodium or mercury lights. The room housing the cultures should be free of dust, so that the exterior of the vessels containing the sterile cultures remain as clean as possible. This is important because external contamination of the culture vessel will be a problem when the sterile cultures are transferred to fresh culture medium. The cultures will need to be transferred to fresh medium every 2 to 3 weeks and the growth promoting substances in the medium (auxins and cytokinins) may have to be changed at different growth stages to obtain the required shoot proliferation or rooting (See Chapter 6 and Fig. 32). It should be emphasized that only one virus-free plantlet needs to be regenerated for the procedure to be successful. It is not, therefore, essential to include a proliferating medium stage as illustrated in Figure 32 in the regeneration procedure. Once a virus-free plant has been obtained this may be multiplied by conventional macropropagation (for example by cuttings), or it may be micropropagated in tissue culture using the scheme shown in Figure 32 when the proliferating medium stage would be required.

If a meristem-tip is growing on a well-balanced nutrient medium it may be expected to regenerate into a rooted plantlet from a freshly cut tip in approximately 8 to 12 weeks. Scrupulously aseptic procedures must be followed (See Chapter 6) at the time the tip is initially cut from the parent shoot and at each subsequent medium transfer to avoid contamination of the culture (See Plate 28).

When good root development has occurred, the plantlet should be transferred to soil. This is always a critical procedure in any plant regeneration programme, for the young, delicate plantlet must be transferred from the very high humidity and protected environment of the culture vessel, to a variable and often harsh environment. The transfer process must be carefully monitored and the high humidity gradually reduced. Plantlets often do well if they are initially transferred to peat 'Jiffy' pots and placed within a plastic-covered seed tray (See Plate 28). A high humidity can be initially maintained within the plastic cover and this can be slowly reduced over a period of 10 to 14 days by first gradually opening the vents in the top of the chamber, and then by lifting one of the sides of the chamber. Finally, the plastic cover can be removed completely. Once the plantlets are acclimatised to the ambient air, the 'Jiffy' pot can be transplanted into a larger pot containing a suitable soil mixture for the species concerned.

Post-Culture Treatment

At the stage regenerated plantlets are established in soil it will not be known if it is virus-free or not, and it is essential to determine its disease status. Because many viruses have a delayed resurgence period following meristem-tip culture and thermotherapy treatments, considerable attention must be paid to testing (called **virus indexing**) the plantlet for virus. The reason why there is sometimes a delay in the re-appearance of virus in regenerated plantlets that have not been completely freed of virus, is due to low virus concentrations. The virus may have been reduced to such a low level by the culture treatments that it is no longer detectable. If the virus is still present in low concentrations, however, given time, its concentration will once again build up to a detectable level.

During this period of virus-indexing, the plantlet should be kept separated from plants that have already been shown to be virus-free and from virus-infected plants. An insect-free glasshouse is essential for this purpose. In addition to frequently observing the regenerated plants for virus symptoms, each plant should be tested for virus several times during the first year following culture. Where facilities are available, the leaves from the regenerated plants should be tested for virus by sap transmission to a susceptible host plant (See Chapter 6) and/or by electron microscopy and serology tests.

Although there is a lot of evidence to show that plants derived from meristem-tips do not usually vary genetically from their virus-infected parents, it is essential to check that no obvious genetic changes have occurred. This should be done by observing the generated plants for any changes in agronomic characteristics over several seasons in the garden or on the nursery, and attention should be paid to small differences in the plants' performance that may result from physiological changes in the plant due to loss of virus. The virus-free plants will usually be more vigorous than infected plants, and this increased vigour may lead to changes in flowering dates, earliness and other minor differences compared with the virus-infected parent plants.

Once it is certain that the regenerated plants are virus-free and that they have no adverse characteristics, they may be multiplied conventionally to produce commercial quantities. It must be emphasized that this propagation should be carried out as far as possible, under virus-free conditions, for the plants although virus-free are still susceptible to reinfection by virus. Consequently, in addition to the healthy plants being multiplied under virus-free conditions, it would also be sensible to maintain a smaller, nuclear stock of virus-free mother plants under virus-free conditions for future multiplication. The virus-free conditions could be maintained, by only growing the plants in quarantine in a glasshouse or gauze-house that is insect-proof, and ensuring that the plants are grown in sterile soil.

CHAPTER SIX

Practical Information

PLANT HEALTH AND CONSERVATION

The import of plants into Britain is governed by two separate types of legislation covering (a) plant health and (b) conservation of wildlife.

Plant Health Import Regulations Background

Many harmful organisms and diseases are absent from some countries. As a result, governments prepare plant health import regulations to minimise the opportunities for their introduction. At one time in Europe, each country prepared its own Plant Health Regulations independently of other countries. However, with the establishment of the European Economic Community (EEC) the regulations of Member States are being revised and unified by means of Directives published in the Official Journal of the European Communities. The Directives describe the import of plant material into Member States from countries within the EEC and other areas of the world ('third' countries). There is the requirement that many plants and plant products can only enter the EEC or be traded between Member States if accompanied by a **Phytosanitary Certificate**. These Plant Health Regulations have two main purposes (1) to minimise the opportunities for the introduction of harmful organisms from non-member to Community States and (2) to re-organise plant health inspection so as to remove unnecessary obstacles to trade between Member States. At one time it was the responsibility of the importing country to inspect plants. However, the intention is to increase the responsibility of the country of origin to ensure that plants for export are free of harmful organisms and to remove the responsibility of the importing country to inspect the plants. This type of legislation is already operated by the USA who employ Plant Health Officials in exporting countries. In 1987, the

European Commission produced a strategy for plant health within the European Community (EC). The strategy included plans for a Community Plant Health Inspectorate and the replacement of phytosanitary certificates with a '**plant passport**'. In the UK plant passports are planned for 1993. Commercial producers will be required to register (at no charge, 1993) with the MAFF; plants will be given a plant passport if they prove healthy when inspected during growth and at harvest. Imports of plants and plant products from non-EEC countries would be subject to standard Community rules and require a similar plant passport.

The relevant current regulations for Great Britain (England, Wales and Scotland) are described in the Plant Health (Great Britain) Order 1987, with Amendments in 1989 and 1990, and the Plant Health (Forestry) (Great Britain) Order 1989. The Orders describe the restrictions on the import of plants, plant products and soil into England, Wales and Scotland. As with the EC, their purpose is to minimise, with as few restrictions as possible, the opportunities for the introduction of pests and diseases which are not normally present in Britain and which would be potentially harmful. Plant products and soil or other growing media infected or contaminated with them are also included. The Orders are summarised in the 'Travellers' Guide to Bringing Plants Back from Abroad (including Wild Plants)' (publication PB0238) and the 'Plant Health Guide for Importers' (publication PB0426). These and the complete Orders are obtainable from MAFF Publications, London, SE99 7TP or HMSO, PO Box 276, London SW8 5DT. Imports into Northern Ireland, the Channel Islands and the Isle of Man are covered by separate legislation.

Plant Health Orders and Regulations are based on sound scientific and commercial considerations and are for the protection of horticulture, agriculture and forestry. It is essential that we are guided by them.

Similar regulations apply in other countries and readers should consult their appropriate authority for exact details.

Scope of the Plant Health Import Regulations

Plants are defined as living plants including seeds, fruit (botanical sense) (other than deep frozen), vegetables, tubers, corms, bulbs, rhizomes, cut flowers, branches with foliage, plant tissue cultures. **Plant products** are defined as products of plant origin which have not been processed or have undergone simple preparation. **Harmful organisms** are defined as pests of plants or plant products, belonging to the animal or plant kingdoms, or pathogens such as fungi, bacteria and viruses.

The Orders distinguish between

- Organisms which are particularly harmful and whose entry into Great Britain is prohibited,
- Organisms which are prohibited when present on certain plants

or plant products,
- Plants and plant products which are prohibited,
- Plants, plant products and other objects contaminated by specified organisms,
- Plants and plant products which require an official certificate describing the country of origin,
- Soil and other media for growing plants.

Prohibited pests are not normally present in Britain but would be potentially harmful if they were introduced; plants, plant products and soil or other growing media which are infected or contaminated with them are also prohibited. Genetically manipulated materials are prohibited. It may be possible to import prohibited materials providing a **Licence** is obtained beforehand from the GB Department of Agriculture or Forestry Commission.

Restricted plants and plant materials are those which have been produced or derived in prescribed conditions. They may be imported but only when accompanied by a Phytosanitary Certificate. A **Reforwarding Phytosanitary Certificate** is also needed if a consignment of restricted material is stored, repacked, or split up in other countries before arrival in Great Britain. Phytosanitary Certificates are only valid when issued by an official of the Plant Protection Service of the country in which the plants are grown; that is to say they may not be issued by a State, department or local government. The Certificates must be written in English or translated. It is difficult to obtain phytosanitary certificates in remote areas. Therefore wild plants may be imported providing an import licence is obtained beforehand and providing they are not endangered species (Appendix 1.2: CITES). Licences are obtainable from MAFF, Plant Health Division, Ergon House, c/o Nobel House, 17 Smith Square, London SW1P 3HY; they cost £31 for amateurs and £215 for scientific or commercial operators (1991 prices). Phytosanitary Certificates are not required for plants or plant products from Northern Ireland, the Channel Islands or the Isle of Man.

Prohibitions and restrictions are based on the country of origin. Three important areas are **Continental USA** comprising the whole of the USA excluding Hawaii; **EC Member States** comprising Belgium, Denmark, France, Greece, Ireland, Italy, Luxembourg, The Netherlands, Portugal, Spain and Germany but not the Canary Islands, Channel islands or the Isle of Man; the **Euro-Mediterranean area** comprising Europe (including the Azores, Canary Islands, Madeira and Western USSR) and countries bordering the Mediterranean – Algeria, Cyprus, Egypt, Israel, Jordan, Lebanon, Libya, Malta, Morocco, Syria, Tunisia and Turkey.

Main provisions of the Plant Health Orders (Great Britain)

Those considered of most importance to gardeners and commercial horticulture are summarised below. The Regulations are subject to change and it is emphasized that full up-to-date details should be obtained from the MAFF.

Allowed at all times

- Flower seeds from any area of the world.

Prohibited at all times

- Annual and biennial plants outside the Euro-Mediterranean area;
- Plants of herbaceous perennials originating outside the Euro-Mediterranean area and belonging to the Caryophyllaceae, Compositae, Cruciferae, Leguminosae and Rosaceae;
- Plants of trees and shrubs originating outside the Euro-Mediterranean area, Canada, Continental USA; there are exceptions for the use indoors or in a greenhouse of ornamental species of Agavaceae, Araceae, Araliaceae – includes *Hedera*, Araucariaceae, Bromeliaceae, Cycadaceae, Gesneriaceae, Haemodoraceae, Palmae, Polypodiaceae (ferns), Streliziaceae, Zingiberaceae, *Ficus* and *Codiaeum*;
- All bonsai plants and any plants from New Zealand of *Camellia*, *Chaenomeles*, *Crataegus*, *Cydonia*, *Eriobotrya*, *Malus*, *Prunus*, *Pyrus*;
- All hosts of *Sclerotinia fructicola* (syn. *Monilinia fructicola*);
- Plants of Gramineae (agricultural and ornamental grasses) originating outside the EC. NB: various bamboos, *Cortaderia selloana* (pampas grass) and *Pennisetum setaceum* originating from New Zealand are not prohibited;
- Plants of Solanaceae originating outside the Euro-Mediterranean area;
- Plants of tuber forming *Solanum* species from all countries;
- Plants of *Citrus*, *Fortunella* or *Poncirus* (other than fruits and parts for decoration) from Florida, Louisiana and Hawaii;
- Plants of *Prunus*, *Cydonia*, *Malus* and *Pyrus* excepting those from the EC, certain countries in the Euro-Mediterranean area, Finland, Norway, Sweden, Canada and continental USA;
- Plants of *Dendranthema*, *Leucanthemella serotina* and *Nipponanthemum nipponicum* (mostly types of florist chrysanthemum);
- Plant of *Fragaria* originating in all countries except Europe and certain countries in the Euro-Mediterranean area, Africa, Australia and New Zealand, Canada and continental USA;
- Plants of *Juniperus* and certain genera of forest trees originating outside Europe. Those of most relevance to gardeners are *Abies*, *Larix*, *Picea*, *Pinus*, *Pseudotsuga* and *Tsuga*;
- Host plants of the San Jose Scale (*Chaenomeles*, *Cornus*, *Cotoneaster*, *Crataegus*, *Prunus*, *Cydonia*, *Malus*, *Mespilus*, *Pyrus*, *Ribes*, *Sorbus*, *Symphoricarpos*) with certain exceptions (see below);
- Soil and used growing media not associated with growing plants or plant products from countries outside the EC;
- Seeds of *Beta vulgaris*, lucerne (*Medicago*), and certain varieties of fodder pea originating from some countries;
- All genetically manipulated material.

Prohibited at certain times of the year

- Plants of *Acacia*, *Acer*, *Amelanchier*, *Euonymus*, *Fagus*, *Juglans*, *Ligustrum*, *Maclura*, *Populus*, *Ptelea*, *Salix*, *Syringa*, *Tilia* and *Vitis* originating in New Zealand and sent between the period 16

October-31 March;
- Cut flowers of *Gladiolus* sent between 1 May-31 October originating from countries outside the EC in which gladiolus rusts are known to occur;
- Host plants of the San Jose Scale sent between 1 October-15 April from certain countries in the northern hemisphere; host plants from elsewhere are prohibited (see above);

Restricted material originating from any country and requiring a Phytosanitary Certificate

- Cut flowers and parts for decoration of florists' chrysanthemum, *Chrysanthemum*, carnation (*Dianthus caryophyllus*), *Gypsophila*, *Prunus*, *Rosa*, *Salix* and *Vitis*.

Restricted material originating in the EC requiring a Phytosanitary Certificate

- Soil and growing media;
- All rooted plants;
- Unrooted vegetative propagating materials;
- Potato tubers;
- Seeds of certain vegetables, lucerne and species of *Prunus* and *Rubus*;
- Most types of raw vegetables;
- Raw fruit of quince (*Cydonia*), apple (*Malus*), apricot, cherry, greengage, peach, plum, bullace, cherry plum and sloe (*Prunus*), pear (*Pyrus*), *Citrus* except lemons and citrons;
- Plants of chestnut (*Castanea*), Coniferae, *Platanus*, *Prunus* and *Quercus*;
- Plant and plant products, but not forestry material, from the Irish Republic.

Restricted material from countries outside the EC requiring a Phytosanitary Certificate

- *Gladiolus*, carnation, florists' chrysanthemum, *Protea*.

Entry to the UK and clearance

- On entry to Britain the original certificates or licences must be given to the Customs;
- Consignments by post or unaccompanied should have the Phytosanitary and Reforwarding Certificates in an envelope attached to the outside of the consignment and marked for the attention of HM Customs;
- Phytosanitary Certificates and Reforwarding Certificates must be stamped on entry to the country;
- All plants and plant materials entering Britain are liable to be inspected on arrival. If the plants etc. are unhealthy or in contravention of the Plant Health Orders the importer may be required to destroy, treat or re-export them at his own expense;
- Plants etc. which enter Britain and which have a Phytosanitary

Certificate are not **cleared** until inspected by an official of the Plant Protection Service.

Concession to travellers. Travellers are allowed to bring with them as passenger baggage and for their personal use, small quantities of certain plants and their products from countries in the Euro-Mediterranean area without the need for a Phytosanitary Certificate. **The concession does not apply to material which is posted or for use in commerce.** The concession comprises

- a total of 2 kilograms (kg) tubers, bulbs, rhizomes or corms;
- 5 plants or parts of plants;
- a small bunch of cut flowers;
- a total of 2 kg raw fruit and raw vegetables;
- 2 kg of raw citrus fruit;
- 5 retail packets of true seed.

Excluded from the concession are: endangered species of plant, any sort of potato, fruit tree or chrysanthemum; plants of forest trees, bonsai trees, *Beta*, vine or *Gramineae*; cut flowers of *Gladiolus*. The concession is limited to materials originating from the Euro-Mediterranean area. The **only** concession allowed from other countries is 2 kg citrus fruit from N America.

This information was prepared during Spring 1992 and the MAFF should be consulted for the most recent information.

Conservation of Wildlife

Endangered plant species. The UK is signatory to the **Convention on International Trade in Endangered Species (CITES)** and consequently importation of some species of wild plant is restricted or prohibited. Details are available from the Department of the Environment, International Trade in Endangered Species Branch, Tollgate House, Houlton street, Bristol BS2 9DJ.

Species of plants (and animals) are classified as 'endangered', 'threatened' or 'vulnerable'. The import and export of endangered species to or from the UK is controlled by (a) the provisions of the regulations of the European Community which enforce the Convention on International Trade in Endangered Species of Wild Fauna and Flora (CITES) within the EC and (b) other national and international legislation on conservation. For example the **Endangered Species Act** controls the UK trade in many non-CITES species of wild life, the **Bern Convention on the Conservation of European Wildlife and Natural Habitats** controls the import and export of animals; the **EEC Birds Directive (79/409/EEC)** controls the import and export of birds occurring in the wild state (not 'game birds') in the European territory of the Member States of the EEC; the **Wildlife and Countryside Act 1981** protects certain animals in the wild in the UK.

Convention on International Trade in Endangered Species of Wild Fauna and Flora (CITES)

The CITES is the most relevant to the alpine gardener of the various regulations on conservation.
Plants species are classified as follows:

AI, C1 refer to endangered species of which the commercial import, export and sale is normally prohibited; AI species are prohibited from display for sale, etc;

C2 species are threatened species which may be traded provided import and export licences are obtained; normally import licences will not be granted by the UK and other EC states unless strict conservation and other criteria have been met;

AII species are vulnerable species which may be traded provided that export and import licences are obtained and an export permit obtained from the country of origin (exporting country);

AIII species are given special protection by certain countries, the standard of protection being similar to that of AII species. AIII species which are imported from a country which listed the species require a CITES export permit from the exporting country; if imported from countries other than those listing them specifically, a **Certificate of Origin** is required. All AIII species require a UK import permit.

Plants protected by the CITES convention

AI (Endangered species – commercial import, export and sale normally prohibited)

AII *Anacampseros* spp; *Lewisia cotyledon*, *L. maguirei*, *L. serrata*, *L. tweedyi*; *Cyclamen* spp.

C1 Primulaceae: *Cyclamen graecum*, *C. mindleri*, *C. creticum*, *C. balearicum*

Orchidaceae: certain species of *Cypripedium*, *Epipactis*, *Cephalanthera*, *Limodorum*, *Epipogium*, *Listera*, *Spiranthes*, *Goodyera*, *Gennaria*, *Herminium*, *Neottianthe*, *Platanthera*, *Chamorchis*, *Gymnadenia*, *Pseudorchis*, *Nigritella*, *Ceologlossum*, *Dactylorhiza*, *Corallorhiza*, *Liparis*, *Malaxis*, *Hammarbya*, *Neotinea*, *Traunsteinera*, *Orchis*, *Aceras*, *Himantoglossum*, *Barlia*, *Anacamptis*, *Serapias*, *Ophrys*.

PROCEDURES FOR VIRUS INOCULATIONS AND TISSUE CULTURE

Introduction

It is intended that the information contained in this section should assist the enthusiastic alpine-gardener, hybridizer or professional nurseryman, in carrying out the virus screening procedures necessary if a resistance breeding programme is being contemplated, and describes to the reader simple methods that might be used to produce virus-free plants by meristem tip culture. The preparation and source of the various chemicals, materials and equipment are detailed, together with the practical procedures required for each technique.

Preparation and Maintenance of Infected Sap Inoculum

This procedure would be used for the following purposes.

(i) To determine if a plant is infected with a virus (for example, to detect the presence of cucumber mosaic virus (CMV) in sap from infected *Viola*. Marrow seedlings which are highly susceptible to CMV could be used for this test).

(ii) To screen a segregating population of seedlings from a breeding programme to determine the resistance of individual plants (for example, testing a F_2 population of *Viola* seedlings for resistance to CMV).

(iii) To propagate and maintain a specific virus for further use.

a. **Solution for preparing sap inoculum**

- 1% di-potassium hydrogen orthophosphate (K_2HPO_4) + 0.1% sodium sulphite (Na_2SO_3).
- prepared by dissolving 1g K_2HPO_4, and 0.1g Na_2SO_3 in 100 ml of distilled water.

b. **Inoculation procedure**

- Take an infected leaf showing virus symptoms and place in a precooled mortar (previously placed in a refrigerator at 4°C). Add ice-cold K_2HPO_4/Na_2SO_3 solution to the mortar in the ratio of 1.5 ml of solution to 1g of infected leaf. Grind until a fine sap-mixture is obtained.
- Filter the mixture through a square of butter-muslin into a 1 cm diameter glass test-tube. Keep the test-tube containing the

inoculum in an ice-bucket (or at 4°C) until used.

- Dust the test seedling with a fine layer of carborundum 300 using a throat spray (see Plate 28) or mix some carborundum with the sap-inoculum and shake thoroughly before use.
- Take a folded 4 cm square of butter-muslin, moisten thoroughly with the sap inoculum and squeeze gently to remove excess sap. Then gently, but firmly, stroke the upper surface of the dusted leaf with the moist pad, supporting the lower surface of the leaf with the free hand (see Plate 28). Ensure that the whole upper surface of the leaf is rubbed. Alternatively, instead of using a muslin pad, a finger dipped in the sap-inoculum may be used to rub the leaf. Hands must be thoroughly washed when the inoculation is completed.
- The inoculated surface of the plant should be rinsed under a trickle of cold tap-water as soon as the inoculation is completed and the plant placed in a cool (22-25°C) glasshouse compartment.
- Test plants should be observed for symptom development from 5 to 6 days after inoculation.
- It is helpful to keep an uninoculated test plant and a plant inoculated with K_2HPO_4/Na_2SO_3 solution alone for control purposes, so that virus symptoms are not confused with physical damage to the leaf caused by the rubbing alone.

c. **Maintenance of virus culture**

For screening purposes, the virus isolate being used must be maintained and multiplied regularly by sub-culturing from infected to healthy plants. For relatively short periods (a few months) this may be done by inoculating healthy young plants with infected sap approximately every three weeks. If the virus culture is to be maintained for long periods (a year or more), the possibility of it being lost or contaminated with a second virus is considerable. It is, therefore, advisable to the store the virus culture in a dry condition. This may be done by taking an infected leaf and drying it over anhydrous calcium chloride ($CaCl_2$) in an airtight, screw-topped tube or small bottle. After several months of drying the dehydrated leaf may be ground in a pestle and mortar and the powder stored in a small sealed capsule and kept in a jar containing $CaCl_2$. Many viruses, including CMV, may be stored for many months or even years in this way.

When a fresh isolate is required, the dried powder is rehydrated in K_2HPO_4/Na_2SO_3 solution and inoculated to a seedling test plant. Known virus-isolates of common viruses are generally available from plant virus laboratories, either as dried powder, or infected fresh leaves that may be sent through the post between sheets of damp blotting paper, sealed in a small polythene bag. Alternatively, some virus isolates, but not all, may be stored by deep freezing. The infected sap should be prepared as if preparing virus inoculum and then stored in a sealed glass or plastic tubes.

Meristem-tip Culture for Virus Eradication

a. **The tissue culture room**

An essential feature of any room used for tissue culture, is a sterile area where the tissue culture procedures can be carried out. Most laboratories used for this purpose would contain a commercially available sterile air-flow bench. This provides a working surface within an open-fronted cabinet through which filtered, sterile air is blown under positive pressure out towards the operator (see Plate 28). Although advisable, a sterile air-flow bench is not essential for tissue culture and a small clean, dry room can be used. This room should have a bench with a work-surface (such as formica) which can be easily swabbed down and sterilised with industrial (70%) alcohol. Alternatively, a small working cabinet could be constructed which should be kept internally sterile by wiping with a sterilant. This should be large enough to house a small binocular microscope and to allow hand and arm movement when the culture explant is cut and transferred. Adequate lighting is essential whatever working surface is used.

All tissue cultures require to be incubated under controlled conditions of temperature and illumination. Most cultures grow steadily under daylight fluorescent tubes. These do not produce as much heat as sodium or mercury lamps. Generally temperatures between 22° and 25°C are suitable for most cultures and daylengths of 12 or 16 hours are suitable depending on the species.

A glasshouse, containing plastic weaning chambers (See Chapter 5), is necessary for transplanting regenerated plants from tissue culture to soil. Consideration should be given to insect proofing the glasshouse to prevent virus re-infection.

b. **Culture medium**

Media based on Murashige and Skoog's (M.S.) or Gamborg's B5 (see Table 44), have proven to be the most suitable for a range of herbaceous and woody species. If the species to be cultured has already been grown *in vitro* by other workers, try following their procedures in detail. If no information is available on the culture of a species, as is likely to be the case with many rock plants, the media detailed in Table 44 should be tried. Preliminary experiments should be made using different concentrations of indoleacetic acid (IAA) and kinetin as shown in Table 41. These experiments should show the optimum concentrations of auxin and cytokinin required for the type of culture growth the operator is seeking. Usually, high cytokinin concentrations favour shoot prolification and cytokinin-free medium favours rooting. Other auxins and cytokinins may be substituted for IAA and kinetin.

The mineral salts complex used in the culture medium may be made up from individual ingredients, but it is much easier to purchase them in a prepared pack which only needs to be dissolved in distilled water. The auxin and cytokinin constituents may also be purchased in commercial packs already combined with the mineral salts, but such packs

Table 50 **Examples of varying concentrations of auxin and cytokinin that may be used to induce different types of culture growth**

Kinetin[b] concentration	Indoleacetic acid[b] concentration			
	0	4 mg/l	8 mg/l	16 mg/l
0	1[a]	2	3	4
1 mg/l	5	6	7	8
2.5 mg/l	9	10	11	12
10 mg/l	13	14	15	16

[a] Number of treatment
[b] Other auxins and cytokinins may be tried instead of kinetin and indoleacetic acid

are often only suitable for the culture of a specific species. The small changes in the organic requirements of individual species, as indicated in Table 41, means most workers prefer the flexibility of preparing their own organic constituents and making fresh solutions of these as required.

Weighing out small quantities of ingredients require a fine balance (scales), if this is not available a coarser balance must be used to weigh the smaller quantity possible, and then the substance must be physically divided to give approximately the required amount of powder. Alternatively, larger quantities of chemical can be dissolved into solution and portions of the solution taken to adjust to the final concentration required for the culture medium. This latter approach is, however, likely to be wasteful.

One litre of MS medium, as detailed in Table 44, may be prepared as follows:

(i) Dissolve one sachet of mineral salts (commercially preweighed and mixed to prepare 1 litre in quantity), 30g sucrose and 100 mg myo-inositol in 800 ml of distilled water.

(ii) Add to this solution:
Pyridoxin HCl: dissolve 25 mg in a few mls of N/10 hydrochloric acid and make up to 50 mls with distilled water (this gives a sol^n 500 mg/l). Use 1 ml (containing 0.05 mg/l) of this solution.
Thiamine HCl: dissolve 25 mg in 50 mls of distilled water (gives a sol^n 500 mg/l). Use 0.2 ml (0.1 mg/l) of this solution.
Nicotinic acid: dissolve 25 mg in a few ml of N/10 hydrochloric acid and make up to 50 mls with distilled water (gives a sol^n 500 mg/l). Use 0.2 ml (0.1mg/l) of this solution.
Indoleacetic acid: dissolve 40 mg in a few mls of absolute alcohol and make up to 50 mls with distilled water (gives a sol^n 800 mg/l). Use 10 ml of this solution (8 mg/l).
Kinetin (6-furfurylaminopurine): dissolve 25 mg in a few mls of N/10 hydrochloric acid and make up to 50 mls with distilled water (gives a sol^n 512 mg/l). Use 5 ml (2.5 mg/l) of this solution.

(iii) Make up the total volume to 1000 mls with distilled water and adjust the pH to 5.7 with N/1 NaOH (sodium hydroxide). Use pH test papers to measure the acidity.
(iv) Add 9g of agar (Oxoid No. 3 or equivalent) and heat the solution until the agar is thoroughly dissolved, by placing the flask containing the solution in a saucepan containing about 2 cm of water.
(v) Add 10 ml of molten solution to 7.0 × 2.5 cm, flat-bottomed glass tubes (or other containers of equivalent size). Seal each tube with a cap or aluminium foil.
(vi) Stack the tubes in a wire basket or glass beaker and cover the mouth with non-absorbent cotton wool and autoclavable paper (strong brown parcel paper).
(vii) Sterilise by autoclaving for 15 to 20 mins at 15 lb pressure in a pressure cooker. The sterilised tubes may be stored in their container at 3° to 4°C in a refrigerator until used.

The culture explant can be supported on a paper bridge as an alternative to using agar. The bridge soaks up the medium from the bottom of the tube and at the same time keeps the roots of the plantlet well aerated. The bridge is folded from a 9 × 4 cm strip of chromatography paper (Whatmans No. 1), or thick blotting paper could be used. The dry bridge is placed in the tube before the culture solution is added.

c. **Culture vessels**

The type of culture vessel used will depend on the individual worker. Disposable, pre-sterilised plastic containers are available, but the use of large numbers may be costly. Also, different workers favour different methods of sealing the culture tubes.

In our laboratory meristem-tips are grown in 7 × 2.5 cm flat-bottomed glass tubes containing 10 ml of solid agar medium, and the tube is sealed with a piece of polypropylene secured with a rubber band (Plate 28). Other workers frequently use plastic tubes and close them with screw tops. Non-absorptive cotton-wool bungs or aluminium foil may also be used to seal the tubes. Larger vessels may be used if more than one culture explant is to be grown in each vessel.

d. **Sterilisation of plant material and removal of explant**

Sterile explants are an important part of any tissue culture procedure. Some material is extremely easy to dissect in a sterile condition, but other explants may be difficult to obtain in an asceptic state. If meristem-tips are taken from a bud that is completely enclosed by numerous leaf primordia (young leaves), surface sterilisation of the shoot and bud may be unnecessary. Simply wiping the shoot bearing the bud with 70% (industrial) alcohol may be sufficient. It is important, however, that the instruments used to remove the explant are kept sterile by dipping them in 70% alcohol and then flaming them by passing through the flame of an alcohol burner, so that the underlying, sterile leaf primordia are not contaminated from the outside as the dissection proceeds. In other cases, more careful surface sterilisation of the shoot or plant organ is required.

The following procedure may be used for this purpose.

(i) Immerse shoot in 70% alcohol for 1 to 2 mins and then immerse in 5% sodium or calcium hypochlorite (bleach) solution, containing 0.1% Tween-80 (or washing-up liquid), for 5 mins.
(ii) Rinse several times on **sterile** distilled water for 3 to 5 mins per rinse.

The treatment of the parent plant prior to removal of the explant may also influence the subsequent level of culture contamination. If the plant is watered by regular overhead irrigation, there is a greater chance of contamination than if the plant is watered only at soil level. This is because bacteria and fungal spores are not then washed over the buds and bud scales.

A binocular microscope or high magnification, mounted lens will be required to dissect the explant from the bud. This should be thoroughly wiped with 70% alcohol to remove any surface dust before starting. To dissect out a meristem-tip, the shoot must be held by sterile forceps, and a sterilised needle used to remove bud scales and leaf primordia, ensuring that the forceps and needle are always flamed and sterilised between each operation. Finally, a tip measuring 0.5 to 1.0 mm should be removed with a piece of fragmented razor-blade mounted in a holder (Plate 28) and transferred to a culture tube. The mouth of the culture tube should then be quickly passed through the flame of the alcohol burner to expel air and contaminants, and the tube sealed with a sheet of sterilised polythene, aluminium foil or other suitable closure.

Cultures should be transferred to fresh media approximately every two weeks and the new media may be modified to change the type of growth should it be required.

e. **Post culture treatments**

Once a regenerated plantlet is ready for transfer from its tissue culture environment to soil (e.g. when the culture has well developed roots and shoots), it must undergo a careful weaning process. The culture must be transferred from the almost 100% relative humidity of the culture vessel to the much lower and variable humidity of a glasshouse. A simple, but effective way of achieving this transition is to transfer the rooted culture into a peat 'Jiffy' pot and place this in a plastic covered seed tray (see Fig. 5.3). Then the humidity in the tray is slowly lowered over a period of 1 to 2 weeks by first opening the ventilation holes in the plastic cover, and then by gradually lifting the plastic cover to allow a greater exposure to the ambient atmosphere.

If the meristem-tip culture procedure has been used to produce virus-free plants from infected mother plants, it will be necessary to monitor the developing plantlets once they are planted in soil to check for the development of any residual virus, and also to maintain the plantlets in a virus-free environment so that they cannot become re-infected (see Section 5.5). In addition to observing the plantlets for any virus symptoms, it will also be advantageous to back-test leaf samples from the plantlets to susceptible host seedlings sensitive to the virus concerned (see above).

f. **Heat treatment of the infected parent plant**

Heat therapy of the infected mother plant is often an essential aid to meristem-tip culture of a virus-free plantlet (see Section 5.5). The infected parent plant, growing in a pot in compost, should be incubated at a temperature between 30° and 40°C in an illuminated chamber receiving 16 hours daylight. A home-made chamber with thermostatic control, a fan heater and illumination with daylight florescent tubes would be perfectly adequate for this treatment.

The minimum treatment period is likely to be 4 weeks, but up to 12 weeks may be necessary. The plant should be treated for as long as possible at the highest temperature it can withstand. A preliminary experiment will be required to determine this maximum temperature and a pretreatment period at a lower temperature (around 30°C) for 1 week, may be helpful to acclimatise the plant for treatment at a higher temperature.

The meristem-tip must be removed immediately the plant is finally removed from the high temperature treatment chamber.

g. **Chemical treatment of virus infected cultures**

Ribavirin (1,2,4-triazole-3-carboxamide syn. virazole) has been the most effective chemical for the eradication of virus from infected plant tissues (see Section 5.5). When incorporated into the meristem-tip culture medium at concentrations between 10mg and 50 mg/l it may block virus replication. The mode of this inactivation and the culture procedures needed to take advantage of it are detailed in Section 5.5. Ribavirin may also be phytotoxic especially at concentrations above 50 mg/l, so preliminaray experiments are needed to determine the maximum concentration that an individual species can withstand.

To prepare a medium containing 50 mg/l, dissolve 50 mg ribavirin in 5 mls of 0.05N hydrochloric acid and adjust pH to 7.0 using 0.05N sodium hydroxide. Add this solution to the remainder of the culture medium to make up to 1 litre.

h. **List of apparatus and chemical requirements**

Chemicals

Absolute alcohol (ethanol) (BDH)
Agar (Oxoid No. 3) (Unipath)
Calcium chloride (BDH)
Carborundum 300 (BDH)
Dipotassium hydrogen orthophosphate (K_2HPO_4) (BDH)
Gamborg's B5 medium (Flow)
Hydrochloric Acid N/1 (BDH).
Indoleacetic Acid (BDH)
Industrial Alcohol (methylated spirit) (BDH)
Inositol(myo) (BDH)
Kinetin (6-furfurylaminopurine)(BDH)
MS mineral salt medium (Flow)
Nicotinic acid (BDH)
Pyridoxin HC1 (BDH)

Ph test papers (BDH)
Ribavirin (Sigma)
Sodium sulphite (BDH)
Sodium hydroxide (BDH)
Sodium hypochlorite (BDH)
Sucrose (BDH)
Thiamine HCL (BDH)

Apparatus

Alcohol burner (Gallenkamp)
Beakers, glass, conical and straight sided (Gallenkamp)
Binocular microscope (Gallenkamp)
Culture tubes, sterile plastic, glass vials (Richardsons or Lab Systems Gp).
Forceps (Gallenkamp)
Filter funnel (glass) (Gallenkamp)
Jiffy pots, 4.5 cm (any horticultural supplier)
Measuring cylinder, glass, 100 and 1000 ml (Gallenkamp)
Mounted needles (Gallenkamp)
Pestle and Mortar, porcelain (Gallenkamp)
Pipettes, glass 1 ml and 5 ml (Gallenkamp)
Sterile air-flow bench (Brassair)
Scalpel blades No. 11 (Gallenkamp)
Scalpel holder No. 3 (Gallenkamp)
Seed tray and propagator (any horticultural supplier)
Tubes, glass, flat-bottomed for tissue culture (Gallenkamp)
Tubes, glass, test-tube (Gallenkamp)
Whatman's chromatography paper (Gallenkamp)
Wire basket (Gallenkamp)

Addresses

BDH Ltd, Fourways, Carlyon Industrial Estate, Atherstone, Warks CV9 1JG

Flow Laboratories Ltd, Woodcock Hill Industrial Estate, Harefield Rd, Rickmansworth, Herts, WD3 1PQ

Gallenkamp, Belton Road West, Loughborough, Leics, LE11 0TR

Lab. Systems Group UK Ltd., Unit 5, The Ringway Centre, Edison Rd, Basingstroke, Hants, RG21 2Y11

Richardsons (Leic) Ltd., Evington Valley Road, Leicester, LE5 5LJ

Sigma Chemical Company Ltd. Fancy Road, Poole, Dorset BH17 7NH

Unipath Ltd., Wade Road, Basingstoke, Hants, RG24 0PW

REFERENCES AND RECOMMENDED READING

ABDUL MAGID, A. G. M. (1981). *Investigations on viruses of pinks* (Dianthus sp.) *and their possible control.* PhD. thesis, University of Exeter.

ANON. (1970). *Narcissus Pests.* Ministry of Agriculture, Fisheries and Food Bulletin No. 51. London: HMSO, 40pp.

ANON. (1985). *Bugs to Kill Bugs. Greenhouse Pest Control.* In: Gardening from Which, April 1985, 106-109.

ANON. (1986). *Directory of Garden Chemicals.* London: British Agrochemical Association Ltd., 45pp.

ANON. (1991a). Garden Chemicals. *A Guide to their Safe and Effective Use.* British Agrochemicals Association, 43pp.

ANON. (1991b). *Pesticides 1991. Pesticides Approved under the Control of Pesticides Regulations 1986.* HMSO, London, 426pp.

ANON. (1991c). *The Gardening from Which? Guide to Pests and Diseases.* Consumer Association and Hodder & Stoughton, London, 144pp.

BECKER, P. (1974). *Pests of Ornamental Plants.* Ministry of Agriculture, Fisheres and Food, Bulletin No. 97. London: HMSO, 175pp.

BLACKMAN, R. L. & EASTOP, V. F. (1984). *Aphids on the World's Crops: An Identification and Information Guide.* John Wiley & Sons, Chichester, England, 466pp.

BOOTH, C. (1971). *The Genus Fusarium.* International Mycological Institute, Kew, Surrey UK, 237pp.

BOS, L. (1978) *Symptoms of Virus Diseases in Plants.* Central Agricultural Publishing Documents, Wageningen.

BUCZACKI, S. T. , HARRIS, K. M. & HARGREAVES, B. (1981). *Collins Guide to the Pests, Diseases and Disorders of Garden Plants.* London: Collins, 512pp.

CARTER, D. J. (1984). *Pest Lepidoptera of Europe with Special Reference to the British Isles.* Dr W Junk Publishers, Dordrecht, The Netherlands, 431pp.

CASPER, D. L. D. (1964). Structure and function of regular virus particles. In: *Plant Virology* (ed. Corbett, M.K. & Sisler, H.D.) University of Florida Press: Florida.

CHINERY, M. (1973). *A Field Guide to the Insects of Britain and Northern Europe.* London: Collins, 352pp.

CLOUDSLEY-THOMPSON, J.L. (1968). *Spiders, Scorpions, Centipedes and Mites.* Oxford: Pergamon Press, 278pp.

DAVIDSON, R. H. & LYON, W. F. (1987). *Insect Pests of Farm, Garden and Orchard.* John Wiley & Sons, New York, 640pp.

DIXON, A. F. G. (1973). *The Biology of Aphids.* The Institute of Biology's Studies in Biology No. 44. Edward Arnold, London, 58pp.

FORSYTHE, T. G. (1990). *Successful Organic Pest Control.* Thorsons Publishers Ltd., Wellingborough, Northamptonshire, 128pp.

FOX WILSON, G. & BECKER, P. (1960). *Horticultural Pests, Detection and*

Control. London: Crosby Lockwood, 240pp.

GAMBORG, O. L. & Wetter, L. R. (1975). *Plant Tissue Culture Methods*. N. R. C. Canada, Saskatchewan.

GARNER, R.J. (1958). *The Grafters Handbook*. Faber & Faber, London.

GARRETT, S. D. (1956). *Biology of Root-infecting Fungi*. Cambridge University Press, UK, 293pp.

GODAN, D. (1983). *Pest Slugs and Snails. Biology and Control*. Springer-Verlag, Berlin, 445pp.

HARRIS, K. F. (1981). Arthropod and Nematode vectors of plant viruses. *Annual Review of Phytopathology* **19**, 391-426.

HAWKSWORTH, D. L., SUTTON, B. C. & AINSWORTH, G. C. (1983). *Ainsworth & Bisby's Dictionary of the Fungi*. International Mycological Institute, Kew, UK, 445pp.

HEATH, R. E. (1981). *The Collingridge Guide to Collectors' Alpines, Their Cultivation in Frames and Alpine Houses*. Collingridge Books, Richmond upon Thames, 543pp.

HORNY, R., WEBR, K. M. & BYAM-GROUNDS, J. (1986). *Porophyllum Saxifrages*. Byam-Grounds Publications, Stamford, England, 372pp.

HUSSEY, N. W., READ, W. H. & HESLING, J. J. (1969). *The Pests of Protected Cultivation: The Biology and Control of Glasshouse and Mushroom Pests*. London: Edward Arnold, 404pp.

HUSSEY, N. W. & SCOPES, N. (Editors) (1985). *Biological Pest Control, The Glasshouse Experience*. Poole, Dorset: Blandford Press, 240pp.

IVENS, G. W. & STUBBS, J. (1990). *Plant Protection in the Garden*. British Crop Protection Council and Royal Horticultural Society. Farnham, Surrey, 151pp.

IVENS, G. W. (Editor) (1991). *The UK Pesticide Guide*. C. A. B. International British Crop Protection Council, 578pp.

JONES, F. G. W. & JONES, M. G. (1984). *Pests of Field Crops*. 3rd Edition. London: Edward Arnold, 392pp.

KLUG, A., LONGLEY, W. & LEBERMAN, R. (1966). Arrangement of protein sub-units and the distribution of nucleic acid in turnip yellow mosaic virus. 1. X-ray diffraction series. *Journal of Molecular Biology* **15**, 315-43.

LARGE, E. C. (1958). *The Advance of the Fungi*. Jonathan Cape, London, 488pp.

LELLIOTT, R. A. & STEAD, D. E. (1987). *Methods for the Diagnosis of Bacterial Disease in Plants*. Blackwell Scientific Publications, Oxford, UK, 216pp.

LEWIS, T. (1973). *Thrips, their Biology, Ecology and Economic Importance*. Academic Press, London, 349pp.

LISANSKY, S. G. (Editor) (1990). *Green Growers Guide. The World Directory of Agro-Biologicals* 1990/91. CPL Press, Newbury, England, 304pp.

MATTHEWS, L. H. (1952). *British Mammals*. Collins, London, 410pp.

MAXWELL, F. G. & JENNINGS, P. R. (1980). *Breeding Plants Resistant to Insects*. John Wiley & Sons, New York, USA, 683pp.

MINISTRY OF AGRICULTURE, FISHERIES & FOOD. Advisory leaflets on many important pests. Published by HMSO, London.

MOREL, G. M. & MARTIN, C. (1952). Guérison de dahlias atteints d'une maladie à virus. *C.R. Hebd Séances Acad. Sci.* **235**, 1324-5.

MOREL, G. M. & MARTIN, C. (1955). Guérison des pommes de terre atteints de maladies à virus. *C.R. Hebd Séances Acad. Agric.* **41**, 472-5.

MORETON, B. D. (1978). *Beneficial Insects and Mites*. London: HMSO, 118pp.

MOUND, L. A. & HALSEY, S. H. (1978). *Whitefly of the World. A Systematic Catalogue of the Aleyrodidae (Homoptera) with Host Plant and Natural Enemy Data*. British Museum (Natural History) and John Wiley & Sons, Chichester, England, 340pp.

MURASHIGE, T. & SKOOG, F. (1962). A revised medium for rapid growth and bioassays with tobacco tissue culture. *Physiologia Plantarum* **15**, 473-97.

NYLAND, G. & GOHEEN, A. C. (1969). Heat therapy of virus diseases of perennial plants. *Annual Review of Phytopathology* **7**, 331-54.

OWEN, J. (1981). Hoverflies in gardens. *The Garden* **106**, 191-195.

PORT, C. M. & PORT, G. R. (1986). The biology and behaviour of slugs in relation to crop damage and control. *Agricultural Zoology Reviews* **1**, 255-299. Intercept, Newcastle upon Tyne.

QUAK, F. (1977). Meristem culture and virus-free plants. In: *Plant cell, tissue and organ culture* (ed. Reinert, J. & Bajaj, Y.P.S.). Springer-Verlag, Berlin, pp. 598-615.

ROTHERAY, G. E. *Aphid Predators*. Naturalists' Handbooks No. **11**, Richmond Publishing Co Ltd., Slough, England, 77pp.

SIMPKINS, I., WALKEY, D. G. A. & NEELY, H. A. (1981). Chemical suppression of virus in cultured plant tissues. *Annals of Applied Biology* **99**, 161-9.

SMITH, K. M. (1972). *A Textbook of Plant Virus Diseases.* Longman, Harlow.

SPENCER, D. M. (1978). *The Powdery Mildews.* Academic Press, London, 565pp.

SUTTON, S. (1972). *Woodlice*. Oxford: Pergamon Press, 143pp.

TOMLINSON, J. A. (1962). Control of lettuce mosaic by the use of healthy seed. *Plant Pathology* **11**, 61-4.

TOMLINSON, J. A. (1982). Chemotherapy of plant viruses and virus diseases. In: *Pathogens, Vectors and Plant Diseases.* (ed. Harris, K.F. & Maramorosch, K.). Academic Press, London, pp. 23-44.

WALKEY, D. G. A. (1991a) *Applied Plant Virology.* Chapman and Hall, London.

WALKEY, D. G. A. (1991b). The micropropagation of rock plants. In: *A Century of Alpines*, Conference Report, Univ. of Warwick, 1991.

WALKEY, D. G. A. & ANTILL, D. N. (1989). Agronomic evaluation of virus-free and virus-infected garlic (*Allium sativum L.*). *Journal of Horticultural Science* **64**, 53-60.

WALKEY, D. G.A . & FREEMAN, G. H. (1977). Inactivation of cucumber mosaic virus in cultured tissues of *Nicotians rustica L.* by diurnal alternating periods of high and low temperature. *Annals of Applied Biology* **87**, 375-82.

WALKEY, D. G. A., WARD, C. M. & PHELPS, K. (1985). The reaction of lettuce (*Lactuca sativa L.*) cultivars to cucumber mosaic virus. *Journal of Agricultural Science, Cambridge* **105**, 291-97.

WALKEY, D. G. A. & WEBB, M. J. W. (1970). Tubular inclusion bodies in plants infected with viruses of the Nepo type. *Journal of General Virology* **7**, 159-61.

WALKEY, D. G. A., WEBB, M. J. W., BOLLAND, C. J. & MILLER, A. (1987). Production of virus-free garlic (*Allium sativum* L.) and shallot (*A. ascalonicum* L.) by meristem-tip culture. *Journal Horticultural Science* **62**, 211.

WATTS, L. (1980). *Flower and Vegetable Plant Breeding.* Grower Books, London.

WEBSTER, J. (1986). *Introduction to Fungi.* Cambridge University Press, UK, 669pp.

APPENDIX

Glossary

Acarology: the study of mites.

Accession: name used by plant breeders for a specific breeding line.

Acquired resistance: (syn. **induced resistance** or **acquired immunity**): resistance response developed by a normally susceptible host following a predisposing treatment, such as inoculation with a virus, fungus, bacterium, or treatment with certain chemicals; this type of resistance is not inherited (see **cross protection**).

Acquisition feeding time: time during which a vector feeds on an infested plant to acquire a virus for subsequent transmission (e.g. to become viruliferous).

Active ingredient: internationally agreed name for a chemical.

Adelgid: a conifer woolly aphid.

Aeciospore: thin-walled, one-celled, binucleate, non-repeating vegetative spore of a rust fungus.

Aestivation: summer resting period of an animal (see **hibernation**).

Aflatoxin: poisonous, carcinogenic chemical produced by *Aspergillus* species growing on peanuts or cereal grains.

Allele: one of two or more alternate forms of a gene occupying the same locus on a particular chromosome (see **gene**).

Alternate host: plant species on which heteroecious rust forms spermogonia and aeciospores, and hence essential for completion of rust life cycle.

Alternation of generations: succession of sexual and asexual stages, or gametophyte and sporophyte stages, in a life cycle.

Ametabolous: life cycle of an insect in which there are no distinct stages.

Anamorph: vegetative, or imperfect state of a fungus (see **teleomorph**).

Anastomosis: fusion between compatible fungal hyphae.

Anther smut: fungus in Family Ustilaginales producing dark ustilospores in anthers.

Antennae: feelers on the head of an insect or other animal.

Aphid: alternative name for greenfly or blackfly.

Apothecium: saucer-shaped fungal disc, often stalked, producing asci on upper surface.

Arthropod: a jointed-limbed animal, for example – crustacean, insect or spider.

Ascocarp: fungal fruiting body containing asci produced by the fungal group Ascomycotina.

Ascoma -ta: fungal fruiting body containing asci.

Ascomycotina: Subdivision of the Division Eumycota comprising fungi which produce ascospores.

Ascospore: spore produced in an ascus by an Ascomycete fungus.

Ascus: tiny specialised cell containing ascospores produced by Ascomycete fungi.

Asexual reproduction: multiplication without exchange of genetic material, usually producing identical organisms.

Assimilate: food or other essential chemical for plant metabolism, which moves through the plant via the vascular system.

Autoecious rust: rust able to complete life cycle on a single host plant species.

Authority: citation of an author's name for the scientific name for an organism.

Bacteriology: the study of bacteria.

Basidioma -ata: fruiting body containing basidia.

Basidiomycete: alternative name for fungi in Subdivision Basidiomycotina.

Basidiomycotina: Subdivision of Division Eumycota comprising fungi which produce basidiospores.

Basidium: tiny specialised cell producing basidiospores.

Big bud: the distorted, swollen bud of blackcurrant caused by a gall mite.

Binomial: scientific name of an organism, comprising a combination of the genus and species.

Biological control: exploitation of natural enemies to control pests, diseases and weeds; natural enemies, sometimes called 'agents', include parasites, predators and pathogens.

Biotroph: fungus whose nutrition is dependant on living tissue i.e. a parasite.

Biotype: a race or population of a pest which can be distinguished on the basis of its reaction to different plants.

Brand name: a registered name for a product such as a pesticide.

Brown core: disease symptom describing discoloured root vascular tissue.

Capsid: a) protein shell of a virus particle;
b) group of plant bugs belonging to the insect order Miridae.

Carpogenic germination: production of apothecium on germinating fungal sclerotium.

Caterpillar: larva of a butterfly or moth.

Chafer grub: larva of a cockchafer beetle.

Chemotherapy: use of chemicals to eradicate a pathogen from an infected plant.

Chlamydospore: resting spore consisting of a vegetative cell, or groups of cells, with thick protective walls.

Chlorosis: yellowing of plant parts which are normally green.

Chromosome: long molecule of DNA associated with proteins and carrying the genes of the organism; they are small rod-shaped structures occurring in the nucleus (see **nucleus** and **DNA**).

Chrysalis: pupa of a butterfly or moth.

Cicadellid: leafhopper.

Circulative virus: virus which is transmitted by an insect in a persistent manner and which circulates from the insect's digestive tract, through the haemolymph to the salivary glands, before being transmitted in the saliva as the insect feeds.

Cleistothecium: ascocarp with no opening.

Clickbeetle: beetle belonging to the family Elateridae.

Clone: genetically identical group of individuals, originally derived from a single individual by vegetative propagation.

Cockchafer: beetle belonging to the family Scarabaeidae.

Cocoon: silken case in which insect larvae pupate.

Coenocytic: absence of cross walls in fungal hyphae.

Coleoptera: beetles order of insects.

Collembola: springtails order of insects.

Compatibility factor: governs the capacity of a fungal thallus to fuse with another thallus during reproduction.

Coremium: bundles of fungal hyphae producing vegetative spores e.g. in *Fusarium*.

Covered smut: dark ustilospores produced inside seeds (see **loose smut**).

Crawlers: newly-hatched nymphs of whiteflies and scale insects which disperse to find suitable sites in which to feed.

Cremaster: horn-like projections on a chrysalis.

Crepuscular: animal which is active at dawn and dusk.

Crioceran: lily beetle.

Cross-protection: reduction in infection by a severe strain of a pathogen following pre-infection by a mild strain of the same or a different pathogen.

Cuckoo spit: frothy mass secreted by froghopper nymphs in which they are concealed.

Cuticle: outermost, protective surface layer of a plant or insect.

Cutworm: caterpillar of certain noctuid moths which feed at ground level cutting through plant stem.

Damping-off: collapse of seedlings shortly after seed germination.

Deuteromycotina: Subdivision of Division Eumycota comprising fungi with no known sexual state.

Deoxyribonucleic acid (DNA): large self-replicating molecule which carries genetic information and is found in all living cells.

Dermaptera: earwigs order of insects.

Diapause: extended resting phase in the life cycle of an insect.

Dikaryon: fungal cells containing two, genetically different, haploid nuclei.

Dikaryotism: conversion of fungal homokaryon to a dikaryon.

Dimorphism: two forms; thus sexually dimorphic moths have males and females which differ markedly in certain characteristics (see **pleomorphic**).

Dioecious: male and female reproductive structures on different plants, or on different fungal thalli.

Diploid: a) a nucleus with twice ($2n$) the basic number of chromosomes; b) two genetically different haploid nuclei in a cell.

Diptera: true flies order of insects.

Dominant gene: gene that is fully expressed in the phenotype of the heterozygote plant (see **recessive gene**).

Downy mildew: fungus in the Family Peronosporaceae.

Durable resistance: resistance which is long lasting.

Ecology: inter-relationships of organisms with their environment.

Eelworm wool: aggregation of eelworms or nematodes in a dormant state which can survive a long period of unfavourable conditions.

Eimer's organ: organ located in the snout of a mole and which is sensitive to humidity and temperature.

Entomology: the study of insects.

Epidemic: repeated cycles of secondary infection by fungi or bacteria.

Epidemiology: the study of factors affecting the outbreak and spread of infectious diseases.

Epidermis: outer layer of cells of a plant (see **cuticle**).

Eriophyid mite: gall mite, family Eriophyidae.

Erysiphaceae: Family in the Subdivision Ascomycotina comprising the powdery mildews.

Eumycota: 'true fungi', usually producing mycelia, but sometimes unicellular, with firm cell walls.

Exoskeleton: external skeleton of invertebrates.

Extreme resistance: very high level of resistance against a pathogen; resistance may also be **moderate** or **low**.

F_1: first generation offspring of a cross between two parents.

F_2: second generation offspring resulting from a cross between **F_1** offspring.

F_3 and **F_4**: third and fourth generation of offspring resulting from a cross between **F_2** and **F_3** parents respectively.

Facultative: fungal nutrition which changes according to ecological conditions.

Fascia: lines on an insect wing.

Field resistance: resistance to infection by a pest or pathogen shown by a host plant under natural field conditions, even though the same host may be susceptible under experimental conditions.

Flagellum -ae: thread-like appendage on fungal or bacterial cells which assists movement in water.

Forma specialis: form of a species distinguished by a difference in pathogencity or host range.

Fungi Imperfecti: fungi with no known sexual state (see **Deuteromycotina**).

Furcula: springing organ of a springtail, Order Collembola.

Gall: outgrowth of host plant cells often caused by fungi, bacteria, insects, mites or nematodes.

Gall mite: mite belonging to the family Eriophyidae (see **Eriophyid mite**).

Gene: inherited factor that determines the characteristics of an organism (see **allele**).

Generation: the full cycle of an organism's life history.

Genome: nucleic acid component of a virus, which may consist of a single (*monopartite*), two (*bipartite*), three (*tripartite*), or more (*multipartite*) molecular species of RNA (see **multi-component virus**).

Genus: a) assemblage of species sharing common characteristics which indicate a close relationship;
b) first taxon of a binomial (see **species**).

Gestation period: the period in a mammal's life between conception and birth.

Ghost flies: the cast skins of leafhopper nymphs which remain attached to the plant after the insect has crawled away.

Grub: the larva of a beetle (Coleoptera).

Gustation: the sense of taste.

Haemocoel: blood of an insect or other arthropod.

Halteres: modified hind wings which, in true flies (Diptera), are developed as balancing organs.

Haploid: a) nucleus with the basic (*n*) number of chromosomes;
b) cell with one genetic type of haploid nucleus.

Haustorium: hyphal branch of parasitic fungus which penetrates host cells to obtain nutrients.

Hemimetabolism: insect having an incomplete metamorphosis.

Hemiptera: plant bugs order of insects.

Herbivorous: feeds on plants.

Hermaphrodyte: animal possessing both male and female sexual organs.

Heteroecious rust: rust fungus needing two, unrelated, host plant species to complete life cycle.

Heterokaryon: fungal cell with more than one genetic type of haploid nucleus.

Heterothallism: fungal thallus which is sexually self-incompatible, hence different thalli of compatible mating types are required for sexual reproduction.

Heterotrophism: use of carbon or organic compounds as a main source of nutrition.

Heterozygote: possession of two different alleles in a single gene pair, e.g. Ss (see **homozygote**).

Higher fungus: fungus in Subdivision Ascomycotina or Basidiomycotina and considered to be more advanced evolutionary-wise than 'lower' fungi.

Holocarpism: whole vegetative fungal thallus which converts to a sexual reproductive body.

Holometabolism: insect having a complete metamorphosis.

Holomorph: collective name for the different states of a single fungal species.

Homokaryon: fungal cell with one genetic type of haploid nucleus.

Homothallism: sexual self-compatibility in fungi, reproduction being possible without the need for different thalli.

Homozygote: possession of two identical alleles in a single gene pair, e.g. SS or ss (see **heterozygote**).

Honeydew: sweet, sticky substance secreted by plant bugs.

Hymenoptera: ants, sawflies, bees, wasps order of insects.

Hypersensitivity: reaction in a host plant resulting from pathogen infection, involving rapid death of the infected tissues. In some instances (as with a virus) the area of dead cells is restricted to discrete local lesions, and in others the pathogen may spread readily through the plant's vascular system causing systemic necrosis and death. Often considered to be a form of resistance to disease spread (see **lesion**).

Hypha: filament which forms part of a fungal body or thallus (see **mycelium**).

Hypopharynx: lobe at the back of the mouth of an insect or other animal.

Hypopus: specialised immature stage in the life cycle of an acarid mite.

Immunity: describes absolute exemption from infection by a specific pathogen. An immune plant is not attacked at all by the particular virus and is a *non-host* of the virus concerned (see **acquired resistance**).

Imperfect fungus: fungus with no known sexual state i.e. in Subdivision Deuteromycotina.

Imperfect state: vegetative state of pleomorphic fungus.

Inbreeding reduction: adverse effects (for example reduced growth, deformity) arising from repeated self-pollination of plants which are normally out-breeding.

Indexing: procedure for demonstrating the presence of virus in a plant.

Inoculation feeding period (syn. **test feeding period**): length of time a vector feeds on a plant during virus transmission experiments.

Inoculum: form of a fungus, bacterium or virus potentially able to infect a host plant.

Inoculum potential: resources of a fungus available for infection of a host plant by microorganisms.

Instar: stage in the development of larvae which occurs between moults (casting of skin).

Integrated control: combined use of more than one method to control a pathogen or pest, such as the complementary use of biological and chemical control measures.

Integument: skin of an insect or other invertebrate.

In-vitro: a) occurring in cells or tissues grown in culture or in cell extracts (virus);

b) experiments not in natural environment (fungi, bacteria and animals).

In-vivo: a) occurring within a living organism (virus);

b) in contact with natural environment (fungi, bacteria and animals).

Isoptera: termites order of insects.

Karyogamy: fusion of pairs of fungal nuclei following plasmogamy, nuclei becoming diploid.

Keel: the ridge running down the back of a slug.

Loose smut: smut fungus which produces dark ustilospores on outside of seed (see **covered smut**).

Lower fungus: fungus belonging to the Division Myxomycota, or to the Classes Chytridiomycetes, Oomycetes or Zygomycetes.

Labium: lower lip of an animal.

Labrum: upper lip of an animal.

Land-race: stock of plants selected on a local basis by farmers over many years, and which are strongly adapted to local conditions.

Larva: immature stage in the life cycle of an animal that undergoes metamorphosis between egg and the adult form. Many larvae are very different in appearance from the adult. It is frequently the main feeding (and therefore the most damaging) stage of insects.

Latent infection: infection of a plant without visual symptoms.

Latent period: period after a vector has acquired a virus before transmission can occur; often observed in the case of persistent virus transmission.

Leatherjacket: larva of a crane fly (daddy long legs).

Lepidoptera: butterflies and moths order of insects.

Lesion: localised area of diseased tissue often referred to as a *local lesion*. The term *primary lesions* may be used to describe lesions that develop on the inoculated leaves at the initial points of infection (see **hypersensitivity**).

Macroconidium: larger of two spore types in fungi which produce microconidia; often diagnostic in *Fusarium*.

Macrocyclic rust: rust fungus with all the reproductive stages present in the life cycle.

Maggot: larva of a true fly (Diptera).

Major gene: gene having large observable effects on the phenotype.

Mandible: jaw of an animal.

Mastigomycotina: Subdivision of Eumycota comprising fungi with motile stages, some forms with filamentous coenocytic mycelium.

Mating type: morphologically identical fungal thalli differing in their ability to fuse during sexual reproduction.

Maxillary: sensory mouthparts of an insect.

Maybug: cockchafer beetle.

Mechanical transmission: used to describe artificial transmission of a virus in which an infectious preparation is rubbed onto a test plant. May also occur in the field when virus is transmitted from one plant to another by leaves rubbing or root contact.

Meiosis: two consecutive nuclear divisions which halve the numbers of chromosomes.

Meristem-tip: meristem dome of cells and one or two pairs of primordial leaves (0.5 to 1 mm in diameter), which comprises the explant removed from a bud and grown in tissue culture to produce a virus-free plant.

Metamorphosis: series of distinct changes or stages in the life cycle of an animal.

Minor gene: gene having small observable effects on the phenotype.

Microconidium: a) smaller of two spore types in fungi which produce macroconidia e.g. *Fusarium*;
b) alternative name for rust pycniospore.

Microcyclic rust: rust fungus with no known aecial or uredial stage.

Mitosis: multiplication of chromosomes without genetic exchange.

Mirid: group of plant bugs belonging to the order Miridae of insects.

Mollusc: animal belonging to the group which includes slugs, snails, oysters, limpets, etc.

Monoculture: the cropping of land with a single plant species.

Monoecious: male and female repoductive structures on the same plant or on the same fungal thallus.

Monogenic: character that is controlled by a single gene (see **oligogenic**, **polygenic**).

Monokaryon: one genetic type of nucleus present in a fungus.

Monophagous: animal which feeds on a single host species (see **polyphagous**).

Mucus: slime secreted by slugs and snails.

Multi-component virus: virus whose genome is divided into two or more parts, each part being separately encapsidated. Hence two or more components are needed to initiate infection. Note that this is different to a multipartite genome where two or more components may be enclosed in a single particle (see **genome**).

Mummification: shrinking and hardening of diseased bulbs and corms.

Mycelial strand: fungal hyphae organised into pale-coloured strands with capacity to grow over nutrient-poor or unfavourable regions and infect neighbouring plants.

Myceliogenic germination: production of vegetative hyphae during sclerotial germination.

Mycelium: aggregation of fungal hyphae.

Mycetophilid: fungus gnat or mushroom fly (see **sciarid**).

Mycology: the study of fungi.

Mycorrhiza: beneficial root-infecting fungus which assists mineral nutrition of the host plant.

Myxomycota: Division comprising fungi without firm cell walls, and which form amoebae or plasmodia.

Necrosis: death of plant tissue.

Necrotroph: carbon nutrition of fungus derived from either dead or living tissue.

Nematode: alternative name for eelworm.

Nematology: the study of eelworms or nematodes.

Nepovirus: viruses characterised by possession of rod-shaped particles and which are transmitted by eelworms.

Noctuid: a large family of stoutly-built moths whose adults commonly fly at night; also known as owlets.

Non-host: plant that cannot be infected by a particular pest or pathogen.

Non-persistent transmission (syn. **stylet-borne transmission**): type of insect transmission in which the virus is acquired by the vector after very short acquisition feeding times, and which is transmitted during very short inoculation feeding periods. The vector remains viruliferous for only a short period unless it feeds again on an infected plant (see **persistent** and **semi-persistent transmission**).

Nucleus: large dense organelle within a cell, bounded by a membrane, in which DNA replication occurs (see **chromosome**).

Nymph: young stage (often the larva) of an insect with an incomplete metamorphosis.

Obligate: fungal nutrition limited to one type.

Obligate parasite: pathogen capable of living only as a parasite on living tissue and which cannot be cultured, or is difficult to culture, on artificial medium.

Olfaction: the sense of smell.

Oligogenic: character controlled by a few genes (see **polygenic**).

Oligophagous: animal which feeds on a specific group of closely-related plant species.

Orthoptera: grasshoppers, crickets and locusts order of insects.

Ostiole: an opening, lined with sterile hyphae in an Ascomycete perithecium.

Ovipositor: an insect's egg-laying organ.

Owlet: large family of stoutly-built moths whose adults commonly fly at night, also known as noctuid.

Palp: invertebrate appendage used for testing the quality of, and for manoeuvring, food.

Parasexual cycle: genetic exchange bewteen filamentous fungi, not involving meiosis.

Parasite: organism infecting living organisms only i.e. a biotroph.

Parthenogenetic: animal which reproduces by asexual means.

Paris green: originally a green dye or pigment made from copper and arsenic and, in the past, used extensively as a pesticide .

Perfect fungus: fungus with a sexual state.

Perithecium: fungal fruiting body with an opening (ostiole) and containing asci.

Persistent transmission: type of vector transmission in which the virus is acquired by the vector only after a long acquisition feeding period, and in which there may be a latent period following the acquisition feed, before the vector can transmit the virus. The vector remains viruliferous for a long period, often throughout its life span. The virus sometimes multiplies within the vector (see **non-persistent** and **semi-persistent transmission, circulative and propagative**).

Phasmida: stick insects order of insects.

Pheromone: volatile chemical released by an animal which influences the behaviour of another animal.

Phialospore: type of vegetative fungal spore.

Phycomycete: common name once used to describe the 'lower' fungi.

Physiological race: fungus differing in biochemical reaction or host range but identical in appearance.

Phytopathology: the study of plant disease.

Phytotoxic: damage to a plant by a substance (usually a chemical).

Plant pathology: the study of plant diseases.

Plant resistance: genetic capacity of a host plant to restrict infection by other organisms.

Plasmodium: multinucleate mass of cell material without a firm wall; found in organisms in the Division Myxomycota.

Plasmogamy: the bringing together of fungal nuclei into one thallus by fusion of compatible hyphae; the nuclei remain separate.

Pleomorphism: production of more than one type of spore by a fungus.

Plurivorus: ability to infect more than one host plant species (see **polyphagous**).

Poikilothermic: a cold-blooded animal.

Polygenic: character controlled by many genes (see **oligogenic**).

Polyphagous: animal which feeds on a wide range of host plant species.

Polyvoltine: insect which undergoes several generations (literally several flights) each year.

Powdery mildew: fungus belonging to the Family Erysiphaceae.

Primary host: plant species on which a heteroecious rust produces urediniospores and teliospores.

Primary inoculum: inoculum which initiates the first cycle of infection on a host plant.

Primary symptoms (infection) (syn. **local symptoms**): the symptoms that develop at the site of virus entry (see **secondary** or **systemic symptoms**).

Proboscis: feeding mouthparts of insects which suck up food – often takes the form of a tube.

Prolegs: stumpy legs on the hind parts of a caterpillar.

Propagative virus: virus that multiplies within its insect vector.

Propagule: infective or survival unit of fungus or bacterium.

Proprietry name: registered name for a product such as a pesticide.

Protoplast: cell of an organism after removal of cell wall.

Pseudosclerotium: compact mass of fungal mycelium, often dark, incorporating host plant tissue, soil or other substrate.

Pseudostroma: stroma incorporating host plant tissue.

Pseudothecium: stroma with tiny cavities containing asci.

Pupa: stage in an insect's life cycle between larva and adult and often a resting stage when the insect undergoes re-organisation; also called a **chrysalis** in butterflies and moths.

Pycnidium: tiny flask-shaped fungal fruiting body which produces vegetative spores.

Rats-tail symptom: protrusion of central water conducting tissue following decay and removal of soft outer layers of roots.

Recessive gene: gene that is not expressed in the phenotype of the heterozygote (see **dominant gene**).

Reduction division: alternative name for meiosis.

Repugnatory gland: gland which produces a repellent fluid which deters predators.

Resistance: a) capacity of a host plant to suppress or retard the activity of a pest or pathogen. Resistance is the opposite of susceptibility and may be high (extreme), moderate or low depending on the degree of protection;
b) reaction of a pest or pathogen to a pesticide which reduces the effectiveness of the compound.

Resting spore: spore adapted for survival.

Reticulate: pattern made up of lines which form a network.

Reversion disease: a virus disease of blackcurrant transmitted by a gall mite.

Rhizobacteria: root-colonising bacteria implicated in protection of plants from fungal infection, or in changes to host growth.

Rhizomorph: dark, boot lace-like aggregations of hyphae growing from a food base of infected woody roots over nutrient-poor or unfavourable regions to infect neighbouring plants; typically produced by the honey fungus.

Ribonucleic acid (RNA): large molecule made up of a single chain of ribonucleotide subunits. It is the main genetic material of some viruses.

Roguing: removal of diseased or infested plants to minimise spread of a pest or pathogen.

Rostrum: beak or snout of a plant bug or weevil.

Saprophytism: capacity of a fungus to grow on, and obtain nutrients from, dead plant or animal tissue.

Scale: flattened nymph of whiteflies and scale insects which is pressed closely to foliage of plants.

Sciarid: fungus gnat or mushroom fly (see **Mycetophilid**).

Scion: donor part of a graft that is inserted into the receiver plant (see **stock**).

Sclerotium: aggregation of fungal hyphae, often enclosed in a protective outer rind.

Screening test: method of assessing the response of a range of plant cultivars or types to pests and pathogens.

Secondary inoculum: inoculum which repeats the cycles of infection on a host plant.

Secondary mycelium: mycelium of a Basidiomycete fungus containing two nuclei per cell, and produced by fusion of compatible hyphae.

Secondary symptom: see **systemic chemical**.

Semi-persistent transmission: virus transmission by an insect vector that is intermediate between **non-persistent** and **persistent transmission**.

Septum: cross wall between adjacent fungal cells.

Sexual reproduction: multiplication involving genetic exchange between nuclei.

Shanking: die-back of *Allium* or *Tulipa* aerial growth caused by *Phytophthora*.

Siphunculi: paired tubular organs on the rear of an aphid's abdomen which release odours used in communication and defence.

Skipjack: type of beetle, family Elateridae.

Slime: mucus produced by slugs and snails.

Smut ball: groups of dark ustilospores.

Sole: undersurface of a slug or snail.

Sow bug: a woodlouse.

Species: a) closely related group of individuals;

b) second taxon of a binomial (see **genus**).

Spickel: gall produced in leaves or stems by nematodes.

Spiracle: external respiratory opening of an insect.

Spiracular line: line running along the side of an insect's body between the spiracles.

Sporidium: basidiospore of fungi in the Orders Uredinales and Ustilaginales.

Springtail: insect belonging to the family Collembola.

Sterigma: minute outgrowth from basidium on which basidiospore forms.

Stigmata: a) coloured patch or ring near wingtip of many insects (also called a Pterostigma);
b) flower part which receives pollen.

Stock: part of a graft that receives the donor tissue or **scion** from another plant.

Stridulate: production of sounds by rubbing parts of the body together – a form of insect communication.

Stroma: mass of dark resistant fungal hyphae, often adapted for survival and often containing reproductive structures.

Stylet: flexible hollow needle-like organ used for piercing plant tissues and sucking up cell contents. Present in plant bugs, mites and nematodes.

Stylet-borne: see **non-persistent transmission**.

Sub-clinical: absence of disease symptoms on infected host.

Subiculum: firm, compact mass of mycelium produced under a fungal fruiting body.

Sub-lethal temperature: temperature which damages, hence weakens, but does not kill, an organism.

Susceptibility: plant readily infected by a pest or pathogen (opposite to resistance).

Syndrome: group of symptoms which, together, characterise a particular disease.

Synergism: association of two or more pathogens acting at the same time.

Systemic chemical: chemical taken up by plant roots or leaves and transported to other parts of the plant.

Systemic (secondary) infection: movement of a pathogen from the site of primary infection into the remainder of the plant.

Taxon: a taxonomic unit e.g. Kingdom, Division, Genus, Species, forma specialis.

Taxonomy: allocation of scientific names to animals, plants, fungi, insects etc.

Teleomorph: sexual (perfect) state of a fungus (see **anamorph**).

Testa: outer hard coat of a seed.

Thallus: body of a fungus made up of hyphae.

Thermotherapy: heat treatment which eradicates a pathogen from an infected plant.

Thigmoreception: the sense of feeling and touch.

Thunderbugs: common name for thrips, so called because they commonly swarm in thundery weather.

Thunder fly: common name for thrips, so called because they commonly swarm in thundery weather.

Thysanoptera: thrips order of insects.

Thysanura: silverfish order of insects.

Tobravirus: viruses characterised by having spherical particles, and which are transmitted by eelworms.

Tolerance: a) host response to virus infection that results in negligible or mild symptom expression, but relatively normal levels of virus concentration and movement within the host compared with a susceptible host (see **vector resistance**);
b) ability of a plant to withstand attack by a pest.

Tortrix: large family of small moths with approximately rectangular wings held roofwise over the body at rest. Caterpillars live in rolled leaves or tunnels in plants.

Trade name: registered name for a product such as a pesticide.

Transovarial transmission: transmission of a virus via the eggs of the infected vector to its progeny.

Univoltine: insect having a single generation (literally one flight) each year.

Ustilospore: dark powdery teliospore (brand spore) produced by smut fungi.

Vector: an organism able to transmit a pathogen.

Vegetative repoduction: multiplication of an organism without exchange of genetic material.

Vertebrate: animal possessing a backbone - amphibians, reptiles, fish, birds and mammals.

Virology: the study of viruses.

Virus indexing: tests carried out to determine if a plant is virus infected.

Volunteer: plant from a previous season's crop that grows in a subsequent crop, e.g. a potato tuber.

Warren: network of tunnels made by rabbits.

Webbing: silk threads produced by insects and mites used for production of life lines, shelters and cocoons.

Weevil: type of beetle, family Curculionidae.

White rust: alternative name for white blister caused by *Albugo*.

Wirestem: collapse of young stem (hypocotyl) of seedling tissue as result of infection by *Rhizoctonia*.

Wireworm: larva of a clickbeetle.

Witches broom: proliferation of twigs often caused by fungi or eriophyid mites, common in *Betula* and *Juniperus*.

Woolly bear: the very hairy caterpillar of tiger and ermine moths (Arctiidae).

Worker: a sterile female ant, wasp or bee.

Zoosporangium: minute fungal sac producing zoospores.

Zoospore: motile fungal spore produced in a zoosporangium.

Zygomycotina: Subdivision of Division Eumycota comprising fungi without motile stages, and producing thick-walled zygospores.

Zygote: thick-walled resting sporangium produced by fusion of zoospores.

INDEX

B

D

E

H

I

O

P

S

T

U

V

W